MOTHERS
and
WIVES

MOTHERS
and
WIVES
GUSII WOMEN OF
EAST AFRICA

Sarah LeVine
In collaboration with
ROBERT A. LeVINE

THE UNIVERSITY OF CHICAGO PRESS
Chicago and London

SARAH LEVINE is a research associate at the Laboratory for
Human Development at Harvard University.

ROBERT A. LEVINE is Roy E. Larsen Professor of Education
and Human Development at Harvard University. His
books include *Dreams and Deeds: Achievement Motivation in
Nigeria,* published by the University of Chicago Press.

The University of Chicago Press, Chicago 60637
The University of Chicago Press, Ltd., London

© 1979 by The University of Chicago
All rights reserved. Published 1979
Printed in the United States of America
83 82 81 80 79   5 4 3 2 1

Library of Congress Cataloging in Publication Data

LeVine, Sarah.
  Mothers and wives.

  Bibliography: p.
  Includes index.
  1. Gusii (Bantu tribe)—Women.   2. Women—
Kenya.   I. LeVine, Robert Alan, 1932–   joint
author.   II. Title.
DT433.542.L49   301.41'2'096762   78–21573
ISBN 0–226–47548–4

In memory of my mother

Contents

Acknowledgments

The investigation on which this book is based was carried out during 1974–76 as part of a larger field project, "Parenthood and Child Development in a Kenya Population," which was supported by a research grant (SOC 74-12692) from the National Science Foundation and a research scientist award from the National Institute of Mental Health to the University of Chicago for Robert A. LeVine. Our American collaborators were T. Berry Brazelton of Children's Hospital Medical Center, Boston; P. Herbert Leiderman of Stanford University Medical Center; and members of their research groups. The project was associated with the Bureau of Educational Research, University of Nairobi, and carried out with the cooperation of D. O. Mulama, then district commissioner of Kisii District. I gratefully acknowledge these indispensable sources of support and cooperation.

Introduction

African women occupy a special place in the annals of cultural variation. As tillers of the soil and market traders, they bear a subsistence burden unique among women of the world. As the wives of polygynists on this most polygynous of continents, they share marital rights to a degree that is rare in other places. Yet their relative freedom of movement and independence of activity and spirit have long attracted the interest of outside observers. The many ways in which this apparent paradox is resolved in the diverse cultural settings of contemporary Africa have been portrayed in detail by anthropological studies of the past fifty years.

We know a great deal about the social lives of African women, and much of what we know is due to women, beginning with E. Dora Earthy (*Valenge Women*, 1933) and Sylvia Leith-Ross (*African Women*, 1939). After 1935, academically trained women, some of whom became leading figures in anthropology, produced ethnographic studies covering women's roles for many parts of the vast continent. These anthropologists included Audrey I. Richards, Monica H. Wilson, Elizabeth Colson, Mary Douglas, and at least thirty other women from Britain, France, and the United States. (A selected bibliography of their works on African women appears at the end of the text.) They and their male colleagues have described how women live in matrilineal as well as patrilineal societies, rural and urban settings, Islamic and indigenous cultural environments.

In contrast with this wealth of sociological and cultural information, there are few psychological studies of African women. The only such studies of which we are aware are those of Robert E. Edgerton (*The Individual in Cultural Adaptation* [Berkeley: University of California Press, 1971]), Maria Leblanc (*Personalité de la femme katangaise: contribution à l'étude de son acculturation* [Louvain: Publications Universitaires, 1960]), and S. G. Lee ("Social Influences in Zulu Dreaming," *Journal of Social Psychology* 47 [1950]: 265–83).

Their social behavior is well documented, but their patterns of personal experience and private feeling have rarely been explored. Even in biographies, African women appear more as informants on their culture than as individual personalities of interest in themselves (e.g., see Mary Smith, *Baba of Karo*). To be able to understand them empathically, i.e., as persons like ourselves, it is necessary to move beyond the sociological abstractions of ethnographic description to actual individuals and how they feel and think about their lives. We must seek to understand their inner experience as we understand our own, not only out of scientific curiosity but to provide the deeper recognition of our common humanity that will help eliminate the misrepresentations of Africans that still abound in Western thought. The present book is offered as a contribution to that search, in this case among rural Gusii women of childbearing age in Kenya.

The investigation on which the book is based was carried out during the years 1974–76 as part of a larger field project, "Parenthood and Child Development in a Kenya Population," involving medical and social science collaborators. That project, located in an area in which Robert A. LeVine had worked from 1955 to 1957, was designed to bring the approaches of anthropology, pediatrics, developmental psychology, and psychiatry to bear on understanding the care and social development of Gusii infants and small children. After making preliminary contacts and conducting initial census and nutrition surveys, we established a pediatric clinic near the market center early in 1975 and began a seventeen-month longitudinal study of twenty-eight infants and their families.

During this period the environmental and developmental patterns of the infants were monitored by American and Gusii fieldworkers, using a variety of observational methods, interviews, and tests as well as ethnographic investigation. This research brought us into close contact with the mothers of the babies, whom I observed in their homes. In order to understand these mothers better, the case studies in this book were launched.

One purpose of the case studies was to understand in depth what childbearing means to Gusii mothers. Ethnography provides the shared meanings, the cultural concepts and ideals of reproduction, but it does not in itself reveal how individuals experience and react to these events; that requires the direct study of individual lives. A second goal was insight into the psychological functioning of these women: the patterns of thought and feeling and action manifested in the management of their daily lives and their reactions to crisis. I was particularly interested in discovering the sources of their self-esteem and other forms of personal satisfaction, and the expectations involved in their contemporary relationships which might have been carried forward from earlier ones. Finally, the case studies were intended to explore the impact of cultural beliefs and socioeconomic change on their experience and behavior during the adult years. Facing unprecedented pressures and choices, Gusii women of this generation cannot rely simply on traditional role definitions for solutions to their problems. In devising or revising their own solutions during the period of field research, they revealed their personal coping styles and the ways they use Gusii cultural beliefs in their adaptive and defensive processes. The overall objective of the case studies, then, was to obtain a perspective on Gusii mothers, grounded in experiential data, in which they could be seen not only as products of the conditions under which they were raised and those to which they must respond but also as individuals striving in diverse ways for survival and satisfaction.

These studies draw their theoretical and methodological inspiration from the Freudian clinical tradition, but they are not "psychoanalytic" case histories; "psychosocial" might be a more appropriate designation. Their focus is on the conscious experience of the Gusii woman in the changing situations and relationships of her current life, including her relationship with the investigator. The emphasis is on presenting the case material in contexts that facilitate the reader's empathic under-standing of the subject. Interpretations are advanced when the material seems strong enough to warrant them. In a culture as different from ours as that of the Gusii, however, clarification of the surface, i.e., of conscious experience, is itself a major task and must precede depth interpretation. This book is above all an exploration of individual experience and personality in another culture, and it is offered to the specialist and nonspecialist reader alike primarily as an account of that exploration rather than as a finished interpretation of its results. In writing the book, my husband and I collaborated on the introductory and concluding chapters; the case studies were written by me alone.

THE GUSII OF HIGHLAND KENYA: THEIR CULTURAL BACKGROUND

The Gusii who currently number close to a million, live in southwestern Kenya, surrounded by Nilotic-speaking peoples (Luo, Kipsigis, Masai), but are part of the great Bantu-speaking majority of Africa south of the equator; their culture has both Bantu and Nilotic affinities. Western Kenya has long been a region where diverse peoples have met, merged, and fought and from which they have subsequently migrated. The Gusii moved to their contemporary highland position (about fifty miles south of the equator and twenty miles east of Lake Victoria) toward the end of the eighteenth century, thereby gaining elevation in relation to their Luo neighbors and putting distance between themselves and the Masai. In addition to relative security from attack, however, migration gained the Gusii a fertile, well-watered, healthy, and abundant land, most of it over 5,000 feet above sea level. They have lived in these green hills ever since, in a busy isolation, expanding their settlements, crops, and (until recently) herds. (For a complete bibliography of the Gusii to 1965, see R. LeVine and B. LeVine, *Nyansongo: A Gusii Community in Kenya* [New York: John Wiley & Sons, 1966]).

Gusii institutions before the British conquest of 1907 were not differentiated into political, economic, and religious spheres; patrilineal-descent groups of varying scope provided the organizational framework for all social behavior, and all functions were vested in kinship roles. The Gusii polity consisted of seven named territorial divisions, each of which was a cluster of intermarrying, localized patrilineal clans without permanent leadership positions or centralization. The clans, and the divisions in which they were located, occasionally fought with one another and united only in the face of external threat. Even lineage segments of a clan conducted blood feuds against each other though these could be settled by informal councils of clan elders according to an established set of rules. In this insecure environment, the homestead of a single patriarch, i.e., a man, his wives, and their sons living in a cluster of houses on their own land, constituted in many respects an autonomous unit of defense and internal governance. The residents of the homestead also constituted a largely autonomous unit of economic production, with the women doing most of the cultivation, the young men and children the herding of cattle, sheep, and goats, and the older men supervision and decision-making in all spheres. The division of labor was entirely by age and sex; each man could build a house and thatch a roof, each woman make baskets—in addition to their roles in primary subsistence activities. The Gusii depended on (part-time) specialists only for iron tools, hide preparation, medical treatment, and some ritual services. Neighbors cooperated in house building, agricultural work, and herding, with young men of a local lineage segment jointly tending and defending the herds in cattle-villages (until their abolition in 1912). Each homestead, however, supplied its own food and met many of its other needs as well. There were no temples or shrines; most rituals were performed at home in the same setting where all other activities took place, often with the patriarch as chief officiant. Thus there was no sharp boundary between the domestic and other spheres of life, and domestic organization assumed functional primacy in day-to-day activities.

This situation was reflected in Gusii views of social relationships. Concepts of social order, for example, drew heavily on domestic imagery. Terms for doorway, house, and hearthstone were used metaphorically to denote corporate group, subgroup, and localized lineage, respectively. The term for doorway is *egesaku*, a word that designates the small door into the man's part of the house from the cattle pen, and is used to signify lineage, tribe, and nation. The word for house is *enyomba*, which means also the mother-son unit within the homestead and similar subdivisions or segments within larger groupings. The word for hearthstone, *riiga*, denotes a localized lineage in which joint cattle herding and other local cooperative ties were maintained; since there are three adjacent hearthstones in the Gusii fireplace, this metaphor seems to be based on the coordinate status of adjacent lineages within a clan. Gusii proverbs and rituals relied on domestic metaphors, representing social and religious experience in a language of familiar physical objects, routine actions, and everyday encounters. It would not be an exaggeration to say that domestic arrangements constitute the Gusii model of the world, an abundant reservoir of prototypes for interpreting the flux and ambiguity of extradomestic relationships. Though their social structure has gradually changed since 1907, these prototypes remain salient in the social thought of most Gusii people.

The Gusii domestic group or homestead as a multifunctional unit and a model for social experience presents a large topic for ethnographic description. The present account is limited to its basic structural features, those economic and social functions that set the background for understanding the Gusii life course. The Gusii term *omochie* denotes a settlement based on primary kin relationships (parent-child and husband-wife), governed by its elder or patriarch (*omogaaka bw'omochie*)—who is sometimes referred to as its owner (*omonyene*)—and cooperating under his direction in a variety of economic, military, and ritual tasks. The males of the homestead, normally the patriarch and his sons, constituted a minimal corporate lineage, an *egesaku* at the lowest level in the genealogical pyramid of patrilineal descent groups sharing that vernacular designation. Polygyny was a cardinal feature of the homestead. The patriarch had several wives—at least two, ideally four, occasionally eight or more. Each wife had her own house with its own yard, surrounded by the fields allocated to her by the patriarch, which she was responsible for cultivating and the produce from which was stored in her own granary. When each of her sons married, he built another house, nearer to the mother's than to those of her cowives, for himself and his wife. There were also children's or bachelors' huts (*chisaiga,* singular *esaiga*), for older boys to live in before marriage; and the patriarch himself—who ideally rotated among his wives but often stayed longer with the youngest—sometimes slept in *esaiga* as a retreat from domestic strife.

Another cardinal feature of the domestic group was its virilocal residence—the men were permanent residents from birth to death, but the women came from other (exogamous) clans as reluctant brides. Since the intermarrying clans occupied distinct territories and carried out military actions against each other, the transfer of women at marriage was heavily formalized and highly coercive (from the bride's point of view). At home, this marital residence pattern meant that men were related by blood to their neighbors, but women were related by blood only to their own children—something they never lost sight of. Despite their initial position as clan strangers, however, women had a good deal of economic and social autonomy (their own fields, granaries, houses) in the circumscribed world of the homestead.

The world of the Gusii homestead as experienced by its inhabitants was a unit of economic expansion and of social control. In precolonial times, land was abundant, and a homestead head had access to as much land as his family could cultivate and use for grazing. The more wives he married, the more land he could bring under cultivation, the more daughters whose marriages would bring in cattle as bridewealth, the more sons to herd and defend the cattle and keep the homestead safe from outside attack. The ideal was proliferation—of wives, children, herds, and crops—and economic conditions permitted these modes of growth to be mutually reinforcing. For many Gusii men, now as then, cattle husbandry is the prototype for expansion in general—a man invests in initial nurturance and supervision, these result in growth and multiplication, he divides the herds and replicates the cycle, and thus the continuing process enriches him through indefinite expansion. The patriarch is the investor in and supervisor of domestic growth in all its forms.

In the past those Gusii men whose investment skills, combined with initial good fortune, enabled them to acquire numerous wives and sons, gained not only in productive labor but in many other ways. The adult sons, obedient to the patriarch, operated as his private army, defending the herds and constituting a military presence in the locality which intimidated potential interlopers into the territory. A man with six or more wives and with grown sons would inhabit an entire hill and become known far and wide as the patriarch of that area. His poorer lineage mates from the surrounding homesteads would visit him frequently, be provided food and drink by his wives, and give support to his prestige, authority, and influence in the settling of disputes. Such a man would play a major leadership role in the mobilization of his clan to meet external military threat; this meant in effect the amalgamation of the various homestead armies together with the warriors living in lineage-based cattle-villages. Since there were no permanent superordinate structures of leadership, the foremost Gusii leaders were well-to-do polygynists whose wealth and power were based entirely on the proliferation of domestic husband-wife and father-son bonds. With many sons, they became the founders of lineage segments named after them and thus achieved the only kind of personal immortality recognized in Gusii belief.

The Gusii homestead also represented a prototypic moral order. It involved a highly prescriptive organization of activities in space, an organization viewed as the embodiment of the highest moral ideals by which Gusii were supposed to live. Moral planning and normative prescription pervaded the design and arrangement of houses, rooms, ornaments, footpaths. Each married woman had her own house, and the patriarch was forbidden to enter the house of his son's wife under any circumstances. The adult son was forbidden to go beyond the entrance foyer in his mother's house—the house he had lived in as a child. The husband was forbidden to climb to the loft in his wife's house. These homestead restrictions, together with others concerning sexual modesty and respect, represented a code of propriety effective throughout the clan, regulating elders and youths alike, and enforcing incest rules, marital rights, respect for paternal authority, and checks on that authority. This system of normative control has more ramifications than can be explored here. Our present emphasis is on its location in the homestead, where many other activities took place, similarly prescribed by custom: for example, birth, male and female initiation ceremonies, weddings, burials (just outside the house), sacrifice. The homestead was a stage on which most of life was played according to a traditional script with specific directions for the design of sets and the locations and movements of the actors.

The traditional social order of the Gusii put women in a distinctly inferior position but also accorded them significant measures of autonomy and respect. Gusii women owned no property in a situation where property was the basis of social power; they were, after marriage, strangers in a community founded on kinship. They were responsible for producing and processing the food supply, but were excluded from most privileged forms of enjoyment. Women were ordered about, first by their parents, then by husbands and mothers-in-law. They were considered morally and emotionally immature, irresponsible, and lacking in sound judgment and were in fact prevented from bearing legal responsibility or exercising judgment in matters of importance. At the same time, they were not required to be demonstratively deferential to men; they were permitted much latitude in their own sphere of the homestead; they were not overtly despised as filthy or polluted; and as they grew older, they could gain power in homestead affairs and ritual performance.

The Gusii structure of sex roles was embodied in the design of their domestic arenas for social action. Each house and its adjacent fields and granaries was associated with a married woman and controlled by her; her father-in-law, patriarch of the homestead, was forbidden to set foot in it. The house itself was divided into two rooms: a woman's room (simply called "house," *enyomba*), in which cooking and sleeping took place, and a man's room (*eero*), in which male entertainment, beer drinking, and most domestic rituals took place. The man's room was regarded as being on the right-hand side of the house, the woman's on the left—a representation of female inferiority in Gusii belief. The woman was buried outside her part of the house (i.e., on its "left"), the man outside his (on its "right"). Men constructed houses and thatched their roofs, women smeared the wattle walls with mud. Men herded and milked cows, women carried the milk from the cattle-villages to the homesteads.

Despite their visible subordination and publicly inferior status, Gusii women were forces to be reckoned with. Senior wives could make it difficult for husbands to become polygynists, and since sons were more loyal to their mothers than their fathers, an elder who antagonized a wife with grown sons was courting rebellion and division in his homestead. Gusii diviners (*abaragori*), who played the most important extradomestic role in ritual, were virtually all women; so were witches, the most powerful personification of malevolence. The acquisition of power was a function of age.

THE ADULT LIFE COURSE FOR GUSII WOMEN

In the Gusii life plan, social esteem for both sexes comes later in life, with grandparenthood rather than parenthood. The labels below show how Gusii divide up the life course for both sexes.

FEMALE	MALE
1. Infant—*ekengwerere*	1. Infant—*ekengwerere*
2. Uncircumcised girl—*egesagaane*	2. Uncircumcised boy—*omoisia*
3. Circumcised girl—*omoiseke, enyaroka*	3. Circumcised boy warrior—*omomura*
4. Married woman—*omosubaati*	4. Male elder—*omogaaka*
5. Female elder—*omongina*	

Except for infancy, the labels are different for men and women, reflecting their drastically different statuses and social roles in a patrilineal society. The specific term for infant is not used frequently unless special emphasis is being put on the young age of the child; otherwise *omwaana* (plural *abaana*), the general term for "child," tends to be used for infants and older children alike. The single term for infants regardless of sex is consistent with the claim of Gusii mothers that they do not behave differently to boy and girl babies. When a baby is born, however, its sex is a matter of primary interest, and inquiries are answered with the terms *omoiseke* or *omomura* (no. 3, above) because the terms for uncircumcised girl or boy (no. 2), though more accurate, have a derogatory connotation that is out of keeping with the pleasantness of the occasion.

Females have four recognized and labeled life stages after infancy, while males have only three, since there is no special term for a circumcised male who is married but not yet an elder. The difference seems to reflect the fact that women undergo a fundamental change in their social status and residence at marriage, whereas men do not.

The *egesagaane* (uncircumcised girl; no. 2), is, like her male counterpart, a hard-working toiler at the bottom of the hierarchy in the domestic labor force, but the tasks she performs are different: carrying water from the stream (in pots balanced on her head), caring for babies, and (later) helping her mother in cooking, grinding, cultivating the fields. (If parents lack children of the appropriate sex, however, boys might be pressed into infant care, and girls might be assigned the male task of herding, at least temporarily.) As with boys, initiation ceremonies involving circumcision are the rite of passage to the next age grade, but girls undergo these at a younger age (nowadays seven or eight; in precolonial times, early to middle teens) and with a ceremonial content that emphasizes themes of sex, marriage, and procreation rather than valor and social autonomy. Of the two terms for a circumcised but unmarried girl, *enyaroka* literally means "a circumcised thing," and emphasizes the ordeal she has gone through; *omoiseke* is the more general term for a marriageable girl. Nowadays, girls are circumcised so young that there are many years elapsing between initiation and marriage, but preparation for marriage is a salient theme of life throughout these years. Parents view the unmarried girl with some ambivalence: the mother knows that however attached she is to her daughter, the girl must leave forever. Both parents feel they have a right to be compensated for having nurtured her but are rightly fearful that she may deprive them of the bridewealth compensation by eloping—thus leaving them with no source of bridewealth for one of her brothers.

The timing of marriage in the Gusii life plan is sharply differentiated by sex, reflecting the fact that wives are in greater demand than husbands in this polygynous society. For a typical young man, the timing of marriage is uncertain; it depends on his family's wealth, his patriarch's willingness to permit him the use of cattle, or the presence of a sister whose bridewealth can be used in his marriage. Wealthy or fortunate young men may be married by the age of twenty, whereas unfortunates must postpone the event until they are able to raise the bridewealth inside the family or through their own efforts—often until thirty or later. For young women, the timing of marriage is not problematic; like circumcision, it is an event that occurs at approximately the same age for all (fifteen or sixteen) and is another predictable marker of graduation to more elevated status, that of *omosubaati*. The problem is not whether or when they will get married but to whom. A young woman is expected to face marriage with reluctance about leaving home and to resist being taken away when the time comes—even though she has agreed to the match. Some are married to men they like in acceptable circumstances; others are forced by their fathers for reasons of bridewealth into undesirable matches with older men, frequently as secondary wives. There is, ideally, a period of trial marriage in which the bride is entitled to call it off if she discovers something terribly wrong with her new home: stereotypically, the husband is impotent or the mother-in-law a witch. Her father, however, may find it inconvenient to return cattle he has already committed to another purpose and may thus refuse to honor her complaint with action. Even if she is permitted to come home, she is soon married again, probably to another stranger and removed to a strange place where she is expected to live and work with strange people.

The young woman as *omosubaati* faces a period of adjustment that is considered by the Gusii to be difficult. She is expected to be exceedingly respectful, quiet, and cautious about violating kin avoidance norms. The "home people" are ideally expected to treat her kindly and hospitably and to make her feel welcome, but they may be jealous of her in one way or another and thus embroil her in controversies before she has developed much support in her new home. Furthermore, her domestic and agricultural skills are scrutinized, and she is criticized, often with mockery, if she is considered lazy, irresponsible, incompetent, or insubordinate. Her progress in gaining respect and social support among women of the homestead and neighborhood depends on many things, including their idiosyncrasies and hers, but in the long run her adjustment requires bearing children early and regularly. As her children grow older, her status increases. The circumcision of her first child of either sex is a joyous event for the mother, a kind of public confirmation of her successful motherhood. When one of her children is married, she graduates to *omongina* (female elder), the highest age grade to which she can aspire. As with the male term for elder, *omogaaka*, however, the use of the term *omongina* within and outside the homestead is distinguished: a woman who is *omongina* through the marriage of her children and through becoming a grandparent (as with men, the confirmation of elder status) is not *omongina* in the sense of the most senior woman in the homestead if her father-in-law has living wives, even though they may be junior wives younger than she in chronological age. Being the oldest chronologically while belonging to the younger generation does count for something, though: people in the homestead may begin calling her *omongina*, saying they are imitating a grandchild who uses the term for the woman who is visibly older.

As *omongina*, a woman has many prerogatives formerly denied her. She can talk more publicly, even to the point of being raucous and openly aggressive; she is permitted to drink beer at beer parties, though not to sit with the men; she can expect a certain amount of help when she needs it from her daughters-in-law and grandchildren. A woman who gives birth at seventeen or eighteen can become *omongina* in her early thirties and be a grandmother as young as thirty-five, when she has another decade of childbearing herself. After menopause, in her forties, she should have circumcised grandchildren, and her primary interests are focused on her son's and daughter's children, some of whom will live with her, visit her, joke with her. At her husband's death, her sons' claims to land will be based on what she cultivated when he was alive, so she is in effect the trustee of that part of his estate belonging to his sons.

This brief sketch of life stages for Gusii women brings some general points to the fore. First, transitions among the life stages of the Gusii are not based simply on chronological age, particularly after marriage. There is a status hierarchy among married adults of each sex; in this hierarchy, those with no married children are at the bottom, those with married children higher, those with grandchildren higher yet; and grandparents with no living seniors of the same sex in the same home-stead are at the top. Within the homestead, seniority is based on generational age and within a generation on birth order. A person moves up by the birth and growth of those below and by the death of those above. Getting older is inherently positive in terms of social esteem if the reproductive cycle is working as it should, i.e., if mating, birth, and death are occurring at expected times and with expected results. If they do not, there is concern, anxiety, potential conflict.

For a woman, progression up the hierarchy of age status requires having at least one son: to take care of her in her old age, to secure the land she has worked for her own progeny (rather than those of her cowives), to bring her a daughter-in-law to help with work, to produce grandsons who will dig her grave. More sons will make her feel more secure in all these ways and bring her more respect. Progression is also dependent on continuing to bear children until menopause. Interruption of childbearing, whatever its cause, is regarded as an unbearable calamity caused by ancestral spirits or jealous witches, occasioning recourse to divination, sacrifice, and antiwitchcraft medicine. Women who have had many offspring, grandchildren, and great-grandchildren are revered at well-attended funerals and mourned publicly to a degree that those with less successful reproductive careers cannot hope to match.

The role of women in Gusii ritual is prominent, pervasive—and too complex to be treated adequately here. On the positive side, there are healing roles—as diviners, herbalists, and performers of special birth ceremonies (or other related events)—available to women in their middle and older years, especially if they have themselves been afflicted and cured. On the other side, invidious distinctions among cowives, sisters-in-law, or other neighbors, concerning the number of children each has or their worldly success, give rise to suspicions of witchcraft and accusations of homicide through poisoning and magic. Finally, there are women in an intermediate realm of legitimacy who sell love magic (*amaebi*)—which is considered more dangerous than its translation connotes in our language—and medicines to prevent magical adultery punishment from taking effect.

CHANGES IN THE POSITION OF GUSII WOMEN

The foregoing account emphasizes traditional ideals, which are still recognized by contemporary Gusii. But the environments of men and women have changed considerably over the last seventy years, affecting their capacities to realize those ideals. To understand the contexts in which the women who were studied in 1974–76 lived their lives, an overview of these changes is necessary.

Population growth represents a major aspect of change. The Gusii have been remarkably successful in fulfilling their ideals of fertility and group proliferation. The postmenopausal women surveyed in 1976 for this study had a median of ten live births, and there was only one childless woman of advanced childbearing age or older in an area of more than 2,100 residents. This high fertility, combined with low infant and child mortality, has increased the Gusii population enormously over the last few decades. "Nyansango," the community first studied in 1955 to 1957, had doubled through natural increase by 1974, even though a number of its residents emigrated during the intervening years. Trees were removed, pastures occupied and cultivated, houses built closer to each other than before. The rise in density has forced people into closer contact than they would choose and has made land scarce, so that holdings now average less than three acres per family. In response to an increasingly difficult situation, the Gusii have reduced their livestock, continued to work hard on the land, adopted agricultural innovations promising higher returns, and sent their men out in search of economic opportunities. With close to 40 percent of the adult men away, the burden of cultivation and responsibility for child subsistence in the area studied falls on women like those portrayed in this book.

This change in the ratio of people to land has occurred rapidly among the Gusii; their economic adaptation to it has not yet been followed by a change in reproductive attitudes or behavior. Children are still regarded as the greatest of blessings, the more the better, though their economic futures are clearly at risk. The reasons for this lie in the domain of basic values, which few Gusii have so far questioned. For women, this situation means continued striving toward high fertility and great concern about reproductive inadequacy. They present the apparent paradox of wanting to bear more children than they can support on a dwindling base of land resources.

Another paradox of population growth is that overcrowding on the land has increased the social isolation of Gusii women from each other. Married women used to spend a great deal of time with their neighbors in cooperative work groups (ebisangio, singular egesangio), which are nowadays rarely activated because each woman's land is small enough to cultivate on her own. These groups have not been replaced by anything as organized, compelling, and enjoyable; the result is a net loss in neighborhood sociability and a diminution in the reciprocal relationships women can rely upon when they need help.

The development of a cash economy has undermined some traditional Gusii social values and transformed others into a more convertible currency. Young men go to work in the cities to earn money that can replace agricultural income and purchase consumer goods newly desired. Their lessened dependence on the patriarchal land and livestock erodes the control of elders over their homesteads and communities. The cultivation of cash crops, now primarily pyrethrum (a flower used in nonresidual insecticides) and tea, makes it possible for women to earn money at home from their agricultural labor—particularly important if the labor-migrant husband fails to send part of his wages regularly. It is also possible to sell food crops—maize, finger millet, and vegetables—at the local marketplace when cash is needed. Now, in contrast with the past, land can be rented and sold; meat and (in many families) milk must be purchased, and beer can be bought by anyone with the money. As late as the 1950s, women of childbearing years were largely prohibited from drinking millet beer (*busaa*) at neighborhood beer parties; nowadays they buy it and even corn whiskey (*changaa*) freely at the many places it is sold in the area. Monetization and commercial development have brought a new freedom from traditional restrictions and introduced new choices which can lead to prosperity and poverty. Gusii women must face these choices with less supervision and control than ever before.

Like population growth and a cash economy, schooling has changed the lives of Gusii women in many ways. First, it changed their economic perspective on child rearing: they are now rearing children to be successful in school and get good jobs, as an investment in their own economic futures. Second, those who have gone far enough in school to be employed at the higher levels are greatly respected and become sources of new values to replace the old; it is they who give women (and men) the idea that in the outside world the kinship values of the Gusii are superseded by more powerful, glamorous, and prestigeful lifestyles worthy of emulation. This trend helps diminish the capacity of elders to enforce traditional morality. Finally, more women have been educated in the late 1960s and early 1970s, with an increasing number in secondary school. For a few, this has meant postponement of marriage as they continue schooling to become teachers and nurses. For others, it has meant premarital pregnancy at about fifteen or sixteen—an apparent consequence of unsupervised contacts with men (both pupils and teachers) in school—and parental efforts at a hasty marriage. Those who have gone to school for six or seven years seem to acquire a new outlook on the world that affects their attitudes as consumers, wives, and mothers, even though their social roles in the economy and the moral order of the domestic group have changed hardly at all. This is a paradox with which some women of the case studies are struggling most intensely.

These changes in land pressure, economic adaptation, and education translate into both burdens and possibilities in the experience of contemporary Gusii women. Their husbands away, their land resources small, their neighborhood support groups reduced, they struggle to feed their children and send them to school, working long hours every day on agricultural and domestic tasks—with less reliable help than before from young daughters, who now go to school instead of spending the whole day in infant care. These women are preoccupied with making ends meet and getting the work done. At the same time their relative isolation, participation in a cash economy, and schooling give them choices Gusii women never had before: to console themselves with a drink, to join one of several Christian churches, to start a small business such as brewing beer, to rent out the land for short-term gain or put in a new pyrethrum crop for a later profit. There are possibilities for pride and satisfaction in this newfound freedom, though the anxieties and burdens often seem to outweigh them. Each married woman is more dependent on her own personal resources than ever before, with consequences that necessarily vary from one individual to another and are represented in the following chapters.

Despite the major socioeconomic changes that have altered the context in which Gusii women live their lives, the normative center of those lives remains in place. Each woman must find a husband whose home, affiliations, and resources become her own. She must leave her parents and go to live with a man who at least promises to pay bridewealth for her. She is given her own house and fields at his homestead, raises her food and children there, and is expected to serve, obey, and be faithful to her husband, respect and help his mother, cooperate with his brothers' wives. There is less uniformity than before in the fulfillment of these expectations, but they are still the standards against which women are evaluated. Similarly, regardless of the husband's employment and her own education, each woman is still a tiller of the soil and manager of the home—whatever else she might do. Thus the norms and obligations of women's kinship and economic roles are largely intact within a restructured socioeconomic environment.

The Gusii system of beliefs and rituals—religious, magical, and medical—also remains largely intact, despite Christian influence, and forms the context for personal belief and remedial action among young women as well as old. Now as in the past, afflictions are seen as due to the righteous anger of the ancestors (*ebirecha*) or the malevolent jealousy of local witches (*abarogi*); diviners (*abaragoori*) are consulted to detect the exact causes; and a variety of measures, including sacrifice (*okogwansa*) and sorcery (*obonyamosira*), are undertaken to effect cures. Antibiotics and indigenous herbs are also used. The women portrayed in the case studies share with their Gusii neighbors the belief that reproductive and mental disorders, as well as other chronic diseases and fatalities, are symptoms of spiritual processes that threaten the self and the family in a fundamental way and require ritual as well as medicinal remediation. Their most serious anxieties, particularly in relation to neighbors and kinsmen, are experienced in these terms.

WOMEN AND THEIR NATAL KIN

The women in these case studies are not *abangina* (female elders); they are all mothers of children yet unmarried. Two of them do not yet even have their marriages socially confirmed by bridewealth transfer. Thus they have not reached the stage of a woman's life which is ideally—and certainly was in earlier years—most rewarding and enjoyable. On the other hand, they maintain something which is easy to overlook in this strongly patrilocal and patrilineal society, namely, ties to the kin in the homes where they grew up.

At marriage a young woman must transfer her loyalties to her husband's patrilineage and clan, but at the same time she is permitted and expected to continue relationships with members of her family of origin. Her social and economic future and her position in the community depend upon her situation in her married home, but still she looks to her own family for various kinds of support, in particular emotional support. It is her father and brothers who, having received bridewealth payment for her, will see to it that she remains with her husband, or else they will be obligated, if she runs away, to repay the cattle. Accordingly, it is in their interests to promote harmony in relations between their daughter/sister and her in-laws, and at times they will intervene as mediators on her behalf. However, a woman often regards her male relatives with more awe than affection; it is her female relatives to whom she is likely to be more positively attached, particularly her mother, her paternal grandmother in whose house she slept as a child, and her elder sister who was her caretaker or, in the event that she was senior in her sibling order, the younger sister whom she herself cared for, whose *omoreri* she was.

Actual frequency of contact after marriage depends on a number of factors, not the least being geographical location. When a woman marries into a clan close to her home, she is likely to meet natal family members on the road or in the market. While custom allows new wives to visit their own previous homes, nevertheless ease of visitation varies considerably. When a young woman is perceived by her in-laws as being especially ambivalent about her marriage, it is probable that she will be refused permission to visit her home for fear she will not return. Thus, even though her own and her husband's homes might be close, a woman might be denied by her in-laws the opportunity to visit her parents. If she were sufficiently unhappy she might take matters into her own hands and run away; otherwise she would have to remain where she is until, having settled down sufficiently, she would at last be allowed to go on a visit to her natal home. There she would be welcomed joyfully and given all the attentions due a "visitor," being recognized now as one who is no longer a resident of the homestead.

Another factor which regulates the frequency of a woman's visits to her parents' home is her work load. Gusii women, especially young women, who must work for their mothers-in-law as well as themselves, are much burdened. Furthermore, it is not customary for a young woman who is nursing a child to sleep at her natal home. Many in-laws insist that she return to her husband's home by nightfall, which might be impossible in instances where the distance between homesteads is considerable and transport difficult. Thus it is frequently the case that women go rarely to their parents' homes and even less frequently to visit sisters who married "out," even though both sisters might have married into the same clan and thus be living fairly close to one another. Unless they meet by chance on the road or at church, for example, their schedules do not permit much contact.

Nevertheless, the importance of a woman's relationships with her female relatives must not be underestimated. Younger women especially are consciously preoccupied with thoughts of their mothers. They worry about them, miss them, and dream about them. They are extremely sensitive about the attention, or lack thereof, which their mothers pay them, especially in matters of obligation and presentation of gifts at the time they give birth. When after a time her mother still has not come to greet her newborn child, a woman will be increasingly anxious. She tries to handle her feelings of rejection by blaming her mother's tardiness on a third party: her father, who will not give her mother time off to come; or in cases where her mother is a widow, her brothers, whose economic support is inadequate, thus preventing her mother from accumulating the prescribed gifts without which she may not visit her daughter. The relationship a woman has with her own mother is of central importance to her feelings of self-worth. If she is lucky and finds that her mother-in-law meets some of her emotional demands, as time goes on she will gradually be weaned from her own mother. Though she will still say, "My mother-in-law can never be a real mother to me," nevertheless she will be secure and reasonably content in a more mature relationship in which ambivalence is kept within comfortable limits. A woman who has borne many children may say that nowadays she is truly at home in her husband's home. However, it is rather unlikely that anyone would express these sentiments as long as her own mother were alive. It was our observation that even postmenopausal women whose marriage careers had been very successful seemed to suffer profoundly at their mothers' deaths, while those women who had lost their mothers in girlhood, or before they were properly established in their husbands' homes, still mourned their losses many years later. It would seem, then, that the attachment of a daughter to her mother is not only central and enduring but is likely to be the most important relationship in a woman's life. In part this situation might be due to the circumstances of a traditional marriage, in which a girl is married before the age of twenty to a man not of her choosing from a clan she has grown up to regard as enemy of her own. In part it may be due to the nature of the marital relationship. A husband does not provide the kind of nurturance a woman found at home, although she may be fortunate and discover in her mother-in-law a source of emotional support. Certain other aspects of the mother-daughter tie in Gusii society must be considered also. It may be that a daughter's feelings for her mother are never fully reciprocated. A mother invests more in her sons, who will stay with her, than in her daughters, who will leave. Thus perhaps a girl, being more heavily invested in an unequal relationship, will always be left wanting. But living in a society that stresses obedience above all else, in childhood she had little opportunity to express negative feelings of any sort. Thus she has little chance to emerge from her unambivalent dependency on her mother while still at home. She takes with her at marriage a still idealized image of her mother which her life experience in alien territory, where she is necessarily an outsider, gives scant opportunity for reworking.

As a child her relationships with her paternal grandmother and her sister were inherently less ambivalent. With both she was once on extremely intimate terms. She gave and was given to without stint, and she carries most pleasurable memories of these relationships her whole life long. When she visits her own home, she often spends more time in her grandmother's house than in her mother's, seeking once again the playfulness of childhood. Yet if she does not see her grandmother or her sister for long periods, she will miss them without experiencing great distress. Should her mother fail to visit her when custom demands, however, a woman will feel bitterly rejected; and her own inability for whatever reason to visit her mother is likely to be a sore trial to her.

THe case sTuDies

My initial tasks were twofold. First, I had to become familiar with the community, and the inhabitants had to be given the opportunity to become familiar with me. My objective was to become as unremarkable as possible. Second, since I wanted to use an interpreter only minimally, I had to learn the language, Ekegusii. Swahili, the lingua franca of Kenya, was not spoken by women unless they had lived outside the tribal area for extended periods and had had intensive contact with other tribal groups. Even those few women who knew Swahili were not fluent and clearly did not think their most intimate thoughts in it. If I hoped to understand their cognitive processes and the subtle shifts of association, quite apart from the reality content of what they said and what they dreamed, it was essential that I tackle their extraordinarily difficult language. There was no dictionary, no literature except an edition of the New Testament, and no grammar other than a mimeographed introduction twenty years old—and already, with the rapid change in the spoken language, out of date. The first task, that of familiarity, was easier than the second, since for five months I was constantly on display while collecting census and nutritional data. The second task was more difficult; but a woman, Mary, was found who had had eight years of primary education and knew Swahili and some English. From her I learned to speak Ekegusii. Subsequently Mary became my assistant. She was a local woman whom most people knew and apparently trusted, and without her this work would have been impossible.

The purpose of the investigation was to try to understand the psychic reality and mode of adaptation of ordinary Gusii peasant women. My position as a researcher was obviously very different from that of a therapist whose help is sought by persons who are suffering. Apart from goodwill, I had nothing to offer in return for the license to intrude at intervals into their lives. I intended to visit them in their homesteads once a week for an hour. Early on, if I sensed my presence was unwelcome, I would desist, but if all went well and a relationship developed, I could increase the number and duration of my visits as circumstances dictated, for example, during periods of stress or illness, or if some ritual were to be performed.

During the course of my other research I took note of women with whom I felt I could work. My judgment depended largely on whether I found them interesting, and to some degree, despite Gusii women's traditional female reticence with strangers or people regarded as powerful, they also showed signs of finding me interesting. In all I began to work with eleven different women, four of whom I soon dropped. The other seven I continued to see as long as both I and they remained in the area.

The amount of data gathered was of course enormous. I therefore decided to select, for each case, a specific issue or incident and to use that as a focus in the presentation of the material. By examining the way in which each woman behaved in a stress situation, I have sought to throw some light generally on the psychological functioning of women in this society.

I have interspersed the narrative with excerpts from my field notes wherever I thought it appropriate. The proper names of individuals and places have been changed in order to insure the anonymity of the persons involved. In instances where individuals were known by their baptismal names, I have substituted accordingly. Likewise, in those instances in which individuals went by Gusii names, I have found Gusii substitutes. The seven subjects of the case studies all had Christian as well as Gusii names, and I refer to each throughout the text by her Christian name to make it easier for the reader.

1

Suzanna Bosibori

I

Suzanna Bosibori, a young mother of four, was the first woman whom I selected and began to visit regularly. My original contact with her occurred when I was doing a community census and at the same time collecting a sample of pregnant women whose infants, after birth, could be included in our longitudinal study. At that point Suzanna had three children, all daughters, the youngest of whom was about eighteen months old. Toward all her children Suzanna seemed to display, for a Gusii woman, exceptional gentleness and warmth. Although communication was difficult, since she knew no Swahili and my Ekegusii was rudimentary, her behavior toward me was also exceptionally warm. She seemed at ease with me. I told her that I had a daughter and a son the same age as Joyce, her youngest child. "Only two children?" she asked, and I said, "Yes, two are enough. Children are so much work. Aren't three enough for you?" She said, "No—I am already expecting a fourth." This she said quietly, but directly, looking me in the eyes.

Later, as we continued our research on the psychological meaning of pregnancy, we discovered that no Gusii woman will ever, except under most unusual circumstances, admit even to her husband that she is pregnant unless her condition is patently obvious to the eye. Even then, when challenged, she will rarely agree to the fact. Her silence must be taken as her assent. The reason for such reticence is that all Gusii believe that any kind of good fortune may arouse jealousy in another, most particularly in one's closest relatives and kinsmen, among whom one invariably lives in a patrilocal society. Anyone whose jealousy is provoked is likely to attempt to bewitch the person of whom he or she is jealous. Among these people, who value above all else the capacity to reproduce copiously, pregnancy is seen by everyone as good fortune, and thus any woman who discovers she is pregnant is highly unlikely to volunteer the fact or even to admit to it if asked. Otherwise, she may incur the malevolence of her husband's brothers' wives or of other women of her husband's family, whether or not they are of childbearing age and regardless of their own ease or difficulty in bearing children. Thus for Suzanna to volunteer to me that she was pregnant, some time before the fact even became apparent, was a most unusual admission. I did not understand the significance of her behavior at the time, but as the months passed and I continued to meet her occasionally on the road or weeding in her *shamba* (garden plot), she would always greet me with a special warmth. Never in the early months did she go out of her way to pursue me, as others in the community in fact did, but when by chance she saw me she behaved as if she had been expecting me to come and she was ready to receive me. In short, I decided to work with her because I liked her and I was attracted by her apparent serenity and graciousness. It was my impression that both were unusual characteristics in Gusii women.

When I first began to visit Suzanna to learn with her help, as I told her, how Gusii women bring up their children, I knew very little about her. Over time, as in the psychoanalytic process, I would learn from her what she allowed me to know, and I would try to understand the significance of information which came from other sources but remained uncorroborated by anything she herself said or did in my presence. However, for the sake of readers who cannot be familiar with either the setting or the typical conditions of life in a remote African tribe, it is necessary to go ahead a little in order to provide some information without which this material would be confusing or incomprehensible.

At the time I worked with her, Suzanna was in her mid-twenties.

She did not know her actual age and claimed initially to be nineteen. She was the second child and second daughter of a tribal policeman, Ochoi, and his senior wife, Moraa. Physically she was of middle height and strongly built, with erect carriage. She was very black. With the Gusii, as with many African peoples, light skin color is prized. Although to the members of our research team Suzanna, with her smooth skin and charming smile, seemed very attractive, I never heard any Gusii say anything complimentary about her appearance. She was poor, even by local standards. She possessed two ragged dresses and one head scarf; her house was not a real house at all but the hut of an adolescent boy. She claimed to have gone to school for five years, but though she could possibly read the vernacular with difficulty, I never saw her write. She even denied that she knew how to sign her name. She occasionally spoke of writing to her husband. However, she may have got a brother to write her letters for her. At any rate, her primary school experience had left her virtually illiterate.

She described her original home as being happy, "much better than this place," her married home. As a young child her mother was her father's only wife. He married a second wife with the cattle he received when his eldest daughter married. Thus the cowife/stepmother, who inevitably brings trouble, did not come into the home until Suzanna was almost grown.

Both Suzanna's parents were converts to the Seventh Day Adventist church. Her father left the church when he married his second wife, but this young woman was also an SDA. There was no brewing or drinking of beer in the home, and both wives were energetic and well organized in their work habits, according to the Calvinist directives of their church. They made the best of the few acres their husband inherited. We found that in our area members of Protestant churches, especially of the Seventh Day Adventist church (which, though claiming a small minority of the total population, nevertheless was the Protestant church with by far the largest following), were often markedly different from their Catholic and non-Christian neighbors in their orientation and the degree of their "progressiveness," i.e., their receptivity to modern values. The SDA church preached the Protestant ethic in its most exacting form and in addition demanded monogamy, teetotalism, and renunciation of traditional "pagan" rituals. Church members, of course, varied in their capacity to live by those precepts.

However, in a society where alcoholism is rampant and the violent behavior which accompanies drinking is a familiar occurrence, children growing up in a family from which drinking is absent are likely to have a calmer early experience than many of their peers. As a child Suzanna kept the Sabbath, although she never was baptized, since she left home before completing the necessary course of instruction leading to baptism.

The social structure of the Gusii is quite simple. The primary relationship of a man is with his patrilineal clan and its component lineages; of a woman (after marriage), with her husband's clan and lineage. The Gusii are exogamous and patrilocal. That is, a man must marry outside his own clan, and he brings his wife or wives to live on the land which his father allocated to him. Early sexual relations may occur secretly within the clan, but marriage is always between "strangers." At the age of sixteen Suzanna had a brief union with a young man. She left him, and on returning to her father's homestead, she discovered she was pregnant and gave birth to her first child, Flora. She remained at home for three years until, pregnant once again, she eloped with William Ongaki, a young Catholic schoolteacher of about her own age. He brought her to his home and installed her in the hut which had been built for his circumcision long ago, when he was about ten years old. Ongaki was an affable young man. His mother's original husband had died, leaving her with two sons. She was inherited by her husband's brother Ogaro, by whom she had three more sons, of whom William was the eldest, and two daughters. While the sons by her first husband went off into the world, prospered, and bought land elsewhere, Ongaki and his two younger brothers, the sons of the leviratic husband, had been much less determined and fortunate. The three of them laid claim to the acre and a half which their social (rather than biological) father left them and which remained undivided and under the control of their mother, Kemunto. From this Suzanna and her mother-in-law attempted to eke out a living. They had a little pyrethrum and some coffee, and the rest was devoted to food crops for home consumption. In no year was their maize supply sufficient, and for months at a time· they went hungry for heavy porridge (*obokima*), their staple diet.

The six years since Suzanna eloped with Ongaki had been filled with turbulence for both of them. Suzanna's second daughter, Jane, was born in Ongaki's home, but the fact that he was now "married" brought little difference in his behavior. He was frequently negligent of his professional duties as a teacher. He drank a great deal and was often absent from school for days at a time. He spent his salary on beer and prostitutes. Ultimately he was fired, just as we started working in the community. He and Suzanna quarreled constantly, and when Suzanna was still nursing Jane she left him and returned to her home. She remained at home for more than a year, but during that time Ongaki was trying to persuade her to return. As a result of an assignation with him, she became pregnant for the third time. She gave birth to Joyce at her own home. Her father told her to go back to Ongaki, "for who else will pay for you?" And thus, when Joyce was three months old, Suzanna did return to Ongaki, bringing Jane but leaving Flora behind with her grandmother. At the end of our time in the field, Suzanna was still living with Ongaki. She had borne him three children and was regarded by everyone as his wife except in one essential aspect: Ongaki had never paid bridewealth for her.

Traditionally very young Gusii girls sometimes engaged in consensual unions, as Suzanna herself did. However, later they expected to be married according to the custom of their tribe: that is, with cattle. The conventional practice in arranging marriages called for an intermediary, who would be sent by a young man to find out if a certain girl were willing to entertain his suit. If indeed she were willing, she would then have an opportunity to meet her husband-to-be (who was often a stranger to her). If she consented to his proposal, the fathers, both real and classificatory, of the young pair would negotiate the cattle payment. Only when the groom had paid the bridewealth cattle either in total or at least in large part would the marriage take place and the bride be permitted to go to her husband's home.

Ten years ago a very large proportion of all marriages were still taking place according to traditional practices. With the extreme shortage of land, however, fewer and fewer farmers have the space on which to graze cattle. Whereas in the past the Gusii took ownership of cattle as a matter of course, nowadays the majority have no cattle at all or have them only briefly when they have received some in payment of bridewealth or have bought them prior to making such payment themselves. The cost of cattle has risen enormously, and young men, unless they come from modern (i.e., educated) families, do not have the resources to buy cattle. Therefore, in the past few years, the custom of making bridewealth payments at the time when girls go from their father's to their husband's home at the outset of their married lives has diminished rapidly, to a point where the traditional practice is now very rare indeed. Young people are not prepared to wait until the boy has earned the money to buy the cattle. Nowadays almost every Gusii girl elopes; that is, she leaves her parents' home, often secretly, and goes to her lover's home, where she immediately starts to behave like a married woman. Nevertheless, parents are often most indignant when this occurs, and no one, neither the girl's parents nor the girl, nor anyone else involved, regards the girl as properly married, however many children she might bear and however many years she might remain, until the cattle have been paid. Owing to economic pressures, the Gusii have thus been forced to alter the chronology of their marriage practices but not the essential procedure, i.e., the transfer of property from the husband's family to the bride's family in compensation for the loss of a daughter to another clan, which from now on will have sole claim on all she produces, notably her labor and her sons.

Ongaki's failure to pay for Suzanna or, while he was employed, to make any efforts to save money to do so was a source of great bitterness and shame to her. As long as she bore him daughters he had reason to procrastinate, but even after the longed-for heir, Ogaro, was born, he talked of paying for her but did nothing to put his good intentions into effect.

On one hand Suzanna dwelt upon the grief which her ambiguous status brought her, and she joyously greeted the birth of her son, who would tie her irrevocably, regardless of bridewealth, to her husband's clan. The birth of her daughters had not forced any absolute commitment upon either Suzanna or Ongaki. Daughters are not valued like sons—they grow up, marry outside, and leave the parents forever. Thus men do not value the mothers of their daughters as they do the mothers of their sons. But on the other hand, at a deeper level, the advent of Ogaro, named for his dead paternal grandfather, precipitated a maturational crisis in Suzanna which I witnessed and struggled to understand during the last fourteen months of my stay.

II

It should be of interest to know something about how my relationship with Suzanna developed. When I had reached a point in language learning where I thought I could manage to go into homesteads alone, without an interpreter, I went to see Suzanna and made an appointment to return another day in order to watch her and her children. I explained that I did not want to interfere in whatever work she was engaged in. She should go about her business as usual. I had observed mothers and children elsewhere in Africa as well as in America, and I wanted to see in what ways Gusii mothers behaved similarly to mothers in other places, and in what ways they were different.

I had originally determined to visit without an interpreter, despite the anticipated impairment in my understanding of what was being said and done, because I thought any third person would complicate and dilute the situation and inhibit the subject. In addition, for many months I was unable to find an assistant who I felt might be capable of the degree of sensitivity necessary for such work.

In America when a patient who is a native English speaker talks in such a way that his foreign-born therapist cannot understand, the therapist may decide that this is "resistance" on the part of the patient. Though I do not deny that this might have occurred in my case with my Gusii research subjects, there were several factors which rendered this possibility less likely. First was my imperfect knowledge of the language, a circumstance that continued throughout my stay. Second was the fact that almost all the women with whom I worked were totally unfamiliar with strangers, European or African, who spoke Ekegusii. Since the beginning of colonial times outsiders have spoken Swahili. A handful of Catholic priests and Protestant missionaries have learned the vernacular, but most Gusii have never in their lives heard their language spoken imperfectly. Thus when they heard me speak Ekegusii they were utterly confused, particularly if I made mistakes. Since my purpose was primarily to listen, my difficulties with speaking their language were not vital. More important was their failure to talk so that I could understand. They had no experience with simplifying their speech patterns and vocabulary for the benefit of a stranger. I worked with only one woman who consistently made efforts to ensure that I could follow her entirely, and she had lived many years outside the district. In general, although I learned fairly rapidly to understand what people said to me specifically, I always had difficulty in understanding conversations to which I was peripheral.

After some time of struggling alone, I decided to try using Mary, my language teacher, as an assistant, and I believe her presence did nothing but enhance my investigations. She had married a man of Bogoro; that is, her husband was of the same clan as Ongaki, and indeed of the husbands of several other women who were in my study. But of course Mary herself came originally from an adjacent clan. She had grown up at some distance from both Suzanna and Ongaki and in addition had lived away for most of the time since her marriage, since her husband had been working outside the district. Thus, though hers was a familiar face in the community, she was certainly not intimate with women in the neighborhood. Moreover, Mary had only one child. In this community where infertility was known but fairly rare, everyone knew that she was unable to have more children. In a way, this might be seen as something in her favor, for as she said, "How can they be envious of me when I am so much poorer than they are?"

However, in my earliest contacts with Suzanna, I was alone. I rejected the idea of using a cassette recorder since Gusii life, weather permitting, is lived in the open and so much of what interested me was visual, not auditory. Apart from the unfamiliarity of these women with a cassette recorder, even the most sensitive machine could pick up what was being said—with the corn stalks crackling in the breeze—at a distance of fifty or a hundred feet. I would make notes only of dreams and associations to them in situ. Everything else of interest I would attempt to remember as best I could, and as soon as I left the compound I would make detailed notes of all I had heard and seen and its proper sequence.

I began by structuring my visits as if I were doing a behavior observation, because it was a way of spending extended periods of time in the compound while being minimally intrusive. Before I could claim to understand what I was seeing and hearing at anything but the most superficial level, I had first to become familiar with the activities and personal idiosyncrasies of Suzanna and her family. For many months I did not initiate conversation apart from the simplest greetings and inquiries as to health, harvest, and the like. If Suzanna or other family members engaged me in conversation, then I would respond readily. But my purpose was to listen and to take note in particular of what Suzanna selected to talk about in my presence to other people as well as to me. In all, during seventeen months I visited Suzanna on seventy occasions for an hour or more and had briefer contacts with her on hundreds of other occasions.

I made my first visit at lunch time. It was March, the beginning of the rains and of the growing season. For diagnostic purposes, I shall give a quite detailed account of my first visit: when I arrived, Ongaki's homestead was deserted. All the houses in the compound were mud walled, with grass-thatched roofs (as opposed to cement walled, with iron-sheet roofs—which is the contemporary ideal). There was a main house fifteen feet square with a smaller separate kitchen beside it. These belonged to Kemunto, Suzanna's mother-in-law. Her walls were quite well maintained, having been recently smeared with clay and decorated with white-chalked pictures of flowers. The other two homes in the homestead were much smaller and not so well kept. These belonged to Ongaki and his two unmarried brothers. Near Ongaki's house was a flowering shade tree with a bench beneath it. I would sit on this bench during my visits while Suzanna usually lay on a piece of sacking at my feet.

On this occasion I sat down to wait, thinking Suzanna had forgotten or purposely remained in the fields. But after a while her neighbor saw me over the boundary hedge and ran off to find her. Within a few moments Suzanna appeared, walking slowly, with Joyce on her back and followed by Jane. She was obviously very tired.

> She is nearly seven months pregnant and has been digging in her garden since shortly after sunrise. She greets me warmly and reassures me that I am not inconveniencing her. She would have come home anyway at this time even if her neighbor had not come to find her, because she is too tired to do any more work. She stands and chats for a moment. She was alone in the garden this morning, she says. Her husband is in Mombasa (on the coast 600 miles away), where he went to find employment. She just got a letter from him saying he's all right, but he hasn't found work. All the same, she is happy to hear from him. Without excusing herself, she goes on past me to take care of her

two little girls. From a pot she pours water into a bowl to wash off the mud from the fields and energetically washes her arms and legs and feet, while instructing the children to do likewise. Jane is a friendly child who shows no signs of being wary of me. She carefully imitates her mother, but Joyce retreats and begins to whimper. She is not yet two. She is a slight little girl, much lighter skinned than her mother or sister. She seems very fragile. Suzanna comments to me that Joyce is sick; she has diarrhea. She talks to the children constantly, in a soft voice, gently examining their hands and feet to check that they are clean. At the same time she talks to me intermittently. When the ablutions are finished Joyce clings to her mother, indicating that she wants to get onto her mother's back again. Suzanna tells her no and explains to me that she has such a backache she can scarcely bend down.

She is ready now to give them their lunch, which is *erongori*, or porridge made from maize meal, similar to semolina in texture. Meanwhile the neighbor who fetched Suzanna from the garden comes into the homestead (to get a closer look at me), followed by some teenagers, a girl and two boys. Suzanna greets them, offers them food, and goes about her tasks. She isn't still for a second. She moves smoothly on from one task to another. Eventually, when everyone has been taken care of, she sits on the ground near me, with Joyce between her knees. She herself ate at a neighbor's house, she says. She is not hungry, only tired. She lays out a piece of sacking in the shade and encourages Joyce to lie on it and take a nap. She sighs, remarking that she wants to sleep but she must go to the garden again if it doesn't rain. If she stays at home, what will the family eat? Where will they find money for clothes?

She lies down beside the children, but in a second Joyce has climbed on her back and started to tickle her mother. Suzanna tells her off, but she smiles as she does it, and the child continues her efforts to get her mother to play with her. Suzanna pretends to put out her breast, "Is this what you want?" she teases. (Gusii women usually nurse their babies for about eighteen months or until they discover they are pregnant again. It is believed that the fetus contaminates the mother's milk. A nursing child must be weaned immediately when his mother conceives. Thus Joyce was weaned months ago.) She turns away from Joyce and attempts to continue her conversation with her visitors, but Joyce insists on having her mother's attention. Eventually she jumps up and runs off. Suzanna remarks without much conviction that Joyce is naughty.

I had many visits like this one, in which I slowly pieced together who was who and listened as best I could to the conversation while Suzanna got used to me and I to her.

On this first occasion I noticed a number of diagnostically important things about her. For one thing, she was attached to her husband. Even though he had gone off and left her in the second half of her pregnancy, with all the farm work to be done at home, and even though he seemed, after almost three months of looking for employment without success, to have gone in vain, Suzanna conveyed the idea to me that she missed him. Clearly, any feelings of resentment she might have about his absence or failure to provide for her and his family were secondary.

She was overtly ambivalent about being pregnant. She was so very tired. Yet the welfare of the family depended upon her, and she had no chance of indulging her desire to rest. She was in need of so many things, but she did not ask me for anything, not even for milk, which women commonly requested for their children.

She attracted visitors—not only her neighbor who had come to scrutinize me but the three teenagers, Ongaki's relatives, whom she entertained as best she could. According to Gusii custom, it is very important to offer food to visitors. These days, when food is less plentiful than in the past, especially during the growing season, long after the last harvest, people tend to be niggardly in sharing food with visitors. But Suzanna brought out what she had—which was boiled corn kernels. Her behavior with her children bore out my earlier impression that she was a gentle person. She talked to them, particularly to Joyce, her younger child, in a structuring and nurturing way. She responded to the child's mood rather than just giving orders. Though she had visitors, she had time for her children also. She had quite a lot of eye contact with them, in particular with Joyce, when she was luring her out of her initial fear of me.

She fitted me into whatever else had to be attended to. There were certain tasks which had to be seen to before she could relax, and these she accomplished before sitting down with me and her other visitors. I was certainly the first white person she had ever met, yet she showed no sign of awe. This might of course have been evidence of a profound lack of sophistication on her part. However, later as I knew her better, I saw that in her relations with other women, European or African, she behaved consistently: having greeted her visitor she always put the tasks at hand first. Then when she had time, she would return to socialize. Responsibilities came first, and though she might complain about how much she had to do, from my observations I would say that she enjoyed her work. She never seemed distressed by the tedious and repetitive nature of her tasks. What distressed her was being tired or sick, because then she could not accomplish them in the smoothly integrated way she expected of herself.

When I first conceived of using an approximation of a therapeutic model with these Gusii women, I was well aware that I would have to make drastic adjustments in the model we are familiar with in clinical work in the West. As mentioned earlier, among the expectable differences was the fact that these people did not view themselves as suffering psychologically. They might expect to gain some form of concrete help from me, or perhaps some support in familial conflicts, but not intrapsychic relief. I could not require them to come to see me. If they could be induced to come to me at the clinic in the chief's camp, their visits would be noted by everyone in the community. Anyone I selected for special attention would be the object of suspicion and jealousy on the part of her neighbors. Thus my attentions had to be as discreet as possible. I would have to go to see my subjects at home.

I could not count on seeing any of them alone, since in their homesteads they had no privacy whatever. They could not turn away a visitor who happened to appear. No more could they exclude members of their families from our conversations. In Suzanna's case, the usual process of developing a relationship was attenuated by the fact that not only was she a sociable person, whom many women liked and trusted and therefore would drop in to visit at all hours, but her mother-in-law, Kemunto, and her unmarried sister-in-law Nyanchama, aged about fifteen, were usually present and included themselves in our discussions. The likelihood of our having an opportunity to be alone together (alone, that is, with the exception of her children, who were constantly present) was especially rare, since Kemunto brewed and sold beer and very often the homestead was full of men and women drinking, while Suzanna ran about attending to their needs. In this way, in order for me to get to know Suzanna I had to get to know her mother-in-law and sister-in-law and induce them to trust me. During the course of my work with Suzanna, I had the opportunity to learn about the social and psychological adjustment of this particular middle-aged woman and her adolescent daughter, but it was at a price. Sometimes weeks would go by during which Kemunto was highly motivated to see to it that I never had a moment alone with her daughter-in-law, and Suzanna and I would be forced into hurried conversations on the roadside. On occasion I felt that my relationship with her, far from being that of a researcher and her subject, was more akin to that between two conspirators.

I met Kemunto and Nyanchama on my second visit. Suzanna, with whom I had made a noon-time appointment, was gone. I found her mother-in-law asleep with Joyce tucked into the crook of her arm. Nyanchama was busy with domestic chores.

The moment I walk in Kemunto awakes, covers Joyce with a piece of sacking, and comes to greet me. She explains that she was sleeping because she is very tired from working so hard.

She is a woman of about sixty who must in her youth have been quite striking. Now her face is wrinkled with a thousand tiny lines. She talks very fast indeed, and since she is missing a number of teeth, her speech is almost incomprehensible to me—and will remain so. She sits herself down beside me and asks me many questions about where I come from, where I married, what we plant there, what we eat. Of Suzanna she says, "I don't know where she went. She is always going about, here and there, who knows where?" She gives me a significant look. Her eyes are piercing under bony brows. In fact, as it turns out, all morning Suzanna has been digging at the far edge of their land near the road, and probably Kemunto knows this perfectly well. However, she implies to me, a stranger, that Suzanna is an irresponsible person. When Suzanna eventually appears, she throws down her hoe and lies beside me. She's so tired! She rested many hours last night, and yet she wasn't refreshed. She doesn't refer to her pregnancy, only to the physical distress which pregnancy induces. She wears a shapeless nylon dress, originally pink, now brown, with dark brown flowers on it. Even at the end of the seventh month her stomach is not much in evidence, owing to the tubular shape of her dress.

As the weeks passed, her direct communications with me were almost all complaints: "Ninchandagete" (I am suffering). She didn't seem to expect me to do anything about her troubles. She was merely presenting the facts:

> "My house is so small, it's just the hut of a boy, not the house of a married man and his wife—it is smoky and cramped and there isn't room for a family of five. The roof leaks; surely you can feel the rain dripping down your neck. Wait until May when it rains from morning until dark. The house may fall down then! You see, Ongaki gives me nothing. I have no sweater to wear in the cold after the rain has gone. Men are all rogues, *ekebago.* My daughter Joyce has been sick for such a long time now. Diarrhea. She cries all night and is so thin. I have no chance to sleep."

She sighed and then smiled, laughing at herself. Hers was a self-pity which sounded qualitatively different from the complaints of other women. She was stating facts. Perhaps once she had been angry and got over it, or perhaps she never was really angry. She told me—or anyone who happened to be there—about her troubles, but her affect belied her words. She accepted and was even rather amused by her lot in life. Though she was cold because it was raining and the roof leaked, and she had no firewood and no energy to go out to look for a few sodden branches after the rain stopped, she did not whine. She was not demanding that I pity her or run out to get the firewood for her, or give her my sweater so her goose bumps would go away. She complained with grace and humor.

By the end of her eighth month of pregnancy, I had begun visiting her with my assistant. Suzanna talked freely to Mary, occasionally glancing at me to gauge my response. She didn't seem to comprehend that I often had difficulty in understanding what she was saying to Mary. She appeared to assume I could follow, even though I frequently asked her to repeat what she said or asked my assistant for a translation. It may be that she was deliberately trying to exclude me, that she was ignorant of my difficulties, or even, perhaps, that she saw me as being so powerful that I automatically had total comprehension.

When she was in the presence of her mother-in-law and sister-in-law, Suzanna appeared to be very much at ease. They discussed problems of the homestead and possible solutions. Apparently the three women worked well together. They rested between tasks, laughing and chattering. My assistant remarked to me, "See how Kemunto loves Suzanna," and indeed, she frequently touched Suzanna, her forearm or her leg, as they lay together under the tree. At first it seemed that she was merely emphasizing a point or, less likely in this culture, making a gesture of affection. It was only over time that I began to understand the intrusive nature of her behavior toward Suzanna. I noticed that Suzanna was markedly quieter when Kemunto was present than when she was not. Perhaps this was out of respect on the part of a young mother for her mother-in-law, or perhaps it was a way of handling more complex feelings.

One day when she was especially tired, I asked Suzanna where she intended to deliver her baby.

"I would go to the hospital in Kisii town, but I haven't any money. If Ongaki were employed, I would go to Mombasa to stay with him. As it is, I have no one to rely on for help in this compound. My husband's brothers are all gone."

This she said in a factual way, smiling as she often did when she was talking of her difficulties. Then she went on, with sudden feeling,

"Even if I had money to deliver in the hospital, I could never leave the children here. My mother-in-law drinks so. She's not the only one here who does. They all drink, all the people in this place. I can't leave the children with the old lady. She will go off to find beer and the children will go without food. So I must stay here, even if I am dying."

When Ongaki suddenly returned from Mombasa, having given up his search for work, Suzanna was briefly radiant.

She presents him to me and stands back, beaming. He is pleasant-looking and wears the same affable expression as his sister Nyanchama.

He gestures for me to sit down and then launches into an account of his travels, dwelling particularly on the climatic differences of the towns along the way. He is determined to speak English. Having demonstrated his knowledge of my language, he then asks me to employ him. I have to tell him that at present we have no vacancy. He does not seem at all put out.

Later I see him going off with a hoe on his shoulder to dig in

the fields, and Suzanna reports that he is a great help to her both
in the garden and at home. He will not cook or fetch water, but
everything else he will do.

However, her euphoria following Ongaki's return from Mombasa
was quickly over. One afternoon we found her in the deserted compound weeping outside her house. This was the only occasion on which
I ever saw her weep.

> She says she is so worried. What will the children eat? They
> have nothing. Their own maize ran out long ago and they have
> no money to buy any in the market. Then spontaneously she
> tells us, "Last night I had a very bad dream. *Nakumirie*. [I am so
> upset.] I dreamed I had trouble breathing and the baby came out
> dead." Now her belly has dropped and she knows she is close to
> delivery. She is so afraid. "Afraid of what?" I ask. "Your three
> previous deliveries were without trouble." "But this time I may
> die, or the baby may die, or both of us together."

I had heard such dreams from others, and we had concluded from the
data we collected from forty other pregnant women that their feelings
about pregnancy were extraordinarily ambivalent. While they longed
to conceive and measured their own worth above all by how many
children they had, nevertheless pregnancy was viewed by the majority
as an affliction. Pregnancy is a period of extreme physical discomfort:
you are tired, your back aches, and frequently, though not in Suzanna's
case, you have morning sickness until the day you give birth. Rather
than celebrating their good fortune in being able to fulfill the most
highly valued female function, Gusii women almost unanimously talk
about their pregnancies at the time as an almost intolerable burden.
Given the fact that they do indeed have to continue working very hard,
life *is* especially difficult for them during pregnancy; however, they feel
compelled to emphasize the hardships to the total exclusion of the
pleasures. The cultural expectation is that all women will envy your
good fortune and therefore you must not reveal any pleasure whatsoever
in your condition. This stricture is so absolute that it appears to be
quite normal, within the context of their culture, for most Gusii
women at a conscious level to derive no pleasure, physical or
psychological, from pregnancy. Pregnancy is a great burden, and they
long for the day when they will be freed. At the same time, they dread

the onset of labor, and I heard Suzanna, like many other women, describe repeatedly and only in negative terms the horrors of childbirth. A woman will rarely admit to having any aspirations for her unborn child. "May he or she be healthy" is as far as she will go. Suzanna admitted to me that she wanted a son, but she did not verbalize any fantasies about what this son would look like or what he would achieve in life. I believe she did not even permit herself to indulge in daydreams about her child.

In the last weeks before she delivered Ogaro, when Ongaki was home and the stage was set, Suzanna appeared to be under increasing psychological duress as well as physical discomfort. She was giving birth during the lean time of the year. In better-off families there was still maize left in the store, but in Ongaki's there was none, and there would be none for at least another three months. From time to time Moraa, Suzanna's mother, would send her a sack of flour, and that was all they had. Ongaki, who had been fired for irresponsibility from his teaching position at Christmas, had been gone in a fruitless search for work for four months and had then returned empty handed. She herself had to produce a son, or else her continuation in this house was in jeopardy. And yet if she did indeed give birth to a son, she would be trapped in poverty, each "hungry" season dependent on the generosity of her parents, from whose storehouse, according to Gusii custom, a married daughter may take maize to feed her own family when the granary in her husband's home is empty.

Suzanna was normally an energetic person, and her exhaustion, though predictable, was also symptomatic of her great anxiety. I believe she sensed she had reached a crossroad. If she had a daughter, she would have to leave. If she had a son, she would remain permanently.

I saw Suzanna for only ten weeks before she gave birth. During that time she was friendly, but she kept me at a distance. She never asked me questions about myself. Nyanchama and Kemunto were both intrigued by me, and even little Jane would touch me and look into my purse and sometimes ask questions. Suzanna, however, did not seem much concerned. If she were puzzled about my purpose in coming to sit in her compound so frequently, she never said anything. She did not seem to expect anything from me. Perhaps she tolerated me partly out of traditional courtesy to a stranger, partly because she was so low in energy that it was the path of least resistance. Eventually I would go away for good. However, other women who wanted to get rid of me did so very effectively. They merely turned their backs on me and went about their chores or repeatedly disappeared to the garden or the power mill. They were not prepared to stay at home for my sake. Suzanna did not exactly exclude me, but after the early visits she seemed to hold back from me. Whether this was due to her self-preoccupation at the end of her pregnancy or to a fear of the relationship, or both, it was hard to judge. I do know that I became very aware of her aloofness, which continued for some considerable time after her baby was born.

There was no lack of people to talk to in the homestead, however. Once or twice Suzanna and I were both present at conversations in which other women talked about intimate details of their sex lives. Although Suzanna did not herself contribute to the discussions and neither did I, the fact that each of us was present, that we smiled and laughed and were obviously engrossed in what was being said, I think was significant. This sharing of profane information brought us closer together. Sometimes she seemed reluctant even to sit and talk to me. According to the open-ended method I had chosen to use with her, I could not specifically request her to sit with me, let alone interpret her behavior as "resistance." Often she would greet me, see to it that I had been engaged in conversation by Ongaki, Kemunto, or one of her sisters-in-law, and then she would disappear, without any explanation. I began to feel very awkward and intrusive and considered dropping Suzanna from my study.

Suzanna gave birth to Ogaro at 1:00 A.M. after four hours of labor, assisted by her mother-in-law and sister-in-law. Nyanchama afterward admitted to being terrified, but nevertheless she evidently managed to be useful.

> The following morning I find Suzanna in Kemunto's house. She has given birth there because it is absolutely forbidden for a mother to enter the bedroom of her son, and thus, if Kemunto were to help her daughter-in-law, Suzanna had to be removed from Ongaki's bed.
>
> She is *radiant*. It is the happiest day of her life. Normally, in the daytime, there is no fire because they cannot afford to use firewood except for cooking, but today a fire is burning, and a dozen women are squashed together in the tiny kitchen, laughing and telling stories of their own labors and the labors of other

women they have attended. Suzanna herself says little. However, in describing the course of her labor, she says that, having spent the whole day busily, in an attempt to master the pains, at nightfall she admitted to Ongaki that she was indeed in labor, and she asked him to go find Sarah. Of course by that time I had gone home and would not be back until morning.

She never stops smiling as she nods in response to the stories and attention of the other women. Her infant son, who looks the image of his father, is constantly passed around to be admired, and Suzanna beams at all the admiration. Ongaki, meanwhile, is being entertained by his cronies in various nearby homesteads. We met him on the road on our way to visit Suzanna. He was wearing his best shirt; he was red eyed from being up all night and was very drunk.

We have brought a towel for the baby and tea and sugar for Suzanna. She is delighted with the gifts and immediately wraps Ogaro in his towel, which henceforth is used as a receiving blanket. And the tea and sugar, which we had intended for her alone, as a small luxury, she gives to Kemunto, who boils water and brews tea which is consumed to the last drop by the visitors.

However, a few days later I found Suzanna sitting despondently outside Kemunto's house. The euphoria had passed. Now she had fever and diarrhea. Maize was drying on two mats on the ground. I was told they had bought it with money they received from the pyrethrum cooperative society. They would not be able to afford to buy more. After five days, when this was all gone, what would they eat? "We are suffering."

In fact, Suzanna recovered rapidly from childbirth and its aftermath. She was soon back in her husband's hut, performing household tasks, although she did not go to the garden until some time later. Ongaki was being a model husband: he went to the garden each day in Suzanna's place; he was gentle with the children. He even took care of them when Suzanna went to the river to bathe. He would not fetch water or cook, but Nyanchama, whose sexual behavior was currently the source of much concern to her mother and to a lesser degree to Suzanna, was at home during the day to perform the tasks to which Ongaki would not stoop.

It appeared that Suzanna and Ongaki were on the best of terms. She had produced the longed-for son, and he was ever in attendance. One day Ongaki talked about wanting two more children, to include at least one more son. Suzanna nodded; of course they must have another boy. What if something happened to Ogaro? And then in the next breath she complained of hunger pains. She was so hungry! She needed *obokima*. Only *obokima* could satisfy her. How would they feed these unborn children, I asked, and they were silent.

III

For six weeks after the birth of Ogaro I found myself continually foisted off by Suzanna onto Ongaki. Ongaki, who had not given up hope of being employed on our project, was perfectly willing to entertain me with his observations, in English, on the national scene. But one day (my fifteenth visit), after I had been entertained in this way for half an hour, Suzanna stopped with us long enough for me to ask her if she remembered any dreams. (Her response for weeks had been, "I dreamed every night when I was pregnant, but these days I do not.") Without any hesitation she answered, "On Monday night I dreamed that you went to Kisumu in the Peugeot."

Her association was that she had seen me at the beer party on Monday afternoon, but not since. Kisumu, the provincial capital, eighty miles away on the shores of Lake Victoria, was the farthest place Suzanna had ever been. She had been there twice. She did not mention the first time. The second time was the previous December, when she had gone there with Ongaki for three days, "just to see the place." They walked about the town and stayed in a hotel. That place was much too hot. She preferred the cool climate of the highlands. She had nothing more to add. It was many months before I could understand the significance of this dream. However, the period of her aloofness was over. From this point onward Suzanna rarely, if ever, left me to talk to her relatives. Slowly, then more and more rapidly she revealed herself to me, until I became something like a mirror, an echo chamber for her fantasies and fears. As time went by and she became more anxious, her dreaming became prolific. On occasion she would recount as many as five dreams at once. All the women in my study knew I was interested in their dreams. Some scarcely ever remembered to tell me what they dreamed; others did so more frequently. But Suzanna far outdid them all. She dreamed in order to communicate the content and sources of her anxiety, and she dreamed to please me, so that the European woman in the large expensive car might protect her and assist her in fleeing this place and her predicament.

On this occasion, when she had finished her meager associations, I told her that on Tuesday, the morning after she dreamed her dream, I did indeed go to Kisumu in the Peugeot. (The project had two cars, the second one being a Datsun, and this I drove much more frequently than the larger Peugeot. Suzanna generally saw me in the Datsun. But the Peugeot 504 station wagon is considered the most desirable vehicle by ordinary Africans. They are used everywhere as taxis, and their owners stand to make very handsome profits, despite the fact that the initial purchase price is astronomical.) When Suzanna heard this, she did not seem at all surprised. "I believe my dreams," she said. "What I dream always comes true." Then she went on to tell me a second dream, that of Wednesday night. Her mother was beaten by a *kebago* (thug).

> She, Suzanna, awoke very afraid. Later that day she heard that her father, not her mother, had been beaten up by ruffians in the market near his home. He was trying to stop them from tearing down the Kenyan national flag, and they turned on him. At the hospital they bandaged him and said he was not so bad. He could go back to work, but Suzanna was so upset. She took Ogaro and ran home when she got the news. (Her home is about an hour's walk away.) "In fact, it is true, he is not so bad. He will be all right, but I hated to see him hurt."
> "Is he getting old?" I ask, and she replies, "No, he is not old at all. I am only his second child, and you see that I am young." Then she says vehemently, "My father has not come to greet Ogaro; he has not sent even a shirt. He won't do anything for my son until Ongaki has paid cattle, and Ongaki has paid nothing at all, not even a chicken. Ongaki dares not go there, to greet his in-laws. He would not be welcome there."

This was an issue which should be dealt with soon, but for a time Suzanna could mark time. Her beautiful son was growing, waving his arms, crowing. She doted on him in front of me, considerably less so in front of her neighbors, who could not be trusted. The sight of the mother's pleasure might make them jealous enough to bewitch the child. However, everybody adored Ogaro: his aunts, his grandmother, his father, and especially Nyanchama, who treated him like a plaything. She wanted a child like him, she said. Jane, his older sister, was also very attentive, although little Joyce was obviously less enthralled.

Now food shortages were a thing of the past. Beans and finger millet were being harvested, and Suzanna and Kemunto brewed and sold beer, and with their profits they bought maize for *obokima*. Suzanna was strong again; she was even fat. Her stomach was so large that she looked eight months pregnant.

For a time the family was absorbed by Nyanchama's pregnancy and subsequent abortion and by Kemunto's illness, an illness which was to take on special significance for Suzanna. Kemunto had evidently suffered many years from some undiagnosed stomach ailment. She had been to several diviners who gave her varying directions as to how to deal with this affliction. One had told her that the reason she suffered was that the ancestor spirits were troubled, and that in order to appease them she must perform a series of sacrifices, culminating in her initiation as a diviner. Among the Gusii, diviners (*abaragori*) are almost always people who at some point in the past were physically afflicted. When, having tried local medicine or even Western medicine in vain, they then sought enlightenment from a diviner as to the cause of their affliction, they were told, like Kemunto, that the ancestors demanded they themselves be initiated in the practices of divination. In times gone by, the cost of apprenticeship and initiation was fairly easily met. Every homestead had plentiful goats for sacrifice, and the senior diviner (*omoragori*) who undertook to train the novice could be paid in finger millet or maize the apprentice had raised herself. The only articles requiring money were a few cooking pots, gifts to the instructor, and the quite elaborate beaded necklaces to be worn when performing the divination ritual. Nowadays senior diviners demand steep fees rather than grain from their apprentices. Kemunto, who owned no goats, was having great difficulty in raising the money to purchase all the livestock to pay the initiation fee, as well as to meet the cost of the other items. She had been instructed to sacrifice six goats, and then she would be eligible for initiation. But the goat she managed to buy had some terrible malady which caused its rectum to bulge out. She could not sacrifice an ailing goat, and according to Gusii custom, she could not even slaughter it in the ordinary way for meat. Thus this useless sick creature wandered around the compound while Kemunto lay under the shade tree and complained of her stomach. One day she saw me wearing a cowrie-shell necklace from the Kenya coast. She begged me for it: she needed one as part of her diviner's costume. So I gave it to her, and she thanked me profusely—she would never have had the money to buy one. "In Gusiiland, so far from the ocean, they are so hard to find and so expensive." Suzanna, I noticed, watched this trans-action without enthusiasm, and if ever I asked her about the time when Kemunto's rare sacrifices would take place so that I could observe them, Suzanna would shrug her shoulders and say she never knew in advance. Her mother-in-law never told her. I was surprised to hear this. When I saw mother-in-law and daughter-in-law together, they seemed the best of friends. Yet Suzanna claimed to know little about this very important area of the old lady's life, which, after all, was going on right in the same homestead. Suzanna was either being ex-cluded from Kemunto's plans, or else she was deliberately excluding herself. After knowing me for six months, Suzanna had scarcely al-lowed herself to criticize her mother-in-law in my presence. Although I sensed that there was more to their relationship than I had so far been permitted to see, my evidence was negligible.

Suzanna was much freer in expressing her feelings about her hus-band, however. During my last visit she reported a dream in which Ongaki had had an accident.

"He was going in a *matatu* [taxi] to Kericho when the vehicle went into the ditch. Some were killed but not Ongaki. He was only hurt. I saw the bandages." Her comment is that Ongaki intends to go on a journey to a Sotik town near Kericho to find work. He had been advised to report to the assistant education officer (a friend) who might hire him, despite his poor record. When she told him her dream (Gusii believe that if you dream about someone's misfortune, even that they have been killed, you must tell them if you should meet them by chance, al-though you should not go out of your way to find them in order to tell them), Ongaki was very upset. He said, "Accidents can happen." He was once in one, although he was not hurt. Suzanna tells us that she too was once in an accident but escaped unscathed. It is as if she is trying to pull back her admission of hostility toward Ongaki. After all, even if her dreams do come true and he does have an accident, it need not be fatal. Then she goes on, remorselessly. She doesn't think he will get work at

Sotik. After all, he was fired by the Education Authority because he failed his in-service course (to upgrade untrained primary school teachers), so why should they rehire him? Since December he hasn't earned a single cent, and even when he was employed he drank so much!

"Please, Mary, if you see him and he has a job, tell him he must not drink!"

Two weeks later, when he was returning from Sotik, where indeed his friend failed to rehire him, Ongaki *was* in an accident. He was unhurt except for a few minor scratches, but Kemunto was seen wailing at the roadside, as if he in fact had been killed, and Suzanna went desperately searching in neighboring homesteads for a white chicken, which Gusii custom dictates must be sacrificed before a man who has just escaped death can reenter his own house. The following morning many people came to pay their condolences to Ongaki. The visitors sat around in silence. Ongaki was unsmiling and silent also, while Suzanna too was very subdued. She remembered her dream. "My dreams always come true."

In the twenty-first session she told me she had dreamed the previous night:

"Sarah's husband, Getuka [the investigator], drove the Peugeot to America." Then she suddenly remembers an earlier dream of two weeks before which she has forgotten to tell me. "I gave birth to a white crippled baby boy. People said I was a bad mother, because the child was crippled." Her associations are meager: Getuka had indeed gone to America a week ago. "In the Peugeot?" she asks. "No, not in the Peugeot, in an airplane. The Peugeot has had an accident and cannot be driven until it is mended," I replied. (The Peugeot had already been out of commission for three weeks and its absence had been noted by the whole community.) "Why was the baby white?" I ask. "Because I had been adulterous." "In your dream did anyone criticize you for this?" "Oh, no, only that the child was crippled."

The Gusii believe that all crippling is caused by witchcraft, which is motivated by jealousy. Why should anyone be jealous of Suzanna? For her relationship with me, perhaps, or perhaps it was I, Sarah, who was jealous of Suzanna's sexual interest in my husband and thus took my revenge. She told both dreams with no affect. The second dream she had in fact "forgotten" to tell me until her conscience forced her to admit having had it. As I already knew, Suzanna's dreams "always came true," and thus, according to the Gusii conception of morality, she was compelled to tell me, as a substitute for the absent Getuka, any dream which presaged his involvement in a potentially hazardous event. Her conscience was punishing her for her fantasy of having an affair with my husband. She gave birth to a son whom she so much desired. In his fair skin was irrefutable evidence of his patrimony, and yet he was crippled.

Once again the car is the symbol of power. White people are powerful, they are wealthy. When things get difficult for them, they can leave their troubles behind. They can even cross the ocean. (Suzanna knew the ocean lay between Africa and America. The ocean was like Lake Victoria, very great.) She also knew, however, that wealth and power are hazardous. The Peugeot had rolled over six times on a wet night and was now lying useless in a garage in Kisii town. Intimacy with powerful people could be dangerous for *her*. Not only might her neighbors or even the women in her own homestead be jealous of her and she would have to content with their malevolence, but more dangerous yet, her relationship with Getuka and his wife would bring forth all kinds of forbidden feelings in her. They wanted to investigate (*ogotuka*) her. But ultimately they had the power to leave her when it no longer suited them to stay. They would abandon her to live alone again without benefit of their protection.

If these considerations gave Suzanna pause, however, it was momentary. Regardless of the dangers, she was ready to climb into our vehicle and risk the slick road on a stormy night. If we wanted to use her for our purposes, she would use us for hers.

We were moving closer now to the issue which was confusing her: the issue of separation from her own family and commitment to her husband's, this process which every Gusii woman must go through with greater or less ease. (My assistant once told me, "From early childhood you know you must leave your home, and you fear that day.")

Until this point I had assumed that Flora, Suzanna's eldest daughter, was illegitimate. She had been born, after all, in Suzanna's own home. Suzanna talked very little about Flora, who only visited her mother briefly during school vacations. The rest of the time she remained with her grandmother, a common pattern for out-of-wedlock children. However, in the twenty-second session I heard the story of Suzanna's first "marriage," which produced Flora.

Once, when she went to help her elder sister, Rebecca, with the *wimbi* harvest, a young man of her brother-in-law's clan proposed to her, using Rebecca as his go-between. He let her know that he was in secondary school, and so he could not marry her until he was finished with his schooling. However, he wanted to arrange things now so that when he graduated they could marry. Suzanna agreed to go with her sister and brother-in-law to visit this young man (an unorthodox procedure; traditionally the suitor should have come to visit the girl), but after they had been there in his house a short while, her sister and her husband disappeared, leaving Suzanna alone with the young man. She attempted to run away, but he and two of his friends overpowered her. Though she struggled and begged to be allowed to go, it was in vain. And so, "against my will" (as is almost always the explanation given by Gusii women of Suzanna's generation, though not of their younger sisters, who are more emancipated from traditional puritanism and can therefore admit to being seduced willingly), Suzanna was forced to have sexual relations. The following morning the young man, who was now her "husband," took her in a taxi to Kisumu, where she discovered that, contrary to his earlier account of himself, he was *not* a schoolboy, with good prospects on completion of his education. He was only a poor migrant laborer. She remained with him for four months. "His penis was very big and I was very small, and he beat me when he was drunk and gave me scarcely any money."

So this Seventh Day Adventist girl, with her fantasies of upward mobility through marriage to an educated husband, saw that her hopes were not about to be realized. She found a classificatory father—i.e., a cousin of her own father—who was also working in Kisumu, borrowed taxi fare from him, and escaped to her home. So much for her first marriage, and so much, also, for her first visit to Kisumu, to which she had alluded in the fifteenth session when describing her dream in which "Sarah drove to Kisumu in the Peugeot." On that occasion she did not tell me the circumstances of the first visit. Now the picture was becoming a little clearer. Kisumu was a town at the limits of Suzanna's world. It was the only large town to which she had ever been. It was the scene of her brief and disastrously disappointing first marriage and also of her vacation with her second, "educated" husband, Ongaki, a last fling following his dismissal from his teaching post.

Suzanna went on to describe the aftermath of her escape. When she gave birth to Flora, her mother-in-law came with all the traditional gifts of meat and flour, sugar and tea, and her husband came with money. They begged her to come back with them, but she refused. Impulsively she had rushed into marriage. She was of an age for marriage; the young man had seemed desirable. Then realizing her mistake—that her husband had deceived her about his prospects—she left him and resolutely refused to return to him, despite his professed intentions to mend his ways. She was home again, with a child to be sure, but a girl child whom her mother was willing to raise along with her own latter-born children. Suzanna had won an extension of her girlhood. But still the pressure, both internal and external, was on her to marry. She was courted by several men who seemed to fit her educational or financial requirements. She was even carried off ("He tricked me") to Kericho by one suitor for a week. But she rejected them all. Eventually she selected Ongaki, who was teaching in a school close to her home. Like her other suitors, he promised her upward mobility, but he did not appear to have the single-mindedness or stability to realize his aspirations. Her father said, "Both times you went to your husbands in the clothes you brought from home [rather than clothes given by a bridegroom to his bride], and thus you have remained." In other words, both times she chose badly. She selected men who treated her badly and who gave her nothing.

"And at home were you happy?" I ask. "At home I lacked nothing," she answers. At home she was *given* to by her father and mother.

When I asked women how they remembered their parents, and which they loved more, almost invariably they would answer, "I loved my mother, of course, because she prepared my food," or else, "I loved them both—my mother because she gave me food, my father because he bought me dresses." When they were sent to relatives as nursemaids to their little cousins, they commented first on what the babies' mothers gave them—food, dresses, soap. When they married, it was the same again in talking of their mothers-in-law: "When I first came here she would [or would not] cook food for me." And of course of their husbands. A man might have other wives, he might stay away for a couple of years at a time, but provided that he sent back money for the children's school fees and for consumer goods, his wife could hold up her head. She was clearly being taken care of.

At home Suzanna was cared for. She was happy there. But she knew she must leave in order to get children, whom she greatly desired but whom her sense of propriety demanded be legitimate, at least by the standards of today (if not yesterday); i.e., she must live with her children's father, as his wife, even though briefly and at intervals. As long as she chose to live with men who were ne'er-do-wells, she could continue her pattern of periodic married life indefinitely. In this, I believe, for a while she had had the support of her father. Though he ultimately told her to go back to Ongaki ("Who else will pay for you?"), for years he had let her stay at home with her "fatherless" children. He could have rejected her. He had many other mouths to feed, and these days many fathers do refuse their adult daughters a home, forcing them either to remain with their husbands, regardless, or to become prostitutes.

Indeed on one recent occasion when Suzanna voiced her intention of becoming a contract laborer in the local tea nursery, in order to earn money for necessities like soap and sugar, her father was so outraged that he declared it would be better for her to come home, where, presumably, he would give her the necessities that Ongaki failed to provide. Thus under parental pressure she dropped the plan.

Though it was not far away, Suzanna rarely visited her father's homestead, and her parents scarcely ever visited her. However, her younger brothers were constantly being sent with news and gifts of flour and vegetables, and Nyanchama, who was a favorite of Suzanna's mother, was as frequently sent in the opposite direction. Thus, despite rare face-to-face contact, the relationship between Suzanna and her parents was still very close. And yet, since her parents never came to visit Suzanna, I ultimately had to request that she take me home so that I could meet these people who featured so vividly in her psychic life. She talked about her parents constantly. She freely described her father's attitude toward both Ongaki and herself, and I got the impression that she did not resent his judgment. Her father saw her as a childish, undiscriminating person, Ongaki as a ne'er-do-well. And Suzanna seemed to agree with him.

IV

After five years of something approximating a
marriage, Suzanna's tie to Ongaki and his kin was still tenuous. At any
moment, she seemed to believe, she could break that tie and go home
to seek some other relationship.

In the twenty-ninth session Kemunto is lying under a tree playing with Ogaro, and Suzanna is close by shelling beans. Suddenly Kemunto remarks, "Ogaro, if you had been a girl, your
father would have sent your mother away. And as for me, I
would have refused to cut the umbilical cord. She would have
had to bite it with her teeth." Evidently I have come into the
middle of an argument. Suzanna rejoins, "But I had a son,
didn't I? And if I have no more, Ogaro will marry and have
more sons for me." In response to the tension, I say laughingly
to Kemunto, "Well, at least you gave her three chances! You
were more patient than Ongaki. What did you tell him when he
sent Suzanna away the first time?" "Ah, he was not the impa-
tient one," Kemunto says. "It was Suzanna who made the mistake. She told Ongaki, when he was sick, not to put his muddy
feet on the bed." Then Suzanna breaks in, laughing and ges-
ticulating as she tells me her version of the events: "He came
home from school in a bad temper and asked me, 'Haven't you
planted those pumpkin seeds?' I answered him, 'No, see, it is
raining!' So he went and planted them himself. Then he lay on
the bed with his muddy feet on the blanket. I quarreled with
him. I told him, 'You find yourself another woman. We are
both young. We can each find someone else!' He tried to stop
me. He said, 'I haven't told you to go,' and he ran to get his
mother. But I started to pack my box. I was crying. I was very
angry and frightened. When Ongaki came back, he said,
'You've taken my shirt.' [Gusii people believe a witch will cut a
piece from the clothing of the person they want to bewitch; this
they boil together with his hair, nail clippings, and feces and use
the brew to kill their enemy. It is thought to be especially
common for wives to steal their husbands' shirts and trousers for
this purpose.] But I remained silent and continued collecting my
belongings. I went to look for the *eriogo ri'emete* [local medicine]
I was giving Jane, for at that time she was sick, and my
mother-in-law, who was in the doorway, shouted, 'That

medicine is *amaebi* [a love potion]. She has used it to beguile and trap my son! She must go to her home.'"

As Suzanna tells her story, her eyes are fixed on my face. She talks very rapidly. This is the first clear evidence of a breach between her and Kemunto I have seen. Suzanna is determined that I hear this tale, regardless. "Then I took a pot I had brought from my own home, filled with flour I had bought with my own money. I broke that pot and poured the flour away [to do this is a sacrilege (*emoma*) according to Gusii custom, and she who does this must make ritual retribution before she can enter her husband's house again], and I poured away all my paraffin. Then I struck Ongaki with a stool and cut his forehead. I took up my child and went home. Everyone agreed that I should go. No one wanted me here." She is interrupted by her mother-in-law. "You struck me also," the old woman says. "Oh, no, you only cut yourself on the metal nailed along the bottom of my door," Suzanna retorts. Suzanna turns away from me now, arguing about whether or not she in fact struck Kemunto on that day four years ago. Finally Kemunto concedes. She was cut *in* Suzanna's house but not *by* her. Yes, there was a difference.

Suzanna turns to me again. "They didn't want me here, they said, but the very next week that 'bad dog' came twice to my home. I refused him. Only later did I greet him, and that is how I got Joyce. For thirteen months I stayed in my mother's house. My father was away at work most of the time, so he let me stay with my mother. Only my mother advised me to return to Ongaki. But now that I am here again with him, I miss my mother so much! I want to go to see her. No one need urge me to visit her. I would go, but it is Ongaki who prevents me. He is a fool." "Why won't he let you?" I ask. Kemunto says quickly, "In this family it is their custom. They [i.e., the men of the family into which she and Suzanna have married] don't like their wives to take their unweaned sons away for the night [i.e., they are afraid their wives may stay, so they hold the babies hostage to ensure the women's return]. Suzanna goes on, "But once I did take Ogaro home for the night, and people said afterward, 'You must wait until next year to go to sleep there again!'" She smiles scornfully. "He says it is the child he would miss, not me, if we were both to go." She falls silent. She is lying next to her mother-in-law, her face averted. Kemunto's forehead is furrowed with rage. She glares at Suzanna's profile. It is time for me to leave.

Suzanna had stated, before her mother-in-law, in the presence of a third party, namely myself, that her primary emotional investment and loyalty was still to her own home. She was welcome there: "I had everything I wanted," but here nobody wanted her. "Everyone agreed I should go." She was speaking, of course, of some years ago when she had only one child by Ongaki, a daughter. Now she had his son, but she still wanted to go home.

In the next session she told me she only came and stayed here with Ongaki because *he* used *amaebi* (a love potion) on *her*. ("And my mother-in-law accused *me* of using it on him! Would I do that? I know nothing of the use of *amaebi!*") She came here with him on a day when Kemunto was selling beer, which her parents never touched. As she walked in, she saw the drunken customers. That same day she had a second shock, for Ongaki had told her he had bought land elsewhere, but when she arrived, she discovered he was lying. His elder brother, Getaya, had bought land in the settlement-scheme area (on a former European-owned farm), but Ongaki had no claim to that at all. When she realized this fact, she told him she wanted to go home again; he had tricked her with false promises. But he went off to Mombasa to visit his brother, persuading her to stay until his return.

> "He said, when he came back, if I still wanted to leave him, I should. I was pregnant, of course. So I stayed, and when Ongaki came back, I didn't go to my home, not until after Jane was born, and you know about that, I told you. But recently I heard from my brother-in-law whom Ongaki had gone to see in Mombasa that at that time Ongaki bought some *amaebi* there and when he returned here he gave it to me, mixed it into my tea. And that is the only reason why I stayed."

In addition, Kemunto was in league with Ongaki to keep her there. She cooked for Suzanna and made her very welcome. It was the two of them together who beguiled her, against her wishes. She took no responsibility for staying with Ongaki. She was trapped, this time by a love potion, just as her first husband trapped her, taking her by force to Kisumu. To me she presented herself as someone prevented from exercising her own will. If it were not for the physical force of her first husband or the magic of her second, she would have run home even more quickly than she in fact did. She described both her husbands in terms of their lying to her, tricking her—about their property or their prospects. It was impossible for her to admit that she went willingly and only later changed her mind and longed to be back with her parents.

> "And you must know that after the last time Sarah was here, when she left me quarreling with my mother-in-law, I told her I was thinking of going to my parents' again. In this place there is nothing, only a broken-down hut without a latrine. There isn't even money enough to dig a latrine!" Next morning Kemunto sent Nyanchama over with porridge for breakfast and in that porridge was charcoal dust. Suzanna recognized that it was *obos-aro*, a medicine Kemunto was using against her. She was uncertain of the purpose of the medicine: whether it was to keep her here or to get rid of her. She showed the porridge to Ongaki, who told her to throw it away. From now on she will refuse to eat anything Kemunto sends her. Her voice drops although the compound is empty. She whispers, "My mother-in-law is a witch. One night I went outside to urinate at dusk, and I saw her standing there in silence. She told me, 'I was coming to borrow something from you,' but that could not have been true. She had not knocked or called to me. No, she had come to listen through the walls to hear what I was saying to Ongaki. She was spying on me."

It would seem that these days the Gusii fear witches more even than they did traditionally. At a time when the basic structure of society has been undermined, people need more than ever to understand what is happening around them. Every event must be explained and must have an intelligible cause. This is particularly true of misfortune. Whereas until a short time ago every Gusii was secure within his kin group, each relationship with its every obligation clearly spelled out, nowadays in a disintegrating society every family is thrown onto its own ever more strained resources. In many instances, especially where no patriarch survives to procure the cooperation of his sons, every man is set against his own brother. With such competition inevitably there is jealousy on the part of those who see themselves as being bettered by others, even on what from a Western viewpoint would seem like trivial terms. If one woman has more and better water pots than another and does not lend them freely, she will fear being bewitched. In confidence she will ascribe any misfortune which may befall her, such as the low yield of her maize plot, to the jealousy and malevolence of her neighbors, who surely must have put down their medicine in her field to make her maize grow poorly. In the same way a man may fear the jealousy of his neighbors if his cows produce milk plentifully, or if his son does too well at school, or even if his little daughter is strong and carries water from the river steadily, without spilling. Any advantage lays one open to witchcraft, worked by those less fortunate than oneself. Magical power is the only recourse of the impotent, of the poorest and the despised. Thus the Gusii will fear any old woman who is ill or neglected. They are especially afraid if that old woman is their mother or mother-in-law and it is they themselves who have been neglectful. They fear those feelings of rage and greed which their behavior has aroused in the old person. However old or enfeebled she may be, they are ready to believe she is a witch. There are indeed people who behave in many respects as witches are believed to behave. While most rural Gusii shut their doors at dusk and, in terror of the dark, stay inside until sunrise, some few others do "run in the night," believing themselves protected by their own magic from mythical beasts (for wild animals were all long ago killed in Gusiiland) and the power of other witches. Some do indeed make potions out of roots and leaves and pieces of cloth, and use these "poisons" (amasaro) against their enemies. In their farm work women may band together in ebesangio (work groups), and the same is said to be true of witches; they too have their groups and go witching together. Anyone who would appear to us to deserve pity the Gusii would suspect of being a witch, for witchcraft is the only weapon of the weak against the strong, of those who fail against those who are successful.

In Kemunto's case she was indeed aging and ill and therefore by our standards pitiable. But in addition she was in control of the meager land her husband had left to his five sons. Two of those sons had bought land elsewhere, but the other three were still landless, waiting for their share. She refused to divide the land. It would be uneconomical to do so. Meanwhile she alone made every decision concerning what crops should be planted and where, and she had no intention of allowing her three younger sons any power of decision making. Thus Suzanna had been brought home by Ongaki only to discover that not only was his patrimony tiny, but he did not have control over it. He could not rent it out for a fee, much less sell it. He could not even plant potatoes if his mother did not agree that the few square yards in question should be used in that particular way. Given that her three younger sons had nothing, the acre and a half she withheld from them gave them reason enough to resent their mother bitterly. Their resentment was something Suzanna could easily share. In general her ambivalence focused on Ongaki, but the question of the land gave her an opportunity to ally herself with her husband against a third party, the old woman, who sat in jealous guardianship over her few coffee bushes and her quarter acre of pyrethrum.

Suzanna told me over several sessions how she came to know Kemunto was a witch. Once when she was pregnant with Ogaro, she was digging in the *shamba* and found a little pot (*egetono*), and she knew immediately that this little pot was the kind of receptacle used by witches for their magical potions, their *amasaro*. When her mother-in-law came back that day, Suzanna gave the pot to her. "See what I found." Kemunto seized it, examined it, and agreed that it was hers. She had lost it long ago and looked for it in vain. As Suzanna described the incident to me, she made it sound as if Kemunto had made no explanation but had run to her house and put the pot away on a ledge in her kitchen. Thus she represented the incident in such a way as to make me think that while Suzanna herself had demanded no explanation as to why Kemunto had originally acquired the pot, Kemunto had not offered any. Each had known what the pot signified, but neither had alluded to its significance. In telling me about the pot, Suzanna became very animated. She asked if I wanted to see it. "You mean you want me to touch it?" I asked. "Why not!" she replied and sent Jane into her mother-in-law's house to find it (Kemunto was out). "The children know where it is, you'll see." And sure enough Jane came out with the little pot; we examined it, and then Jane replaced it carefully. My assistant was frightened by this display and refused to touch the pot herself.

Later Suzanna told me that recently her brother-in-law Getaya, who had bought land on a former European-owned farm, was distressed because his son was very ill. The family went to an *omonyamasira* (a sorcerer, i.e., someone who has the knowledge and power to counteract witchcraft and to protect and relieve those who have been bewitched), who told them the child had been bewitched by his grandmother. When they asked the sorcerer to give them *emesera* (a potion) to kill

Kemunto, he refused: "Let her die in her own good time. She is old now. She will die soon." He added (as an afterthought), "Besides, it is very bad to kill your mother." So they had spared her. "Why had she wanted to kill her own grandchild?" I asked. Suzanna shrugged. "Witches are like that." Meanwhile, as the weeks passed I learned of the mysterious illnesses of several more members of Kemunto's family. Getaya's child recovered, but then I heard in more detail the story of Omae, Kemunto's fourth son, who was living in Mombasa. He had become dumb and refused to eat. He had been working in some menial job and evidently, as far as I could tell from the symptomatology Suzanna described, had become schizophrenic. At one point he did come home, and I remember having seen him a few times. He was silent and brooding. Suzanna reported that while at home he had improved a little so that finally he returned to Mombasa, but he did not recover sufficiently to be able to work. When we left the field he was still "resting" and drinking only a shilling's worth of milk a day (about a pint), without any other food. Then about this time the wife of Kemunto's second son, Isaac, who lived two miles away on his own land, became pregnant and suffered terrible stomach pains. Last, Suzanna herself began to suffer from an excruciating eye infection, as well as several other, more transitory complaints.

One must ask why it was that a year ago, on "discovering" that her mother-in-law was a witch or at least owned the paraphernalia commonly believed to be used by witches, Suzanna was not panic stricken. When Omae had come home from Mombasa so withdrawn, I heard that his mother had gone to *abaragori* (diviners) on his behalf; indeed I once accompanied her myself when she went to consult a diviner about her own illness primarily, but also about Omae's. I remembered very well when Getaya's child had been sick. And since I was friendly with Martha, the wife of Isaac, I knew she had been ill also. Suzanna had talked to me about these illnesses and had represented them as *afflictions;* that is, she appeared to believe that these people, her husband's relatives, were suffering because their ancestors were displeased. The ancestors were demanding sacrifices which, if performed correctly, would relieve the sufferers of their afflictions. It was only after many months that Suzanna suddenly began to talk of her mother-in-law as being the *real* source of these illnesses. The sacrifice of goats was all in vain. The ancestors could protect none of them from the malevolence of the *omogina,* the old woman Kemunto. Why, then, did Suzanna come to this conclusion? Why had her anxiety suddenly risen so sharply that her longstanding ambivalence about her mother-in-law had rushed into a full-blown paranoia?

After Christmas Suzanna suddenly started going to church. She had not kept the Sabbath since she married. Ongaki was a nominal Catholic; if Suzanna wanted to go to church, then she should go to mass, he said, not to the services of the Seventh Day Adventists, who refuse to work on Saturdays. Suzanna would be "wasting precious time" which she should be spending in the fields. But one Saturday she defied him. "Why shouldn't I have one day's rest in the week? Even if I dig every day, we never have enough to eat. So let me dig six days and go on the seventh to church and hear what they have to tell me there." Keeping the Sabbath meant, of course, that she must give up brewing and selling beer as well as drinking it. She was thus depriving herself of the only steady source of income she had during the dry season, when the pyrethrum plants bloom sparsely. Kemunto and Ongaki watched in fury as Suzanna joined other women in the neighborhood and went off to spend four hours in prayer, hymn singing, and instruction as to how to live a productive life, without fear of witchcraft.

Why this sudden zeal?

She reports a dream she had on Christmas Eve. "Ongaki went to Nairobi, but on reaching there he turned round and came back and beat me up." On Christmas Day he refused the beer they had in the house, which Kemunto and Suzanna had brewed themselves, and he went off looking for beer in other homesteads. When he returned he was not only drunk but in a rage. He said he had been in a fight out on the road. Suzanna retorted, "Why can't you stay at home and drink our beer instead of going out and getting into fights?" He pushed past her and removed some water Suzanna was boiling on the fire, and in doing so he scalded his thumb. Ongaki exploded, threw the precious meat and bread which Suzanna had bought for Christmas under the bed, pulled his wife outside the house, away from the baby, Ogaro, who screamed, and started punching her. She hid in the banana trees until midnight—then went to sleep elsewhere. Next morning Ongaki had forgotten all about the fight. "He was surprised when he awoke and found I had not slept with him. At first I thought to myself that I should pack my things and go home. But I forgave him and we are friends again." However, she sent a message to her mother to tell what had happened, and her mother replied, through one of her brothers, that Suzanna should come back to the church. Though she could not stop Ongaki from drinking, at least if she gave up beer herself, when Ongaki was drunk and in a vile mood, Suzanna would be sober and thus could avoid being dragged into a brawl. "If you are both drunk, each is as bad as the other," she says. "And, Sarah, does Getuka get drunk? Do you get drunk together and have fist fights? Ongaki beat me above my heart and I fell down. Only Nyanchama saved me from him. Has Getuka ever knocked you down like that?" I told her we didn't fight physically, but we argued, and that could be bad. "Ah, but you do not beat each other as Ongaki and I beat each other. You and Getuka do not get drunk as we do." Or as Ongaki does. Now Suzanna has resolved to let him drink alone. She wished he would go away to look for work: "I vomited the other day. How I dread being pregnant! But I cannot refuse Ongaki. He would beat me to death! If only he would go away and leave me, at least until Ogaro is bigger."

Ogaro was trying to pull himself up now. He was nearly eight months old. Before long Suzanna would menstruate again and conceive another child who would bind her yet more firmly to this place and this man. And yet her ambivalence about her marriage was as strong as ever, and so she attempted to elevate herself above Ongaki and his drunken family. She declared her intention of becoming a Christian, of giving up *amarua* beer, which at this time of year, after the maize harvest, was almost the staple diet of Ongaki and Kemunto. She would be a Christian, like her mother; she would outwit her drunken husband; like Sarah, she would quarrel only with words. If she had to live here, she would not be like "these people." She would be morally superior.

But there was something else apart from abstinance from beer which made her different from these people. She had prolific dreams, and her dreams came true. I asked her whether she used to dream as a girl, and she said no. She only started recently, when she married. What, one might ask, did she mean by "married"? Perhaps she did indeed start her clairvoyant dreaming when she first came to Ongaki, but apart from a single dream she had reported to me during her pregnancy, it was not until Ogaro was three months old that I became aware that she was troubled by this tendency to dream. I believe that being "married," for her, really began when she had recovered from the birth of Ogaro and realized she was trapped. About this time she also became convinced that her mother-in-law was trying to kill her. Kemunto sent her poisoned porridge, and shortly thereafter Suzanna dreamed she was struck dumb, as Omae, her brother-in-law, had been struck dumb. In her associations she did not say it was Kemunto who bewitched her, only that her head ached from worrying. She wanted to go to see her step-grandmother, Nyagitari, who was a famous diviner, and confide in her that she was being afflicted by dreams. Thus she asked Ongaki if she could go, but although he was very aware of her dreaming and admitted to being alarmed by it, he was afraid that, given the currently turbulent nature of their relationship, if Suzanna were to go home on the pretext of seeing her grandmother, taking Ogaro with her so the old lady might greet him for the first time, she would not return.

> Suzanna launches into a tirade against him: "He has stopped helping me in the garden. Instead he gets little jobs to do on other people's land. Then he drinks away the few shillings he earns and comes and takes the money I get from pyrethrum, which is so little now. Flora will be circumcised this year, in December. But where will the visitors sit, what will they eat? Where will Flora sleep? You see, Sarah, how I am living, in *esaiga* [a circumcision hut], and I am not yet paid for. I suffer more than anyone in the world!" I say to her, "But now you have a son to kiss." (She is hugging and caressing Ogaro.) "Ha! But he will grow up to beat me and smother me with a blanket, saying 'Mother, where is there land for me to inherit? There is none, and so I must revenge myself on you for having given birth to me in vain!'"

I was very curious to see Suzanna's home and had hoped she would take me on an occasion when she visited her parents. But Ongaki adamantly refused to let her go. Eventually, after some weeks, I proposed that we go together, by car, so that I could ask Suzanna's mother some questions about the upbringing of children. We would be back by the late afternoon. If there was time we would also visit Nyagitari, the diviner, who lived close by. Ongaki, meanwhile, had left home to seek employment again, so we set off without his permission. This was the first of several visits.

Suzanna had talked much about her family, describing her home in glowing terms. I was skeptical, however, given the nature of her marital relationship; she was highly motivated to represent her original home in a sharp contrast to Ongaki's. But I was wrong. The homestead of Suzanna's father, Ochoi, was as she had described it. While not an affluent village, it was well ordered, and the atmosphere was warm, with children of all ages playing and laughing and interacting freely with Moraa, Suzanna's mother, and Ester, her "stepmother" (mother's cowife). The vivacity of the younger children in particular was unusual, especially in the presence of visitors. The two wives of Ochoi—who was not there that day; I did not meet him until some weeks later—had known we were coming and prepared a feast for us. Throughout our visit Suzanna smiled joyously, and all her siblings as well as her mother and stepmother responded to her delight. On that occasion I had little opportunity to talk to Moraa, since she was busy in the kitchen; however, I was entertained by her children and her cowife's children also, none of whom were at all inhibited in their curiosity about me and their eagerness to talk to me.

When the feast had been eaten, we went en famille to see Nyagitari. She was unaware that we were coming, and as we came up the steep hill to her house we heard the rattling of gourds and the sound of the *chinsembe* (diviner's shells) scattering over skins. "She is at work," Suzanna said. "We must wait our turn." Indeed there were a number of the afflicted sitting in a row with their attendant relatives and we sat with them, in complete silence. Nyagitari did not even acknowledge our arrival. She was deep in consultation with a psychotic woman, whose fearful daughters were sitting mute beside her, transfixed by Nyagitari's insistent voice: "A Masai died in your grandfather's house, and no sacrifice was ever made for him. The ancestors [*chisokoro*] must be satisfied." When at last all the supplicants had been attended to and she was free to talk to us, one of her small granddaughters suddenly had an epileptic fit, and much of the time we had remaining to us before nightfall was spent discussing the onset and treatment of the illness of that little girl. Suzanna never had an opportunity to tell her grandmother of her own affliction, the clairvoyant nature of her dreams. Nyagitari did, however, describe briefly how she had become a diviner, and in the course of this account she alluded to the fact that she had for many years foretold the future not only by divination but in her dreams.

When she said this, Suzanna and I looked at one another. Later Suzanna told me that until that day she had not known about Nyagitari's gift. And it was clear that Nyagitari did indeed look upon this power as a gift, not as an affliction. Thus Suzanna went away from her grandmother's relieved. It comforted her, she said, that the old lady, a grand imperious woman whose reputation as a diviner was known throughout the location, should be troubled at night in the same way Suzanna was, and yet not really troubled because, unlike Suzanna, Nyagitari did not fear her dreams; she valued them. Suzanna's father was the son of his father's first wife, whereas Nyagitari was the third wife. However, Ochoi's mother had died long ago, and Nyagitari had taken on the role of grandmother to Ochoi's children. Suzanna was deeply attached to her, even though Nyagitari did not seem to have behaved in the customary way of a grandmother to her grandchildren. Gusii grandmothers are indulgent of their grandchildren in a way that mothers rarely are. In reports of their childhood adults often describe their grandmothers as having been the most loving and lovable person in their lives. Clearly, in keeping with her role as a diviner—that is, someone who is somewhat apart from other people—Nyagitari was not the warm, indulgent traditional grandmother. Nevertheless, she was a very important factor in Suzanna's life.

Though she had only mentioned her grandmother occasionally before this visit, afterward Suzanna talked about her often. She had known for some time (though I do not know since when exactly) that her father was clairvoyant. Now she suddenly heard that her grandmother, whom she had always respected and idealized, was clairvoyant as well. This comforted her. Now, it seemed, she could tolerate the burden of her dreams. In the six months which remained of my stay, during which time Suzanna was dreaming prolifically, she did not go again to consult her grandmother. Perhaps the knowledge that Nyagitari was like her in this crucial respect was a source not only of relief but of strength. Henceforth, despite the frequently traumatic content of her dreams, she could dream with abandon, with curiosity, and even relish.

In the session following this visit, I found Suzanna with multiple physical complaints, including malaria, nausea, and conjunctivitis. She was wretched.

She told me Ongaki had found work in Kisumu in the bar of a kinsman. The money was very poor, but it was better that he go to Kisumu than stay at home and use Suzanna's few shillings for beer. However, in the bar he would be subject to the temptation of prostitutes, a temptation to which he would inevitably succumb. She, Suzanna, on the other hand, could never be adulterous, however much she were tempted. I asked her what would tempt her, and she replied no man could attract her now. "I could not open my legs except to Ongaki." But there are so many women in the neighborhood who seek other men, even when their own husbands are at home. She talked about a relative who had been recently caught in adultery. "She did it because of beer. You see, if you drink then you're bound to get trouble. A man offers you beer, and then, when you are drunk, he'll get you in return." Suzanna would never let herself be seduced for beer or for anything else, however poor she was. Indeed, recently a shopkeeper in the market offered her soap when she was penniless. She refused him. She told Ongaki about this man, and Ongaki swore to kill him or at least beat him up. But he changed his mind and left the man alone. She would go dirty rather than perform a service in return for goods.

As time went on I realized that Suzanna, with her charming smile and ample figure, was sexually a most moral woman. Traditionally the Gusii were a puritanical people. Only a generation ago sexual mores were so repressive that after circumcision the only sexual outlet available to young men was by physical assault on a girl from another clan. Indeed twenty years ago the Gusii had the highest incidence of rape in British Africa, a reflection of the sexually repressive nature of the culture. During the circumcision ceremonies older girls, already circumcised but not yet married, who were living in seclusion with those who had recently been circumcised, would allow themselves to be "taken by stealth" (ogochoberwa) by young boys. But this was the one occasion in the whole year when young people were permitted sexual relations prior to marriage. Assignations were supposed to be conducted in the utmost secrecy, despite the fact that the parental generation was well aware of the likelihood of their taking place and in many instances turned a deaf ear to the scufflings.

It seems that a generation ago the age of menarche was considerably later than today, and many girls menstruated for the first time at seventeen or eighteen, whereas today it is thirteen or fourteen, so the chances of girls becoming pregnant as a result of these encounters was slight. As soon as a girl was considered "big enough," however, even though she might not yet have menstruated, she would be married. She would then be taken with much protest, usually unfeigned, to live among a clan traditionally hostile to her own, whereupon she would resist intercourse with her bridegroom as long as she possibly could, even for as long as three days and nights, until eventually, exhausted, she succumbed. I believe that the cultural ideal that a woman be faithful after marriage was formerly often realized. Gusii women commonly looked upon sex as an obligation and regarded women who "liked men" with distaste. However, today many married women of Suzanna's age are flagrantly adulterous, and perhaps a majority of unmarried girls are sexually quite free.

But Suzanna grew up before the rather recent fundamental changes in rural society had made much impact; she was the daughter of God-fearing parents, members of a church which preaches eternal damnation to the sexually immoral. Her mother, while adopting "progressive" ideas about farming and education, insofar as she was in a financial position to do so, had remained thoroughly traditional in other respects. Suzanna claimed that her only premarital sexual experience was at *esubo ya chinyangi,* the circumcision of a schoolmate, to which she went against the ambiguous advice of her elder sister. There she was taken by stealth, an event she described as traumatic. She claimed not to have known this might occur; had she known, she would have remained at home like her sister. Afterward she was overcome with humiliation as well as anger at the mother of her friend, who not only failed to protect her and the other girls but even colluded with the marauders. She did confide in her sister but never had the courage to tell her mother or, when she married, her husband. Even now she remembered the incident with shame. The young man in question lived not far away, and she passed him frequently on the road. Sometimes he greeted her mockingly. I have heard similar accounts from other women as well as many accounts of extreme sexual naiveté prior to marriage, and I am inclined to believe Suzanna's story. The other two sexual relationships which she admitted to were with Flora's father, who treated her badly and whose "thing was so big he hurt me," and with a well-to-do businessman who took her forcibly to a town in another district, and from whom, on discovering he had two other wives, she immediately ran away.

Now she was with Ongaki. Why did she choose him? She was always reticent when the general conversation turned to sex. Her sisters-in-law, Martha and Nyanchama, would rattle on about their pleasures and pain, but Suzanna was profoundly discreet. Once, however, when she was trying to clarify why she rejected another suitor in favor of Ongaki, she remarked, "My blood did not warm to his as it did to Ongaki's." In other words, whatever the complicated motivation for her choice, sexual attraction was definitely an important factor, and once having made her choice, having fallen in love, she was physically committed to him alone. During the latter part of my stay when Ongaki was away again, Suzanna would periodically describe the propositions she received from neighbors. Despite the fact that she was bitterly angry that Ongaki, who, though now employed in a factory, was not sending any money home, Suzanna apparently did not succumb to these advances.

A year after I began working with her, Suzanna was again living apart from her husband, but now she was nursing his son, Ogaro, who was already taking his first steps down the path toward his grandmother's house. Still the cattle had not been paid, not even a calf. Ongaki was far away, enjoying himself with prostitutes and sending nothing home to his wife. Suzanna had been left once again with her mother-in-law Kemunto. She had many physical complaints; most of these she was rid of after a time, but one, the eye infection, remained with her for a long period. This frightened her very much. She went in vain to the district hospital for treatment as well as to a dispensary a few miles away; our project doctor failed to help her. Meanwhile her dreams became so disturbing that she dreaded the night.

In the fortieth session she reported she dreamed she was sent for from home because her father died. Then, in reality, three days later her uncle suddenly died; he was one of Ochoi's half-brothers. She remarked that she had not seen her father in a long, long time. On her own rare visits to her parents' home, he was never there. And yet she thought about him constantly. A few days later she reported another dream.

> "My mother had been divorced by my father. She came here weeping, her clothes dripping with blood. She carried in her arms her baby son, who was wrapped in a cloth which Ongaki had given her at the child's birth. That cloth was soaked with blood also. My mother cried, 'Ochoi is divorcing me because of you, Ongaki. You have not paid for Suzanna. See how I bleed

where Ochoi beat me!' In the dream I escorted my mother to the road and I saw water lying on each side of the path. At the road my mother and her child got a ride to the hospital. Then I came home and found Ongaki. I told him I was leaving him because he has brought so much trouble to me and to my parents. He cried and begged me not to take the children from him."

She tells me that nowadays her father is angrier than ever about Ongaki's failure to pay bridewealth. Before Ongaki went to work, whenever he and Mwamba met by chance, Ochoi would demand, "Where are my cattle?" Only if they met at a funeral would Ochoi, out of respect for the dead, keep quiet. She laughs wryly and recounts that once when she was *enyaroka* (a young girl), a boy offered eight cows for her, but her father refused. "He said they were too small. I was very sad because I loved that boy, but my father was greedy even then. It is true that my father once beat my mother over Ongaki's not paying, for all my brothers and sisters need school fees, and if my father received cattle for me he would sell them and use the money to send his children to school. Even Joseph, my brother, is at home these days. He should be in the secondary school, but this year they could not afford to send him. But I do not want to leave here now, even though my father is angry."

Suzanna had no more associations at this point, but I was curious about the fact that in the dream Moraa was carrying a baby boy wrapped in a cloth, a gift from Ongaki—who I know never produced so much as a shirt for his own son. Currently Moraa's youngest child was about five years old, but her lastborn children had in fact been twin sons who had died a year or two ago, in infancy. Later in this session, Suzanna said that despite the impression of harmony between cowives with which I had come away from her home, Moraa and Ester had never gotten along well, except in front of visitors, since the death of the twins. At that time Moraa accused her cowife of killing them with witchcraft, and Suzanna believed this to be true. "That woman looks good, but she is not. My father has a plot of land elsewhere, and soon he will put her there, away from my mother. Perhaps then there will be peace."

Suzanna's own son was now about the age of her mother's twins when they were bewitched. Up until that time Moraa and Ester had been the best of friends. Ester seemed like a replacement for her elder daughter, Rebecca, with whose bridewealth cattle Ochoi had married Ester. Then suddenly, when Moraa's sons began to go to secondary school, Ester, whose children were still very young, became furiously jealous that Ochoi should be spending so much money on the children of her cowife. Thus from *engareka* (jealousy between cowives) she killed the twins.

In this same session Suzanna suddenly remembered another dream in which she was coughing and a woman came to her and said, "That cough will kill you!" She awakened in terror, knowing that she had been bewitched and she would surely die of the bronchitis from which she had been suffering for some days past. To increase her terror, a few hours later, at mid-morning, a neighbor actually came into the homestead, and seeing Suzanna lying still sick under the shade tree, she said to her, just as in the dream, "That cough will kill you."

Nowadays Suzanna was preoccupied with sickness and death: first she dreamed her father died, and straightaway her father's brother, her classificatory father, died. Then she dreamed that she herself was dying. She was suffering from numerous complaints, some more serious than others, but each day there was a new one. Now she reported she had a bladder infection. She was debilitated and unable to work. The rains were imminent, and she should be preparing the ground for planting. Even Ogaro was no longer the robust little boy he once was. He, too, had a bad chest cold. When somebody is chronically ailing, the Gusii will always look for the cause close to home, for that is where hatred and jealousy (*endamwamu*) lie. Thus just as Suzanna assumed it was Ester, the erstwhile loving "daughter," who killed her cowife's children, now she did not doubt that her mother-in-law (of whom my assistant Mary once said, "Is it not wonderful how much Kemunto loves Suzanna") was bewitching her. "But why should your mother-in-law be jealous of you?" I asked. "What have you got that she wants?" Suzanna shrugged. "Could it be that she fears Ongaki loves me more than her?" Perhaps Kemunto believed that Suzanna, despite the tempestuous nature of her relationship with Ongaki, now reigned supreme over his heart.

Shortly after this session, the forty-first, Suzanna appeared at our clinic early in the morning. This was most uncharacteristic behavior. Using the privilege of her relationship with me, she had come to rely on sending messages to our doctor if she or someone in her family needed attention. Today she had come because she wanted to speak to me privately.

> She tells me she had been feeling so afraid that she sent word to Kisumu for Ongaki to come, and when he arrived two days ago they went together to a diviner living some distance away. They dared not go to Nyagitari since Kemunto and Nyagitari were friends: it was Nyagitari who had directed Kemunto to undertake instruction in divination. So they went to another diviner. He told them that Kemunto is indeed trying to bewitch Suzanna and Ogaro in revenge for Ongaki's refusal to join her *egesangio* (witches' club). Each one of her sons in turn has refused to join her, with the exception of Obao, the youngest, who has recently gone off to work in the Tanzanian forests (possibly to escape his mother). And each one has had to pay for his refusal: Omae has been struck dumb, Getaya's son almost died, Isaac's wife has been ailing for months, now Suzanna and Ogaro are sick. It is out of jealousy and rage that Suzanna has more influence over Ongaki than she herself that Kemunto has turned her malevolence against Suzanna.
>
> The *omoragori* instructs Suzanna to refuse all food from her mother-in-law, for clearly Kemunto is determined to poison Suzanna and her family: did she not put poison in the porridge which she sent to Suzanna a little while ago? The diviner gave Suzanna amulets (*erisi*) to put around her own waist and the children's, to protect them all from witchcraft. He also told them that Kemunto has taken several objects, including a shirt of Ogaro's, and from these she is preparing *obosaro* (a potion) with which she intends to kill them all, even Ongaki. In addition, Kemunto has already hidden *amasaro* (the implements of witchcraft) in the walls and rafters of Ongaki's hut. The diviner instructed them to hire an *omoriori* (witch smeller), who will come and remove these lethal objects.
>
> She cannot stay longer with me or her absence will be missed, and Kemunto will be suspicious. Before she runs home she remarks that she does not know how she will be able to stop the children from eating in her mother-in-law's house. Every day Kemunto feeds them; indeed it will be thoroughly inconvenient for her if she can no longer rely on Kemunto to take care of the children when she needs to go somewhere. Nyanchama is always off with boys these days!

When I went to the homestead the following day, I found Kemunto lying close to Suzanna, touching her, caressing her ankles. At one point she asked Suzanna to cut her toenails for her. She talked obsessively about trivial matters. I wondered if she would ever leave us alone together. But eventually she went off to the market, and we were free to talk.

> I ask Suzanna how she felt when she was cutting Kemunto's toenails. "I don't think. I do as she asks." Then she smiles. "I hate it in my heart, but could I refuse? I must keep quiet. One day, Sarah, when you are in America, you will hear that I have died, but perhaps Ogaro will be permitted to live and have the sons I had no chance to bear." She proceeds to fill in various details about their visit to the *omoragori*. She swears neither she nor Ongaki told him anything or gave him any hints. "He told us everything from what he read in the *chinsembe*." In fact they went to a second diviner yesterday. They wanted to make sure the first one had not lied. The second *omoragori* told them the very same things as the first. So the *chinsembe* were telling the truth! Then, when they came home yesterday evening, Ongaki's brother, Isaac, came to see them and told them that because one of his sons was very ill he had been to the very same diviner whom they had consulted. He told Isaac also that Kemunto was bewitching the boy, out of rage at Isaac's refusal to join her witches' club. "But you were there to consult him two days ago," I say. "Of course he remembered what you told him about Kemunto." Suzanna denies this: "He knows nothing about our family, we are strangers. He could not guess Ongaki and Isaac are brothers!"

Evidently in Isaac's case the hiring of a witch smeller was not necessary, since Kemunto, who lived two miles away, had not had an opportunity to put *amasaro* in his house. *Erisi* would be sufficient protection for Isaac's son. However, Isaac was willing to lend Ongaki 150 shillings to hire an *omoriori,* and he went off immediately to find one. "If Kemunto goes on a safari, Sarah, then you must come and see how he does his work," Suzanna promised.

I gathered that Suzanna had not kept these revelations to herself, for she told me that yesterday she spoke to Kemunto's cowife, Nyanduko. In fact they were not exactly cowives. Nyanduko was the wife of the senior Ogaro, who became *omochinyomba* (leviratic husband) to Kemunto when her original husband died. However, Kemunto had seven children by Nyanduko's husband, so for very many years the two women were in a cowifely relationship, even though officially they had been married to different men. Suzanna reported that Nyanduko told her that when Ogaro was alive he was impotent with her a large part of the time. "His thing could not stand up, whereas he played very well with Kemunto. You see, I knew long ago that she was a witch, for she spoiled our husband for me." Ogaro died before we began our work, but he left the reputation of a much respected elder who handled his domestic affairs well. Suzanna remembered him as being protective of her when she first eloped with Ongaki: he would defend her when Ongaki was drunk. The family idealized his memory, and some of the dissension I observed in his *omochie* (village) must have been in reaction to his death, for he left two wives and many sons on a very small piece of land. It seems he kept disputes to a minimum during his life time, but after his death the tensions surfaced rapidly, especially between Nyanduko's sons and of course between Kemunto and her sons.

Apart from confiding in her stepmother-in-law, Suzanna had also shared the diviner's revelations with Dina, a daughter-in-law of Nyanduko. However, Suzanna claimed that Nyanchama knew nothing. I was skeptical, but Suzanna continued to insist that Nyanchama not only did not know that Kemunto was attempting to bewitch Suzanna and her children but even had no idea, despite the little pot (*egetono*) in the rafters of the house, that Kemunto was a witch. Suzanna agreed that it was Nyanchama who had brought over the porridge with the *obosaro* (medicine) in it and that Nyanchama had seen Suzanna throw the porridge away untouched, but she was adamant, the girl knew nothing. "She is too busy with boyfriends," and indeed I noticed Nyanchama was scarcely ever in the homestead. I felt she knew quite well what was going on and she intentionally stayed away from home as much as possible.

Thus Suzanna was alone with her mother-in-law for long periods, without even the presence of Nyanchama to reduce the tension. "I am afraid all the time," Suzanna told me. "Last night when I was in bed, I heard the door rattle. That was the *omongina* [old woman]. I said nothing. I kept silent." I asked her where Kemunto would be likely to hide the articles of clothing which she had taken from Suzanna's hut.

"In the rafters [*rirongo*]." I offered, jokingly, to search for them. Suzanna was horrified. "You will be struck dumb if you do!" she gasped. I was powerful, but evidently not powerful enough. I was not immune to the malevolence of a witch. No one was. Moraa, Suzanna's mother, had been anxious to see Kemunto's little pot which Suzanna found in the *shamba,* and yet somehow she had never managed to come to see it. She was afraid of her *korera,* the mother-in-law of her daughter, even though on the surface they were great friends. Indeed Moraa always bought beer with which to entertain Kemunto, despite the fact that she did not drink herself. Then Suzanna told me her father had advised her not to confront her mother-in-law, which was why Suzanna had not called out to her in the night, when she heard the door rattling.

> "He says that to let the old woman know I am aware she is a witch would be madness. She will surely kill me then. Up to now I have been spared because she is afraid of my two uncles, my father's brothers, who are *abanyamasira* [sorcerers]. Up to now she has only made me sick. But if she knew I suspected her of witchcraft, she would believe I had asked my uncles for *emesira* [medicine to counteract witchcraft] and that would make her try even harder to harm and even kill me first before my uncles kill her."

Suzanna had not been to see her father, nor had Ochoi come to Ongaki's homestead. Indeed he was away at the chief's camp, where he worked as a tribal policeman. Suzanna must have sent a message to him through one of her brothers who frequently visited her. At any rate, her family already knew all about her visits to the diviners.

She was telling me she was in mortal danger, and yet as the afternoon went on I watched her become more and more animated. She was especially warm and loving to me. She hugged Ogaro repeatedly and sang to him about Sarah and Getuka. "If you stay until December, you will hear this at Flora's circumcision." She glowed. She was luxuriating in all the attention and support she was receiving from those whom she loved. Even Ongaki, at her request, soon came from his prostitutes and liquor in Kisumu, risking his life in the face of his mother's jealousy and rage to be with her. Each person she called on had responded immediately. She had so many allies and friends, while Kemunto had none except perhaps one or two other old women reputed like herself to be witches; "but they do not go witching together," i.e., they would not come to Kemunto's aid in harming Suzanna. Perhaps the power of one beleaguered old woman was not so great after all.

A few days later I learned that Isaac had made arrangements for the *omoriori* (witch smeller) to come.

> "The *omoriori* will come on Thursday evening, at nightfall, and if the old woman sees or hears him, that doesn't matter. She is already very afraid. I let her know that on Sunday Ongaki and I did not merely go for a walk, as I had told her. We went to see a diviner to discover why Ogaro and I have remained sick for so long. And the diviner told us, 'Someone in your village is doing you harm!' So now she knows we are aware she is a witch."

For a day or two Suzanna was in good spirits. After some delay the *omoriori* came with his wife unexpectedly, and thus I was not after all able to watch them. Kemunto and Nyanchama were both out at the time. Suzanna reported that the *omoriori* extracted many objects, including medicines in *ebitono*, little pots like the one in Kemunto's house, and the tails of various small animals. All these were thrown in the latrine, from which even a witch would shrink from retrieving them. I gathered from other sources that it is generally the case that an *omoriori* will delay his visit. This is to give him the opportunity to acquaint himself surreptitiously with the layout of the homestead and at the same time to conceal the objects that he will "smell out." But when I saw Suzanna the following day, to my surprise, instead of being relieved that she was now free of those nefarious objects, she was much more upset than on my previous visit.

She told me Kemunto still had no idea the *omoriori* had come. However, today the old woman had informed Suzanna that she herself had been to a diviner who told her, "Suzanna and Ongaki are trying to kill you!" Now Suzanna was more terrified than ever, for she was certain her mother-in-law would straightaway engage a sorcerer to reciprocate. She and Ongaki had no intention of attempting to kill Kemunto. "As that *omoragori* told Getaya, 'She is old, so let her die in her own good time.'" They only sought *erisi,* medicine to protect themselves from witchcraft; they did not seek to use *emesira* (sorcery) in retaliation against the old woman. But now Suzanna was too afraid of Kemunto's sorcery to sleep at night. She was exhausted, and her eye infection was still plaguing her.

Later that same day, I saw Kemunto looking equally exhausted and nervous on the road with Moraa, Suzanna's mother. Moraa had come, ostensibly, to consult our doctor because of the pain she was suffering in her fingers and hands. She was unable to work in the fields, for she could not hold a hoe. Her complaint was later diagnosed as rheumatoid arthritis. Suzanna was convinced that her stepmother Ester was to blame for Moraa's affliction. Moraa's second reason for making one of her rare visits to her daughter's married home was to find out for herself what was going on between Suzanna and Kemunto, but the old woman never left them alone together, so Moraa went home without speaking privately to her daughter!

During the month which followed, Suzanna was in a state of almost incapacitating anxiety. She did scarcely any farm work at all. Her dreams, which were prolific, graphically illustrated her turmoil and terror. In the forty-seventh session she reported a dream in which her mother had died.

> In the district hospital she found the corpse with hands tightly clenched. She weeps and cries out: "Who will pay for the education of my brothers now?" Her father tells her roughly, "It is your responsibility, not mine, to take your mother's body home," and she realizes that Ochoi and Ester, his junior wife, have together killed Moraa by witchcraft. Then the next day she hears that a neighbor died with fists clenched, just as her mother's had been clenched in the dream.

When Suzanna saw her mother (on the occasion when Moraa had come in vain to talk privately with Suzanna), she recounted this dream, and her mother tried to reassure her: "Perhaps you were really dreaming of someone else." But Suzanna was not comforted. Her ambivalence about her father was now clear. How could she trust him? On one hand he would not permit her to humiliate herself by working as a contract laborer in the tea nursery, insisting that she come home, where he could take care of her himself. But on the other he now told her, "You stay where you are, in the place to which in your foolishness you eloped." She should stay to make sure her cattle are paid. If her brothers were not educated, it would be Ongaki's fault for not providing bridewealth for Suzanna. Only the sale of Suzanna's cattle would ensure that Joseph, Simeon, and Musa did not grow up like *amachara* (idiots). But ultimately the blame would be Suzanna's—for eloping with a shiftless fool. It seems, then, that in this dream Suzanna saw that her father had become her enemy. Her stepmother, whose jealousy at Ochoi's spending money on Moraa's sons' school fees had been so great that she killed Moraa's babies, had won their husband over to her side. Together they eliminated Moraa. But in fact Moraa was not the real root of Ochoi's troubles. Suzanna was the true object of his anger, Suzanna who had failed to fulfill the primary obligation of a daughter, namely, to attract salable cattle in payment of her bridewealth. In the dream in revenge Ochoi killed her mother, who was dearer to Suzanna than anyone else on earth.

In this same session Suzanna recounted three other terrifying dreams:

> In one she hears Ongaki has been killed: "I fell to my hands and knees and crawled like a little child, crying, 'Who will take care of these children now? [Who will pay for them and legitimize them?]'" In another dream she sees a corpse being carried home from the hospital in a truck. "The legs were waving out of the back. Thump, thump, thump they went against the metal. In the morning I saw just such a sight."
>
> Then in the third dream she has gone blind. She sends for two married women nearby who are cousins of hers. They weep to see her thus sightless. One of them sends for her parents, and her mother arrives immediately and proposes taking her to the hospital. But Suzanna then awakens to find Ogaro with a high fever. As Suzanna is telling me this dream, Kemunto comes up to us, and Suzanna remarks, "Let her who is bewitching me, allow me to die," i.e., let her put me out of my misery once and for all. Kemunto listens with narrowed eyes, turns and goes back to her own house in silence.

Suzanna's associations to the last dream went as follows:

> She tells a long story in which a relative of hers, a young woman, was similarly afflicted with an eye infection and despite medical treatment ultimately died. She goes on, "Once I was sitting here under this tree and my mother-in-law, pretending to look for fleas on my head, removed a hair. I told my mother about this and my mother warned me, 'Do not allow her near you. She may bewitch you.' Then when the *omoriori* was here he told me, 'Kemunto took a hair from your head and used it against you!' So my mother had been right all along. The old

woman used that hair of mine to make *obosaro* to cause me to become sick as I am now."

These days Ongaki's homestead was a sorry place. Kemunto, whose chronic stomach illness had been worsening for months, despite the expensive sacrifices she made, dozed most of the time on a ragged cloth in the grass near her house. Across the compound Suzanna lay under her shade tree, a fretting Ogaro cradled against her side. The two women continued to interact when necessary; there was no real confrontation. But to any visitor who knew the place in other days, the change in atmosphere was chilling. Suzanna and Kemunto watched each other surreptitiously, while feigning uninterest. They strained to catch what each said to those who came to commiserate. It was difficult for me to speak with Suzanna. Kemunto's eyes gleamed twenty yards away. However, we persisted as best we could in lowered tones. Each woman was convinced the other was trying to kill her. Given this state of affairs, Suzanna believed she had little to lose by talking to me. She was even willing to talk to me in front of Nyanchama (who still officially knew nothing). When Ongaki came home, having lost his job, Suzanna's fears and depression were intensified.

In the forty-ninth session, she recounted one dream in which, once again, she found herself blind and a second in which her house was burned to the ground, her few precious possessions all destroyed. Ongaki could not ward off these night terrors. She awakened screaming, clutching at him. But he was almost as afraid of Suzanna's dreams as she herself. In addition, it seemed that Suzanna's fears of witchcraft were now more generalized.

> She dreams that a neighbor, Nyaminsa, a quarrelsome crank, who is thought by many to be a witch, comes to the compound in the night. Suzanna calls out to her, challenging her, "Why do you come here? What do you want?" and then awakes. She recounts how she opened her door to see if anyone was outside, but the yard was deserted. However, when she tried to sleep again a piece of iron sheeting fell from the rafters into the fireplace. "I felt something pass over my face. I could not sleep; I shivered and held Ogaro close to me. I thought perhaps a witch had thrown a stone against the roof and it had dislodged the iron, so I made myself get up once more and open the door. Outside in the moonlight I saw a man standing. I shut the door and fled

into my bed. But in the morning I saw footprints in the dust and I recognized the pattern of the rubber soles of the shoes of Getango [a well-known witch]. Perhaps he was only passing through our homestead, for a woman in his *egesangio* [witches' club] lives close to us. But perhaps he truly intends us harm. He is unpredictable and very dangerous. He struck Apoko's son dumb last year [indeed, Mary and I had heard the story from that boy ourselves] just because the boy annoyed him."

In this same session Suzanna reported yet another dream in which one of her sisters-in-law (the wife of Ongaki's half-brother), Drucilla, gave her porridge to drink, and after she had drunk it, Suzanna saw there were worms creeping out of her own hand. She realized that Drucilla had given her the evil eye, and she awoke weeping.

Drucilla was famous in the locality for having the involuntary power to afflict people, especially light-skinned children, with the evil eye. This meant that anyone she looked at might subsequently find himself incorporating thousands of tiny objects and particles into his body: in particular insects, charcoal dust, maize kernels, pieces of thread, and the like—all of which combine to clog the veins and swell the abdomen and ultimately bring about death. Drucilla had a hyperthyroid condition which caused her eyes to protrude. We later arranged for her to have surgery to correct her condition, but I do not know whether the normalizing of her eyes had any effect on the way her neighbors regarded her, which was with extreme cruelty and hostility. Suzanna lived a short distance from Drucilla, who passed through Ongaki's compound twice a day on her way to and from the river. The Gusii believe that someone who has the evil eye is only really dangerous during the two periods each year when the maize is very high. Suzanna, a dark-skinned adult, was the one person in the neighborhood who treated Drucilla reasonably during the "safe" months of the year. She admitted, however, to avoiding her for the month in each growing season when the "cornsilk hangs from the cob," and her light-skinned daughters were forbidden to play up the hill near Drucilla's house.

I was spending a good deal of time with Drucilla, and, although she never referred to it, Suzanna knew this very well, for she would see me on the path. In fact the afternoon preceding the night when Suzanna had this dream she had seen me coming from Drucilla's house. Suzanna was subject to the fears of supernatural perils to which most Gusii are subject, however fervid they might be in their devotion to Christianity. But I, who spent long hours with Drucilla, continued to come away unscathed. Perhaps I was exempt. In this session, in her associations Suzanna did not refer to my relationship to Drucilla, but in the following session she suddenly remarked, "You took Drucilla to the hospital, didn't you?" I.e., you are not afraid of her, indeed you are even willing to help her.

While according to the manifest content of her dream about Drucilla, Suzanna seemed again to be in mortal peril, at a deeper level the dream pointed to other issues. First, did not Sarah disregard the dangers of the evil eye and behave kindly to the unfortunate woman who happened to possess it (by no fault of her own, as the evil eye is inherited or acquired by chance)? Second, did not Sarah in addition brave the malevolence of Kemunto (who would surely strike her dumb if she tried to examine the old witch's paraphernalia) to come to talk to Suzanna? Last, Sarah was attempting to help Drucilla rid herself of a dreaded condition. (The evil eye was known to be almost as destructive and onerous to the possessor as to the one whom it afflicted. Everyone knew that Drucilla had been divorced three times because of her eyes and that Ongaki's half-brother Getono only kept her because she bemused him with *amaebi,* a love potion.) Perhaps Sarah would save Suzanna also from her illnesses and, more important, from her ambivalence: Should she take leave of her parents and commit herself finally to the feckless Ongaki or retreat from the hardships of her marriage and run home?

But why, one must ask, should Suzanna's anxiety be suddenly so intense? Why all these dreams of blindness and death? Did not the witch smeller remove the lethal *amasaro* from her house and throw them into the latrine, from which Kemunto could not retrieve them? Moreover, he brought Suzanna medicine for her eyes, and this seemed to be improving her condition, while Western medicine did nothing for her. Though Suzanna promised me that she and her husband had no intention of trying to kill Kemunto, in fact if they wanted to change their minds on that score, they could very easily consult a sorcerer themselves and get medicine to use against the old woman. A short while ago Suzanna had seemed much more at ease; indeed she was radiant with relief. Why this abrupt new descent into terror?

I believe Suzanna's state of panic was precipitated by the appearance of a suitor for Nyanchama, a suitor, moreover, who was prepared to pay cattle for her. If the transaction were to go through, Ongaki would immediately deliver those cows to Ochoi, and Suzanna would be paid for at last. On the conscious level Suzanna was delighted at the prospect. "The day Nyanchama goes to her new home, I will give her a dress, I will cook *obokima* for her, I will dance for her and escort her all the way to her husband's place. I will love her until I die!" she exclaimed. When the young man, who was uneducated (and therefore Nyanchama did not take to him at all), came with his many friends to look over his "intended," Suzanna, despite her poor health, managed to cook for them and wait on them. She used her precious pyrethrum money to buy meat. She watched the dancing into the early hours of the morning, when, exhausted, she left the young people and went off to bed. Then in the days following she waited anxiously for the go-between to come to continue the marriage negotiations. "When will you be invited to inspect the cattle?" I asked. "We do not know, we have heard nothing." Ongaki smiled pleasantly and went to look for beer. Nyanchama wasted no time in waiting for her uneducated suitor to make up his mind. "He hasn't married me yet, has he?" she said as she tied a colored cloth around her head and went off to the market to continue her numerous flirtations.

One day Ochoi sent a message that he was at home; would I visit him?

> Word has gone ahead that we are coming, and when we arrive at Moraa's house there are many relatives assembled to greet us. Suzanna whispers to me thumbnail sketches of each one: "She is a witch, that one is a harlot," and so on. She seems unusually critical of her relatives. She is tense and anxious, in contrast to the occasion of our first visit. There is no food for us today. Moraa and Ester, who is with us throughout and is friendly as before, apologizes. Eventually the neighbors all leave, and Ochoi is to be seen coming across the meadow to Moraa's house. He greets me and starts to talk to me as if he's known me for years. His physical resemblance to his daughter is extraordinary. They both have the same black skin and wide, beautiful smiles. Their styles, of course, are different. Suzanna is always gentle and graciously controlled. Her father is self-confident and direct. He leans toward me, talking intensely. He is careful to speak so that

I have no difficulty in understanding him. His wives sit beside him, and from time to time each offers her comments. They are deferential to him but apparently uninhibited about joining in the conversation. Suzanna remains silent throughout, but she seems delighted that Ochoi and I are getting along so well together. We cover a wide range of topics, from a review of his life history to the latest developments in a particularly violent family dispute in our research area. At one point, however, the conversation suddenly shifts. He remarks, apropos of nothing, "It will be good when Suzanna is paid for!" and then we discuss briefly the delays in Nyanchama's marriage before proceeding to another topic.

I was left with the impression of an energetic and dominating man. He asked many questions. He considered it his right to know about me, my work, and my family. I had been summoned to meet him, and yet he was not there to greet me. I had to wait for him, and when he arrived he let me know that his time was limited. He had other business to attend to that afternoon. I met him subsequently from time to time in the market or on the road. He could spare me a moment or two, but no more. He was always in a hurry. As yet, he had only a foothold in the modern world. If he could not advance himself, then he must ensure the advancement of his sons. He was an operator, but he did his operating with a certain humor. He once tried to sell me a lion skin he had got from a Tanzanian Masai. He came very close and whispered in my ear. When I said I could not export it without a license and where could I get a license for the skin of an animal which had been shot by poachers, he laughed and conceded, "I just thought I would ask you anyway."

Thus the meeting took place between Ochoi and myself. Perhaps Suzanna had fantasized that an alliance between us for her protection would ensue. A short time after I visited her father, Suzanna told the following dream:

Suzanna, her sister Aska and her child, Sarah, and her assistant Mary were all in the Peugeot. We had been to her home and were on our way back to Morongo when the car stuck in the mud. Everyone got out of the car but Suzanna, who refused, crying, "Let me rest here first!" Then Ochoi appeared on the scene and ran off to ask the subchief to pull us out with his car.

However, when the subchief drove up, he skidded, and his car rolled down the bank into the river. The onlookers all cried out, "Bobee [alas]!" and then Suzanna awoke.

She had no associations to the dream, but the implication seemed to be that nothing I did in terms of using my power resources on her behalf and nothing her father did could save her from being trapped. She had hoped to escape her quandary by her relationship with me, i.e., in the Peugeot, the symbol of my magical power. In this instance the Peugeot also seemed to represent modern life and upward mobility, such as she thought she was getting by marrying Ongaki, the educated schoolteacher. However, the Peugeot stuck in the mud. I would be going away in a few months, and there she would be, stuck with Ongaki and his tinsel dreams. Her sister Aska, on the other hand, in reality had just run home from her husband, and their divorce was being negotiated. Aska was much better educated than Suzanna. She had had three years of secondary school when she came down with a disease which, a diviner told Ochoi, had been inflicted upon the girl by a relative who, jealous of her academic success, bewitched her. The only cure was to terminate her education. Ochoi had recently agreed to a divorce and even to repayment of her bridewealth, because Aska was educated and her father believed she would be capable of supporting herself. She and her child would not become a burden to him, as Suzanna with her four children would. Thus Mary, Aska, and I, all of whom had other options, escaped, leaving Suzanna to her fate.

Her fate evidently terrifies her, for in this same session she reports two other dreams. In the first the local incorrigible thief, Orindo, is being chased by a furious crowd. He jumps over the fence surrounding Ongaki's homestead and collapses in front of Kemunto's house. There his pursuers catch him and kill him. Suzanna hides in her house, not daring to help him, for she knows the crowd would kill her also if she went to the thief's rescue.

Why does she identify so closely with a man who is regarded by everyone as a social outcast? Her associations are as follows: "I don't know him well. He is a neighbor of ours, but he has never stolen from me, as he has from Dina, my sister-in-law. Indeed, since he came out of prison last year he hasn't stolen anything from anyone. Even in the dream he was innocent." And yet he was murdered for crimes he had committed long ago.

In the second dream she went to visit a woman friend, a neighbor, and found her selling and drinking *changa* (raw alcohol). "Everyone was drinking, including my mother-in-law, except me. Then the police raided the homestead and arrested everyone. I begged the officer to let me go: 'I have drunk nothing,' I told him, and he answered me, 'Then why ever did you come here?' and continued to arrest people, my mother-in-law as well. Everyone was wailing and crying." She awoke without knowing if she were to be arrested or not.

She comments only that her parents *never* drink.

Though Suzanna did not drink at this time, she had done so until the previous Christmas. Despite her strict upbringing, as soon as she eloped with Ongaki she "fell from grace." I saw her drinking many times, and I saw her giving beer to Joyce and even to Ogaro. Frequently on the days Kemunto sold beer, Suzanna's children would lie giggling drunkenly in the grass, with beer sediment all over their faces.

Thus again, as in the first dream, she was in danger of punishment for past transgressions. What was the nature of the transgression? At the manifest level it was something which was forbidden by her father. Indeed Ochoi was a tribal policeman, just like the policemen in the dream. His job was in part the prevention of the brewing and sale of native beer. But at another level, perhaps, both these dreams signified punishment for oedipal wishes. In the first dream she identified with a thief—a thief, however, who in this instance just happened to be innocent. Although he no doubt coveted his neighbors' property, he did not in fact steal it. In the same way, in the second dream Suzanna went to the drinking party, wishing to join in, but she controlled herself. "Why ever did you come," the policeman asked her, if not to drink? The intention was there; and even though she did not succumb to it, she should be punished for it anyway.

In all three of the dreams Suzanna reported in this session, she found herself trapped. In the one instance in which her father did try to help her, when the Peugeot was stuck in the mud, his efforts were abortive. In the other two dreams the "policing" figures were all hostile, in one case murderous. There was no help for her. She was cast out.

Meanwhile, in the realm of physical reality, Suzanna complained of a series of afflictions. Her stomach, her head, her back, everywhere she was ailing. She told me she was so wretched the previous night that Ongaki, not daring to ask her to have intercourse, went off in the morning to the local "bar" to make good her omission with a prostitute. In his absence, Suzanna told me the witch smeller had come the previous evening to perform *okosaragwa* (scarification) on her shoulders and back. Into these cuts he rubbed a stinging medicine to protect her from witchcraft. The witch smeller told her that she must on no account take any Western medicine. If she wanted to be cured of her multiple ailments, she should take only *his* medicine. While she was telling me this, Nyanchama and Kemunto appeared, and hearing Suzanna groan and complain, Kemunto urged me to take her to the hospital. Next Ongaki returned from his sojourn at the bar and joined his mother and sister in pressing me to help Suzanna.

I found myself in a ridiculous situation, for Suzanna and Ongaki were perfectly aware that a visit to the hospital was out of the question. The *omoriori* had forbidden it. And yet Ongaki was apparently urging Suzanna to go. Suzanna, determined to resist, tried to mollify her mother-in-law with an alternative plan: she should be taken to her home, where she would be able to rest, for her mother and stepmother would take care of her. Ongaki, who as always was afraid that if Suzanna went home she would not return to him, refused this plan outright. I watched him, a really rather comical sight, torn between wife and mother. He knew neither plan was operable but felt constrained to support his mother, and so he continued to urge Suzanna to go with me. Eventually I said to him in English, "You know Suzanna isn't sick; she's nervous. Going to the hospital won't help her, will it?" So we achieved a compromise by which I offered to take Suzanna into the hospital when I drove to town later in the afternoon. However, she had to find the money to come back in the bus, for I would not drive her home myself.

When I returned to pick Suzanna up, I found the hospital plan had been abandoned because the family "could not raise the bus fare." Since the bus fare was only two shillings, a trifling amount, it was obvious that Suzanna and Ongaki had gratefully used their poverty as an excuse.

The following day I found Suzanna apparently in better health. She was washing vegetables prior to cooking them and seemed in good spirits. She told me,

"Last night Getaya [Ongaki's elder brother] came unexpectedly and found me lying in front of my house. He did not think it was right that I should be still sick. Had not the *omoriori* discovered all the things which were harming me? It seemed he had not. So Getaya went off immediately and found another *omoriori,* who found that it was indeed true that the first *omoriori* had left something behind. This second one found a stone wrapped in rags under my hearth. As soon as he put it outside I felt much better. My mother-in-law did not see any of this, for it was night. The *omoriori* told me, 'Now you cannot die.'"

However, despite his assurances, Suzanna was still upset. The family had heard nothing more from Nyanchama's suitor, and Nyanchama looked depressed. Indeed the whole family was apprehensive. Ongaki was waiting around in the hope that he would be summoned to look at bridewealth cattle, but no message came. Suzanna's anxiety persisted even though many of her physical complaints disappeared.

In the fifty-fifth session she reported that on her return, after dark, from the funeral of a kinsman's child, she heard a witch calling, "Bosibori, Bosibori!" She bent down and looked beneath the door. She saw someone standing in the dark, but she could not tell whether it was a man or a woman. She kept silent, for the Gusii believe that if you answer when a witch calls to you, you will be struck dumb. Then just before dawn the following morning, Ongaki went outside to urinate, and he saw a woman behind him. He called to Suzanna to come out with him. They screwed up their eyes and made out Areri, their neighbor, going into her house. They heard the door creak behind her. Areri is a great friend not only of Getango, whom Suzanna had seen outside her house on another occasion some weeks before, but also of Kemunto. Although Suzanna believes Kemunto worked alone in the past, perhaps now that her sons have refused to join her, except for Obao, who isn't even at home, she has formed a witches' club with Areri and Getango and is using them in her struggle with Suzanna and Ongaki.

Meanwhile, Kemunto is complaining as much as ever about her stomach (our doctor believes she has an ulcer). Yesterday evening, when Suzanna came from the fields and was washing her legs, Kemunto asked her for the dirty water she had been using. The old woman said she was going to mix it with beer she intended to give to Okaru, the husband of Areri. Okaru was about to cut Kemunto's hedge, and the beer was in payment for his labor. Kemunto told Suzanna, "Okaru has joined Areri and Getango. He is a witch now also." Ongaki, who overheard his mother's request, prevented Suzanna from giving the old woman the dirty water with which, presumably, she would have made bad beer, thereby causing Okaru a stomach upset. Suzanna cannot tell the real cause of Kemunto's antagonism to this man, whether he is the old woman's longtime enemy or whether he was formerly a companion in witchcraft and only recently have they fallen out. Nor does she know whether she should fear Kemunto alone or, in addition, these neighbors who have taken to terrorizing her at night. Perhaps she is caught in the middle of some quarrel between Kemunto and Areri, and really the quarrel has nothing to do with her. How can she know? Meanwhile Ogaro is ill again, Ongaki is out of work and shows no sign of trying to get employment, and her eyes are beginning to bother her again. Her nights are filled with dreams of the death of members of her own family.

In the fifty-eighth session she reported a dream in which Ongaki was employed in a town far away.

She took Ogaro to that town to visit his father, and when they arrived she asked two men in the street where to find Ongaki. One told her he was staying with Ongaki; he would take her to him. But the other warns her not to go with his companion. "This man lives at a distance from here and if you go with him he will kill you. He's already murdered many people." So Suzanna started to run away and the first man, the "murderer," ran after her. But Suzanna ran faster than he did and escaped. In her dream she wept and cried out, "Why must I come so far to find Ongaki, only to be killed?" She told Ongaki the dream when she awoke, and he made no comment. "But he is very worried by my dreams," she adds.

All the supports in Suzanna's life seemed to be crumbling. Her mother's rheumatism was excruciating. Suzanna heard she was unable to weed her maize. Her father was also suffering. His knees were giving him trouble. An *omoragori* told him he needed to make an elaborate sacrifice for *erioba;* that is, his grandfather must once have seen a ring of fireflies on the path at dusk and then failed to sacrifice a goat as he should have done according to Gusii belief. Thus Ochoi would be afflicted until the necessary elaborate and costly rituals were performed. I was told that when all was prepared I would be summoned to attend, but I never heard anything more. I presume Ochoi was unable, before I left the area, at any rate, to raise the money necessary for the perfor-mance of the *erioba* ritual. Meanwhile, he continued to be in pain and more resentful than ever that Ongaki had not paid for Suzanna. The proceeds from those cows could have been used not only to send Suzanna's brothers back to secondary school but to pay for sacrificial goats.

Once at this time I happened to meet Ochoi in the market, and I told him how much Suzanna was suffering, physically and mentally. I described in detail her fears concerning her mother-in-law, and he appeared to listen. I am certain he had already heard all I was telling him, for his wife Moraa had been informed of Suzanna's suspicions from the start. I was well aware that I was in a way committing a breach of confidence by talking directly to Ochoi about what had been happening to his daughter. But I decided to do so in order to gauge his response. I knew very well the strength of Suzanna's attachment to her father, but what of his to her?

When I finished what I had to say, Ochoi was silent for a second and then started talking about something else entirely. In effect he behaved precisely as a Gusii man is expected to behave when forced to receive information of a distasteful nature: he acted as if nothing had been said. In this way I was able to experience vicariously something of what Suzanna must have experienced frequently of late with her father: he would listen to her, either in person or through a go-between, and would then behave as if he had heard nothing, neither the factual nor the emotional content. His message was clear: she had made her bed, now let her lie in it. As he left me on this occasion he mumbled, as an afterthought, an apology, something about intending to visit his daughter, but both of us knew he would never come to Ongaki's homestead until the day he was called to inspect Suzanna's bridewealth. When I told Suzanna later that day about my encounter with her father, I watched her face carefully and saw her expression change from tremulous expectation to gloom. Not so long ago her father would have rescued her from Kemunto's malevolence and told her to come home. But that was before she had a son. Now even Sarah's advocacy on her behalf stirred no pity in his heart.

But then I would be leaving in ten weeks' time. If I had no influence with her father, at least I had chloroquine to give her when she had malaria. In the garden she had been feeling cold and dizzy: "Won't you leave me medicine to take when you are gone? And a blanket? Have you no old blanket in which I may wrap myself when I have fever?" she asked mournfully. At Christmas I had given her some of my son's cast-off clothes for Ogaro, and she had been surprised and delighted. Now she did not ask for anything for herself. Perhaps our relationship had been a blanket to wrap herself in when she had fever. She had seen me almost daily for more than a year. Though we might not have any conversation, we would wave and call out greetings to one another. Ten months ago, in the fifteenth session she had reported her first dream about me. Since then, there had been many more, almost as many as about her parents. Her reserve with me had vanished, and I had become a haven, a vehicle which she used to travel away from the attachments of her childhood to the new ones of her marriage and maturity. Never, either in our conversations or in her dreams, had she asked me to take care of her. Her behavior toward me had always had a certain slightly distancing quality. I approved of her, I endorsed what she was so that she could be at liberty to change and grow, even though the course was perilous. She appeared always to be saying, "Listen to me, bear with me, and I will have the strength." When the time approached for me to go, she seemed to say, "Leave me something so that I may continue as I have begun with you; leave me the capacity to manage on my own." At times she laughingly offered Ogaro to me, saying, "Take him with you to America and bring him up to be *omongaine* [a clever person]. Let Ogaro learn the power of Europeans." She asked me when I would come again. How much did the airplane cost? When I came back I should build a house near the main road and live with the Gusii people forever. My son Alexander and Joyce would marry, and she and I would call one another *korera*, "mother of my daughter's husband," "mother of my son's wife." But she never asked or dreamed that I take her with me.

V

In the last weeks before my departure, we spent a little time talking about my travel plans. Suzanna was interested in the logistics of how I would disassemble my household and how I would get myself and my family to Nairobi. She did not ask about what would become of me in Europe or America, places she found impossible to imagine. On the whole, although I raised the subject at regular intervals, I had the impression that Suzanna was doing her best to retreat from me before I actually left her.

Meanwhile, through a relative, Ongaki heard of a factory job in a distant town. Initially after his departure the tension between Suzanna and Kemunto remained high. For some days the old lady was not told where Ongaki had gone. Suzanna let her believe he had gone to Nairobi, because, as she explained to me, "If she knows Ongaki's destination, she may bewitch him so that he meets misfortune on the way. If she must know where he is, let her discover from someone else." I pointed out that many people, including women with whom Kemunto was friendly, knew Ongaki had gone to Eldoret, not Nairobi. In a day she would be bound to hear the truth. "But by then he will have reached the place where his cousin has found work for him. The old woman will not be able to harm him." Meanwhile Kemunto would come over to Suzanna's hut and say to Ogaro, "Where is your father?" and Suzanna would be silent.

The old woman was still complaining about her stomach and had not been out of the compound in weeks. Private conversations with Suzanna had become impossible. One day when we had arranged to meet at another homestead in order to secure half an hour of privacy, a rain storm began just as I was passing Suzanna's house on my way to our rendezvous, so I ran inside to shelter. Almost immediately I was followed by Kemunto, who squatted down between myself and Suzanna and remained there until the rain stopped, when, having given me a detailed account of the condition of her stomach, she left us. I noticed, however, that during the fifteen minutes we were together, Suzanna was more talkative, less tense than she had been of late in the presence of her mother-in-law. As soon as we were alone I remarked, "You aren't afraid of her, are you?"

At first Suzanna contradicts me. "Yes, of course I am!" But
then she laughs. "When she complains like that, can she really
last till morning, or will she die during the night?" Evidently
Suzanna has heard that Ongaki is employed again. She cannot
really be afraid now. She kisses Ogaro. "I am happy! For so
many months Ongaki would be telling me, 'I must have your
pyrethrum money for cigarettes,' and I couldn't refuse him.
Perhaps now I will save enough to buy a new dress to replace
these rags you see. Last week I asked a neighbor at the river if I
might borrow a dress in order to go to a funeral, but she refused
me. She laughed at me and said rudely, 'How can I agree? If I
wanted to borrow a dress from you, you would have none to lend
me!' But soon I too will have a pretty dress to wear and lend. I
shall not be *omotaka* [a beggar] much longer." She goes back to
talking about Kemunto's illness and the possibility of her dying,
and she remarks, "If she dies I will make people think I am
weeping for her, but in fact I shall be laughing. How I shall
laugh! I used to be so afraid of her, but I am no longer. It used
to be that if Ogaro awoke sick in the night, I would not dare to
light my lamp for fear the old woman would see it and know her
witchcraft was taking effect. But last night Ogaro was sick, and
I lit my lamp. I didn't care if she saw. The *omoriori* gave Ongaki
medicine with which to find a job, and you see now, that
medicine did its work. Soon I will have a new house, not just
live in it. Oh, no. We'll leave it, and we shall go to live where
Ongaki is working. We will live as a family in the town. You
see, the *omoriori* is more powerful than my mother-in-law. He
gave me other medicine, you remember. He made cuts in my
back and rubbed his medicine into my flesh. If Ongaki's
medicine worked, then mine must also. My mother-in-law cannot harm me now!" And so when Kemunto comes into the hut
Suzanna is unafraid.

From this time onward I saw the tension between them gradually
subside. Ongaki, over whom they had been embattled ever since his
return from Mombasa the previous year, had left the scene. Both
women wanted the job to be permanent. Suzanna, however, was apprehensive.

She reported a dream in which she sees Ongaki running after a
young girl who has eloped with a boy. Ongaki has been sent by

the girl's father to catch her and bring her home. Suzanna calls out to him, "Why have you left work? You should have stayed in the factory at Eldoret!" To which Ongaki replies, "I haven't come home for nothing. I have come to get a letter of recommendation."

Her associations are as follows: she does not really know the girl in the dream, except by sight. That girl is always causing trouble for her parents, and perhaps she has it in mind to elope with an unsuitable man even now. As for Ongaki, "it isn't in his character to resign from his work. When he was a teacher he neglected his work, but he did not leave it of his own free will. He was fired. This time, if he loses his job, it will be nobody's fault but his own."

In fact an influential relative had found this factory job for Ongaki. He did not need any further recommendation. He had been accepted. As Suzanna knew so well, however, Ongaki could make a mess of even the most secure position. But ironically, in the dream, in trying to bring back an impulsive girl to her father, he was acting as an arm of the law. Had he himself not eloped with a girl from a family marginally better off than his own? The girl in the dream had long been the subject of gossip in the community. She eloped three times with boys who did not meet with the approval of her ambitious father, and each time he forced her to come home, on one occasion with her child. So it seems that, although Suzanna was skeptical about Ongaki's capacity to stick to his job, she was also revealing two fantasies, first that Ongaki might become a responsible, law-abiding, and law-enforcing person (like her father), and second that her own father, like the girl's father, might send someone after her to force her to come to her senses and bring her home. However, as far as I know Ochoi never made any attempt to make Suzanna give up her husband. He grumbled for years, but he was interested in her staying and being paid for instead of leaving Ongaki. In other words, the task of her dream work was, "Let her make the best of what she's got."

Meanwhile, no word had ever come from Nyanchama's suitor, and Suzanna and Kemunto had concluded that the marriage would not be taking place. The chances of another such possibility coming Nyanchama's way were slight. Perhaps an old man might want a junior wife, but these days few young girls are prepared to accept such an offer.

Thus, unless Ongaki managed to earn enough money to buy cattle, Suzanna could remain safely in limbo for years to come. The condition of the not-yet-paid-for wife had its discomforts, but as we have seen, it also had compensations, at least for Suzanna. As always, she was ambivalent about most aspects of her current life, but these days it seemed she was slightly less so. One afternoon when she had no soap, she said to me, "If Ongaki were here I could have sent him to perform some small task for a neighbor so that he might earn two shillings with which to buy soap. How wonderful it is to have your husband home with you! He is the *omotobwa* [central pole] of the house!" In fact when Ongaki was at home he usually spent what little money he earned from felling trees and thatching roofs on himself. At such times Suzanna was angry with him, but she could think more gently of him now he was gone.

She offered further indication that she was feeling safer in mind and limb. She reported a dream in which a witch, Nyaminsa, about whom she had dreamed on a previous occasion, came to Suzanna's hut, asking for food; but Suzanna and Kemunto sent the woman away, saying, "This is not the time for us to cook. We have nothing to give you."

Suzanna's associations reveal that Nyaminsa had a grudge against Ongaki, and recently she refused to greet Suzanna when they met by chance. Since Gusii people always greet each other except during periods of outright hostility, Nyaminsa's failure to do so alarmed Suzanna very much. She might be wise to expect attack at any moment, and yet in her dream she refused Nyaminsa food. Traditionally the Gusii cannot refuse requests for food, especially not to a relative, and Nyaminsa was the wife of a relative. Moreover, I had often seen Suzanna share what little she had with neighbors who happened to be passing and who called over the hedge, "Have you something to eat?" But of special significance was the fact that she and her mother-in-law had evidently closed ranks again. Together they rejected the demands of a woman whom everyone in the neighborhood, even in normal times, agreed was a witch. But in telling her dream Suzanna seemed unconcerned about her personal safety.

These days Kemunto's health had also improved. She still had a backache, but she was working in the fields again and going about her business. When I visited Suzanna, I missed seeing the old woman glaring at us from across the compound. Once, when I was questioning Kemunto about her initiation as a diviner, she revealed a very important fact of which hitherto I had been totally ignorant. Namely, when she was a young woman with only two children, she had trouble conceiving a third child, and she was instructed by an *omoragori* to seek initiation as a diviner. She therefore did indeed become an *omoragori* and practiced for a couple of years, until she gave birth to another child. Some time during the nursing period, she gave up divination. "All was well with me." But at some point her house was burned, and she lost her equipment in the fire. She built another house nearby, but when she began to suffer from a stomach complaint, years later during Nyanchama's infancy, she knew she should begin again to practice divination. She did not do so, however, because she was unable to replace her equipment. She mentioned to me that a year ago Suzanna had found a little pot on the site of her old house. "Perhaps you would like to see my *egetono?*"

So this was how Kemunto, according to her own testimony, happened to have had the pot in her possession. Not only witches but *abaragori* (diviners) also use such pots. I think it very likely that Suzanna knew Kemunto had once been *omoragori*. She knew a good deal about diviners, since her grandmother was one, and she must have been aware that *abaragori* use *ebitono*. It seems that initially she had not been especially upset by her discovery of the pot, but a year later, after Ogaro's birth, her anxiety in relation to her marital status had caused her to interpret the significance of Kemunto's pot in quite a different light, and it was this interpretation which she had given me. It is very common for a Gusii woman to believe that her mother-in-law is a witch. Many women said this. But since a mother-in-law and daughter-in-law must somehow coexist for many years, the intensity of the younger woman's suspicion is not constant. Generally it rises and falls, reflecting the interaction of a complex set of social and psychological factors. Often a woman may tell you, "Yes, my mother-in-law is said to be a witch, but she has not harmed me"; i.e., her potential for malevolence must be borne in mind, but it is of no immediate consequence right now. Or again, as in Suzanna's case, after a period of mutual enmity and terror the relationship may revert quite abruptly to one of routine cooperation, albeit with periodic expressions of suspicion. Thus Suzanna got more medicine from the *omoriori,* the witch smeller, when her eye infection returned briefly, and every week she boiled up another potion he gave her and sprinkled it around her house as protection against Kemunto's witchcraft.

But Kemunto was no longer the focus of Suzanna's anxiety. In reality members of Nyaminsa's family had begun to threaten her, as Ongaki's wife, in retaliation for the part Ongaki had played in securing their kinsman's imprisonment. Once Suzanna found a man lurking outside her hut, in the dark, and several times she was threatened on the road by other members of that family. But she confided in her stepbrothers-in-law, and they gave her advice about what kind of lock she should get for her door. Currently only these young men were at home, since all Kemunto's sons were gone, and even though in the past Suzanna had been sharply critical of their indolence and drunkenness, nevertheless in a crisis she could depend on them for support. Despite the supernatural hazards involved in giving blood to someone with the evil eye, they gave blood to Drucilla when she had her thyroid operation. Surely they would do as much for Isaac and Getaya, Ongaki's eldest brothers. They had been consistently helpful to Suzanna and would continue to be so even though Ongaki himself might neglect his wife.

When payday came and went and she received nothing at all from Ongaki, Suzanna was enraged and told a whole raft of stories about how he squandered money on prostitutes. "He will always see other women. Even here when he is with me, he runs after women. But why must he spend money on them?" she cried. Gusii women do not expect their husbands to be faithful and have no culturally prescribed right to demand fidelity, but they do demand that their husbands conserve their resources for consumption within the family. "One of these days, when I have menstruated three times again, I will go to Eldoret and tell him, 'I am not a truck which can be parked at home without oil or petrol!'" In the last weeks I never heard her say, as she used to say so frequently, that she was thinking of going home to be "given to" by her mother and father. It seemed as if the focus of her life had shifted at last. Whatever she needed and wanted she would get from Ongaki; failing him, from his brothers or by her own efforts. As she said, "I have some land here. It is only a little, but I will plant pyrethrum and earn extra money. I may not earn enough money to feed and clothe and educate my children, but it is all I can be sure of. It is too late for me to linger at home or to try to find another man. What man would take me now?"

VI

When the day of my departure arrived, I gave Suzanna a dress and some underclothes. This had to be done in secret, with the understanding that she should not wear the dress until the beginning of the next month, so that relatives and neighbors, long jealous of her relationship with me, might believe her clothes were brought by Ongaki with his pay packet. Suzanna had assembled a few of her friends, all of whom I knew well, and she served us roasted maize and sodas. She talked to me very little. She escorted me to the road and looked tearful as we parted.

Kemunto had earlier presented me with a beautiful gourd, but Suzanna significantly gave me nothing. Consciously she no doubt believed she had nothing to give me. Perhaps she reasoned, Why should I take beans or vegetables with me to Nairobi where I would stay in a hotel? Nevertheless, she might have offered these things to me, but she did not. Possibly this omission was some indication of her anger at my abandoning her. We left the field at the time of harvest, when food was becoming plentiful again, and local people loaded us with gifts. Suzanna was generally meticulous in the way she carried out the requirements of the traditional Gusii woman's role, which demanded in this case that she send a traveler on her way with provisions; and yet she let me leave her empty-handed. Despite the fantasies she verbalized about my return, I do not think she believed these fantasies would come true. She knew if I ever came back it would be for a brief time, and our relationship as it had been would not be reconstituted. In the last weeks I had the distinct feeling that she was talking past me, avoiding my eyes, in a word, withdrawing. She even arranged my last visit so that we would not be alone together, and so we were inhibited from making any real statement about the significance of each to the other.

I am well aware of how important my relationship with Suzanna was to me. She took me by the hand and led me through the Shades. Her dreams revealed to me a realm of which I had previously been scarcely aware. I had known, of course, that beliefs in witchcraft and sorcery were widespread among the Gusii. However, my work with Suzanna convinced me that in the 1970s a Gusii does not care to differentiate clearly what is "real" from what is "supernatural." The two are inseparable. The smooth social relationships which outsiders see and in which people invest so much to maintain scarcely reflect the ambiguities just below the surface. Suzanna had mastered the external behaviors expected of a Gusii woman. She was competent, hospitable insofar as she was able, responsible, generally placid. How could I ever have guessed at the degree of her preoccupation with the supernatural or the terrors and longings with which she struggled?

In what way was I important to Suzanna? I believe I provided her with a structure in which she could explore her ambivalence, essentially about becoming a woman. She was able, after months of caution, to commit herself to using me as a sounding board. I was a stranger, the details of whose life and purpose concerned her very little. I was neutral. When she longed for Ongaki and condemned him almost in the same breath, for example, I accepted this. I kept coming back repeatedly to hear her cover the same ground. Had I not been there, I doubt if she would have remembered her dreams, in which so much of the work of ambivalence resolution was done. In the event she *had* remembered them and unburdened herself to Ongaki or one of her sisters-in-law, their alarm at the content would have almost equaled her own. They would not have been able to reassure her. Sooner or later she would have prevailed upon her mother to let her stay. As it was, I was not afraid of her dreams, and gradually, through repeated recounting of the same themes, Suzanna too became less afraid of the content. She was able to stand firm, and in the end she came to understand the reality of her situation: though she might literally be able to go home again, to do so would accomplish nothing. She must stay where she was married. The fact that she was not yet paid for was really an irrelevance.

Given her parents, it is likely that even ten years ago, when most Gusii girls were still being married according to custom, i.e., to strangers after payment of bridewealth, Suzanna would have experienced considerable psychic pain in transferring her commitment from her own to her husband's home. Ochoi was a very compelling man. It was easy for me to see him through Suzanna's eyes, larger than life. His first three children were all daughters, and when they were young, before his career as a policeman began, he was living at home on his farm. No doubt he paid more attention to his daughters than is perhaps usual for a Gusii man, who generally is more interested in his sons. His daughters might find separation from this idealized yet intrusive father very difficult. At the same time, Moraa, their mother, was a warm and thoroughly mature person, a great contrast to Kemunto. When I knew her, Kemunto was in poor health, but I have no reason to believe that even at the best of times she was much less self-absorbed or prickly. It was easy for Suzanna, after she eloped with Ongaki, to make a split. Moraa was the good mother, Kemunto the bad. I am not at all sure that Suzanna's two sisters, Rebecca and Aska, have had an easier time than Suzanna in settling into their married homes. Aska was seeking a divorce while Rebecca, who had also been married with cattle, was still with her husband but frequently returned to her parents' home on long visits. Unlike her sisters, Suzanna of course eloped with a man of her own choice. The difficulties Rebecca and Aska had with their husbands were partly the result of chance, since they had no opportunity to discover whether or not they and their husbands were compatible (okoigwana) before marriage.

Suzanna, however, one must assume, was highly motivated to select a man who would not compete with her father for her affections and primary commitment. Marriage was traditionally regarded with great ambivalence by young girls. They desired it, but they dreaded the separation from family which it entailed. However, the culture provided for this. To begin with, many allowances were made for a bride, but before too long she was expected to settle down in her new home. Suzanna's initial behavior, therefore, had been well within the cultural norms. But as she grew older, had more children and finally a son, she was if anything less comfortable than ever in her role as a wife. A psychological conflict, which is probably found in all young Gusii girls and which is normally resolved with time, she handled in part by deflecting her feelings of rejection by and hostility toward her parents onto her mother-in-law, whom she came to view in a way which her culture legitimized, namely, as a witch. She used her relationship with me to explore the terrors of her ambivalence with its extremes of love and hatred, and ultimately her emotional crisis eased.

No doubt she will undergo similar periods of great tension and conflict in the future, but perhaps they will be less intense and less protracted. One day soon Kemunto, the bad mother, will die, leaving Suzanna with a little more control over her own destiny. At least she will have some powers of decision making as to what she will plant on her land. No doubt she will continue to have children until such time as the government institutes an effective birth-control program. Meanwhile the lean time times will get leaner and longer. Ongaki may or may not be permanently employed. In any case, given his character, it is doubtful that Suzanna will be able to rely on him financially. "He gives me nothing but children," she would say. This is a reality with which she will have to make peace. Her emotional support must come in the future, as in the past, from her sisters-in-law, from her female cousins who are married close by, and for a time from her mother, but not from Ongaki. However, Gusii women do not expect emotional support from their husbands. They may these days hope for it, but that is a different matter.

2

Trufena Moraa

I

Trufena Moraa lived in the furthermost corner of our research area. Her homestead was a three-mile walk away, but in my initial encounters with her while I was census taking, she had struck me as so unusual that the prospect of trekking on a regular basis so far out of my way seemed reasonable and worthwhile. What attracted me to her was her volatility: she could be enormously exuberant and utterly depressed within a very short time. Such overt extremes of feeling were unusual, to say the least, among the Gusii. She was also unusual in that, with two years of secondary education, she was the most highly educated married woman in our area.

When I first came to know her, Trufena was twenty-one years old and was living with her only child, a son named Johnathan, who was just eight months old. Her husband, Philip Ombui, had gone off as a recruit to the air force training college the previous week. Trufena did not expect to see him again for several months, when the first part of his course was over. Although she missed him, she was delighted that he had been taken into the air force (indeed, as I heard from another source, Ombui received the best marks of any candidate from this province in the entrance examination), because his acceptance ensured him permanent employment and opportunities for advancement and promotion. Ombui, who was a couple of years older than Trufena, came from a more traditional home than hers. After a very short time in secondary school, he had had to drop out for lack of tuition money. He had then spent some years sitting at home or working in menial jobs such as tea picking on the Brocke Bond tea estates in the adjacent district before being taken into the air force. He had left Trufena behind in the little house he had built before his marriage at the bottom of his father's land. This house was unexceptional apart from the flower garden which surrounded it. Ombui had seen the gardens of Europeans who worked on the tea estates and had laid out similar flower beds around his own little house. These he had planted with a variety of flowers, including roses, and while he was still at home he had tended them with great care. In the neighborhood there was only one other such garden, and this belonged to a cousin of Ombui's, a young man who had also lived at Kericho near Europeans.

Trufena had eloped while a student in a girls' secondary school a short distance away. An uncle, her mother's brother, lived close by, and she would see Ombui on the path on her way to visit her uncle. She remained with him for a month initially and then ran home to her parents. She was pursued there by Ombui and his father, Mogaka. They persuaded Trufena, who was pregnant, to return with them.

At the time I began working with her, Trufena had been in her husband's house for seventeen months, and she found her new home quite inferior to that of her parents. Her father had graduated from secondary school long ago in Uganda and was currently secretary of a coffee cooperative. He had three wives, a shop in a market town near his home, a large farm, many cattle, and a car. He was a lapsed Seventh Day Adventist, but his two elder wives were still regular church goers and subscribed to all the precepts of that rigorous Protestant sect. Trufena was the firstborn child of the senior wife. Her father was a force for progress in his area, which until very recently had been remote and backward as far as cash-cropping and educational facilities were concerned. Regardless of their own inclinations, he had insisted that all his daughters as well as his sons go on to secondary school. The boys were evidently more highly motivated, if not necessarily innately more intelligent, for they gained places in government schools, whereas the girls attended inferior *Harambee* or "self-help" community schools, into

which those children who did poorly in their primary school examinations were channeled. Trufena had not been interested in her
studies, and for the six months before she ran away from school to be
with Ombui, she had thought of nothing but love. Her father was
furious when she eloped and had remained so, since to date he had not
received bridewealth to compensate for his financial investment in
Trufena's education.

Ombui's family was nominally Catholic, although Mogaka, his
father, had never set foot in a church of any kind. Mogaka had one wife
whom he had married traditionally and by whom he had eight children
(Ombui was the third) and two leviratic wives, that is, women who
were widows of kinsmen. The Osoro family, of which Mogaka was the
eldest surviving male, was notorious in the community for its intra-
familial conflicts and lawsuits. Mogaka struggled to control his
brothers and to maintain some semblance of peace, but his attempts
were often futile. He spent a good deal of time drinking and smoking
enyasore (marijuana), and he relied almost exclusively on his youngest
brother to pay for the education of his children. These children were in
fact all quite able. The girls had married educated husbands, and the
boys, despite their lack of formal qualifications, were doing well at the
time we left the field. However, when Trufena first eloped, Ombui was
unemployed. He did not even have title to his land, as his father still
maintained control of his acreage.

When I began to visit Trufena, I was still working alone. Johnathan
had been selected as a sample child for our larger study and I often went
to the homestead in the course of my other work. I noticed that
Trufena, whose house was about 400 yards from that of her parents-
in-law, almost never had visitors. The nearest house was only ten yards
away. This belonged to a man who, though of the same clan as the
Osoro family, was of a different lineage; i.e., he was a rather distant
cousin. Trufena would chat across the boundary fence with this man's
wife, but I never saw the woman inside Trufena's compound or vice
versa. The logistics of arranging to see Trufena alone were thus no
problem. On the occasion when I first told her I had come to talk to
her, rather than to observe her child, she immediately said,

> "I am giving Johnathan *erongori* [porridge] mixed with milk in
> a bottle. I mix it so the liquid is very weak. Is it good to feed a
> small child thus?" She flops down beside me and asks me to give

her a piece of chewing gum. I oblige. At this point Johnathan,
who has been sleeping, awakens crying. Trufena brings him out
from the house and tells me he has an eye infection. "Hear him
cry," she says. "He's not hungry, he's sick," she adds, and
immediately attempts to give him the bottle of porridge, which
he does indeed reject. Thereafter Trufena pays spasmodic attention to him. She will excite him and then, losing interest, look
away, leaving the baby initially puzzled and protesting and ultimately quiet. Meanwhile she talks to me at a great rate until,
just as abruptly, she puts him down again and turns back to me.
She is extraordinarily vivacious. She speaks in a mixture of
Ekegusii and English, which, it is apparent, she remembers
poorly. She does not take any pains to ensure that I follow what
she is saying. I continually have to request that she repeat
things. She runs on about how much she loves and misses her
husband, while continuing to try to get Johnathan to drink from
his bottle. Ultimately he gets his way. He bangs her breast and
she nurses him. When he is satisfied, she jumps up and gets a
homemade rattle for him, which he seizes and bangs vigorously
on the ground.

In this first session I was again impressed by Trufena's boldness. Not
only did she request information and chewing gum, but she volunteered that she loved her husband. I never heard another young Gusii
woman make such an announcement. Was this a "modern" way to
talk, the new mode among secondary school girls? Possibly, but I
doubted that it was usual for such an admission to be offered in almost
the first conversation a schoolgirl had with a strange older woman. I
knew Trufena was a little younger than most of the women I was
working with at that point; she was also more educated. Was the
striking difference between Trufenna's straightforward admission of her
feelings for her husband and the reticence of other women concerning
such feelings due to the former's youth and superior education alone? I
left her house halfway seduced and yet cautious. What was she really
telling me? I was also struck by the way she handled her baby. Much of
the time she ignored him, but it seemed the child must be used to
getting a good deal of attention, for he appeared to be persistent, very
alert, and closely attached to his mother. When Trufena did play with
him, she would rush at him and excite him violently. She generated a
feeling of wildness, particularly when she played with her son. There

was a self-consciousness about her also, as if she were watching herself in a mirror.

But a week later her mood was totally different. She was sitting in front of her house with Johnathan on her lap. He had been scratching up soil and eating it, and as soon as I appeared Trufena asked me how to stop him from doing that. But she scarcely attended to my reply. Johnathan went crawling off into the thorn hedge, from which she retrieved him, whereupon he expected to play with her, but she plumped him down beside her and ignored him.

"What is the use of my education?" she exclaims. "Here I am at home doing nothing. I am getting more and more depressed and bored. I'd do anything, even sweeping floors. Couldn't I sweep your floors?" Then she goes on, "I'd like to be a teacher or a nurse, but I have not got a sponsor, someone of influence to get me into a training course. You have those young assistants working for you. When they go to the university, may I take their place?"

This is a request which I frequently encountered, and I explained firmly why it would not be possible for us to employ her. I managed to do this without saying specifically that her English was inadequate. Indeed she did not speak English as well as Ombui's fifteen-year-old sister, who was only in the fifth grade. Trufena listened to my explanation and then went on to talk about another topic, how she happened to come to this "poor little house" in the first place.

"I eloped and my parents were so angry, my father in particular, that I thought he would kill me. Ombui has not paid anything so far. My father wants five cows; it doesn't matter what kind, whether native or grade cows." "Grade cows" are those of a European breed such as Jersey or Holstein, which are very costly and require intensive care but are already fairly common in Gusiiland. Only a young man from a wealthy home, marrying a girl of a similar economic background, would be required by the girl's father to give grade cows in payment of bridewealth. Thus by even offering a choice, "native or grade," Trufena's father revealed his aspirations for his daughter. He expected her to marry a man from a "good family." Ombui did not approximate his requirements in any way. "My parents are not quite so angry now, but still my father does not care to see me. He would never come here. When I went home at Christmas time, he was living at the market with his new wife. I scarcely saw him." She stares gloomily in front of her at the overgrown flower beds. It is the early part of the rainy season, and everything is growing abundantly, but Trufena has neglected Ombui's flower garden, and the weeds are choking the roses. Suddenly she lunges at Johnathan, places her head against his and trills in his ear. He laughs and pulls on her blouse. She jerks away and lays him on his stomach across her lap; grabbing his feet, she blows on them for an instant, then she stands him upright again and bites his shoulder. "Stand alone," she cries, releasing him. He falls to the ground, she tickles him, he shrieks with laughter, rolls away from her, inviting her to tickle him again. She seizes him, snuggles his stomach, trills in his ear in response. He makes a kissing noise into the air. "Did you hear that?" Trufena exclaims. "He means he loves me." She lets him move away from her—he is just learning to crawl—and abruptly turns from him, ignoring his efforts to keep her attention and continue their game. She slumps down, her back against the shade tree. "My sisters and brothers are all going to school still, and look at me! When I ran away with Ombui I spoiled my life, didn't I?"

When I came away from her house that day I was thinking, "This girl is like me. She feels the way I might feel." I had not expected to find anyone like Trufena. I was blinded by the familiarity and for a time chose to ignore the difference.

About this time I started taking my assistant, Mary, with me on my visits. As it happened, Mary was an aunt to Trufena by marriage. She was married to Mogaka's youngest brother, Nyagama, who, having only one child of his own, had been called upon to pay for the education not only of Ombui but of most of the other children of Mogaka as well. Using Mary, a local woman, as my assistant and interpreter was potentially problematic in general and in this case was particularly so. Mary and Trufena had a relationship dating from the day of Trufena's elopement, when Ombui had brought his bride to his uncle's house for her first meal. He had received much more support from Nyagama and Mary than from his own parents. However, as an aunt by marriage, Mary was a member of the parental generation, and thus, despite their closeness in age, she and Trufena had to show *amasikane* (respect), as each expected to experience *chinsoni* (shame); thus they should avoid all mention of matters relating to sex within one another's hearing. Furthermore, although their homesteads were not close together, they of course belonged to the same network of gossip, and thus I could anticipate receiving all kinds of information about Trufena from Mary herself and also from other members of the family whom I had already come to know. It was almost inevitable then that Mary's presence would complicate the development of a relationship between Trufena and myself. Both were vivacious, somewhat garrulous people who might unintentionally exclude me from their conversation unless I was very insistent about being included. However, despite many misgivings, I decided to continue visiting Trufena. She was sufficiently different from other young women in the neighborhood to make the investment of time and energy worthwhile, despite the risks. I saw her on a regular basis for a period of about eleven months and much less frequently toward the end of my stay. In all, I saw her for fifty-one sessions over seventeen months.

From my contact with Trufena I believe I learned something about what it is like to be caught between traditional and modern life. Most other Gusii women whom I came to know well identified thoroughly with the traditional woman's role. Even though it might bring them much unhappiness at times, they could not imagine any alternative. If they were mistreated by their husbands or their in-laws, they complained, but they scarcely expected anything else. "Men are like that" or "The world is like that," they would say, and absorb the latest disappointment.

Trufena, however, was of a new generation. I watched her endure a great deal of suffering, much of it, it must be said, self-generated; but she was never for a moment resigned to it. She had grown up in the hills overlooking the great Mara which falls away to Tanzania and the Serengeti plains. Her home was a bush place where the cattle must be protected day and night against Masai raiders. Her father's father had moved there, to the frontier, because he had seen opportunities which no longer existed in his congested birthplace, and there he and his sons had prospered. But all his grandchildren were being given the directive, "Go out into the world." Trufena, as the eldest, heard it first. The others came fast on her heels and seemed to have caught up with her and passed her by. But the mistake of her youth was not going to stall her permanently. The little house at the end of a muddy path in Endege would only be a way station for Trufena. She had learned her father's lessons well. She could never be like Sabera, her sister-in-law, Ombui's elder brother's wife, who was demure and competent, the loving mother of two little boys and the worshiping wife of a mostly absent husband, content to use her considerable intelligence in farm work and making good the daily omissions of her drunken parents-in-law. Trufena, who so far had never been out of the district, acted as if Nairobi were her home away from home. In school she had been idle. She could not conduct a simple conversation in English. She could not read the newspaper clippings or the copy beneath the magazine illustrations which decorated the walls of her sitting room (divided from the place where she cooked and slept by a mat, not even an adobe wall). So far her "modernness" was a veneer. But she was determined to leave this peasant life behind. Whatever, whoever came her way she would use, including myself.

But it was many months before I comprehended what kind of a person Trufena was or what kind of game she played. Meanwhile I found her fascinating, essentially because I did not understand her. She seemed very sociable, yet she had an impressive capacity to live alone, apparently relying upon herself almost to the exclusion of anyone else. She could endure long periods of rejection and depression, but unlike other women she refused to be passive; rather, she fought back every step of the way. "You see, she is not a Gusii." Mary would say, ashamed and mortified by Trufena's latest indiscretion. Of course, as the girl's aunt, Mary was particularly affronted when Trufena did not conform to Gusii norms of discretion. Although Mary herself often privately found fault with members of their family, she never quite got used to Trufena's criticisms, especially of people of the parental generation. Mary's self-restraint was remarkable, however. Never did she leap to the defense of her husband or anyone else when, as so frequently happened, Trufena criticized them harshly.

The first time I went to see Trufena with Mary, we found her with a female secondary school cousin named Selina. They were having lunch as we walked in and had almost finished their food. It struck me that Trufena was high, whether on alcohol or on her father-in-law's marijuana, I could not tell. She danced up to us, thrusting the last scraps of boiled cabbage in our mouths. She was wearing a very short dress, a foot at least above her knees, and sweat stood out in beads on her upper lip. She bumped and ground her way round the room, singing as she went. From time to time she would let out a little scream. "Ombui, I am waiting for you. When will you come? Come soon, I am waiting for you," she sang in English.

Selina, wearing her best dress and a little woolen hat, stared at her cousin in wondering silence. Mary was sitting with her hands folded, her eyes on her lap, rigid with horror. For her sake I engaged Selina in conversation about her school, to which she was about to return after her Easter holidays. We spoke in English, and Trufena, who stopped dancing after a while and came to sit at the table with us, could not follow what we were saying. Or perhaps she might have been able to, had she been concentrating, but she was swaying on her stool, absorbed in the rhythm of her dance. Mary stood up abruptly and announced, "We should be leaving." Trufena jumped to her feet and bumped ("bumping" was the current dance craze in the marketplaces) her way through the yard in our wake. She appeared completely unfazed by the impact her behavior was having on her aunt. Afterward Mary assured me that Trufena was certainly not drunk. As an SDA she had never touched beer in her life. *Enyasore* was out of the question. "That was Trufena. That's the way she is. She has no respect. She is not like a married woman. Young girls today are different from you or me."

Only a few days before, Trufena had been envying her sisters and her cousins who had their lives before them, in contrast to herself, who had spoiled her chances. That day her depression had been profound. But perhaps today's manic eroticism in front of Selina was a desperate attempt on Trufena's part to convince herself that she had something better after all.

In subsequent sessions none of us referred to the occasion with Selina. Trufena was expecting Ombui to come on leave, and she was cheerful and lively. We would find her in the *shamba,* and she would come willingly back to her house to talk. She treated us as equals, and I wondered a little about this. Even if, since I was a white person, she was at something of a loss as to how to relate to me, nevertheless Mary was her aunt, and she knew quite well that she should offer her respect. She would always bring out chairs for us to sit on, but apart from the time when we came upon her having her lunch, she never offered us any kind of refreshment. At first I imagined that this was because it was the lean time before the harvest and thought no more about it. Her sister-in-law Sabera, whose child was the same age and was also in our sample, was already, at age twenty-two, the consummate Gusii house-wife, hospitable and gracious. As Mary would say, "Sabera really knows how to entertain visitors!"

But Trufena still had the abrupt manner of an adolescent—not, of course, a traditional Gusii adolescent; rather, of a girl brought up in the city (although she had never in her life been to a city), coquettish, abrasive, self-confident. She still wore her old school skirt and blouse for digging. One felt she continued to wear her uniform, and for this particular purpose, out of defiance, not just frugality. In Kenya students treasure their uniforms as a badge of privilege. Trufena muddied hers daily. It should be mentioned that she was not a good-looking girl either by Western or Gusii standards. She was stocky, black, and heavily muscled. Her features were large and rather coarse. When she was dressed demurely in her best clothes and was on her good (i.e., traditionally approved) behavior, she made a fair impression, however, and one did not notice her ungainliness. At other times she often seemed to present her physical self badly on purpose, as an act of defiance familiar among teenagers in our own culture. I found myself biting my tongue to avoid saying, "Trufena, you could be attractive if only you'd try."

In the sixth session she reported that she dreamed of Ombui nightly.

> "I see him coming down the hill. I run to him and kiss him." Mary grimaces, "In the daytime! I would never do such a thing." In Gusii culture love making between married couples during daylight hours is frowned upon, at least by women. "When Trufena was first married, if you came to the house by day the door was always locked," Mary says. "She loved her husband so, she agreed to *ogotomaana* [to have sex] whenever he wanted." Trufena grins and rolls her eyes. "Why not!" Mary explains that if you shut your door during the day and you are known to be at home, then you are advertising to all the neighbors that you don't want to be disturbed for one reason only, sex. She would die of shame herself if people were to know that was what she was doing. If her husband were working out of the district and came home once a month for the course of an

afternoon only, then she would agree to sleep with him, if he insisted, but he never has insisted. He understands her feelings.

As we were leaving, a young man, Ombui's cousin, came into the house. It was late in the afternoon. Mary said to me, "You see what Trufena does? Soon it will be night and she is entertaining a man." I remarked that Trufena's visitor was only a cousin whom she knew very well. "But I never invite any man of my husband's generation into my house [i.e., any man with whom sex would not be incestuous]. I would not even invite my brothers-in-law inside if it's already late in the afternoon. But Trufena is a modern girl. She will do anything she pleases."

As the days went by and Ombui did not come for his leave, Trufena became depressed again.

> She reminisces about when she first eloped. "It was a Sunday that I did not return to school, and after a while the house-mother heard where I was and came to visit me with some of my classmates. The housemother said, 'Women are women, be happy with your husband,' and went back to school. After a while I began to have pains in my stomach." "I remember," Mary laughed. "I told you those weren't stomach pains, you were pregnant, that's all, so you didn't bother going to the hospital to check."

It seemed Trufena wanted to clarify for herself as well as for me how she got "caught" in her current situation. She talked about Ombui, what kind of man he was and whether or not she could trust him.

> "Do you hide any secrets from your husband, Sarah? Of course you must! Surely men don't tell their wives everything either. People tell me Ombui is a good man. Now he's shut up inside the camp. There are no women there. He earns sixty shillings a month, and he's got nothing to spend his money on."
>
> She seems to be trying to convince herself that Ombui is all hers, sexually and financially. Her doubts are a constant source of anxiety.
>
> "I'm so bored, I can't be bothered to weed his flowers. I don't go visiting other homesteads. My mother-in-law is no companion. Anyway people say she's a witch," Trufena remarks casually. "Why go visit her? My house needs smearing [with fresh

mud], but I can't be bothered to do that either. I'm alone with my thoughts all day." She looks down at Johnathan, who is banging her breast. She pulls down the neck of her dress and allows him to nurse, then she tells us that a younger sister came to see her recently. "She's about to finish secondary school," Trufena says, and then offsets any admiration we might have for the girl or any envy she herself might feel by adding, "but she's not very good at school work." As we leave her, she struggles to her feet to escort us to the gate. She is full of lassitude. I wonder how she occupies herself through the long day all alone. When she chooses to interact with Johnathan Trufena is very lively, but then, suddenly losing interest in him, she lapses back into self-absorption.

Shortly after this session, Ombui came home for a weekend. I met him briefly when I went to take photographs of the family. He looked good in his uniform and was obviously taken with himself. He was quite patronizing to me. He was a man and I was only a woman, after all, so he made jokes about my work, which he thought pointless. During the photographic session Trufena wore the dress and new shoes he had given her (sensible safari boots; I was impressed that he had not bought her light sandals, which would have been pretty but useless, given where she lived). She scarcely spoke at all while Ombui and I parried with one another. I came away feeling vaguely annoyed that I had been forced into having a sexist conversation by a man ten years younger than myself.

When I next visited Trufena, she was in an ambiguous mood. I noticed she had grown fatter, and I teased her that Ombui made her pregnant again. She shook her head. Johnathan was still small. He was nursing. She ate a lot of *obokima* (maize meal) while Ombui was at home, that was all.

"We had a good time. I love my husband, but he says I cannot join him in Nairobi in December when he finishes his course." This is evidently a disappointment to her. "Ombui used his pay to rent some farm land, and he says I must stay here to dig it." She laughs bitterly. "As you see, I haven't got an *omoreri* [a babysitter], so of course I cannot go to that land, taking Johnathan with me. He will crawl everywhere and hurt himself. So Mogaka will plant maize there, and I will wait until I find a babysitter. Then I will go with him to work. Meanwhile, I am here at home, as before. And I am fat because I eat nothing but *obokima*. Europeans mix their foods, and that is why they stay slim. I cannot do that because if people knew I ate differently from the way they ate, they would be jealous and bewitch me. People don't want their neighbors to do better than they themselves are doing."

She felt rejected by her husband and deprived because her diet was so plain—not, presumably, what she had been used to at home. She was tied to her house and her child without a babysitter to relieve her. At night a young sister-in-law slept with her, but the girl was at school all day and no help to Trufena. She went on to talk about a relative, a girl living close by who very recently gave birth illegitimately.

"That girl has nothing to give her child, and nothing for herself, either. Her father hates her, and her mother is too bur- dened by her sons to have money left over for Miriam."

She talked with much affect about a girl in very different circum- stances from herself. Miriam had no husband. Trufena had a husband whom she loved and who apparently loved her ("We had a good time together") and who, moreover, had used his earnings to rent land for the benefit of herself and her child. The reason she gave for eating only *obokima* was not poverty but the wish to avoid the jealousy of her neighbors (a legitimate concern). And yet if she were so concerned with Miriam, she must also have identified with her.

"Why did I marry Ombui? I wish I never had! I shall have one more child only, and then I shall go to work. I'll do any- thing at all. I don't care how ordinary the work is."

She was trapped by her child and her responsibilities, and she spent time fantasizing about another kind of life in the working world which, like Nairobi, she dreamed of but knew nothing about at firsthand. She did not tell us whether she fantasized herself going to work within the context of her marriage or whether this was what she intended to do when, having left Ombui, she ventured forth as a divorcée. She was overtly ambivalent about Ombui. "I wish I'd never married him," she said, and yet later on, when we talked about women who entertained men while their husbands were away, she said, "What brings trouble is when they drink beer. Then they become confused and are seduced by their visitors. I don't drink myself, and I would never commit adultery."

She went on to talk about Mogaka. I had wondered about her feelings for her father-in-law, a man who in social and economic status was so different from her own father. But like her father, Mogaka had recently acquired a third wife, admittedly a leviratic wife, but he had access to her bed, which was the crucial matter.

> "A month after her husband died, Mogaka went with his oxen to plow Moraa's land. The first evening she made beer for him. The second evening he proposed himself as her *omochinyomba* [husband] and was accepted. They could not even wait until two months had passed, as is the custom among the Gusii!"

Mogaka's success with women was the envy of many men. He took a good look at all women, myself included, and doubtlessly also at Trufena, who had been left in his care. Now Ombui had ordered her to work with Mogaka on a plot he had rented far from home. She would have to spend many hours alone with her father-in-law, who told me himself that he awakened every morning to a pipeful of marijuana and some leftover *busaa* (native beer). He was drunk even before the day began. Once his brother Ondari, with whom he was engaged in a dispute, shouted so everyone in the neighborhood could hear, "You degenerate! You who are the husband of your son's wife!" People thought Ondari was referring to Sabera, the wife of Mogaka's eldest son, but he could as well have meant Trufena.

These days Trufena shifted from topic to topic, avoiding whatever it was that was bothering her, if indeed she knew herself. In the ninth session she told me a dream in which her mother was very sick and her eldest brother had come to tell her the news.

> "I awoke sweating with fear. Then I lit my lamp and read my Bible until those thoughts went away. Eventually I was able to sleep again. I am still very frightened."

She recalled that she had gone home a month ago and found her mother in a great deal of pain. Since that time she had heard that her mother had recovered. But now she was afraid that her dream had foretold some new illness. She said sadly that she did not hear regularly from her mother. Her home was a long way away; if someone from home were passing Mogoro, he might stop to see her, but probably not. I gathered she was feeling very isolated and cut off from her family.

"Nowadays," she says, "my old school allows pregnant girls to return after they give birth. But when I eloped that was not yet the case." I ask if things had been then as they are now, would she have acted differently? "Of course! I would have left Johnathan with my mother and continued my education. But now Ombui has me [i.e., I am considered to be his, I am married]. It is easy to leave a boyfriend and go back to school. You can always find another boyfriend. But another husband after you have lived as I have with Ombui, that is different. I have a son, and a man will not take another man's son. Girls who have sons rarely find husbands. They must become bar girls and prostitutes. Men do not often want to marry prostitutes for fear they cannot trust them to be faithful wives. Some girls who have been prostitutes do settle down, but they find they have diseases and cannot conceive again." Then abruptly she becomes animated: "Ombui must cool himself until he comes home again to me and not go catching diseases. If he is a proper man, he can wait."

II

Ombui came home unexpectedly for a week's leave and during his stay he told his elder brother, Mwamba, that Trufena was pregnant. Mwamba told Mary, who of course told me, a fine example of the indirect way by which news of pregnancy gets about among the Gusii. Mary and I felt rather foolish. We had noticed that Trufena was fatter than before and had talked about this with her. We had even teased her a month ago about looking pregnant. However, despite what we had seen with our eyes, we had accepted Trufena's denial, because she was still nursing Johnathan. According to Gusii custom, a woman will nurse her child until she becomes pregnant again. There was a possibility, of course, that Trufena had not known she was pregnant and had continued in ignorance to nurse Johnathan. Women had told us of conceiving without ever menstruating after the birth of their previous baby, and this might be true of

Trufena. On the other hand it was known that some women, either out of shame that they had conceived again so quickly or because they were too poor to be able to afford cow's milk to give their child, delayed weaning for as long as possible, until the new pregnancy was obvious to everyone.

When we went to visit Trufena, I asked her laughingly, "When will you give birth?" In fact I had greeted her thus on two previous occasions and she had denied that she was pregnant, just as she did today. When Johnathan awakened from his nap I said to Trufena, "Go ahead, nurse him." I was feeling warmly toward her and assumed that we had a secure relationship in which my teasing was acceptable. But she replied, "He's not hungry," and it was true, he made no attempt to go to her breast, which indicated that if he were weaned, the weaning had occurred long enough ago so that the transition had been accomplished and he was comfortable again. Trufena, however, insisted that Johnathan was still too young (at eleven months) to be weaned.

> "But why is your maternity dress hanging on your clothes line?" I ask. Then it becomes obvious that however lighthearted I might feel about the issue, Trufena feels very differently. She is extremely angry and upset. Mary says, "Why couldn't you tell us you were pregnant? When you knew you were pregnant with Johnathan, I was the first person you told." "I don't know if it is so." Trufena refuses to look at either of us. "I had a period last month!" "How could you have?" asks Mary. "You must be four months pregnant at least, or you wouldn't need a maternity dress. You conceived this baby before Ombui went away, didn't you?"

Evidently I had precipitated a very bad situation. These women, Mary and Trufena, who for almost two years had had a great deal to do with one another, ostensibly within a relationship of mutual trust, were suddenly adversaries.

> I try to redeem myself by saying, "This is my fault. I have known other Gusii women deny they are pregnant the first time I asked them, but later on they admitted it freely."
> "But Gusii women cannot be trusted. They are always jealous. You cannot talk about your pregnancy to them. How can you know what kind of women they are in their hearts? A 'good' woman may really be a witch. You cannot know that, so you

must keep quiet when you are asked about pregnancy." Trufena's eyes flash. "Europeans are not jealous people. *You* may not be a jealous person, but let me tell you, *all* Africans are jealous."

Mary breaks in, "Not I! Everyone knows I have only one child. I had only one when you came here. I had only one when Sabera came five years ago. Even then I was already in difficulties. That is an old story. You and I are friends. We have never abused one another, so why should we do so now? Why should I be jealous of you? I am used to my sorrow. It is nothing to do with you. I am only happy for you."

"I *know* you are jealous of me. How can you be otherwise? All women who have few children are jealous, and even some who have many are too." When Johnathan cries, Trufena feeds him with a bottle. "I don't know if I am pregnant or not. When I am sure, I will tell you both. When I was a girl, I used to have my period regularly, but not now. The bleeding is uneven nowadays. I cannot go by that."

Her face was flushed as she watched her son drink from his bottle on her lap. I tried to mollify her by saying that abroad women can go to a clinic and have a pregnancy test to confirm their suspicions, but here it is different. You have to wait and see. I said repeatedly that I had not meant to upset her. I thought we could joke together as women who stand in a certain relationship with one another can speak of things they would not mention to others. We joke about so many things, about sex and our husbands. I had believed we could joke about pregnancy also. But I had been mistaken, and I was very sorry. She replied, in essence, that she was afraid if she told us she was pregnant, Mary would spread the rumor around that she was *boasting* of her good fortune. In addition, women in the neighborhood were always asking, "Why does Sarah go to your house and not to ours?" and she would reply that she did not know. She said, "They are jealous that you are my friend and not theirs." There were plenty of women nearby who were jealous of her for one reason or another and who would eagerly seize on an excuse to accuse her of boasting.

I tried to explain my reasons for coming to see her. To deny that there was a possibility that "other women" (I presumed she meant her sister-in-law Sabera in particular) might be jealous of her friendship with me would be pointless, since I imagined this was true. So I told her why I had chosen to get to know her better than her neighbors. I said that I studied mothers and little children, but I could not know everyone equally well or visit them equally often. I had to choose a few. I liked her, and she had seemed happy to see me when I was first going about the neighborhood. Some women were dour or too busy to talk to me, but she had welcomed me. That is why I had continued to come so often. Trufena listened and seemed reassured. When we got up to leave, she begged us to stay longer, which we did, and then she escorted us a long way along the path, something she had not done before. However, she offered us no refreshment, which she certainly could have done, since Ombui was on leave and had brought her tea and sugar as well as money.

Already her behavior toward Mary hinted at Trufena's eccentricity, particularly in relation to a senior in-law. Given the fact that not only was Mary of the parental generation but, as I came to understand, along with Nyagama her only supporter in the family, Trufena was extraordinarily lacking in the respectful attitude which was demanded by her culture and which, moreover, would have been very much in her own interests to present. I already knew she was rebellious, and I suspected that in fact she deliberately set out to shock. Having been somewhat socialized into Gusii ways, I too had been made uncomfortable by Trufena a number of times. After this episode, however, I saw that I probably would not be able to develop an independent relationship with Trufena. The prior constrictions imposed on her by her kinship tie with Mary were so compelling that there was little chance for me to differentiate myself from my assistant and persuade Trufena to relate to me separately. I had the option of resuming my visits to her on my own, but by doing so I would not fool her that my association with Mary was ended. I decided, therefore, to continue seeing her with Mary, believing that even though the likelihood of developing a relationship of mutual trust with her was slight, I would nevertheless learn a great deal of value from this young woman, who had already shown some deviant personality traits.

A day or two after this session, in my absence, Trufena asked one of the Gusii female assistants on our project to intervene with me on her behalf. At the time she made this request our pediatrician was working with Trufena and Johnathan, but Trufena was so agitated that the session had to be halted so that she could unburden herself. She wanted our doctor's assistant, acting as her intermediary, to explain to me why she had denied the fact of her pregnancy. Presumably Trufena wanted to make these explanations to me alone, without Mary present. However, when I next saw Trufena she made no mention of her wish to see me alone, nor did she refer to this incident again.

I believe Trufena denied to herself for a very long time that she was pregnant. I do not know whether she conceived without having menstruated after Johnathan's birth or whether she merely "forgot" she had had a period in order to discount the possibility of pregnancy. However, given what I had seen of her depression after Ombui went off to the air force, I gathered that in his absence she was highly ambivalent about her marriage. She regretted her elopement and envied her siblings who were still sensibly studying at school. Contact with our project and with the unmarried female assistants who were waiting to go to the university no doubt heightened her ambivalence and her regret at having "ruined her life." Her husband was no longer at home to sustain her erotic excitement. She daydreamed about leaving Johnathan with her mother and resuming her old schoolgirl life, which appeared from her current vantage point, at which her sleep was being interrupted by her sick child and her days were being spent in the performance of dull chores, infinitely preferable, even glamorous. She was highly motivated to deny as long as possible that she was going to have a second child who would further commit her to a humdrum life.

I do not believe Trufena deliberately ignored her pregnancy. Although in certain situations she sometimes behaved unacceptably, nevertheless she was still a Gusii girl who had had exposure only to those beliefs and customs prevalent among the Gusii. It is doubtful that she would question the belief that for a woman to nurse a baby when she is pregnant may harm either that child or the child in her womb. Unlike some others, she could afford cow's milk. She had money from pyrethrum and could have used it to buy milk with which to feed Johnathan. Indeed, once she "went pregnant," she immediately started to buy milk from a farmer nearby. Her failure to admit her condition to her family, to me, or even to herself must have reflected her ambivalence about her marriage as well as her shame at having two children so close together. (This is something which educated Gusii women are doing more and more frequently as they come to rely upon bottle feeding, which reduces the prophylactic effect of lactation. However, though Trufena might aspire to becoming an educated Gusii woman, she was not yet one, nor did she, after her marriage, associate with educated married women. She had used a bottle to feed Johnathan watered-down porridge from the age of three months and had therefore presumably become fertile again in short order but was probably unaware of the connection between bottle feeding and conception.) Last, her response when we confronted her with the fact of her pregnancy was so striking that it must have arisen from a profound terror of her aunt, Mary, her only female supporter in her husband's home. Trufena had been close to and very dependent on Mary. Her fear not only of incurring Mary's jealously but of losing her emotional and financial support was great enough for her to suppress the knowledge that she was far along in her pregnancy.

I tried to placate Trufena in the aftermath of exposing her. I gave her a packet of biscuits and repeated that I was sorry about what had transpired. Having heard my speech, she accepted the gift but did not allude to her feelings of the previous session or even to her pregnancy. Dressed now in her maternity clothes, she was in excellent spirits and completely self-assured. She treated Mary and me once again like peers, or perhaps something a little less than peers. She swept about her yard like a grand lady, to Mary's barely concealed disgust.

As we were leaving, Mary whispered to me that a few weeks ago her husband, Nyagama, had gone to Trufena's house asking to polish the furniture he had lent the young couple after their elopement. However, Trufena, giving some inconsequential excuse, had refused him entrance. I then heard that all the furniture in the house other than the bed had been provided by Nyagama. He had looked upon Ombui as a son and had willingly fed, clothed, and educated him. At her marriage to Nyagama, Mary had been obliged to accept Ombui as part of her husband's household and had found him to be responsible and rewarding. From her point of view their relationship had become problematic only after Ombui brought Trufena home as his wife. Trufena's behavior to everyone in the family seemed inconsistent and unpredictable, though on the whole less so toward Mary and Nyagama than the others. Nyagama tried to overlook Trufena's arrogance, saying she was immature and would learn to behave in time, and for his nephew's sake he tried to meet any demands she made on him. These demands (for money) had increased since Ombui's departure, and Nyagama had done his best to take care of them, without, however, receiving any thanks from Trufena.

This was really the first time Mary had indicated to me that Trufena's behavior toward herself and Nyagama, as distinct from other family members, was objectionable in any way. Until now Mary had kept her own counsel and left me to get to know Trufena in my own time. Now that I was discovering Trufena's obtuseness for myself, she warned me, "That girl is not like other people. It seemed that she was glad to see us today, but how can we tell what she was thinking in her heart? She wears that big dress of hers, and yet, even after all our talk last week, she says nothing about her pregnancy. Can she be trusting us and yet say nothing?"

Even a week later Trufena said nothing directly about her pregnancy. However, we had a conversation about how the sex of a child is determined. At school Trufena had learned about chromosomes and had been taught that it was the father's seed and not the mother's egg which determined the baby's sex. She had also learned that a woman conceived when she became fertile at a point in between periods. But could she believe these things, she wondered. Gusii people say the woman is responsible for her child's sex, and that is why men send away wives who have only female children. Furthermore, the Gusii say you conceive *while* you are menstruating.

> "I learned these things at home. Can I also believe what the teacher said at school?" I ask her whether she thought a woman might conceive without menstruating (as she herself, at one point in our earlier discussion, claimed to have done), and she looks blank. Then she tosses her head, "It's impossible! Such a woman bled but she forgot about it."

It is evident, therefore, that despite her schooling, Trufena subscribed to the same beliefs about women's physiognomy, and presumably about other things, as her neighbors, whether educated or not. Her reference point was Gusii life and culture. If she had some notion of an alternative, it was vague. Her behavior reflected the predominantly traditional situation in which she had grown up. Sometimes she talked and acted like a city girl, but how significant could that behavior be if she had never lived in a city? Despite her intensively Seventh Day Adventist childhood, she did not question the prevalence and power of witchcraft. She was merely a little more discreet than others in talking about it. Her religious upbringing and her youth—which had allowed her fewer opportunities to confront witchcraft—might explain her relative reticence. But she was as persistently wary and potentially as afraid of it as any other Gusii, man or woman. One might assume, moreover, that whatever concerned others in Gusii traditional life would most probably concern her also, even though she preferred to talk to me about dancing and romantic love, and schools, and what she heard on the radio, thus giving me the illusion that she was different from her sister-in-law Sabera and the other young wives in the neighborhood.

I found her very puzzling. She seemed determined to keep our relationship on the superficial level of one outsider commiserating with another about these "bush" people among whom we lived and worked. However, interspersed between long periods in which she orchestrated a smooth "peer" relationship came explosions of feeling. Then in the next session she would be back with her customary vivacious, cheerful manner, and I would be left feeling foolish for having been caught up in her fleeting turmoil.

The instance of our discovery that she was pregnant was a case in point. Within a few days I found her wearing her maternity dress with the assurance and matter-of-factness of a woman who has been publicly pregnant for months, but despite this she still could not bring herself to mention the fact that she was expecting a child. However, in that session she talked freely about her dislike of intercourse during menstruation. Whatever feelings of shame she might have had in talking about sexual matters in front of her aunt, they did not seem to inhibit her. She went on to talk about the way in which she experienced orgasm, something which, incidentally, I never heard another Gusii woman mention voluntarily. She was reluctant to let me leave that day. She knew I was going away on vacation for two weeks:

> "I shall be looking across the fields for you, searching for you on the paths, but in vain. I must wait until August to see you again," she says, as if August were an immensely long time in the future and she will really miss me. In the aftermath of our rather intimate conversation, I feel at liberty to ask her when she thinks her baby will be born. "In January," she answers in a flash. (It was then July!) "I have a long way to go," she adds in exactly the same way a Gusii woman of an older generation would have replied.

Trufena was a great deal more pregnant than the three and one-half months she claimed, but she was not about to admit it to me or, rather, to her aunt, my constant companion.

When next I saw Trufena, she was in the fields harvesting finger millet. We came upon her singing loudly. A little way away, on her own plot, Sabera flinched in horror and turned her back on her sister-in-law. I called to Trufena, "Why are you so happy? Is Ombui home?" "No, but he shall come soon and I'll be hot for him," she called back over Sabera's bowed head. She danced up to the boundary hedge to shake my hand. "Come, let us go to my house," and she danced out of the field, with Johnathan, who had just learned to walk, stumbling along behind her. She whispered to us when we came together on the path that she and Sabera had quarreled, and nowadays, though they worked together on the farm, they did not visit each other's house. What had they quarreled about? Trufena shrugged. "Nothing much. Sabera is always finding fault. Why should I bother going to greet her?"

If Trufena had quarreled with Sabera, of whom at the best of times she saw little, I wondered whom she did see. While Mary as usual was disturbed by the vigorous sexuality of her niece, I was wondering how in such a social vacuum Trufena could generate so much vitality. Who made her feel that good? Was it the absent Ombui? What about her own family? I asked her whether her mother knew she was going to have another baby.

"Of course not! I haven't seen her since May, and I did not know I was pregnant then. I would not go to my home now. I would be ashamed to appear thus before my parents." So this girl who danced and sang in full view of her neighbors did not want her own parents to see her condition. Traditionally married Gusii women were expected to experience *chinsoni* (shame) if they should be seen by their fathers or fathers-in-law when they were pregnant, but nowadays young women tended to be less self-conscious. Some reported to me that though they knew they should experience shame; nevertheless, they did not. "My father is used to me. So is my father-in-law." However, Trufena was not so emancipated. She was not prepared to risk being seen even by her mother (who would transmit news of the pregnancy to her father). Her inhibition also no doubt reflected other factors—that she had not been paid for, that her father was still unreconciled to her marriage, that she had become pregnant again so quickly—as well as that of the desire to hide from her father the consequences of her sexual activity.

Mary urged Trufena to write to her mother. "You don't have to see her in order to let her know you are pregnant. My mother is living far away, but I would write to her immediately to tell her my news." Trufena blushed. "You are different from me"; i.e., Mary, who is known by everyone to be infertile, would have a right to "announce" the news of a miracle pregnancy. No one would begrudge her her joy, but in Trufena's case women would condemn her boastfulness. Her own mother would condemn her daughter for not behaving in the prescribed Gusii manner. As far as I know Trufena's mother never did know of this pregnancy until she received news of the birth.

These nights Trufena was alone. She and Johnathan slept by themselves because Trufena had quarreled with Ombui's young sister, who used to sleep in her house. Mogaka, her father-in-law, had never built a house for his circumcised daughters (who are forbidden to sleep in the same place as their parents), and thus the girls were always sent to sleep with relatives at night. Trufena was annoyed by Mogaka's negligence. Self-respecting men built houses for their daughters. The fact that he had depended for so long on relatives she found outrageous (his eldest girl was circumcised seventeen years ago!). Her own father had provided a fine kitchen for herself and her sisters. But in her married home Trufena had to contend with one, sometimes two of Ombui's sisters, who would come at dusk and leave again at dawn, hardly helping her at all with her domestic chores. She had quarreled with the younger one, Cecilia, because the girl complained that Trufena gave her only rags to sleep on, while for her part Trufena accused Cecilia of using the grass around the house as a latrine. While Mary agreed that Cecilia should be forced to improve her toilet habits, she urged Trufena to give the girl a decent blanket.

"You have three of them. Ombui brought them to you last time he came. You cannot continue alone at night. You have said you vomit every evening and in the morning you awake in pain. You must have someone with you. Trufena, for your own sake, give Cecilia a blanket. Then she will come back and stay with you." But Trufena is adamant. "I have no blankets. What do you mean, Ombui brought me blankets? I sleep on rags, too. I don't want that little animal here at all." Mary sighs, "Ombui wrote to us to make sure you aren't alone at night. You should do as he says and let Cecilia stay with you." "You try and train that child! Do I urinate and defecate in the yard? No! I won't go to the latrine either, there are so many witches about in this place. Who knows, I might meet one on the path to the latrine.

So I use a *omokebe* [a tin] and empty it in the latrine in the morning. But that child is a bush person. Can she use a tin?"

Trufena refused to discuss the subject further. However, this brief interaction had given me some insight. First, I heard Trufena lie to us, determinedly and unambivalently, about the blankets. Of course she had several good blankets. We saw them airing on the hedge in the morning. She knew we had seen them, and yet she stuck to her story. Why? Perhaps if I had been there alone she could have said, "I don't want that girl, whom I dislike, to use my good things. She is of no help to me and she doesn't wash. Let her sleep on *ebichanchabe* [torn clothes and pieces of old blanket]."

But the expectation in a Gusii family was that one should share possessions however much one resented doing so. For many reasons Trufena had not taken to her husband's family, whom she considered inferior to her own. She seemed to look upon her marriage as a relationship between herself and Ombui, not between herself and all Ombui's relatives. She resented having to relate to them at all. However, I was with her aunt and thus, rather than being straightforwardly selfish, as she possibly could have been to me alone (and I could see her point: Cecilia was dirty and distinctly unhelpful), she preferred to lie and be caught at it than to commit overtly another kind of immoral act, that of refusing to share. She had told us once before, "The Gusii are always jealous. They don't want you to have anything better than they. Thus I must eat just *obokima* every day, even though it makes me fat," because to eat other foods would invite jealousy and, consequently, witchcraft. Blankets were an important currency in Gusiiland. Everyone talked about needing them and wanting them (but never of having them). Trufena craved many things: a radio, a cement house, a hat from Nairobi; but by giving her blankets Ombui had at least supplied the first thing on her list. Though at the moment Ombui was only a trainee in the air force college, nevertheless he was employed, he had prospects. He had brought his wife, who considered herself above these bush people, three blankets.

The neighbors were less knowledgeable about the modern world than Ombui was already, after only five months in Nakuru. But while they might be ambivalent about him, they were surely most eager to find fault with Trufena, the outsider, who made no attempt to hide her distaste for them. When Ombui was home he spent all his time visiting relatives, mending his fences, in essence assuring them that he was not proud. But Trufena resented her *egesangio* (communal farm work). She quarreled with her sisters-in-law, she listened in hostile silence when Mogaka told her to help his wife Francesca with the harvest. She kept to herself as much as possible, but her aloofness had a price. Once she remarked, "Francesca is said to be a witch," and another time she admitted she never went out at night for fear of witches. "I've never seen one in this place, but I know they exist, and no fence can keep them out if they want to get in." Though she did not gossip about witchcraft, she was continually on her guard against inviting jealousy. She hid her pregnancy; she lied about the blankets Ombui brought her. She did not offer us any of the tea he provided her, perhaps because if she were to do so, she would be accused of boasting that her husband was employed. And yet, even though she was scrupulous about concealing her good fortune from potentially malevolent neighbors, at the same time she did nothing but antagonize those people in other ways. She was uncooperative, unfriendly, inhospitable, rude. Did she not anticipate the consequences of such behavior? Could she control herself? If she so wished, could she have behaved differently? She made no attempt to ingratiate herself with anyone, even with me. It was harvest time, and wherever we went women offered us food, but though we walked down to Trufena's house through an avenue of ten-foot-high stalks, laden with ears of corn ready for roasting, she never offered us anything.

After a while Ombui's uncle, Nyagama, forced Trufena to patch up her quarrel with Cecilia. The girl was grudgingly lent a blanket and resumed sleeping in Trufena's house. However, Trufena had her there on sufferance only and never gave her a dress, for example, which might have lured Cecilia into being more helpful with Johnathan. Child nurses expect to be given something for their pains. Little girls of seven or eight knew their own worth and refused to work if their expectations were not met. But Trufena, who badly needed help with her very active toddler, refused to provide Cecilia with anything more than the loan of a blanket, and so Cecilia naturally would run off at dawn. As the weeks passed and Trufena got heavier and slower, she became moody and depressed. She was told at the maternity clinic in town that she was anemic and should do as little field work as possible. We found her sitting at home, staring angrily over her neglected flower beds.

"Not working is terrible. I am always lonely in this place, but at least when I am digging and weeding, I don't worry. I am idle on the Sabbath, but then sometimes I have visitors, my cousins or Ombui's cousins. Now that I am idle all day, it is very bad to be left like this with my thoughts. In labor will I die and leave Johnathan alone? When I came to this place Sabera and I were friends, but no longer. I never visit her or my mother-in-law.

"Once or twice I went there, but they did not visit me, and how long can you keep going to see someone if that person isn't interested in you? I have no friends here. Before I married I knew nothing about loneliness. I've had a hard and lonely life since then. Even before Ombui went to the air force he was away all day. I didn't see so much of him. He even worked for a while and did not come home to sleep. No one cares about me here. Even though I am pregnant no one comes to see if I am well or sick."

I knew other Gusii women who were isolated by their own suspicions. However, in every other instance these women seemed to have one friend in the vicinity upon whom they relied for psychological support. Trufena, on the other hand, seemed friendless. She had a cousin, Rebecca, whose home was nearby, but this girl had eloped not long ago. As Trufena talked bitterly about her isolation, Mary looked increasingly uncomfortable. She knew all that Trufena had done to alienate the family, herself included, and yet now the girl was talking as if she herself had contributed nothing to this atmosphere of distrust. "In five years I expect no change," she said, "except that Johnathan will be older and more of a companion." She was implying that Mary, as a classificatory mother-in-law, had also contributed to her misery. Mary squirmed in her seat. She hastened to reassure Trufena, "If you have trouble when you give birth, I will be here to help you. People love you. You are safe with us."

Mary was always the peace maker, the go-between, the only woman in her extended family who managed to maintain relationships with everyone at once, and now she was terrified of the anger underlying Trufena's depression. I had heard much about Trufena's rudeness, her tantrums, the confrontations into which she forced her husband's relatives. She had been extremely angry with us both on the occasion when we discovered she was pregnant. This time, however, I was an on-

looker: her anger focused on Mary, as representative of the whole band
of women whom Trufena believed had rejected her without due cause.
In response Mary fussed about her in a vain attempt at placation.

As we left, Mary burst out, "When Trufena gave birth to Johnathan,
Ombui was away, so Nyagama and I took her to hospital. We hired a
taxi and took her, and afterward we never got a word of thanks. Had it
not been for us, the girl could have died and the child too!" Unfortunately, our visits to Trufena put a severe strain on Mary. In the usual
course of things, their relationship would have been more formal and
distant. As Ombui's uncle, Nyagama had been left in the role of
guardian of Trufena and her child, and it was Nyagama, not Mary, to
whom Trufena appealed for aid of any kind and to whom she brought
her complaints. But because of our work Mary could not remain at a
safe distance from her niece who had antagonized all her female in-
laws, including Mary herself. During our sessions Trufena had an
opportunity to vent her grievances, and Mary was obliged to listen,
under the fiction that the situation was somehow different from ordinary everyday encounters. In the course of our time together, Mary saw
and heard much which shocked and upset her. I tried to syphon off
some of her feelings in between sessions by letting her talk about
Trufena, and by and large she was able to absorb most of what Trufena
said and did in our presence without comment at the time. However,
inevitably our sessions became one more arena in which the struggle
between Trufena and her in-laws and later, her husband, was acted out.

At no time did the consequences of her attitude and behavior re-
bound upon her more dramatically than the day on which she gave
birth to her second child. She had convinced me that she would give
birth at the end of November. She was not particularly large, and
perhaps she really did not know when she was due. At any rate, in the
first week of October we went to visit her as usual and found her lying
on her bed.

> She gets up and walks into the *eero* [living room] where we
> are. "I was planting beans yesterday, and I'm very tired today. I
> was resting." As she sits she grimaces, and Mary exclaims in
> astonishment, "But you are in labor!" Trufena shakes her head.
> "How can I be? I am not due for months." She can barely speak;
> she is in the midst of a contraction.

Trufena, Mary her aunt, of whose jealousy Trufena is so afraid, and
I, the persistent meddling European, were all sitting at the table.

Trufena was in hard labor while denying this fact as vigorously as she could through teeth clenched in pain. When the contraction passed, she got to her feet and attempted to fill Johnathan's bottle. This was the last thing she was able to do and at our urging went back to bed. Meanwhile nothing was prepared. There was neither water nor firewood in the house. Mary ran off to the river while I collected wood from under the eaves and built a fire. Trufena lay mute upon her bed a few feet away from me when Mary returned from the river. We heated some water and washed Trufena's back and stomach. It was a dark, cold afternoon, and we were crowded into a tiny windowless space. Trufena was completely silent. It was as if there were only two of us, not three.

> Since I have little experience in the delivery of babies and could scarcely be relied on as an assistant, I suggest that Francesca be summoned. Whereupon Trufena comes to life and calls out, "No, don't tell her! I don't want anyone to know I'm in labor!" Mary convinces her that we must at least find someone to take care of Johnathan. Trufena eventually agrees that the message should be, "Trufena is sick because she worked too hard yesterday planting beans." Mary goes off to deliver this message, hoping to get Cecilia to come back with her; however, she returns with Teresa, the elder sister. Mary tells us, "Your mother-in-law says she cannot spare Cecilia. *She,* Francesca, is sick also. Mogaka beat her up last week and she is still stiff and sore. She sent Teresa instead." But Teresa, having washed a couple of plates, remarks, "There's nothing wrong with you, Trufena," and leaves summarily.
>
> For a while we are alone again, but then Sabera appears, encumbered by her two small children. By now Trufena has shifted off her bed to a stool. Mary sits behind her on a paraffin tin, and whenever Trufena has a contraction, she reaches backward to grasp Mary round the neck. Mary tells Sabera to hold Trufena's legs apart, and Sabera obeys. However, after one or two contractions, she stands up. "Trufena is afraid," she says, meaning she, Sabera, is not prepared to continue the task, whereupon I am detailed to take her place, and Sabera retires thankfully to the living room on the other side of the matting partition. I hold Trufena's legs apart in case the baby is about to fall out. However, since it is quite dark and Trufena is mute, neither Mary nor I have any idea how imminent the delivery might be.
>
> After what seems like a very long time, Francesca appears, reeking of beer. She brings with her two women who are

classificatory mothers-in-law of Trufena. This means that they cannot enter the bedroom of their "son" Ombui, for to do so would be *emoma* [a violation of the laws of *chinsoni,* avoidance]. These two women, therefore, can be of no assistance unless Trufena moves into the living room, a more neutral space, which she shows no sign of being about to do. Francesca, who is also forbidden to enter her son's bedroom, looks around the partition and then retires to discuss noisily with the other women the details of their own multiple deliveries.

Of course Mary was also a classificatory parent to Trufena, and she admitted that she, too, experienced some embarrassment and apprehension about entering Trufena's bedroom, but being a less traditional person, she compromised. She said that as long as she did not sit on the *bed* of her "son," she was not committing a sacrilege. Even very traditional women on occasion could ignore the restrictions of *chinsoni* if they were inclined to do so. But it seemed that the women of the Osoro family were so ambivalent about Trufena that they gladly seized upon an excuse to delay and avoid being helpful to this girl whom they disliked.

> Meanwhile I am handed a flashlight by Mary and told to see if the baby is crowning. All I see is the water bag bulging through the vaginal opening. I notice that indeed Trufena had a "very good circumcision," just as she had told me during a raucous conversation some months before: her clitoris and labiae minorae are completely gone.
>
> Suddenly Francesca appears in the bedroom, pushes Mary off her paraffin can and sits down in her place. She seizes Trufena, who moans, "Taata, Mama Ominto," that is, "Daddy, Mummy," in fear perhaps as well as pain. It seems obvious that Francesca is the last person Trufena wants helping her at the birth of her child. First she tries to stop us from calling her mother-in-law, and then when she comes anyway, Trufena remains in the sanctum of her bedroom, thus delaying Francesca from joining her for a couple of hours, until she is close to delivery. Eventually Francesca breaks in. She scolds Trufena, singing, "You are refusing to deliver, you are afraid! If you can't do your work alone, you must go to the hospital and ask for help." (I.e., what coward runs to the hospital? Trufena, of course, had her first child there. Francesca, on the other hand, has managed to

approximate the ideal of Gusii stoicism, for on at least one occasion she has given birth all by herself.)

I was aware both from accounts I had heard from other Gusii women and from the one delivery at which I had been present previously that mothers-in-law tended to be rough and unsupportive at such a time. Indeed, despite their own multiple childbirth experiences, older women often appeared disorganized and hysterical to a point of panic. It was as if they had repressed any information which could be of use to the girl in labor and remembered only their own pain and fear. Presumably their behavior was an expression of their ambivalence about the younger woman. They mocked her, they might even beat her, they deprecated her genitalia, they told stories of past traumas which had occurred to them or to others.

Her [Francesca's] intoxicated state no doubt licenses her to be as hostile as she wishes. She yells repeatedly at Trufena to push, even though my periodic examinations indicate that the time for pushing has not yet come. From my vantage point at one extremity, I do my best to nurture Trufena by talking to her reassuringly, but I doubt if she hears anything I say. Sabera has vanished altogether, but the two older women are still chattering away in the living room and Francesca continues her songs. Trufena groans and writhes with the contractions but never cries out. After an hour or so Francesca announces abruptly that the baby is stuck. Trufena cannot deliver the child without help (i.e., she is a failure) and I should go to find the nurse who works with us on our project.

When we return with the nurse the scene is chaotic. There are many neighbors there. Everyone, regardless of *chinsoni* [shame], is now in the bedroom. They are yelling and beating Trufena, telling her to push. The baby's head is half out while Trufena lies limply in the arms of her mother-in-law. The older women are all arguing and pushing one another, behaving in effect as if none of them has ever been through this ordeal before. Sabera's four-year-old son George is stationed at Trufena's left foot, fascinated by what is going on between his aunt's thighs. No one pays any attention to him. Johnathan, who is being entertained by Cecilia, seems unperturbed by the excitement. Apart from George, no one is within arm's reach of Trufena's vagina. The women are all grouped around her head and shoulders. None shows the least intention of being ready to catch the baby. While I hold the flashlight, the nurse takes out the child and hands it to Mary. Immediately attention is focused entirely upon the child, a son, and Trufena is left in a naked heap by the fire, which has been allowed long ago to go out. Francesca leaps into a wildly erotic dance and appears not to hear when we ask for a razor blade with which to cut the cord. After five minutes a blunt one is brought from a neighbor's house, the cord is sawed through, and the baby is washed by the older women. No one does anything about finding a cloth in which to wrap him, and he lies squalling on Mary's lap. I search about in the boxes under the bed until I find a towel, and the baby is wrapped in that. Meanwhile, Trufena is sitting literally on top of the placenta, vainly trying to wipe her blood-streaked legs with a cloth she pulled out from beneath her mattress.

I left the house forty-five minutes after the baby was born, by which time the matting partition had been jerked down to make a bed for Trufena. She lay on it half covered with a blanket. The placenta was still lying on the hearth, and the fire was still unlit. I had bought some sodas and some tea in the market when I had gone to fetch the nurse. Trufena complained of thirst but was ignored. The other women drank all but one of the sodas, and while I was there no one lit a fire to make tea for Trufena. I urged Francesca to throw the placenta in the latrine, as it is customary to dispose of it there immediately, but we discovered later that it had remained in the house until morning.

I was rather shocked by this experience. For one thing, I had not expected Trufena to give birth so soon. Nor had I expected Francesca and Sabera's hostility howard Trufena to have been so obvious. I had imagined that under the circumstances such feeling would be controlled and modified. It is true that Trufena came to no harm. Everything which needed to be done was done, but inefficiently and in a way to maximize Trufena's physical discomfort and emotional distress. She later told us that at the point when Mary and I went off to find the nurse, Francesca also left her to join her friends outside. Trufena was alone when her water bag broke, and it was not until the baby was actually being born that anyone came to her. Of course, I have only Trufena's account of what happened, but it sounds likely, given all else I observed of Francesca's behavior. I had to wonder what would have happened had we not by chance happened to come upon Trufena when she was in labor and remained with her. She might have called to her neighbor across the boundary hedge, but on the other hand she might well have given birth alone, a not uncommon occurrence among Gusii women who did not trust their husband's relatives. Some women freely chose to give birth alone, and this was considered an accomplishment, but others did so merely out of fear. The particularly unhelpful behavior of Trufena's female in-laws might have been a reflection of their special ambivalence toward her, as someone whom they had long viewed with suspicion and dislike.

I wondered how Trufena perceived her experience, but when I later questioned her, she replied nonchalantly, "What else do you expect? Those old mothers always behave in that way." And indeed a couple of weeks later I attended the labor of another young woman who in this case was well liked by her in-laws, and I witnessed the same kind of chaotic scene, in which the girl's mother and aunts-in-law mocked her and pushed and pulled at her and, once her baby was born, virtually ignored her. Then I realized the close similarity between childbirth and circumcision. On the latter occasion also, older women behaved to the novices in what to Western eyes and ears appeared to be a most cruel and hostile manner. While the little girls cowered in their blankets, women abandoned themselves to wild dancing and obscene songs. Evidently childbirth, like circumcision, afforded these postmenopausal women an acceptable opportunity for venting their feelings of anger and envy at being sexually displaced by younger women. But those young women were capable of bearing the pain and mockery without complaint because as eight- and nine-year-olds, they had already experienced and mastered it.

Early the next morning, we found Trufena washed and dressed and the house clean again. Francesca had slept in the house, Trufena reported, but had left shortly after dawn to go to find beer. One gathered that the strain of being in such intimate contact with her daughter-in-law had told on her. Apart from Cecilia, who had been detailed to take care of Johnathan, no other relative had come to greet her, bring her food, or offer any help at all. However, despite her awareness that the family was not treating her as they should, Trufena seemed in excellent spirits. She asked for a stamp and some paper so she could write to Ombui and inform him of the arrival of Jared, whom our nurse had weighed and pronounced, at seven pounds, a full-term baby.

The following day I visited Trufena by myself at lunch time, and soon we were joined by Francesca. At first Francesca lay on the grass outside the door, groaning and complaining of her stomach. "I have worms, and they are giving me such trouble! I'm in no fit state to do anyone else's housework!" Eventually she picked herself up and came in to cook some vegetables which I gathered Sabera had brought. While she prepared them, Francesca talked at breakneck speed to Johnathan and myself; she never said a word to Trufena, who lay on her bed with severe afterbirth pains. We ate our lunch very quickly, and then Francesca ran out, leaving the dishes to be washed by someone else. (This was the only occasion on which I ever ate a meal of any kind in Trufena's house, and it was at her mother-in-law's invitation.) Thereafter Trufena was left to her own devices. Even Cecilia was withdrawn by Mogaka, who needed her to herd his cows. Mogaka himself did not come to greet the child, saying he had no money to offer as a birth gift. It was weeks before he laid eyes on his new grandson. Again, it is not expected of a Gusii elder (*omogaaka*) to take much interest in his infant grandchildren. It is enough that he be gratified a male child has been born. However, Mogaka was unusually tardy. Ombui's family were well aware of their obligations to Trufena, and when they failed to fulfill them, they did not pretend they had forgotten. Rather, they made weak excuses: they said they experienced *chinsoni;* they had no money; their maize needed weeding; they could not cook or fetch water from the river; and so on. Meanwhile, in the case of another family member about whom they were less ambivalent, they overlooked the inconveniences and did whatever needed to be done.

Next day, when I was again visiting without Mary, I witnessed a rather surprising conversation between Trufena and a stepuncle of Ombui, a man of about thirty years of age named Nyachai. Trufena was trying to do her chores alone when Nyachai came in to greet the baby. He examined the child carefully and expressed amazement that Trufena had given birth. He lived some way away and had not seen her for several months, so he had been unaware that she was pregnant. He then questioned her closely about her delivery and sympathized with her over her afterbirth pains, which she complained were worse than the labor pains had been. She described her delivery graphically, including the behavior of her mother-in-law. "When my water bag broke, she was under the shade tree in the yard drinking beer. When Sarah was with me, she didn't run in and out, attending to her own business. She stayed with me all the time. It is very good to have white people with you when you are in labor, for *white people are not jealous*"—i.e., Francesca's negligence was not due to her inebriated condition but to her jealousy of Trufena, who comes from a superior family, who is better educated than any of Francesca's children, and who, moreover, has married Ombui, who looks as if he will go farthest of any of her sons. "Most people," Trufena and Nyachai agreed, "cannot bear to see even their brother better off they they are. Parents are jealous of their own children if they think those children aren't helping them as much as it is within their power to do." Each gave illustrations for my benefit of what could occur between one brother and another or between fathers and sons. However, none of these illustrations was an incident from their own personal experience; rather, they told stories about neighbors and relatives at some safe distance from themselves. At one point the baby, Jared, awoke in the bedroom, and Trufena went to nurse him. She was followed immediately by Nyachai, who sat by the hearth and questioned her about her milk and how well the child was sucking.

I was most curious to know who this man was who had violated so many of the rules of avoidance. Surely he was a "father" to Ombui, and therefore to Trufena as well, and yet he talked freely of her pregnancy and delivery and then pursued her into her bedroom where he questioned her closely about her milk flow. As for Trufena, she seemed to be perfectly at ease. I doubted that such a discussion would have taken place had I been there with Mary, whose censorious silence would have inhibited the other two. Afterward, I discovered that Nyachai was a drunkard who a few years ago had murdered his father. The incidence of patricide and matricide is thought to be very high in Gusiiland; however, as in this case, the murderers are rarely prosecuted, as the family almost invariably closes ranks, concealing from the police the crime and the criminal, even though everyone in the community knows the murder has taken place. The belief is that such a crime is so great a sacrilege (*emoma*) that the ancestors will inevitably perpetrate terrible punishment upon the murderer and his descendants: they will go mad, their wives will be infertile, their children will die. Whatever punishment the law of the land might exact of the criminal can be nothing compared with the retribution the ancestor spirits will ultimately exact. Thus the Gusii believe it is of primary importance to make peace with the ancestors, who must be placated by multiple sacrifices. For the murderer to be handed over to the courts and ultimately sentenced to die would in no way save his family from the blight resulting from his crime. In this way, Nyachai had remained from the legal standpoint a "free" man. However, he was paying a price: he was an alcoholic, his maize business had come to nothing, he had taken as his wife a *ritinge* (divorcée). Any children this woman bore were not legally his, because she had been paid for by another man. Though he lived in the community as before, people regarded him as deviant. People feared him, not just because he was a violent man but because of the sacrilege he had committed.

This was the man, her classificatory father-in-law, whom Trufena welcomed into her house and into her bedroom. It seemed to me that I had watched one pariah comforting another.

III

Trufena recovered remarkably quickly from childbirth. She claimed her family gave her no help, though this was not strictly true, since Mary's son brought water twice daily from the river. However, even in front of Mary she complained of being left to cope entirely on her own.

If Johnathan suffered from the trauma of replacement, in my long hours of observing him during this time I could not detect it. He was his usual alert, independent self. When he wanted attention—which was relatively rarely—he knew how to get it without antagonizing or irritating his mother. As for Trufena, her manner did not change. When it suited her, she played with him and delighted in him, and the rest of the time she ignored him, and he seemed to do very well under this system. He scarcely ever whined. Whoever came into the compound he would engage, if they were willing to be engaged. If not, he entertained himself. Three weeks after the birth of Jared, Trufena's stomach was flat. She had started weeding the beans she had planted the day before her delivery, and her only physical complaint was toothache. But she still received no reply from Ombui to the letter she had written to him telling him of Jared's birth.

At the twenty-first session we came into the compound and found Trufena obviously upset.

> Her face is closed and very black. She scarcely greets us but when we are seated beside her on the grass, she bursts out, "I hear Ombui has married. His cousin, Peter, told me this when he came to build a storehouse here. As he was building he said to me he has heard Ombui has taken a new wife in Nairobi." She recounts how when she heard this she wept, but she did not think to ask Peter who had given him this information.

I could so well imagine the scene: Peter, his back to Trufena, busily lashes poles together to make the walls of the storehouse. He remarks casually that he has heard Ombui has a new wife. Trufena stares at his back in anguish, but he does not look her in the face. Having heard his announcement made, as it seems, inadvertently, as is always the case when Gusii people make important communications, she then weeps, but her misery fails to elicit any further information from Peter, who no doubt shares the general family feeling about Trufena and quite relishes his role as deliverer of bad tidings.

When I heard the news, I was astonished. I had been led to believe that Ombui was as passionately attached to Trufena as she to him. Mary also seemed surprised. Together we tried to comfort and reassure her: Ombui lived in the barracks, he could not have a woman live with him as his wife. Perhaps he had a girlfriend, as men do when they are far from home, but a girlfriend was not a wife, and so forth.

As we talked, Trufena's misery receded somewhat, and she started to be indignant. She said a week ago Nyagama gave her fifty shillings which Ombui had sent to his uncle (who works in the town and has access to the post office, where money orders are cashed) for her and Johnathan. Though he asked Nyagama if Trufena had given birth yet, he enclosed no letter for her. He asked his uncle to insist that Trufena let his sister Cecilia come back to sleep in her house at night, regardless of her past behavior, because Trufena should not be alone. Apparently he was very annoyed that Trufena had sent Cecilia away.

> "He told Nyagama to tell me that this is not my house. It is his, and I have no right to deny his little sister room." She rushes on, "I don't care if that's what he thinks. I will pack up my things and go home. When he comes here he'll find his

beautiful house empty! If he doesn't want me here any more, then there's always a place for me in my mother's house. I'll leave the children with her, and when the new school year begins, I'll go on with my education." Her eyes flash. But then she falters, shaking her head. "Can I do that? I have two sons now. It is very difficult for a woman with two sons to find another husband." Her anger slips away, and she is wretched again. She talks of the friendship Ombui has always had with his cousin, Peter. "They write many letters to one another. I have not asked to see those letters. I don't want to know what's in them." Mary says sagely that if she were in Trufena's place, she would behave as if she had heard nothing. She would wait until her husband came on leave, and then she would greet him and cook for him as if everything were as before. Only after he was satisfied (sexually) would she ask about this other woman. "Perhaps it is true, he *does* have a girlfriend, but a girlfriend is not a wife, is she?"

Having left Trufena a little comforted, Mary told me she had known about this latest development for some days already, for she had seen Ombui's letter which Peter brought to Nyagama. It was true, in it Ombui wrote he had a girlfriend whom he wanted to marry. The girl was a stenographer, whom he visited on his days off. He directed Peter, "See to it that Trufena goes to her home. She has a bad character. I do not want to find her again in my house." So much for Ombui's letter to his cousin and age-mate. But to his uncle, Nyagama, whose opinion he respected and feared, he wrote very differently. In this letter he said he would come on leave in December, and meanwhile Nyagama should see to it that Trufena had help in the house. While he expressed his annoyance at the way Trufena had treated his sister, the overall tone was one of formal solicitousness for his wife. In neither letter, however, did he indicate any awareness of the birth of Jared. "He must know perfectly well," Mary said, "but can he chase away a wife who has borne him two sons?"

During our previous session, Mary had in no way hinted that she knew anything more about Ombui's feeling than what Trufena had told us herself. At that time Mary had behaved as if the news of his disaffection was as astonishing to her as it was to me. "But Ombui loves you, Trufena," she exclaimed. "I know how you two are when you are together! Even last time he was here it was the same as always between you and him." She had hastened to reassure and comfort Trufena in a way which I, at least, never doubted was genuine, and Trufena seemed to have been relieved by unburdening herself to us. Although I understood why Mary had had to feign ignorance of any prior knowledge, nevertheless I was perturbed in retrospect by the smoothness of her performance. However, I came to realize that on this occasion and in the weeks to come her motivation for taking Trufena's part and protecting her (even though by doing so she often concealed information and sometimes even lied) sprang from the commitment she shared with her husband to maintain order in the extended family. Ombui might want to reject obligations to his sons, or Trufena might contemplate leaving them with her mother, to be brought up fatherless and unwanted, but Nyagama and Mary were not willing to let the irresponsibility of the young parents play havoc with the lives of these two little children. The children were sons of the Osoro family regardless of whether or not their mother had been paid for, and they had a right to be brought up in their father's home. The drama which ensued between Trufena and Ombui put a severe strain upon Mary. Because of my work, she was forced to be Trufena's confidante; however, like the other women in the family, she had frequently been manipulated and ill used by the girl and therefore had plenty of reason to dislike her. All the other women were encouraging Ombui to get rid of Trufena, but in part because of her work with me, in part because she was the wife of the most respected and respectable man in the family, Mary had to take a mediating role.

In the twenty-fourth session, that is, a month after the birth of Jared, Trufena told us she had at last received a letter from her husband, in which he made no reference to the birth of his son and sent neither money nor baby clothes. He told her she could expect to see him at the end of the year, i.e., in two months' time, but not before, because he has been sent on another course.

"That's a lie!" Trufena exclaims. "He said nothing about any course to Peter or to Nyagama. Why should he mention it only to me? Even if he were on a course, he'd get the weekend off, and he could come home then." She sits down abruptly and starts weeping, the tears plopping into the grass. "When I had Johnathan, my mother provided me with everything, even though she had not been happy that I'd run away with Ombui in the first place. Ombui was unemployed, so he couldn't buy the child's clothes himself. But now he has a good job, and all he sends is fifty shillings, and that not even directly to me. He sends it by his uncle, pretending he doesn't know I've given birth. Well, how am I supposed to feed Johnathan? I cannot nurse both children at once, can I? I owe the man who has been selling me milk so much money, and he's refusing to let me have any more unless I pay him."

But as she weeps, her sense of hurt and humiliation turns to anger. "It is these women here who hate me and who set Ombui against me. Long ago when I was pregnant with Johnathan, Sabera came here to me and told me, 'Go to your home, nobody loves you here. Even Ombui [who was working away from home at the time] has ceased to love you.' I should have listened to her and gone to my home. I shouldn't have stayed to bear a second child and watch Ombui's feelings turn away from me." She stands up, tears streaming down her face. She seizes the branch of a sapling and stands a moment, staring out across the valley. Suddenly she picks up a machete lying at her feet. "Would that I could cut Sabera!" she cries and slashes off the lower branches of the tree, even in her rage neatly, adroitly pruning it as it should be pruned. Then, as she releases it, the sapling springs back, whipping the air.

Mary was horrified by this performance. Later when we were alone she burst out, "Trufena has no respect [amasikane]. You saw how she cut that tree? And how she wept in front of us?" "Well, that is how she feels," I said. "She has no one to talk to about these things except ourselves. She got that letter from Ombui four days ago, and she has been keeping it to herself all this time." "Then she should sit on the ground and quietly tell us her story. She shouldn't pretend to be attacking Sabera."

Trufena goes on, "I think I will go to my home. I will ask my mother's brother for my bus fare. Perhaps he knows what has happened already anyway, for Peter will have told everybody. And no doubt they heard it happily. Nobody here cares for me." She chokes on her tears. She come and sits beside us. "I ate nothing last night, and I am so tired. Jared cried all night. I couldn't sleep. Ombui used to remember me. When he first went to be trained, he used to send me something. Now he has forgotten me, and even when Nyagama writes to tell him I have a new baby and he should send me clothes for the child, he ignores his uncle and sends nothing. There is a young man, a neighbor, home on leave now, but when he returns to Nairobi, I could send a letter for Ombui with him, to make sure Ombui receives it and cannot later make excuses that the letter was lost in the post. But I cannot write such a letter. I have many thoughts. I would write a bad letter which would only make things worse for me with Ombui."

I ask her whether, when he was last at home, she had any notion that Ombui loved her less than before. "No, we loved each other very much. And so I knew that it was all right for me to stay here, even if no one else loves me." Then I ask if she could ever consent to having a cowife. "That woman must have her own land," she replies. "There isn't enough here for more sons."

She tells me she would not consent to a division of resources, but she has avoided saying how she would feel about sharing her husband with another woman.

As we are leaving, I say to Johnathan, "Take care of your mother," to which Trufena responds, "She is going to hang herself, that's what his mother is going to do!" Mary looks at her in alarm and disapproval. Trufena backs off a little. "Then I won't hang myself; I'll go to my home. I don't care about Ombui! He won't find me here to greet him when he next comes. Why should I stay here for him when he cannot even tell me what he wants? It would be better if he wrote to me, 'I have another woman; I don't love or want you any more,' but he doesn't do that. He doesn't send money to me either, and he doesn't come to greet his child, but until he tells me he wants me to leave, I have a right to his money, and I have a right to expect him to come home if I bear him a son!" Mary makes one last attempt to mollify Trufena and to restore order in this most unsavory situation. She tries to make light of Trufena's fears. "You wait until the end of the year. He will come and say he loves you. He'll seduce you and make you pregnant again!" We leave Trufena shaking her head, "If he tries to do that, I shall weep." "What will you mean by your tears?" I ask, and she shrugs and turns back into her yard.

At the time I could not be objective about the situation. I was too closely identified with Trufena. I had been through an emotionally trying delivery with her and had seen how callously she had been treated, particularly by her mother-in-law. Then subsequently, for more than a month, she had received no communication from her husband. Meanwhile his cousin told her that Ombui had married a second wife. It is every Gusii woman's great fear that her husband may do this, and although older women usually accept it with bad grace, young women like Trufena fight tooth and nail to thwart their husbands' plans. I could empathize with Trufena's feelings of hurt, humiliation, and rage. For a long period I had seen her as intriguingly idiosyncratic. For the most part I made the mistake of interpreting her behavior and her feelings, insofar as she shared them with me, in the light of her being "more modern" than her neighbors. Inadvertently I measured her against a Western yardstick.

Of course I was aware that she was a Gusii girl from a quite traditional background, but I was overly impressed by her eccentricities and tended to overlook the wide areas in which she conducted herself in a perfectly conventional Gusii manner. Thus I preferred to see her not as, for example, a cultural misfit or an especially immature person but as a girl striving for autonomy, with whose direct emotional reactions in periods of stress I could empathize. In times of profound social change, when people are in the process of shifting from an extended kin group to a nuclear-family orientation, it may be that those who accomplish the shift first are marginal in some way—socially, emotionally, or both—and the fact that they do not make the shift gracefully must not necessarily be held against them. For a long time I saw Trufena in just this light. Although I believe this interpretation of her behavior and personality has some validity, nevertheless, while sympathizing with her rebellious attitude and her emotional directness and "honesty," as I saw it, among other characteristics, I often disregarded the norms which she violated. It was only in retrospect that I paid more attention to Mary's reactions to and comments about Trufena.

In this particular instance I "heard" Trufena's sorrow and anger at Ombui's not loving her any more, and I felt I understood why she should want to go home and start life anew. I thought I was observing the type of case so familiar to Westerners in which two young people are infatuated with one another, marry, have children too rapidly, and then one of the partners falls out of love, finds someone else, and demands to be allowed his freedom to pursue his new infatuation. In response, the other partner retreats to her family to recover from the rejection. Then, after a healing period, she takes up her life again, having matured, it may be hoped, as a result of this painful experience. At one level, this is how Trufena talked of herself and Ombui; they were two young people deeply involved with one another, while their relationships with their families were much less important to them.

Since I scarcely ever saw Trufena with either her own or Ombui's relatives, I was rarely reminded to put this marriage into perspective. I mistakenly assumed this was a love match in which the regulation of the marriage, particularly since no bridewealth had been exchanged and Trufena's father had cut her off, depended on the two of them alone. Trufena talked in terms of having or not having Ombui's love. With it she was strong and capable of tolerating loneliness and hostility from his relatives. Without it she, like a Western girl, was devastated. However, it was quite some time before I understood that this was not just a love marriage. Indeed when things began to get difficult for Trufena, the claims of love receded quickly into the background, and she began to talk instead about children and the rights of male children to their father's property.

Originally Trufena had been infatuated with Ombui and had eloped with him, but from the start she, and not just her parents, had been concerned about solidifying her position by payment of cattle. She ran back to her parents after only a month with her lover, but Mogaka and Ombui had come to persuade her to return with them. Because she was pregnant they were successful, but her parents fully expected to be paid for their daughter in due course. Thus, although the original relationship had been between Trufena and Ombui alone, shortly thereafter the families of both young people had been drawn in, and at the point at which Trufena was being rejected by Ombui, whether or not their marriage had been completed by cattle payment, it was nevertheless no longer their concern alone. Rather, it was the concern of both families. Whatever the women of Ombui's family might say, the senior men, the elders, were committed to seeing that the interests of the two small sons of the young couple be protected, regardless of the disaffections of their parents. Thus, when Trufena responded to my question, "Would you consent to having a cowife," with a remark about the paucity of land rather than with any reference to her feelings about having to share the affections of her husband, she had already shifted the basis of the marriage from the insubstantial ground of mutual attraction to the material consideration of property rights.

In the turbulent months that followed, when I wondered continually why Trufena did not pack up her children and her belongings and go to her home, what kept her was the assumption, which she shared with the senior members of both families, that in the end Ombui would have to let her stay because of the rights she had through her sons to his part of Mogaka's land. If he wanted another wife, he would first have to provide that woman—through purchase—with land elsewhere. However, he was not now, nor would he be in the foreseeable future, in a financial position to do this. Thus, if Trufena could tolerate the pain of personal rejection (a loss of love which, I believe, she experienced differently from the way a Western girl would have experienced it), she held most of the cards. After all, she was already installed and entrenched. Apparently Ombui also, despite his modern veneer of tea plantation and air force life, expected of himself that he provide land for a second wife. By the time he was financially able to support another wife, this particular Nairobi girl, about whom he had sent word to Trufena through his cousin Peter, would be long forgotten. Hence when Mary joked with Trufena, "In December Ombui will seduce you afresh and you'll go to his bed as usual," in a manner which I felt was inappropriate and even rather cruel, this was because her time perspective was different from mine. Mary reacted with disgust to Trufena's overt expression of hatred for Sabera, in part, no doubt, because her own defenses were threatened by such strong emotion, but perhaps also because she felt the extremes of Trufena's feeling were not justified. It was Mary's assumption that this squabble would in time be resolved. For reasons only marginally dependent on the wishes of the young people themselves, Ombui and Trufena would ultimately settle down together, and everyone else in the family would learn to live with the situation, just as Mary and Nyagama had already learned.

These perceptions of mine, however, are from hindsight. At the time, I identified too closely with Trufena and visited her more frequently than usual because I believed her to be beleaguered, and I wanted to offer support. But Trufena's behavior never ceased to surprise me. For example, in the session two days after the one described above,

I made my way anxiously through the mud and rain only to find Trufena in the best of spirits. She greeted me,

"That girl who was crying here two days ago was my sister. Why should I care about Ombui? If he marries again, let me dance at the wedding. Ombui can only make me sad when my stomach is empty. But now it is full. I have eaten well." She pats her stomach, seizes her infant son and twirls him around. She starts to sing and to "bump" most erotically. Mary turns away, shocked, as usual. It is not merely the dance in itself. It is the fact that Trufena has no sense of shame and appropriateness. Except at ritual occasions such as circumcision, she should not display herself thus before a female relative of the parental generation. Trufena is wearing a mini-dress turned back to front and unzipped half way so that she can nurse Jared. Her breasts are partially uncovered, and she wears no head cloth. She is truly a spectacle. Lost in her dance, she has nothing to say to us.

Afterward Mary commented, "What can you say about that girl? I do not understand her. One day she weeps, the next she dances. She is like Erena Kemunto" (a woman we know who is despised and distrusted by everyone for her failure to behave, despite her advanced age, like a mature person). "Why should she dance? Is it because my husband gave her money to pay for her children's milk? Is that reason enough to dance?" Of course, Trufena did not mention to us that her milk bill, about which she had been so anxious, had been paid, and she certainly did not express any thanks to Mary. However, it is hardly surprising that she did not say thank you, since it is commonplace among the Gusii for people who have money to be continually besieged and plundered of their resources by their relatives, from whom they receive no thanks whatever. But Trufena's defiantly hedonistic dancing was extraordinary. What did she mean by it? I think Mary was right; the fact that she had been given money to pay her milk bill by her uncle Nyagama had improved her spirits enormously.

I was often bewildered by Trufena's volatility. Her mood swings seemed to depend on such trivial factors. I would search for some important determinant to explain these swift alterations in her spirits—important, that is, from my point of view. In the early days her periods of euphoria would directly follow the receipt of a letter from Ombui. In an instant she would shoot skyward from what had appeared to me to be the depths of depression. This I could understand, but later, when her relationship with Ombui deteriorated drastically, I would still quite frequently come upon her in a state of euphoria which I could not have conceived possible, given the deep depression I had seen her in in the preceding session. However, from my work with other Gusii women as well as Trufena, I am convinced that the self-esteem of these women depended to such a great degree on being given to, that to receive something of relatively slight value from *someone of psychological importance* had an almost miraculous effect. It apparently provided enough narcissistic gratification to allow them to reintegrate, to experience triumph (over their would-be detractors or those whose malevolence they feared), and also, as in Trufena's case, to achieve a defiant sense of completeness and autonomy. Nyagama, her husband's uncle, had ensured one of her most basic needs: a continued supply of milk with which to feed her prematurely weaned (by Gusii standards) son Johnathan. Nyagama was the most respected member of the Osoro family, and thus if he did not stint her, despite Ombui's rejection, Trufena knew she had a very strong ally in her current struggle. She knew that, given the fact that she had two male children, Nyagama would do his utmost to ensure she not be displaced.

Traditionally, a Gusii man knew he could never really divorce a woman who had borne him sons, for even if she were gone for many years, when her sons reached maturity, she would return to live and be protected and supported by her husband's family, regardless of her husband's feeling for her. All the people involved in the dispute between Trufena and Ombui were traditional people, despite the fact that some, like Nyagama, were literate and were even employed in government service. Thus, although for months everyone in the family was involved in a tug-of-war during which each had an opportunity to vent extremely negative feelings against one or the other of the main parties, nevertheless I believe that the basic psychological reality was that this marriage was a permanent relationship. Nobody said this to me, however, and since I knew of a number of instances of divorce between other young couples, where bridewealth had not been exchanged, it was reasonable for me to believe that I was probably about to witness a divorce in this case also.

I had good reason to flounder in my interpretation of Trufena's behavior, for it continued to be mystifying. For example, a few days after the session in which Mary and I were spectators to her euphoric dance, we met Trufena on the road, wearing a very pretty dress, very much the young matron on her way to market. She looked at us haughtily and said she had received a letter from Ombui in which he had enclosed money. She did not say how much money and seemed reluctant to talk to us further. The following day we found her at home, extremely depressed.

> We sit in semi-silence. In an effort to elicit some life from her, I ask about her letter from Ombui. She replies in monosyllables. "Yes, he said he would come before Christmas, but he did not send any money." "Why did you tell us otherwise yesterday?" I ask. "I didn't say anything about money." "You most certainly did." "You misheard me," she replies, her voice flat.

Since I was certain I did not mishear her, the question was, did she lie the previous day when she told us she had received money, or on this occasion, when she denied it? Given her current depression today, I think she lied about the money earlier when she was in a public place. She feared loss of face, even though no one except ourselves was within earshot, and so she claimed to have received money from her husband. Later Mary shrugged off the lie. She was used to lies and expected them, even from people she was closest to, with the exception of her husband. She remarked, however, that Trufena seemed better today. "Better!" I exclaimed. "She seems more miserable than ever! Why, she was barely able to speak. We didn't have a chance to cheer her up, since she wouldn't make any effort to talk with us." Evidently what Mary meant by "better" was that Trufena was *quiet.* She was no longer expressing strong feelings, neither the rage nor the euphoria which Mary found so distressing. She had control of herself now, she was keeping quiet (*ogokira*). No Gusii would castigate another for that.

The first stage in Trufena's reaction to the news of Ombui's disaffection seemed to be over. She settled down to wait for Ombui to come. She told us that in his recent letter he did finally acknowledge Jared's birth and asked the baby's name. She had decided to call him Kibarua (Swahili for someone who is employed part time) as his second name, after the man whose wife, Moraa, Mogaka had recently inherited. It is the custom to name children after someone who has recently died, but several male relatives had died lately, and I could not help wondering why Trufena chose to name her child after that particular man, whose name had rather derogatory connotations.

Trufena's family, however, had not acknowledged Jared's birth. A month earlier Sabera had met Trufena's mother in the market and told her that her daughter had given birth, but she had sent no word to Trufena.

"My father must be preventing her from coming. He is very cruel. He used to love me very much, as his eldest child, and I loved him too. But now his love for me has turned to hatred. This is all because the cattle have not been paid. If he meets someone from Ombui's family in the street, he will not greet that person. But he is only *angered* by them. It is me whom he *hates*. I cannot leave this place and go home. He would refuse to let me stay in his *omochie* [homestead]. He prefers that I become a prostitute. Well, he will have to wait a long time for his cattle. First Sabera must be paid. Only then will it be my turn. I wonder what Ombui is doing with his money these days. At least he isn't sending any to me and the children! Can he be saving to buy cattle? No! He must want to build a cement house, and he's saving all his salary for that! Meanwhile my children grow, and my father never comes to visit them. He has never laid eyes on Johnathan, his eldest grandchild. He's never shown any sign that he even knows the boy exists." As she talks so sadly and bitterly, Johnathan is playing at our feet. He is such an appealing child, and I feel almost tearful, for his sake, that his grandfather has refused to be exposed to his charms. Trufena, however, is dry eyed. I may see her weep in anger, but never in sorrow. She goes on. "He used to love me. When I had been here a week, he sent my mother to bring me home. And I hid. I sent Mary and Ombui's aunt Martha to talk to my mother. But as for me, I would not speak to her. I hid in this house and wept. I wanted to go with her, and yet I wanted to stay. She left without seeing me. Whatever was I thinking of then, to stay with Ombui? I should have gone back with my mother, but I didn't, and now my father hates me."

A few days later, Trufena was suddenly euphoric again. She had been, without the children, to a relative's funeral, and there she had seen both her parents and one of her sisters.

She tells us gaily, "My father refused to greet me, but my mother told me she would come to see Jared soon. She heard the story of Ombui and me, and I think she will help me. My father is still angry with me. In fact he threatened to beat my sister if she came back here with me after the funeral. But my mother thinks that though he won't let me stay if I come home of my own accord, if Ombui *drives* me away, then my father will allow me to stay at home."

She was so delighted at seeing her mother that she went two days running to the funeral and made herself uncharacteristically useful to the family of the dead relative in order to be able to see her mother (who slept overnight there) a second time.

Afterward Mary remarked, "Can it be true that her mother will help her? If so, why did she not pass by to see Jared and Johnathan on her way home from the funeral? Can she be so afraid of her husband, even now that she is a big lady [i.e., past childbearing]?"

At this point I had to go to England following the death of my mother, and I did not see Trufena for nearly a month. When I returned I found I had missed two important events that had left Trufena with a sense of well-being and self-worth verging on arrogance. (She was aware of the reason for my absence, but she made no reference at all to it. She did thank me, however, for the Christmas presents of tea, sugar, and clothing for Johnathan which Mary had delivered.) Shortly before Christmas Ombui had come home for two days. He brought with him many gifts, including clothes for the children and milk money. Trufena related how when he first arrived, she went into the bedroom and he had to lure her out from there to greet him, "but that did not take long." He asked her what was the meaning of her letters in which she had written harshly to him, demanding to know about the woman he had married. He asked her how he could have married anyone when he was off on the Somalia border. Evidently, his excuse for his failure to respond to her letters for so long was that he had been sent on an alert to a remote part of the country, where he received no mail. "Whatever Peter told you was a lie," Ombui said.

Mary reported that Ombui's mother, Francesca, hearing that he had been seen on the path, came hurrying to his house to greet him, and there she overheard him "persuading" Trufena, i.e., trying to calm her as she wept and complained that he had left her alone too long. But Francesca recounted that he quickly stopped her tears, and these were followed by silence as he took her to bed. For the rest of his stay, Trufena claims, she and Ombui "were exactly as before, not one thing had changed," and when he went back to base, he left her his radio, which she played so loudly that it was difficult for us to have a conversation with her. Indeed she had little interest in talking to us once she had informed me of her triumphant reinstatement in her husband's affections and had recited to me a list of the presents he brought to her. She retreated to the other side of the partition, from which she reemerged periodically, dancing to the radio with an abstracted expression on her face.

Once Trufena was in possession of so much visible evidence of her husband's attachment to her, she had no intention of jeopardizing her position by asking him any more questions or making any demands. She admitted that she did not even ask him when he thought he would get leave again. She described how she had accompanied him to the bus stop on Sunday afternoon (proudly dressed in her new clothes, carrying her new handbag, as other women reported to me) and bade him goodbye without daring to ask when next they might see one another. Although he claimed to have been on the Somalia border, and thus out of touch for some weeks, she never attempted to determine the truth by asking him to describe the country, the people, or what he was doing while there. "It never entered my head to ask," she said. Indeed, despite the anxiety the matter had caused her over a long period, she never once asked him how, when, or even if he was planning to pay for her. She kept turning up the radio, effectively drowning out my questions. Mary remarked later, "She was ashamed that she gave in to Ombui. I would never make love to my husband after we had quarreled until I had talked to him and asked him to explain many things." However, there was another major event Trufena was happy to tell me about, and this was the arrival of her mother, the day before, accompanied by four other female relatives. She brought with her large quantities of the foods prescribed for such an occasion, including ten loaves of bread (bread is a luxury). Trufena described the excitement and exultation with which the food was consumed, adding, "I don't know if my father has forgiven me or not, but I don't care." Now she was replete, and her repletion made her arrogant and effectively removed her from my reach.

In January Ombui came home again, this time for two weeks' leave, bringing with him still more gifts. I met him on several occasions, always accompanied by his cousin Peter, the go-between and Trufena's archenemy. One day I found all three in the compound and heard Trufena asking Ombui if they could go visit her mother. Now that Trufena's mother had been to greet the child, Trufena was at liberty to reciprocate the visit, and she was most eager to do so, no doubt to display her new clothes as well as her new son to the people at home. Ombui, however, flatly refused to accompany her. "You go alone if you want," he said. He was lying under the shade tree with Peter. The two of them got up and went off saying they had promised to meet a friend. As they left, Trufena's expression was stony.

A few days later Mary told me that Ombui had come in secret to Nyagama and had made a series of complaints about Trufena. Chief among these was the charge that she frequently claimed to his relatives that she had not received any money from him when she in fact had: she would come begging to Nyagama, causing Ombui humiliation and shame. Second, she had refused, during this period of leave, to be hospitable to his friends and guests. She maintained that it was enough for her to make tea in the morning, and when it was finished, as she told him in front of his guests, "You know how to make it; go make it yourself!" Finally, she had tried to conceal from him the full amount of money she had received from the pyrethrum cooperative. She told him she had received considerably less than in fact was the case, and she had spent the difference on new clothes for herself. She was unaware that the cooperative society always sent Ombui a statement of earnings. He told his uncle he needed advice as to what to do about such behavior. This was the first time Ombui had himself spoken to Nyagama about his dissatisfaction with Trufena. He made no mention, however, of his relationship with another woman, nor did he say directly that he wished to divorce Trufena. Rather, he listed his complaints: she was inhospitable, she did not tell the truth, she misappropriated his money. To Nyagama these were familiar complaints; the whole family, including himself, had suffered from Trufena's behavior. No doubt Ombui misrepresented the facts at certain points, but his uncle was not primarily concerned with determining the truth or falsity of details. He heard his nephew out and cautioned him against acting in haste.

The following day our doctor and his assistants found Trufena weeping as Ombui and his younger brother were about to set fire to the clothing Trufena had bought with the "undeclared" pyrethrum money. One of the assistants, a woman, dissuaded Ombui, telling him that "to burn your wages is foolish."

The next day Trufena explained to me that Ombui had given her the choice of either going home to her parents as a divorced woman or burning the clothes she had bought. She had chosen to give up the clothes. And she went on to describe with great bitterness the scene our doctor had come upon. She denied there was anything reprehensible in her behavior. Ombui, on the other hand, not only almost destroyed her clothes but had refused to allow her to reciprocate her mother's visit. "She was so good to me," Trufena protested, "and yet he won't give me a single cent with which to buy a gift for her to show my thanks."

As she talked, Ombui came silently into the yard. He ignored Trufena and went to play with Johnathan. (The child had been ill, and Ombui had taken him to the hospital that morning.) After a while he asked me, "Who do you think is right, she or I?" My reply, that each had his own story, evidently displeased him. He looked at me stormily for a moment and left again. On the path he called out a greeting to some men walking ahead of him up the hill and Trufena remarked,

> "You see he is a pleasant person the moment he leaves here, but at home he is completely changed. Yesterday I asked him about that woman of his in Nairobi and he answered, 'When you heard about her, why didn't you go to your home? You should have gone. I wish you had!'
>
> "And yet," she says, "never a day goes by without his wanting sex. Even after we have quarreled and sat all day without saying a good word to one another, he still makes me do it." She starts crying. "I want him to make love to me as his wife, not just because I'm someone lying next to him in the bed. I find no pleasure in it, not any more." Wiping her eyes on the edge of her skirt, she tosses her head. "Well, from this day onward I refuse to weed his pyrethrum! If he won't let me keep any of the money, let it rot in the fields!" She walks up and down in angry silence. Then she says, "We have always quarreled. Three months after I came here, we started to quarrel. In those days it

was because people said bad things about my character and Ombui believed them and came home to complain to me. He is always gossiping in the villages, hearing things which are untrue. Mary, you're lucky, Nyagama never goes gossiping in other people's homesteads. Sarah, would your husband listen to his relatives?"

At first, when Ombui had rejected her, Trufena had been bitter and at times very depressed. However, now her mood had changed markedly. She emerged from her depression to do battle.

"After your people dissuaded Ombui from burning my clothes, he packed up all my belongings and told me, 'You go from here. Don't let that baby stop you from going!' But I refused to leave. Have I not got two sons? Can he send me away? Let those who have gossiped to him about me stand before me and say what they have to say to me. Then I will tell them such things as they will never forget their whole lives long! Even witches, and I am no witch, do not deserve the kind of abuse I have received!"

In the early weeks of the rift, Trufena had seemed stunned. The central issue at that point had appeared to be Ombui's withdrawal from her and his desire to marry another woman. However, when she realized Ombui was not in a position to marry a second wife, she understood also that she was considerably more powerful than she had hitherto believed, for her position and tenure did not just depend on his whim but, rather, on the strength of her determination to cling to it. And it was clear now how extraordinarily determined she was.

"I will stay until the end of my life, if that is what God intends." "If *God* intends," I repeat. "But what about your *husband's* intentions to divorce you?" "How can he do that? He could try to make me leave by refusing to give me any money; however, as you have seen, there are women who never receive help from their husbands. And yet they stay. I have pyrethrum. It is the dry season now, but the rains will come, and I will pick again and I will sell it in the market, not to the cooperative. I will get only a little for it, but that money I will take and spend as I think fit, and Ombui will have no record of it. I have no friends here, no *omoreri* [babysitter]. But I will fetch water from the river while the children sleep. I can get along without Om-

bui's sister. Once Ombui and I were like crazy people, we
wanted one another so. Even though we quarreled, we loved
each other madly. Now we only quarrel. When I see him, I do
not think that man is *omwancha one* [my lover]! He has become
like any other man, of no interest. But I have two sons, and
whoever suggests I should leave here, damn them!"

This proud, cold girl is almost unrecognizable as the one who
wept in anger and danced euphorically a little while ago. She has
a plan, an emergency plan, and she hastens to put it into effect.
"My mother told me she would help me. Perhaps she can find
me an *omoreri*. Now that Ombui has gone away again, there is no
one to stop me from going to see my mother. At least if I could
find a babysitter before the planting season, I would be less burdened. I could do my work."

And so a few days after Ombui left, I drove Trufena to her home.
According to Gusii custom, she could take only one of her two children
on the trip. She took Johnathan with her, leaving the unweaned child
with a young sister-in-law. Had she taken Jared and left Johnathan
behind, Ombui's family might have believed they had got rid of her,
and she did not want them to have even a momentary sense of triumph.
On the day she left, Trufena wore one of the dresses, a sweater, and
some shoes that Ombui had given her, and Johnathan had on a new
suit, also a present from his father. We stopped along the way for
Trufena to buy some tea and sugar as a gift. Where the money for the
purchase came from I do not know. Trufena had told us repeatedly that
Ombui had gone back to Nairobi without leaving her a cent. However,
lately I had ceased to pay attention to her remarks about money.
Neither she nor Ombui seemed capable of reporting their finances
accurately.

As we drove along, Trufena was very excited. She had not been home
for nearly nine months. She pointed out landmarks along the way,
including a certain bald hill "where Ombui and I used to walk together
when we were young, when he was courting me. Ombui and I were
like crazy people in those days!" she exclaimed, laughing at the memory. The grimmer realities of their current relationship seemed to have
slipped away. Throughout the visit she acted the part of the young
wife, delighted to be briefly in her own home but at the same time
eager to return to her husband's place, where her real commitment lay.
Meanwhile, without actually mentioning all the new clothes, evidence

of her husband's attention and attachment, she made absolutely certain that everyone in her parents' home had an opportunity to see them and absorb their significance

For some months I had been eager to meet Trufena's mother, and as I had expected, our visit shed light on the probable outcome of Trufena's marital difficulties. At the time, I had not yet grasped the strength of Trufena's position. Her recent resolution I saw as whistling in the dark. She might say she had resolved to remain in her husband's home, but given his determination to get rid of her, how long would she cling to that resolve? I believed that in the face of the almost united front Ombui's family presented against her, she would be forced to go to her home. Therefore, I did not doubt that the objective of our trip together was not to secure a babysitter but, rather, to wangle her return to her mother's house, despite her father's opposition.

Trufena's home was as prosperous as she had described it. As we drove up, we were stopped for some minutes by her father's large herd of cattle which blocked the road. Her mother's house was made of stone—almost the only private stone house I saw during my entire stay in Gusiiland. All her siblings were well fed and well dressed, and the older sisters spoke good English and behaved in the competent and gracious way of privileged boarding school girls. Her mother, Abigail, who had not known we were coming, greeted her daughter with surprise and pleasure but also a slight reserve, as if she immediately suspected that Trufena was coming with an unwelcome request of some sort. However, she and her other daughters killed chickens and prepared a feast for us. Eventually, when the time was approaching for us to leave and still no mention had been made of what I assumed had been the reason for our coming in the first place, I said to Trufena, "You haven't told your mother of your troubles," whereupon Trufena recounted the incident in which Ombui had accused her of misusing their money from the pyrethrum cooperative. She told of Ombui's threat to burn the clothes she had bought, but she did not mention any other cause of dissent between them. Her mother responded with a speech in which the message was unambiguous: resolve your differences with your husband and stay where you are.

"Once I tried to persuade you to come home with me, Trufena, and you refused. A little while later you ran back here of your own accord, and I welcomed you. You were pregnant and I told you, 'Many girls have children out of wedlock these days. Is it such a terrible thing? Stay with me until you find another and better husband.' But you left us and ran back to him. You made your decision then. You complain that he does not let you spend the fruits of your labors as you wish, on dresses, but does he not bring you dresses himself? See, you are wearing one now! See what Johnathan wears! Many husbands do not bring their wives anything, ever. They spend their salaries on themselves. As for the pyrethrum money, your father never let your stepmother Paulina [her cowife] and me have that money. He would collect it from the society himself, and we would see nothing of it. Only very recently has he relented. Then, again, if women gossip and take stories about you to your husband, be careful whom you talk to and to whom you show yourself. If you must have a confidante, choose one who lives at a distance. I myself have two friends, but they live far away. If they were to tell my secrets, my neighbors and those who could use those secrets against me are not likely to hear them. And last, Trufena, you are *omochege* [a fighter], a tough girl. You always have been, since you were young. You must learn to obey Ombui, even as Paulina and I have learned to obey your father. We have endured mistreatment. I have learned to live with him, and he doesn't worry me as once he did, for I have been with him many years now. I have eight children. Paulina still allows herself to suffer, but she too in time will learn not to be bothered by him. So you also must learn. As you know, your father is not willing to see you in his homestead."

Trufena listened with head bowed, and when her mother had finished she was silent. Mary whispered to me, "Abigail knows her daughter's character," and indeed it seemed that we had just heard some blunt talk of a kind quite familiar to Trufena. In this same firm tone mother had told daughter to face up to other inevitabilities of childhood and adolescence. As we left Trufena said wistfully, "Why did I ever leave my home?" but she collected her belongings together, bade her family goodbye, and willingly got herself and Johnathan into the car. On the way back she said she was very grateful to me for making the trip possible. She sang to herself as we drove along, and when I dropped her off she appeared unusually content. I had expected that on this visit she would try to persuade her mother to help her leave

Ombui. It was only later I understood that, to the contrary, she sought her mother's support in holding her ground. Her parents did not represent a haven, and Trufena did not want one. She wanted to add their support to her resolve to stick with her rights, regardless of Ombui's wish that she take her children and go. Thus her silence after her mother's speech reflected not dismay or disappointment but relief. She had come on this visit as the wife of a young man with good prospects. In no way, until I forced her to introduce the subject, did she allude to the possibility that her marriage was in jeopardy. Then she heard her mother tell her that basically, if her marriage were endangered, it was up to her to strengthen it, not to leave it.

IV

Following our visit to her mother, the relationship between Trufena and myself or, more accurately, between Trufena and myself by way of Mary, dwindled almost to nothing. I continued to visit her, but I saw her interest in talking to me or in seeking my support speedily diminish. Our conversation was superficial; she talked about the crops, the weather, odd bits of gossip (although Trufena, who led such an isolated life, knew very little gossip). Frequently she was away from home working the land Ombui had rented at a distance, and she made no effort to try to return later in the day in order that we might talk again as we had been accustomed to talking for so many months. Thus I saw her much less frequently than before, and when we did meet her manner was cursory, a determined denial of what we had been through together. It was as if we scarcely knew one another at all.

While her position in her husband's home was in jeopardy, she had needed me and used me, but that period of her dependence on me and her aunt Mary had not produced the kind of enduring bond one might have expected. It is true that she had thanked me whenever I did something for her, whether it was providing her with medical care, or helping to deliver her baby, or driving her to various places. But even if her words reflected genuine gratitude, this had not provided a base upon which a feeling of trust in me could grow. Even though she was much younger than I, she always presented herself as a peer, and her determination to do so was so consistent that I found myself accepting her as such. In the earlier period she seemed to anticipate my visits with pleasure (despite her confessed fear that her neighbors would be jealous of my attentions to her). Her pleasure was in the expectation that I would gratify various needs, emotional or practical. It became evident, however, that a feeling of mutuality, of liking and being liked and finding pleasure in one another was not one of her emotional needs, or not one at any rate that she expected I might gratify. Though I was sometimes very concerned about and even burdened by Trufena, I was never permitted to feel close.

Once her determination to remain with Ombui had won her mother's endorsement, once all other options were closed to her, Trufena settled down, grimly at first, to her life as the mother of sons and protector of their interests within her husband's lineage. Ombui did not come for three more months, and during that period her financial situation was unclear. She claimed he sent money to her only once, and then only a small amount. She may well have lied about this, however. Her regard for truth seemed to become more and more dubious. In several instances it was obvious that her version of events was untrue, and yet she stuck to it. Thus at this time, when she was waiting for Ombui's furlough, her ability to give an accurate account of her finances, never very reliable, became even less so. Although Mary reported that Trufena had received nothing by way of Nyagama, Ombui may well have sent her money orders directly, which she then had cashed herself in town. The children throve; obviously they were well nourished. Johnathan was getting cow's milk regularly, and somehow Trufena was paying for it. I did once see her run off to sell some pyrethrum in the market, at a very low price, because she needed cash immediately and could not afford to wait for the much higher return the cooperative society would give at the end of the financial quarter. So perhaps during these months she was living from hand to mouth, relying upon the cut-rate sale of her only cash crop, and not upon remittances from Ombui at all. I could not know, just as I could not know about many other aspects of her life. She was very secretive. She did her best to obscure the details of her everyday life from the women of her husband's family as well as from me. They watched eagerly for any sign that her resolution to remain where she was not wanted was being eroded.

But this desire of theirs was not gratified. Although she was unable to find an *omoreri* at her own home, she found a succession of marginally competent young girls to take care of the children in return for their food. Two of them, at least, were retarded, and none of them stayed for long, but somehow Trufena was able to find time enough to plant her rented land and thus ensure a food supply for herself and her sons for the coming half year. Once I saw her working with her in-laws, and I concluded she had decided to swallow her pride and, in an effort to secure their favor, had offered to work for them, as a young wife should work for her husband's parents. But I was mistaken. I discovered she had been ordered out to work by Mogaka, and he had literally chased her from her house into his fields, where she had dug angrily among the hostile women. Trufena's way of entrenching herself did not include overtures of peace to her in-laws. If anything, she was more remote and arrogant than ever. Once, when Trufena and Sabera were planting together and their children were playing at the edge of the field, Johnathan knocked down his little cousin, Evans, Sabera's son of the same age. Sabera, Trufena reported, shouted, "Does that child resemble his father or his mother? His mother, of course! He is *omochege* {a fighter}. He has no respect, just as you have no respect, Trufena, either for your husband or for anyone else." Whereupon Trufena flew at Sabera, and the two could have murdered one another with their hoes if Francesca had not pulled them apart. "She loves Sabera. She would not have her favorite harmed," Trufena snorted in disgust. "Every year we have fought, we two. Sabera always says the same thing, that I have no respect for my husband, unlike herself, who is the most perfect wife a man could wish for! What has any of that to do with two little boys pushing one another down?" What difference did it make if those women hated her? She was damned if she cared!

One day we found Trufena in mid-afternoon, washed, oiled, and dressed in her best; her children were also in their best. She was singing to them under the shade tree. Where could she be going, looking so beautiful, we asked, and after many evasions, she told us she had received news of the date when Ombui would get his leave. It was still a month away, and yet she was exultant, for not only was Ombui coming home, but he had written of his intention not to his uncle nor to his cousin Peter but to *her*, surely an indication that he recognized and accepted her intention to stay. She was winning her battle. During the course of the afternoon's conversation, Trufena mentioned that she did not want to get pregnant "at least until next year," from which I concluded that she fully expected still to be Ombui's wife at that time.

As his arrival came closer, she became anxious, although she denied any connection between her anxiety and the confrontation with her husband which was about to take place. She talked blithely of her desire to get further education or of finding some kind of employment. It emerged that her father had obtained for her a junior secondary school certificate. She had of course never taken the examination, since she had eloped with Ombui a few weeks before she had been scheduled to sit for it. Actually, her father had paid another girl to sit for the examination in Trufena's name (a common practice in Kenya) and had offered Trufena this certificate as an inducement to persuade her to leave Ombui soon after her elopement. When she refused to give up her lover, her father, in a fit of pique, had given the certificate to a relative, who had used it to secure employment as a primary school teacher. It was Trufena's fantasy, however, that she could persuade her father to obtain another such certificate. Then she would be able to go to work. It seemed, in effect, she was saying that if she became financially independent she would even be impervious to the loss of Ombui's interest and affection.

Her fears proved groundless. Ombui arrived loaded with gifts, and Trufena announced to us the next day, "I am happy up to here," indicating the top of her head. Ombui too seemed in the very best of spirits, not only because, after only a year, his career was going very well and he was already a "caterer second class" and slated for rapid promotion, but also, no doubt, because his decision not to divorce Trufena had reinstated him in the good graces of his uncle Nyagama, whose esteem Ombui valued above all else. If Nyagama disapproved of the behavior of Ombui the Kenyan, the detribalized, urbanized man, then the self-esteem of Ombui the Gusii, the son of the family of Osoro, suffered. One could speculate that his chances to regain avuncular approval rapidly improved once his infatuation with his girlfriend waned. However, he still had to deal with the hostility, often justified by her behavior, of his female relatives toward Trufena. As long as her behavior continued to be as unacceptable as it had been in the past, Ombui's resolve to keep her as his wife would be constantly assailed by his mother, sisters, and sisters-in-law, not to mention his father and brothers, who, though less outspoken than the women, were no more favorably disposed toward Trufena. In addition, he would still have to deal with Trufena's objectionable behavior toward himself—for example, her refusal to provide hospitality to his friends.

What motivated this behavior on her part? It seems that in many ways Trufena's behavior deviated from acceptable Gusii norms. It might in fact be exactly this which had appealed to Ombui in the first place. She had a self-confidence which might certainly attract a young man as ambitious and as determined to get on in the world as Ombui, while such a young woman, with her capacity to tolerate being alone, might ultimately thrive in the "modern" world he intended to live in. However, at this point, when she was living on the ancestral land, surrounded by her husband's kin, her self-confidence seemed very much like arrogance and her determination to have things her way like obstinacy. Why was it that she consistently antagonized her in-laws; why was she incapable of conciliation when to be conciliatory and respectful would have improved her situation so dramatically?

I believe that her behavior, so apparently shortsighted and self-destructive, must be interpreted in the larger context of her traditional culture. Within living memory, though not perhaps within Trufena's lifetime, it was a common though not universal practice for brides in the midst of the marriage rites to disrupt the ceremony. This behavior, described by Philip Meyer in his paper *Privileged Obstruction of Marriage amongst the Gusii* (1950), centered upon the cattle which the groom was offering as bridewealth. Meyer interprets the bride's refusal to continue the marriage ceremony, until certain demands had been met by her future in-laws, as a manifestation of her ambivalence about complying with her elders' wishes in an arranged marriage. In Trufena's case, of course, hers was a love marriage which initially was satisfying to both parties. At that point Trufena was ambivalent about her in-laws, but those feelings, and the way she displayed them, were within the normal range. She did indeed come from a better home than Ombui, and what is more, the area where the Osoro clan lived was infamous for the number of witches living there. If she did not know this initially, undoubtedly she soon heard about it. Rightly or wrongly, she came rapidly to fear and despise the neighborhood and the people in it. But it was only after Ombui left for the air force that Trufena's recalcitrant behavior became extreme and consequently intolerable to her in-laws. In part this might be because Ombui had left her alone among his relatives, whose malevolence she feared, and thus her self-exclusion was motivated by a desire to withdraw as much as possible from them. In part it might have been due to her awareness that her new pregnancy bound her yet more strongly to his unsavory family. Thus she acted out her reluctance to commit herself to them by being aloof and uncooperative.

But perhaps Trufena's uncooperative behavior was the only way she had of exacting demands from her husband and his family. She had one son already and was shortly to give birth to a second. Their very existence precluded her ever withdrawing definitively from the marriage, and yet the marriage had not yet been properly concluded. No bridewealth had been paid, even though her husband, now permanently employed, was in a position to start paying for her. As long as Ombui had her without payment, Trufena's father would have nothing whatever to do with her. As his favorite child, Trufena found this situation painful. It would appear, therefore, that Trufena's main goal was to secure her own bridewealth payment. Sabera had waited nearly six years, meekly, obediently, respectfully, to be paid for. (This was accomplished only in the last few months of our fieldwork.) But after a year and a half, Trufena was not prepared to wait much longer. She was entrenched, she had a son; but until she had been paid for she would make life unpleasant for everyone. If she suffered very much in the process, she had little to lose and, with luck, a lot to gain.

It would seem that eventually this is how Ombui interpreted her behavior. During his last leave before we left the field, something very important transpired between Ombui and Trufena's parents. Certainly no cattle were given, but some financial agreement must have been concluded, for suddenly Trufena not only visited her mother, this time taking with her all the prescribed gifts—i.e., she was going as a beloved and properly married daughter—but shortly thereafter she announced her father had given her another (purchased) junior secondary school certificate, and she requested my help in securing her a place in a nurses' training program. When I asked her how she had persuaded her father to give her the certificate, she smiled enigmatically and said, "Ombui asked him," presumably following some preliminary payment of bridewealth.

Thereafter, on the few occasions when I saw her, Trufena was composed and remote. She asked me formally when I expected to return.

She thanked me politely but without warmth for the blanket she, like all the mothers in the sample, received from the project. Such a gift seemed superfluous: there were many blankets already airing on her garden hedge. I left her singing a Seventh Day Adventist hymn as she collected her clean dishes from her draining rack. These days she kept the Sabbath scrupulously. She had even attended a four-day-long "retreat" at her church where the select of the neighborhood learned the lessons of progress and prepared themselves for entry into the modern sector.

Now that her traditional place as wife and mother was about to be secured, Trufena could think again about a wider world. Quite soon, once Ombui achieved enough seniority, she could expect to go to live with him on the air force base. Perhaps in the mean time her behavior at his home would improve, become less combative, more conciliatory. She might go more willingly to her *egesangio* and quarrel less with Sabera once they were on the same footing, both with their bridewealth paid. But before too long Trufena would come here only for short periods, accompanying her husband on his leave. If his relatives disliked her for her arrogance and were jealous of her education and good fortune, she would not have to see them often. Like most other progressive people from this district, she would escape and henceforth come only as a visitor, to oversee the construction of a cement house in which she would rarely live, to supervise her laborer during the planting season, to attend the circumcision of her children, and from time to time to pay her respects at the funerals of her husband's dead relatives.

3

Phoebe Bonareri

I

Phoebe Bonareri was a woman of exceptional competence and self-confidence. As I came to know her, I realized that she, more than the other Gusii women I visited, approximated the contemporary ideal of an energetic, resourceful, and respectful young wife. Though she generally welcomed me and allowed me to spend long periods of time in her house, however, she permitted the development of only a rather superficial relationship. There seemed to be no special place for me in her psychological life, perhaps because her needs for support and stimulation were being met elsewhere.

I met Phoebe shortly after we came to the field. It was Christmas time and her husband, Kepha, was home from Nairobi for the holidays. He was a gentle, well-spoken young man who knew good English. He was the youngest of four brothers, two of whom had remained at home at Morongo while the other two, of whom Kepha was one, worked in Nairobi for a government agency. My task at this point was to identify all the pregnant women in our area, and being still naive about the Gusii attitude toward pregnancy, I questioned Phoebe directly about her condition. She laughed gaily and replied, "My son, Evans," indicating the toddler beside her, "is still young."

Kepha, who was listening to us, laughed also. "Can you not tell us about family planning?" he asked. "People here need fewer children, not more." But when I passed through the homestead a few weeks later, Phoebe was wearing a maternity dress. She shrugged impatiently when I reminded her of her earlier ambiguity, "Well, now you have seen for yourself."

Phoebe, a pretty and unusually light-skinned girl of about twenty-three, had eloped with Kepha, her long-time sweetheart, five years before. Kepha had paid bridewealth for her within a year, and she had two little boys, Johnson and Evans. She came from a strict SDA family and had married into a family of equal religious orthodoxy. Her father, an elder of the church in a neighboring locality, had been a big cattle farmer when Phoebe was growing up, though recently all his cows had died, and he was currently in much less prosperous circumstances. He and his wife had eight children, of whom Phoebe was the eldest daughter. She had had seven years of education, had failed her primary school leavers' certificate, and had been repeating her last year of schooling when she eloped with Kepha, who was working at the time as an untrained teacher in another nearby school. They went immediately to live in Nairobi, where Kepha had procured a permanent job through influential relatives.

Phoebe had had one child and was pregnant with the second when she eventually came back to Morongo to supervise the cultivation of her husband's land and also the land of her mother-in-law, Kwamboka. For some reason, never entirely clear to me, Kwamboka was unable to do any farm work herself. Local people said she was *richara* (feebleminded), but her conversation seemed appropriate enough, and feebleminded-ness would not necessarily prevent anyone from doing farm work. In former years the property of all four brothers had been cultivated in common by their wives and laborers. But more recently they had decided to go their separate ways and farm independently. Their father, Chweya, who had been dead many years, had had three wives, of whom Kwamboka was the youngest and the darling of his old age. At some point Kwamboka and her children had been converted to Christianity; specifically, they had become Seventh Day Adventists. While the sons of Chweya's other two wives remained non-Christian or became nominal Catholics and were apathetic about education, Kwamboka's sons were among the most progressive men in the community. While their half brothers, several of them notorious drunkards, lived close by in traditional houses, Kwamboka's sons built cement houses of European design, with large windows and plentiful bedrooms, and stores. All had outside incomes. One owned a store, one was a schoolteacher, two worked for the government, and none of them, at any rate officially, touched alcohol.

When I first knew Phoebe, she was still living in the small, neat house which had been built originally as the *esaiga* (boys' house) of her husband and brothers-in-law, but the ground was already cleared and measured for her new cement house, the construction of which would begin shortly. Above her house, a hundred yards away, lived her mother-in-law, a large, slow, but congenial woman, and at an equal distance to one side lived her sister-in-law Dorothy, mother of ten children. Dorothy's husband also worked in Nairobi, while she toiled from morning to night with total single-mindedness. Although in her mid-forties, she was very slim and energetic, and as she passed at noon on her way between the two farms her husband owned and required her to take care of, Dorothy looked fifteen years younger than her actual age. She was always so busy that she had little time to spend socializing with Phoebe, even though they lived so close to one another.

I selected Phoebe for my study because she seemed representative of the more progressive element in the community. There was an air of self-confidence about her which was unusual in one so young. She appeared quite unimpressed by me. Though friendly enough, she was largely uninterested in whether I came to see her or not. Since we had not been long in the field when I first met her, I was willing to entertain the possibility that her apparent casualness toward me was common, if defensive, behavior in a young person toward someone she was still sizing up. My hope was that over time Phoebe would become less guarded, and indeed this was the case, but I doubt that I ever acquired special meaning for her. I continued to visit her, however, for a period of eighteen months, though with less frequency than some other women in my study.

I felt that it was important to have as complete a picture as possible of the behavior patterns of a woman who, within the demands and constraints of her culture and environment, functioned very well. Hers was a situation potentially full of familiar hazards: her husband was gone, her children were small, she was forced into close proximity with her mother-in-law, she had to make daily decisions about the management of her farm and her laborers. Many women much older than Phoebe were in a state of perpetual turmoil in response to such pressures. But Phoebe, though she sometimes admitted to experiencing stress in certain specific situations, always had a clear sense of her goals and how to accomplish them. She was an unusually mature young woman who, for example, while not above resorting to magical thinking, seemed to do so but rarely. Of course she was a product of her culture, but within its confines she was more flexible than most, less afraid of malevolence, freer to assert herself when self-assertion was called for. She was a reflective person who enjoyed, when she had the time, educating me about her world. I felt, therefore, that my contacts with her were valuable, and long after I had recognized that the chances of her developing an especially meaningful relationship with me were remote, I continued to visit her.

II

I began originally by explaining to Phoebe and her husband that I wanted to learn about how Gusii people brought up their children, and I wondered if I might spend time with Phoebe, watching her with her children and talking to her. Kepha seemed quite pleased and agreed to the arrangement. Then he went off to Nairobi for five months. Phoebe, however, who was in the eighth month of pregnancy, seemed less pleased. Her *omoreri*, her youngest sister, was at school a large part of the day, so that at hours when I saw Phoebe she was burdened with her children, Evans, the younger one, especially. He trailed after her, and the more he whined, the less patience she had for him. It was the planting season, but because Phoebe had no babysitter during the morning and early afternoon, she had to stay at home instead of going to the fields to work herself and to supervise her laborer. This circumstance irritated her, and little Evans seemed to have to bear the brunt of his mother's irritation.

One day he had an abscess behind his ear, and Phoebe, who had doubtlessly been wondering what useful purpose I could possibly be performing as I sat idly in her yard while she dashed about trying to accomplish her chores with a small child tripping her at every turn, said brusquely, "Can't *you* do something for him?" So I went off to find a doctor, who sent a message that Phoebe should bring the boy up to the clinic right away. On hearing this Phoebe retorted, "I can't go now. I'm doing the washing. I'll go when I'm finished." At another session she demanded to know why the clinic only operated on Thursdays. "It should be open every day," she said. I wanted to point out that before our arrival there had been no clinic at all and that its being open even one day a week was a great improvement, but I refrained from saying this.

Phoebe was in a generally bad humor at that period. She was tired and cross, and she did not hide her impatience with me. Once when I came by myself she said, "I don't understand what you're saying. You should bring someone to translate." Even though she knew Swahili well, from having lived several years in Nairobi, and certainly she had learned English at school, she was not going to speak either language for my sake. Nor was she prepared to waste a moment while I struggled to make myself understood. She seemed not the slightest bit impressed that I attempted to speak her language, though I doubt she had even heard a European try to do so before. After a while she softened, however, began to speak more slowly, and even took a little time—provided there was a job to be done somewhere in my immediate vicinity—to teach me the vocabulary of turkey farming, for she and her sister-in-law Dorothy raised turkeys for sale to Nairobi hotels. But up until the time when she gave birth, Phoebe seemed preoccupied and irritable.

As I was discovering, Gusii women experienced the later stages of pregnancy with profound ambivalence. Indeed the younger women often expressed their resentment quite explicitly. They went into a sort of physical and psychological collapse in which they demanded to be taken care of. If they were fortunate in their relationship with their mothers-in-law, these dependency wishes could be fulfilled in large part. If they were unlucky, then they would complain to anyone willing to listen, in the marketplace or on the road. But Phoebe resolutely refused to complain, even though it was obvious from her cold and touchy manner that she felt burdened, especially by her children. I wondered whether this was her usual mothering style or whether she was short-tempered mainly because of her trying physical condition. Dorothy was too busy with her own work to help Phoebe, and the old lady Kwamboka was herself a dependent character and not about to take care of her daughter-in-law. Since, as Phoebe snapped at me one day, her husband had gone to Nairobi to earn money so they could eat, it was useless to miss him. She had no option other than to do herself whatever work had to be done.

But eventually her day came, and Phoebe gave birth at home to a daughter, whom she named Sally Mokeira. She was delighted to have a girl child and for a day or two seemed transformed by happiness. Wearing her maternity dress, for her figure was not yet observably any different from before the birth, she swept about her yard entertaining the women who had come to greet the new baby.

> Phoebe hands me Mokeira, her eyes shining. Immediately Evans rushes over and pulls frantically on the shawl in which the baby is wrapped. "He's afraid you're going to steal his sister," Phoebe laughs. (This is what Gusii people always say when the child who has just been replaced tries to prevent a stranger from greeting the new baby. That the two-year-old might have another motivation for interfering, for example, jealousy that the baby is receiving all the attention, is unacceptable.) She squats by the fire in the kitchen to prepare food for us, a task which a mother-in-law might be expected to perform for a woman who had just given birth, but Kwamboka is waiting for her meal, not helping to prepare it. Evans leans on Phoebe's lap, gazing up into her face. From time to time she whispers to him, and he smiles.

Suddenly she could allow her child to be dependent in a way she had found profoundly annoying while she was pregnant. Indeed, immediately after giving birth, Phoebe was a changed person. She was as task oriented as ever, and yet her spirit was light: she laughed and called greetings across the hill side to her neighbors. Johnson, aged four and a half, was already quite self-sufficient, and neither before nor after Mokeira was born did I see him staying close to his mother unless he was waiting for her to prepare food for him. He was off playing in the meadow with his cousins almost all the time. But Evans was bound more closely to his mother. Although she had no time nor, perhaps, any inclination to play with him as her husband played with his sons when he was home, nevertheless, as Phoebe did her chores, Evans trotted about after her, chatting away. He amused his mother, and frequently I heard them laughing together. Though I often noticed Gusii women withdraw from their youngest children during the last phase of their pregnancy, I rarely saw the kind of rapprochement which took place between Phoebe and Evans after Mokeira's birth.

Three weeks after her delivery Phoebe was slim again, like a young girl. Kepha had not yet come home because, as she told me, "If a husband comes to greet his child, he would want to taste of the child's mother, and this he cannot do until a month has passed." Kepha had, however, sent a complete wardrobe for his daughter, who was light skinned like Phoebe and promised to be as pretty. Phoebe handled Mokeira with pleasure, but it seemed to be pleasure of a rather impersonal sort. This baby was hers, of course, but a child like any other. Before the birth she had expressed the desire to have a daughter, but now that her wish had been granted, could it be that she was too constrained by her fear of provoking jealousy to display her joy? It is true that she and Mary had had long discussions concerning Mary's inability to bear more children. Thus she might indeed have been inhibited in front of us from truly showing how she felt.

As I came to realize, however, understatement was Phoebe's style. She was a thoroughly practical person, happiest when she was very busy, completing one task after another. Her time with Mokeira was limited. There were always a dozen matters waiting for her attention. If Mokeira was content, then Phoebe was free to run out into the meadow to secure the cow's tether or to wash a heap of dirty clothes. One sensed in her a compulsion for order which scarcely ever allowed her to be still. When it was raining and there was literally no single other chore to be tackled in the house, then she would work on an elaborate weaving project, the frame of which she kept nailed to the living room wall. She had learned how to make this sort of decorative hanging from a handicrafts instructor in her church group. But even working on this, her "leisure" activity, required long hours of standing. It was scarcely relaxing physically. But Phoebe had learned young that the just demonstrate their faith by good work. There is a time—rather precisely demarcated—and a specific place for everything.

One day we were all shelling beans into a big bowl in the yard. Since Phoebe herself never sat idle, we felt constrained to follow her example and keep our fingers busy. By this time Mokeira was seven weeks old, and Mary teased Phoebe that when Kepha finally came he would be in such a hurry he would not bother greeting the baby. He would want to make love to Phoebe first.

> Phoebe laughs and shakes her head. "In the daytime? I'd never let him do such a thing. He would have to wait until nightfall." Then she and Mary agree on how much they fear and resist having intercourse with their husbands in the daytime. "I have only consented twice since I was married. Once Kepha took me to a hotel in town. You pay five shillings for a room for an hour. The other time was here at home, in the morning. We shut the door and went into the bedroom and within two minutes Dorothy came knocking at the door, asking for flour. At least that is what she said she wanted. In fact she knew, when she found the door shut, what we must be doing and so she decided to interrupt us." Mary agrees, "Everyone would know what we were doing if they saw the door closed. It would be a dreadful thing for them to know." I try to find out what is so dreadful about it. "A man comes home on leave. He hasn't seen his wife for months. If his neighbors guess he is sleeping with his wife at midday, what would their reaction be? Would they be jealous?" "Perhaps. Then they might bewitch you or maybe they would simply gossip about you. In town," Phoebe says, "no one cares what you do. But in the countryside women [bw'amasikane] don't do it. Such behavior is for unmarried girls and for *abatari* [prostitutes]." Then Mary tells a story about a cousin of hers, a wealthy man who took a divorced woman as his second wife. "They would go to bed together during his lunch hour. They even had intercourse in his car, but in the end my cousin threw her out, without a cent, her dress torn. He sent her out into the rain and the dark." "Yes," Phoebe nods, "that kind of woman always comes to a bad end."

In the ninth session, when the harvest was still several weeks away and most people in the highlands were hungry when they went to bed at night, Phoebe reported a dream in which she visited her home and her mother gave her a basket of maize to bring back with her to Morongo.

> "The load seemed so real that when I awoke I was surprised to feel the weight of it vanish. Then I felt very sad." She says that these days her supplies of maize are finished and she must buy it from the traders in the market. "I wish I had my own maize,

but my store was empty two months ago." Currently maize is selling at twenty shillings a tin, and a tin lasts a week if she is lucky. But I don't think it is the cost which worries her so much as her failure to be productive enough to ensure her self-sufficiency. "Why I should dream of going to my mother for maize, I don't know, because my parents are buying maize themselves these days. They raise cattle and grow pyrethrum. They plant very little maize, and so they always have to buy, every hungry season."

Despite the reality that her parents never had maize enough for themselves, let alone for their married daughters, unconsciously Phoebe longed to be able to take advantage of the traditional Gusii practice that allows a woman in hard times to take grain from her mother's granary without having to seek permission. As it was, she was living far from home, next to her sister-in-law Dorothy, who already had harvested a little maize (for roasting, not drying and grinding into flour). But Dorothy would never offer to share what she had with Phoebe. Phoebe would have to wait another month until she could harvest her own maize. A woman's married home was not like her original home, where whatever her mother had was hers. Each married woman had her own plot, and sometimes she might offer another woman something of hers, but if she chose not to, then there was nothing anyone could do.

Phoebe talks wistfully of her home. "I have not been there since I knew I was pregnant with Mokeira. I have *chinsoni* for my father. Since Mokeira was born my mother has come to greet me, but my father has not come. He still has *chinsoni*. Once, when I was a little girl, I was his favorite, but as my younger sisters were born he came to love them more, so that by the time I was big and ready to be married I was no longer close to him, that is, he did not talk to me often, though he was very strict and watched me closely to see I did not get into trouble with boys. I still miss him. I doubt he'll see Mokeira until she is quite a big girl because he'll never come here to see me. He used to pass this way to Kisii, but then the other, more direct way was improved, and so he doesn't come this way any more. He'd never come here specially. The last time he came, Evans was a baby. My mother doesn't come here often either. She usually sends my sister Naomi, who is my *omoreri* now. I miss my mother a lot." Phoebe smiles wryly. "I've never in my life got maize from home. Sometimes Naomi has brought beans or potatoes, but maize, never."

The staple food she either had to grow or buy for herself now. She was a big person, a married woman with three children. She had no business expecting help from her parents.

"It is a bad habit, getting food from home. You should provide enough for your needs yourself. But," she excuses herself for her wish, "sometimes Getutu, where my home is, gets better rains than we do here in Nyaribari, and so their crops do better than ours." She pauses for a moment, fingering a bean pod. "After I married, I was homesick for a year. We went almost directly to Nairobi, Kepha and I. I didn't have a chance to get used to this place. We used to come here for holidays, just a few days at a time, but it was almost three years before I came back here to live. By then I was no stranger. My mother-in-law and sisters-in-law made me welcome, but they are not the same as my own mother and sisters. That would be impossible. It took me time to get used to living here. There was so much work to be done."

Indeed, Phoebe's work increased every year as Kepha became more prosperous. First he bought one piece of land, then he rented another. Now he wanted to build himself an elaborate house. Phoebe was waiting for him to come not only to greet Mokeira but to start the construction of the house. Then one day we read in the newspaper that a cousin, Daniel Ogoro, with whom Kepha had been sharing a flat in Nairobi, had been criminally indicted. The charge was a serious one, but perhaps only the tip of the iceberg. At Morongo the gossips said that what was really at issue was a bitter struggle between two branches of a lineage, in which case Kepha too might be implicated. The date on which Phoebe expected Kepha home came and went. She heard he had been detained in Nairobi for questioning by the police. One day we found Phoebe sitting under the eaves. For once she was not working, just worrying. She told us what she knew about the background of the case and its political and familial ramifications. It seemed that the accused man was the junior partner in an extortion racket with a powerful member of his lineage. The current case was a trumped-up charge brought against Daniel Ogoro by this influential relative when he discovered Ogoro was double-crossing him and taking more than his fair share of their "business." Everyone was asking whether or not Kepha was involved in the extortion business also. He had always been close to Ogoro.

"I've told you all I know," Phoebe says. "Men do not tell their wives their secrets in case, if they should fight, their wives would then go telling those secrets to their husbands' enemies."

Later my assistant wondered aloud how Kepha became prosperous so quickly. He had a clerk's job in Nairobi, living was expensive there and he could not earn much, and yet he had been able to buy land and now planned to build a house which could not cost less than 20,000 shillings. Could one do all that on a clerk's salary? Did Phoebe know the answer, or was it that, as she told us, her husband did not share his secrets with her: he bought land and she was thankful and went quickly to cultivate it without questioning where he got the money for the purchase. The days dragged on, and Kepha did not come home. Phoebe heard from her brother-in-law Isaac in Nairobi that Kepha had been taken by the police to make a statement. Isaac reported that though Kepha had not been jailed, perhaps he was still under suspicion. One day we found Kwamboka, a stout woman with a large face and wide arms, slouched miserably on a pile of lumber which was to have gone into Kepha's grand house. When she saw us, she dragged herself to her feet and went away, leaving us alone with Phoebe. Phoebe, who had been looking as wretched as her mother-in-law when we first walked in, suddenly tossed her head and smiled.

"Life is like this," she says, "sometimes good and sometimes bad." She admits that she isn't sleeping well at night these days. "I stay awake with worry," but in the daytime, tired or not, she must be as active as ever. "There's work to be done. The children are sick; they cry at night and keep me up, but shall I not work when morning comes?"

Whatever was happening to her husband in Nairobi could not be allowed to interfere with the accomplishment of her tasks at home. Her mother-in-law moped about the homestead asking piteously for comfort. One of Phoebe's brothers-in-law spent hours in her house talking to her, but while Phoebe listened respectfully to these two, she darted about washing, sweeping, giving orders to her laborer.

Eventually the Ogoro case went to court, and there was no mention of Kepha playing any role at all. Ogoro alone was charged, convicted, and sentenced, and Kepha was free to come at last for his much delayed leave. When he came he evidently had money in his pocket, for during the three weeks he was at home he erected the main structural beams and supports of the house and hired a contractor to do the wall-building work. When he returned to Nairobi, he left Phoebe her usual energetic, smoothly operating self. Whatever anxiety she had suffered during the weeks of waiting to hear whether or not Kepha was implicated with Ogoro had vanished. Meanwhile Ogoro was indicted for another crime, and again his story was all over the newspapers. This time Phoebe could laugh. "He is my husband's relative, not mine. I don't know him well at all." She was immersed in the construction of the house, in worrying now about the contractor and why he did not show up for days on end. She discussed intensely with Mary the rising price of cement. She was indignant about costs, but with the privileged assurance of someone who knew that whatever the cost, she would not have to do without. The only time I saw her truly anxious, thrown off her stride, was on one occasion when Mokeira had an ear infection. Coming into the compound one day, I heard the baby screaming in her mother's arms. Phoebe literally wept as she begged me to help her. Then later, when Mokeira had been medicated and was getting better, Phoebe expressed her thanks repeatedly.

It was difficult to find Phoebe at home. In the morning she was in the fields. She came back late for lunch, and then, as soon as the dishes were washed, she changed into one of her pretty mini-dresses ("All my dresses are like this," she says; "I have only modern dresses") to go to the market to visit her sister-in-law, who served behind the counter of her husband's shop. Phoebe had a schedule, and I could rarely persuade her to deviate from it for even half an hour. "Come tomorrow at noon," she would tell me, and then at noon the following day she would still be in the fields. There was no point in her changing her plans in order to waste time talking to me.

But one morning we found her in her yard cutting kernels off corn cobs. She was sitting on the ground, and beside her on a chair was a middle-aged man, Obongo, dressed in an old raincoat and a black hat. He looked rather self-important. Phoebe did not introduce him, and it was only after much talk that we realized this man was neither her husband's uncle nor any senior relative to whom she must give respect but her laborer, who had come to quarrel with her over the amount of money he received in payment for last month's work. It seemed he had just been fined for growing *enyasore* (marijuana) and was completely broke. Of course, he said, it was not his but his brother's *enyasore,* but his brother was a cripple, so the police let him off and arrested Obongo instead. He was jailed for two days and had to bribe his way out. Now he had come to Phoebe, in the middle of the month, to demand some back pay. He argued that Phoebe had not paid him for three days when he was attending a funeral. One had to go to funerals of clansmen, especially in this particular case, where the dead man was killed by an act of God. The man died under special circumstances, Obongo said. How could anyone stay away from the funeral? It was his business to go each day, and it was wrong of Phoebe to dock his pay. The argument went on for a long time.

Phoebe won't budge. "You never even sent word to say you weren't coming. You just didn't appear. And anyway, what kind of a person comes asking for his salary in the middle of the month, as it is now? The custom is to wait until the end of the month, is it not? Besides, I haven't any money; my husband hasn't sent me any." "Oh, yes, he did," says Obongo. "He sent 400 shillings." Phoebe doesn't deny this, though one must wonder how Obongo got this information, if it is correct. "You must give me sixty shillings." "Sixty shillings for three days' work you didn't do. I'll give you thirty-five shillings, and then you can do some weeding for me, and I'll pay you for that at the end of the month." "Even sixty shillings isn't enough," Obongo sputters. "You'd better take that baby of yours to the fields, put her under the hedge, and do your own weeding. You have nothing else to do. You just sit at home in the house. Take your child, go and weed." Neither looks at the other. From time to time Obongo's face twists in scorn, and Phoebe looks a little overheated, but it seems their argument is something of a ritual. They don't expect it to be concluded quickly. Phoebe, who isn't even half Obongo's age, refuses to give ground, though Obongo is very persistent.

We left before anything was resolved, but a few days later Phoebe said, "He left without getting anything from me. Anyway, I really had nothing to give him." "And if you *had* had money, what would you

have done?" Phoebe shrugged, "Perhaps I would have given him
something." Her husband would not be back until Christmas, but
Phoebe was well able to take care of herself. She gave respect when
respect was due to an older man (*omogaaka*), but she was not about to
allow him, despite his age and sex, to bully her or take advantage of
her. She did not say, as do so many women as a last resort, "I must ask
my husband," or brother-in-law, or whoever the most senior male
might be. She used her own authority to refuse him. She had been
given responsibility for everything at home, including how and when
to dispense money. She was sent back from Nairobi for this purpose,
"and the work was hard," as she told us. But after three years she was a
veteran of arguments in which she knew, without raising her voice, and
while giving all due respect, how to stand her ground.

With the approach of the circumcision season, several of Phoebe's
nieces and nephews returned from Nairobi for their initiation. All of
them would be circumcised in the hospital, Phoebe said. For some
years past boys had been circumcised by medical practitioners under a
local anesthetic in Kisii hospital. Girls had continued to be initiated at
home, because there was as yet no nurse who was offering to perform a
secularized cliterodectomy. This year, however, there was a woman
offering such a service for the first time, and Phoebe's niece would go to
the hospital along with her cousins. Then the children would return by
car, but a mile or two away from home they would get out and walk the
last part of the journey, so that the women of the family could taunt
them and sing all the traditional songs. At home the children's parents
would entertain their guests with meat, *obokema,* and sodas. As Seventh
Day Adventists they could not provide beer.

Thus the occasion, in its modernized form, would be very different
from the traditional ceremony. At most the children would be in
seclusion for ten days—rather than the traditional month—and then
they would emerge, without any special ritual, and return to Nairobi
for Christmas. Their parents still considered circumcision an essential
rite of passage, but they would tolerate only a much abridged form. As
for Phoebe, her ideas on the subject seemed rather hazy. Of course at
her own circumcision no beer was drunk, and she only went to
circumcision ceremonies held by SDA families, where sometimes beer
was provided for drinking relatives, but more often sodas were the only
beverage. Would she want Mokeira to be circumcised in the hospital?

"Who knows? By then things may have changed altogether," she replied, and I gathered she meant that in eight or nine years' time Gusii people, or Gusii people of backgrounds similar to her own, might have given up circumcision completely. On only one aspect did she have a definite opinion: a child should be brought home for circumcision. If the initiation were performed elsewhere, at the father's place of work, for example, then people at home would not be convinced that it really took place. They had to be present to believe it. In recalling her own experience, Phoebe said it hurt dreadfully, and I gathered that she wholeheartedly endorsed the modern practice in which girls are now circumcised with a razor rather than a harvesting knife, as was traditional, and only small parts of the genitalia are removed.

> "Long ago old mothers said you had been well circumcised
> only if you were left with a hole and nothing at all around it.
> But these days they just nick the ends, and the *chinsama* [labia
> minora] grow again, for the children are young; their bodies
> haven't finished growing."

I had the impression that if people should cease circumcising their daughters altogether and begin circumcising their sons in infancy, Phoebe might welcome the change. Maturity was gained not by enduring a rite of passage at the age of eight but by shouldering the responsibilities of adulthood. Traditionally at circumcision a girl would be instructed by her seniors in the lore of her people, but Phoebe frequently said of herself, "I don't know the customs of the Abagusii. Nobody taught me." Or, "You must cut the skin of a pumpkin in a special way when you give it away as a present, but I don't know why you do this or what the cuts signify." Circumcision for her had been a painful experience. She conceded that it was an important experience also but had difficulty in defining in what way it was important, except that the ordeal was physically traumatic. It seemed that whatever instruction she received in the customs and secrets of the tribe was superficial and quickly forgotten. Her knowledge of her own traditional culture was patchy, perhaps because she was still a young woman who had not yet had to act as *omokorerani* (guide) in any ritual (and until someone had the responsibility of teaching others how to do something, she often did not really know herself). On the other hand, her ignorance might have been a more pervasive reflection of the particular family she grew up in, which, as I learned for myself when I visited her parents, differed drastically in important ways from the great majority of Gusii families.

In the days before the circumcision ceremonies started, a sister-in-law came to collect Phoebe's own little sister Naomi, who had been helping her with Mokeira. She was to be taken to her home for her initiation. Naomi was about ten years old. Her father had delayed her circumcision for as long as he decently could, but now her turn had come. Naomi seemed more excited than apprehensive. We were all in the house, since the sun at noon was so strong, discussing the upcoming ceremonies. Phoebe's sister-in-law asked what it was like where I came from, how were we circumcised? When I explained that I had never been circumcised at all, and my son was circumcised at the age of three days, this woman was surprised, but Phoebe, on the other hand, was not. Unlike our much more highly educated assistants, she was apparently aware that Europeans do not perform cliterodectomy. Her sophistication must have come from having lived in Nairobi among people of other tribes, some of whom formerly practiced female circumcision but had more recently largely abandoned it.

The conversation shifted to a discussion of the ways in which white people differed from Africans. Phoebe said that when she was a child European agricultural officers used to come to see her father about his crops and his cattle. Though she never spoke to them, she would stare at them, and she was impressed by how clean they were. Gusii people were usually muddy and sweaty. She realized that Europeans were cleaner only because they had piped water in their houses and had the chance to wash whenever they liked.

> But Gusii people, many of whom want very much to be clean, have to haul their water long distances. "I can't afford to wash as often as I would like." She believes also that Europeans treat their children differently. "In what way?" I ask, expecting her to mention something of an interactional nature. "They give them a varied diet, many different kinds of good food." Once at the hospital she was instructed how to cook meat and potatoes. "They tasted delicious, but I've never tried to do that at home. I haven't got enough cooking pots." "Would it really take so many? You have a lot of *sufurias* [cooking pots]. I've seen them,"

I tell her, but she shrugs and says nothing. Perhaps the new method is too much trouble, too time consuming for a woman who has so many chores to get through each day. "Europeans are different from us in yet another way," she says. "They quarrel as we do, but they don't get divorced." She is surprised when I tell her divorce is very common and on the increase in the Western world. But then she nods. "I think I understand why women in America can leave their husbands! It is because they are all educated, and they can work in an office or in a school if they want to. They don't have to depend on any man. In America married women can earn money and spend it as they wish, without worrying about what their husbands want. If a woman has her own money," she reiterates wistfully, "then *she* can make the decisions," without, presumably, being accountable to her husband, unlike Phoebe, who is no more than a cashier. Kepha gives her instructions about how she should spend every shilling he sends to her; if on occasion she exercises her own discretion, she will worry about how he'll react when she tells him what she has done.

"You Europeans are lucky. It is easier for you. You aren't suspicious of one another as we are." "What do you mean, suspicious? Of course we are suspicious." "No, I mean you aren't thinking all the time that someone close to you is be-witching you. You don't have *endamwamu* [jealousy] as we have it. *Endamwamu* means that you are so angry with someone that you wish that person were dead." "We have jealousy too." "No, no, not as we have it. You have it only as our children have it. You are angry, you envy your brother or your neighbor, but you do not wish that he should die. In your country there is no *endamwamu* as we know it, and therefore you have no witchcraft. Among the Gusii, children grow up free of it but then it seizes them later, when they are big people. A young man will begin to feel it when he wants to marry but his father or his brothers deny him cattle, though they have cattle enough to give him if they chose to do so. A woman starts when she marries and is in her new house. Then she will see others, her sisters-in-law, eating better than she does and having better clothes. She'll start feeling jealous, and though she may not go so far as to become a witch herself, she'll go to witches to buy *obosaro* [medicine] to use against those women. All adult Gusii feel *endamwamu* to some degree. It is not possible to escape it. But it depends what you do with those thoughts. Some can control them, others cannot."

"Is everyone afraid of jealousy, even those who are faithful Christians?"

"Yes, everyone. There is no one in Gusiiland who is not afraid. Those progressive farmers who go to the Sabbath and have permanent houses and cars and many cattle, whose children go to the university and even to your country later, they are not free from fear. They don't show it, of course. They don't stint in their attempts to get richer, but every one of them has medicine to protect himself against witchcraft. They buy it secretly and hide it in their houses, and outside too. Those Christians, though some of them may renounce sacrifices, though they may even in their hearts cease to believe in the ancestor spirits, nevertheless they haven't given up believing in witchcraft. Some of the best-known Seventh Day Adventists are witches. They come to the Sabbath and sing those songs, and yet the rest of the week they are practicing *oborogi* [witchcraft]. The pastor in our church tells us not to believe in witchcraft, but no one believes him, and he doesn't even believe himself!"

Phoebe's sister-in-law was nodding vigorously. "It is true, it is as you say."

"How is it," I ask, "that a woman becomes a witch?"

"Sometimes you come from a family of witches. You learn those things at your home, and when you are married you may go to a place where you are the only one. But you work by yourself and slowly you persuade others to join you. You get your *egesangio* [group]. Or maybe you come as a good person to your married home and find others there are witches. Then they will try to make you join them. But in order to join, first you must give them a child. You'll see, all witches have lost children. At my home there was a woman who had many daughters but only one son, a bright boy who was in form III in the secondary school. Her mother-in-law and sister-in-law urged her to join them. They told her, 'You must give us your son, a daughter won't do!' In the end the woman agreed, and when the boy came for vacation he had an ear infection, and though they took him to the mission hospital, the doctors could do nothing for him. He died so that his mother could be in *egesangio* with the other women of her husband's homestead."

Phoebe had been talking in front of her own brother's wife, not her husband's brother's wife. She could speak freely with a woman from her own home, but I doubt she would have talked in this way before Dorothy or her sister-in-law Phyllis, neither of whom, incidentally, I had seen inside Phoebe's house. Sometimes I saw Dorothy in the meadow or the yard, and I often saw Phoebe talking with Phyllis at her shop, a neutral place, but never at home. Once these women had worked together in the fields, they had had *egesangio;* but a year or two back they gave it up. The strain of cooperation had shown. Though Phoebe never even hinted to me that either of these women was a witch, I imagine they split up and took to working alone or with hired labor because each knew her own threshold. "All Gusii have *endamwamu. It depends on what you do with it. Some control it, some cannot." Later Phoebe told me, "I used to be very close to Dorothy. Now we are not so close." Phoebe explained the decline in their friendship by the fact that Dorothy was always running off to dig her distant piece of land. They no longer had the chance to see one another as much as they had done formerly. That was the ostensible excuse, but then later still, when Phoebe was toiling alone on the construction of her house, she whispered, "Dorothy won't help me. She is jealous, I think." And so they learned to keep their distance. The price each paid for protecting herself against the force of her own feelings was isolation. I began to suspect that one very important reason why Phoebe worked so hard was to escape from loneliness. If she were busy all the time, she would not notice that her sisters-in-law didn't come to visit her. She would not miss the companionship of adult women quite so much.

It was a month before I had a chance to see Phoebe again, and by then the children of this homestead who were circumcised had all gone back to Nairobi. (Isaac's two sons were the only boys from Morongo to be circumcised in the hospital, but at the last moment the little girl was put under the knife not of a registered nurse but of a woman whom the Seventh Day Adventist elders of the area had appointed as circumcisor for the girls of that church. This woman, by all accounts, was old and profoundly unproficient. People doubted that she would be reappointed the following season.) We found ourselves talking about *ogochoberwa* (taking girls by stealth), which traditionally occurred while girls were recuperating after circumcision, and from there we went on to the sexual behavior of Gusii children in general. Phoebe laughed at her own memories.

"The preacher tells you not to, but you don't listen. All
children play at sex when they are young. Saint Paul tells you,
'Better to marry than burn,' and I think that applies to children
too. They aren't old enough to marry, but they feel that they
want sex, so let them have it. It does them no harm. Before
circumcision children have little sense. They play sex with their
half brothers and sisters, but by the age of seven they should
know not to, that they should go to neighbors. My father
had cattle, and when I was young I used to be sent to herd them
with my brother and my cousins. There were no adults to see
what we did in the bush."

"I never did those things in my life!" Mary exclaims, quite
shocked. "I never had a chance, though. My mother wouldn't let
me herd cows. She kept me at home. My Tommy is at home all
the time, too, after school. It is children who are unsupervised
who do those things."

Phoebe laughs. "Well, if you don't watch them, children will
do what they want. I would have sex three times in a week with
three different boys. Little girls don't know their own minds.
It's not possible for them to have one special boyfriend. They're
always changing. Today you think this boy is handsomer than
the boy you were with yesterday. When you're little you play
with uncircumcised boys. Then once you're bigger, with only
circumcised boys your own age. From twelve to eighteen, your
need is great. You have a great deal of sex, and each time you
feel better. After eighteen or thereabouts you stop, but not
altogether. You're afraid you'll get pregnant. [It seems that girls
of Phoebe's generation reached menarche late, between fifteen
and eighteen years of age, and for a time after onset they were
protected from conception by adolescent sterility. At a point
when they became fertile, they expected to be married and free
to give birth legitimately.] So you daren't continue as you did
before. But you can't stop completely. You have sex once a
month and hope you'll be lucky."

I ask whether parents knew what their daughters were doing
and if they attempted to stop them.

"To start with they know nothing. They don't see you in the
bush."

"But nowadays houses are so close together, there is no bush
left."

"Well, if during the day they see you going into a boy's house [*esaiga*], they don't stop you. They know it's natural." She goes on, "A boy will always begin. He is the one who asks the girl, not the other way round. But he can tell if she is willing. At dusk, if they should meet on the path, he will push the girl down, and if she doesn't resist, then everything is well for him. In the daytime he will bring his friend to his hut and close the door so that it is quite dark inside."

"When Mokeira is a big girl, will you worry about her if she goes with boys?"

Phoebe shakes her head. "Why think about it?"

Today she seemed very content. Thinking back over her girlhood, she said,

"Then I knew nothing. I am happier now than then. Now I know how it is that a woman conceives, in the middle of the month, but I didn't know that when I was younger. Like most ignorant people, I thought you conceived while you were menstruating. If you stayed away from boys at that time, you'd be safe. I enjoy sex more now than I did before I married. I was always afraid of getting pregnant. Even so, I did have sex from time to time because I liked the feeling. I had a boyfriend who was away at a boarding school, so I only had sex in the vacations. I loved him; I thought I'd marry him eventually. My parents suspected I had a boyfriend, but they didn't know for certain because, though I went to his house by day, I never spent the night there; he always escorted me home before dark."

"Why didn't you marry him?"

Phoebe smiles. "It was the arrangement of God. When I first was married to Kepha I used to think of that other boy, but then I forgot him. I love Kepha now."

"Do you miss Kepha when he's gone so long in Nairobi?"

"No, I don't miss him much. Of course," she laughs, "I like sleeping with him better than with Mokeira [who, though she normally sleeps with her mother, is removed to her crib when her father is at home]. After all, he is the one who has the seeds, isn't he, and he should plant them as he wishes, even if they never germinate! I used to fight him when he wanted sex, but I don't any longer."

Phoebe felt free to talk about sexual matters to Mary and myself. She was at ease with us, and yet she never said, as other women in the community said, "Where have you been? I missed you." But she claimed not to miss her husband, either, even though from her own account and from my observations of the two together, and also from what neighbors said about them, they were very compatible. If Kepha came home, if her mother-in-law dropped in to chat, if we came, then Phoebe was pleased. To the degree that her work permitted, she was generous with herself. She enjoyed our company, but it was only her parents whom she admitted missing. Perhaps her extraordinary competence and capacity for self-reliance stemmed from the fact that at one level she was still so closely identified with her parents, especially with her mother, that provided she was continually busy, she did not experience loss or loneliness.

In the new year the construction of the new house began in earnest, and from this time until we left the field Phoebe spent every spare moment working on it. The task of packing mud for the walls into the wooden framework the contractor had built was awesome and was Phoebe's alone. Once that was done, she had to plaster the walls, first with mud, then with clay. Then came the floor. Finally, at some point in the future when Phoebe and Kepha could afford it, the contractor would cement the walls. But for now Phoebe was pleased to talk to us as she worked. One morning the children were playing in and out of the house, and Evans, aged two and three-quarters, was overheard asking his cousin, "What is *embere* [vagina], and what is *emboro* [penis]?" Phoebe laughed; she was embarassed. I told her my own son, who was exactly the same age, used those words when he was angry. Perhaps little children did so everywhere. "What do you do? Do you beat him?" I said I did not. I confessed I actually found it rather funny but agreed that when my older child said "fuck" (*tomana*), I used to get upset. Since coming to Kenya she had stopped saying it. "Children here don't stop," Phoebe laughed; "they just learn not to say it in front of their parents!"

This led to a discussion of what children did when unobserved by adults. I had once asked Phoebe if she had ever heard of male or female homosexuals, and she had denied it, but on this occasion she described what children did when they were herding cows.

> "There is a tree called *omoneke* which has soft leaves. You pull off the leaves, leaving only the stem, and girls push it into one another's vaginas." Mary corroborates this. She says she once saw

two uncircumcised girl cousins doing it. "They would push and push until they were satisfied." They had offered to include her, but she refused.

"You say that boys also play sex together," Phoebe breaks in. "How do they do it?" When I explain she is aghast. "Wouldn't that leave the anus very wide?" She can believe, she says, that children do such things in play, but why should adults ever want to? Again I attempt to explain in terms which might be familiar to Phoebe. She nods slowly. "You say these things were done in secret in your country. Perhaps in Kenya also, and that is why I have never come across grown women loving women like themselves, or men loving other men. But tell me, here in Gusiiland, men are known to have intercourse with animals. Why do they do it? It is *emoma* [a sacrilege]. Such people, if they are caught, must sacrifice."

I say possibly they do it for reasons similar to those involved in homosexual behavior, because of fear of the opposite sex, or a lack of opportunity to find women.

"Well," Phoebe laughs, "I think different things. You know, in Nairobi we lived next door to a Kikuyu woman. I think she was *richara* [feebleminded]. Her husband worked at night, so when he came home in the morning they would sleep together. She cried all day. Then, when her husband went off to work, another man would come, and she'd start crying again. She would cry all night! A young cousin of Kepha's used to eat his meals with us. He hated to hear that woman crying. He would eat his supper and run out. If she'd been a Gusii I would have asked her to have respect, but she was a Kikuyu, and I was afraid she might hit me if I spoke about such a thing. If she disliked sex so much, why did she spend so much time at it?"

"She wasn't crying from pain," Mary giggles, "but from pleasure. I, too, when I first married lived next to a Kipsigis woman who cried all night. Once I said to Nyagama, 'How is it that she cries—yet in the morning she appears quite normal?' Nyagama had respect and he didn't answer, but I understood then that the woman cried from pleasure."

"Well, I'm not that kind at all," Phoebe says emphatically. "When I first married I cried, but it was from fear. Men like to think you are afraid. It makes them more excited. But I've stopped that. Now when I have sex I lie as if I am dead. I make no noise at all."

Phoebe was more explicit about her sexual experiences than any other woman in my study. Though all of them were overtly preoccupied to varying degrees with sexuality (their own and especially their husbands'), sexual matters involved such excitement and anxiety that they found it almost impossible to discuss the mechanics of sex. They would talk about *chinsoni* (shame) and *amasikane* (respect). Their concern with these concepts prevented them from discussing their experiences explicitly. Since they took no responsibility for their own sexual behavior ("It is the man who insists," or "my husband," or before him, "boyfriend"), they were almost incapable of admitting sexual desire, let alone of discussing it aloud. Although Phoebe too contended that boys—or men—initiated sexual contact, she admitted that such overtures were often responded to willingly. "My body felt good," she said of her youthful response. Her sexual experiences were much better integrated into her psychic life than seemed to be true of other women I knew. Sex was not something that just happened to you. It was something you wanted, something you could have or refuse. As a young girl she did not *have* to "lie down" in the bush, she did not *have* to be led into a darkened hut unless she wanted to. As a married woman, pregnant with her third child, she once told me that she disliked having intercourse, and when Kepha approached her when she was in her eighth month, she kicked him away. But once she had recovered from childbirth, sex was agreeable again. Not so agreeable, however, that she could not do without it for long periods, not so agreeable that she was ready to sleep with her husband in the daytime. She had desires, but they should be assuaged in the right place at an appropriate time.

As far as I was able to tell, Phoebe was at ease in talking about these matters to Mary and me. She showed not the slightest trace of shame. However, at the end of the session in which we had been talking, among other things, about homosexuality, I teased her, "What would Dorothy think if she had heard what we were saying?" and Phoebe grinned, "She would laugh so hard she wouldn't be able to attend to her business." In this society laughter often indicates psychological distress. Between sisters-in-law like Phoebe and Dorothy there are few cultural regulations concerning shame and respect, but the anxiety arising from this kind of wide-ranging discussion of sexual matters would be great, and thus women voluntarily invoke rules of avoidance.

I had heard something of Phoebe's home, and I had met a few of her relatives, but I was most eager to meet her parents and see her home for myself. When I raised the subject with her, Phoebe was at first unwilling to agree to a visit. At Christmas time the Nairobi house in which Kepha was living burned, and all his possessions were lost. Thus he brought very little cash with him when he came home, because his money had to go toward replacing clothes and other essentials which he had lost in the fire. Phoebe said she had nothing with which to buy gifts for her mother. "I can't go empty-handed. The price of sugar has risen," she said. "But you have sweet potatoes and maize." "No, I must take sugar. Anyway, I was at home at the New Year. It is too soon for me to be invited again, and I can't go without an invitation." But after some consideration she brightened. "My sister left some clothes here when she went to be circumcised. I could use them as an excuse. I could tell my parents I had come to find out whether or not Naomi is going to come back to live with me here."

So Phoebe chose a day, and we set off with Mokeira and Evans, Johnson having been left at home as a "hostage." Phoebe had sent word that we were coming. She was dressed in all the trappings of the wife of a well-to-do man: patent leather shoes, a "poor boy" sweater, a gored midi-skirt and a blazer, all presents from Nairobi. The children too were in their best clothes. The weather was perfect, and the countryside in the highlands round her parents' home looked bountiful in the morning sun. The farms in that area appeared, without exception, to be models of progressive husbandry. I saw little arable land. Most farmers concentrated on cattle, tea, and pyrethrum. We stopped at a signpost which said, "George Onchari Gesuna, Plot 201, Progressive Farmer," and there beside it stood Phoebe's father, a magnificent figure of a man, wearing a suit, white shirt, and tie.

He shook hands with all of us, including his daughter and Evans (his *chinsoni* did not affect greetings, i.e., he was a "modern" man), and led us into his courtyard. The fences were repaired, the hedges were trimmed, the cattle pen was in perfect condition. The iron-roofed house itself, though built of mud, not cement, was spacious and cool. Beside it was a large kitchen, separate from the main house. The living room resembled a small church or chapel. Beautiful patterns had been worked into the clay while it was still wet. In the middle of the room was a long table, surrounded by ten carved chairs, all with arms.

Phoebe's father told us his home was frequently used for religious retreats, and at such times people would come to stay for several days, sleeping, eating, and holding their meetings in his house. I asked to be shown the farm, which, he told me, was nine acres in extent, a large holding at this time for Kisii District, where plots of two acres were common. So far he had not divided it between his two sons but farmed it all himself. He explained how formerly he had had a sizable herd of European cattle, but both his mother and his wife had been ill, requiring hospitalization at the Seventh Day Adventist mission hospital, and so he had been obliged to sell many head of cattle to pay their bills. His mother was now dead, while his wife was still not very much improved. She suffered from arthritis in her feet. The year before disease had killed his five remaining dairy cows, and he was only just beginning to build up his herd again. However, he also had an acre of tea—the most remunerative crop in the area. "My older children only finished primary school," he said, "but now that I have tea I hope to give all the younger ones a secondary education. Tea pays much better than cattle." Throughout our tour he was courteous, smiling, and very formal. Although we were speaking Ekegusii, not Swahili, the language he must surely have spoken with British government officials in the past, nevertheless this did not set him at ease.

Meanwhile, Phoebe had remained at the house with her mother and two younger married sisters. One of these young women, we learned later, had eloped to become, to her parents' horror, the fourth wife of a clerk in the local tea factory. "Did we bring you up to be the fourth wife of any man?" But they had reasoned with her and browbeaten her in vain. Then we discovered that while their father's vigilance had been sufficient to make the adolescent Phoebe reasonably cautious in her sexual activities, this sister, Ruth, had been less cautious or less lucky. At any rate, she had had a child out of wedlock. ("My father beat her terribly when he discovered she was pregnant," Phoebe told us, "and my mother supported him. But my mother insists on bringing up that little girl herself. She has refused to let her go with Ruth to her married home.") Thus becoming the fourth wife of an employed man (as opposed to an aging illiterate farmer) was about as well as Ruth could do.

Phoebe's mother, a matron in her late forties, was well dressed, and as formal toward me as was her husband. She cooked an enormous meal, which we ate at eleven o'clock in the morning, to the sound of a battery-operated record player which played church music. The food had been blessed in the kitchen, I was told, before it was ever brought to the table.

Throughout the day Phoebe was radiant. I had rarely seen her so at Morongo. Her two sisters, who had also come home as "visitors," i.e., to be waited on, were much more reserved. Phoebe was their parents' favorite. Her mother called her by a pet name, "Little Butterfly," and when she heard this Mary whispered to me, "You see how much they love one another!" Indeed Mary was quite overwhelmed by what she saw and heard in Phoebe's home. She said to me, "Did you see how Phoebe's father shook Phoebe's hand, how he talks to her, eager to hear her opinion? I tell you, he loves her! Those parents are like modern people, one husband, one wife. He helps her—you saw how he poured the water into our glasses at lunch, and how he collected the plates afterwards." All this was so different from her own home where her father, an illiterate alcoholic, had four wives and more children than he bothered to count. She said wistfully to Phoebe, "You were lucky, Phoebe, growing up with such parents who love you and one another." Phoebe's mother happened to overhear, and she retorted laughingly, "Don't you know we don't quarrel in front of visitors!" But clearly both parents were most attached to Phoebe, their eldest daughter, the one who, of the three girls already married, had done best for herself. Kepha was viewed by her parents as an entirely appropriate son-in-law. All three girls had eloped originally, but unlike Kepha, the husbands of the other two were considered less than ideal, one being a polygamist, the other a traditional peasant farmer. Indeed the parents had been disappointed also by their firstborn, their elder son. Though a policeman in Nairobi, he had recently married a second wife and thus been driven from the church.

I came away from this homestead with some inkling of what it must have been like to grow up there, being evaluated by the most exacting standards of godliness. These standards must have been intimidating to a young child. Both parents were admirable in many ways, but I found their demands and expectations, both explicit and implicit, chilling. They reminded me of characters in Victorian fiction. Mary saw only the order and harmony in this family, which contrasted so sharply with her own. She envied Phoebe. But what struck me was the price Phoebe's family paid for achieving that order. The exuberance as well as suffering which was so manifest in Mary's home and in others I knew was absent. But while Phoebe's parents appeared somewhat bland in affect, obviously the children did suffer. Neither of Phoebe's sisters had fulfilled the parents' hopes. They had perhaps acted upon their self-perceptions in marrying badly, thus committing themselves irrevocably to hard lives, while Phoebe, though a success in her parents' terms, was forever burdened, constricted, and driven by their work ethic, for her sense of well-being depended on meeting their standards.

Her parents had been brought up in an entirely traditional society. But when as young adults they became Seventh Day Adventists, their church demanded that they renounce many of the values and beliefs of their culture in order to be born again as Christians. It was expected of them that in their everyday lives they would struggle to approximate alien standards. That they were able to make this giant leap from a traditional lineage-bound life to one in which they became members of a universal community is astonishing and to their credit. But whereas they themselves had undergone the conversion experience and had made the decision to renounce alcohol and polygamy, among other features of traditional life, their children had been born into the church. As was true of the offspring of many Adventist parents, some of these children, as they matured, had not found the moral character, the passivity, or the determination, depending on how one looks at it, to live by the church's precepts. Among her adult siblings Phoebe most closely approximated the Christian ideal. As I watched her over the months she showed herself, for one so young, to be already a competent, level-headed woman. Her compulsive style was highly adaptive: she accomplished a great deal, and she warded off loneliness, and yet not far below the surface of the pragmatic, energetic farm manager, mother, and housewife, "Little Butterfly" was looking over her shoulder, making sure she had the approval of her perfectionistic parents.

A Christian is justified by faith, and his faith is made manifest by his good works. Phoebe's personal interpretation of this concept seemed to be focused upon the accomplishment of tasks; no task, once identified, should be left unattended. There were other aspects to life, admittedly, but they were minor. One needed companionship, but if, as in her case, one's husband was away, one's mother-in-law was a childlike person, and intimacy with one's sisters-in-law was not really desirable, then one got by as best one could. Despite her obvious pleasure in some of our conversations, Phoebe never alluded to having enjoyed them. She made me feel she was doing *me* a favor, that the gain was entirely mine. In the last months, when she was spending every available moment at the interminable task of smearing her new house ("This work is not hard if you enjoy it—and I do enjoy it," she said), she would remark testily as I came through the door, "More questions!" or "I'm working too hard and sleeping too soundly to have time to dream." Then if she was not successful in driving me away and I managed to engage her in conversation, she would say with relief, as she noticed me preparing to leave, "So now you are finished with your questions!"

She herself had a specific goal in mind, and she expected me to be the same way. Even after so much contact with me, she still did not perceive our conversations as occasions on which there could be a degree of give and take on both sides, while I continued to gather the information I had primarily come for. Long ago I had said I wanted to learn about Gusii mothers and their children. That was my task. If I wanted to go beyond my original definition, then Phoebe was not at all sure she had the inclination—and she most certainly did not have the time—to accommodate me.

4

Consolata Nyaboke

I

Consolata Nyaboke was married to Kepha's cousin. She lived directly behind the marketplace, little more than a stone's throw from Phoebe. Unlike Phoebe, however, who was unusually mature for her years, Consolata was a chronically disorganized, dependent, and angry young woman who derived minimal satisfaction from her situation. But if I failed to develop a relationship of any depth with Phoebe, I was no more successful with Consolata, though in Consolata's case my failure was due not to her self-sufficiency or lack of a conscious need for support and friendship but, rather, to her excessive self-absorption and inability to empathize with or be close to other people.

When I met her, Consolata was in an advanced state of pregnancy. She had not laid eyes on her husband since the week he had come home during the previous harvest time with the express purpose of providing her with another child, her fifth. Several years before, Consolata had been visiting at the nearby home of her eldest sister, Mokeira (who had been Consolata's *omoreri* and with whom throughout life she would have a special relationship), when an intermediary had approached her on behalf of James Nyamwange. After she had met Nyamwange a few times, Consolata eloped with him. Two years later, shortly after she had given birth to her first child, a son, Nyamwange received bridewealth from his sister's marriage and thus was able to pay eight cows for Consolata. She now had two more sons and a daughter. During the early part of her marriage, she had lived with her husband at Kericho, where Nyamwange was working on the tea plantations, but for the past several years she had been at home, helping her mother-in-law, while her husband held a series of jobs at Mombasa, 600 miles away on the Indian Ocean. Currently Nyamwange was unemployed. He was living with a younger brother, a permanent employee of the Port Authority.

Nyamwange was the eldest son of Kwamboka, the second wife of Oyugi. In the course of a long life, Oyugi had acquired five wives, all of whom were still living. He had long ago given up conjugal relations with Kwamboka. "I have forgotten all about sex," Kwamboka told me once. "If the *omogaaka* came here I would not know what to do. I would run away! I do not cook for him any more because my cowives say if I offered him food, then he would be obliged to sleep with me. But neither he nor I have any interest in that!" Sometimes if she made beer, he would drink some of it, but in fact he was rarely at Morongo; he preferred to live with his youngest wife on a farm he owned in the settlement scheme. Even though Kwamboka was not more than fifty, her youngest child was sixteen years of age, which would indicate that her marital relationship had come to an end, for all intents and purposes, long ago. She received no financial support at all from Oyugi, though of course she had her allotment of land. She had had to rely on her own resources to educate her children, and this fact must in part explain why Nyamwange, the eldest, had been the only son not to finish elementary school. His mother had expected him to find a job and remit a major part of his earnings to help pay for the schooling of his brothers. Thus, after four years of primary school, he had gone off to Tanzania to work with a lumber company on the forested slopes of Mt. Kilimanjaro. He had been confined to various semi-skilled or unskilled jobs ever since. It was also apparent, however, that Nyamwange had had little aptitude for learning and had been thankful to leave the strict Catholic school he had been attending.

That he was a Catholic was purely an accident. Neither of his parents had been baptized, and Nyamwange had become a Catholic only so that he could attend the local school, which happened to be operated by the Catholic diocese of Kisii. (Before independence, almost all schools were offshoots of missions.) Consolata's parents were also non-Christians, and she was the only one of her eight siblings to be baptized. When her closest childhood friend was attending catechism classes, Nyaboke had asked her parents to be allowed to attend as well. She was subsequently baptized Consolata. In order to become a Christian she had had to tolerate being "different," but how much significance she attached to being a member of the church was hard to tell. She attended mass from time to time, but she once said that as far as she could see God had done little for her other than ensure her survival, for what that was worth. "I pray to Him, of course, but doesn't everyone pray to Him, even pagans? Everyone, pagans and Christians, prays to the same god."

She volunteered very little information about her own family. Her father, whom she remembered as being "very kind," was now dead. He had been a cattle farmer, "but mostly those animals died." Her mother had been his only wife. Apart from Mokeira, from whose home she had eloped, Consolata scarcely ever saw anyone from her own family. "My mother comes to greet me after I have given birth, but my brothers and sisters have never been here at all." She seemed, in her more open moments, to regret this. "When we were children we were close, but now nobody cares about anyone else. This is a pity. Brothers and sisters *should* continue to visit one another after they've grown up." By her own calculation, which I think was accurate, she had been about fourteen when she married. "I was very young. I hadn't finished growing. I hadn't started my periods, nor did I until I had been married more than a year." Thus, by the time I knew her, Consolata had been married ten or eleven years, and although she perceived her original home as being a more prosperous place, at least in her childhood, than her married home, her ties with her widowed mother and her siblings other than Mokeira were tenuous.

I saw Consolata for the first time in the prenatal clinic, but as soon as she identified herself, I realized that I already knew her mother-in-law, Kwamboka, one of the most garrulous and amusing women in the community. Kwamboka would pursue me down the road with a stream of chatter, generally related to her bodily ills, but at the same time she was very entertaining. At the first meeting, Consolata also seemed unusually vivacious for someone of her age. Vivacity (*ogokwana*) was generally a characteristic developed—or allowed to emerge—later in life. In this, her first personal contact with a European, she was outspoken and apparently reflective as she answered a standard set of questions which often reduced women to the merest monosyllables. In my view Consolata was very good looking. She had beautiful teeth and a rather arrogant bearing. At first I thought of her as queenly. Later, as I came to know her, her behavior tended to remind me of that of a petulant princess.

She and her children lived about a hundred yards away from the matriarch Kwamboka. I call her a matriarch because even though her husband was still alive, she lived independently of him and appeared, in the tradition of Gusii women, thoroughly to enjoy her status as *omosubati omonene*. I had become used to her endless stream of talk and laughter. I recognized that advanced status did not mean for her that she should relax and gossip with her age-mates, safe in the knowledge that her sons were supporting her. She was certainly very gregarious and spent a fair amount of time socializing, but she was also intimately and actively involved in the care of everyone in her homestead. In her brusque way she ordered everyone about, but her manner was not simply a reflection of her pleasure in the exercise of power. She was anxious about the welfare of her children and grandchildren, and she saw herself as taking primary responsibility for all of them.

As for Consolata, she did not complain that her mother-in-law dominated family life; rather, she asked why Kwamboka, given the authority she retained, for example, over the use of land, was not a better provider. But Consolata did not talk of wanting a greater share in decision making for herself, though at twenty-six she was of an age where many other women around her already had years of burdensome responsibility behind them. Despite her many children, Consolata looked—and behaved—like a newly married girl in the presence of her mother-in-law. She even seemed to abdicate charge of her children to Kwamboka. My first impression of Consolata when I saw her in the clinic was of a thoughtful young woman, open and eager to relate to an outsider. I could scarcely have been more mistaken. Her reflectiveness, at closer quarters, was self-absorption, her queenly manner was the defensive arrogance of the thoroughly insecure, her vivacity she used to engage others in her obsessive ruminations about her own problems.

Indeed, in all the time I knew her I never discovered that she had a single woman friend. She described herself as being close to one of her sisters-in-law, Jane, who at eighteen already had an illegitimate two-year-old. But Jane was a schoolgirl, and she lived in the homestead. Consolata had known her since early childhood and maintaining a friendship with her required minimal effort.

Thus my earliest impressions of Consolata were erroneous. By the time I realized how mistaken I had been, however, I was intrigued by her childishness and by her apparent rejection of any personal responsibility for her troubles. I knew her over a period of fifteen months, though she was gone for five months of that time. In all I visited her on thirty occasions. She lurched from one crisis to another, and each she experienced as an affliction, a visitation from without. To begin with I naively expected circumstances to ease, so that periodically at least Consolata might enjoy a respite. I found her lack of delight in anything, her determination to suffer, angrily wearing indeed, for as she talked obsessively about her burdens, describing how she suffered and was misused, I was equally obsessive in my efforts to keep up with her. Though all the women I worked with complained to a greater or lesser degree, all of them had greater personal resources than Consolata, whose fury at having her dependency needs thwarted was bare and blatant.

II

The very first time Mary and I went to see Consolata, she emerged, after a long delay, wrapped in a blanket. A week before, she and I had had what I had assumed was a mutually pleasurable conversation in the clinic, on the strength of which I had decided to include her in my study. On this second occasion, however, she did not indicate any memory of our previous meeting. It appeared that she was absorbed in her physical condition: though she was not in labor, she had such severe backache and stomach cramps that her mother-in-law had taken her off that morning to a diviner.

"The *omoragori* told us to sacrifice a goat, but my mother-in-law replied, 'Why now? We'll wait until the child is born and have something to be thankful for!' She says she can't afford to buy a goat at present, so I'm no better off than before. I still have backache." Her two elder boys, in their school uniforms, were lying under a bush at the edge of the yard. "They refused to go to school today," Consolata explained. "They are afraid when they see I am in pain. They wanted to stay at home to watch me."

Consolata did not seem to experience their concern as solicitous of *her* welfare. In fact she seemed annoyed that they were not at school. On the basis of what I later learned about this family, it seems likely that the boys were periodically phobic about school. Perhaps they were so ambivalent about their mother that they stayed at home to make sure that, in her weakened condition, their hostility toward her was not lethal.

The familiar stance of a Gusii woman in pain is that of an afflicted person. She suffers, but the anger that her suffering generates is well hidden. Not so with Consolata. While Mary and I did our best to engage her and improve her spirits, Consolata sat hunched up at the edge of her yard. She did not offer us chairs, nor did she get her children to bring them out to us, so we sat beside her on the grass. She claimed tersely that although she disliked childbirth, she was not afraid of it; had she not had four children without mishap? She seemed determined to reject our clumsy but well-meaning efforts to empathize with her condition. After a time, however, she unwrapped her blanket and spread it over a low bush to provide us with some shade. She looked less angry and admitted to feeling better. But when we left she said goodbye peremptorily, turning away long before we had gone out of the compound, as if she were dismissing us before we could reject her.

In the following week we checked on her several times. Her back pains seemed to have eased. One afternoon, however, we found her in labor. Though she must have been in fairly heavy labor, for one of Kwamboka's cowives was already installed in the living room, ready to assist in the delivery, she was vague about the timing of her contractions. Kwamboka rushed in and took control. She had been drinking, but she quickly sobered up, lit a fire, and heated water, talking rapidly to Consolata meanwhile, as if containing her daughter-in-law's pain and anxiety with her flow of ridicule and encouragement. As is quite usual for Gusii women in labor, Consolata did not utter a word as she squatted naked on the kitchen floor, straining against her mother-in-law's firm hold. Unfortunately I had to leave before the baby was born, but our doctors, who arrived in time to observe the delivery, reported that Kwamboka's performance as a midwife was practiced and proficient.

A week later we noticed Consolata standing in the *shamba* as we climbed the steep path up to her house. She had evidently seen us too, for she vanished into the stand of bananas, and it was some time before she reemerged to greet us. She began by saying she still had afterbirth pains and she was hungry. No word about the baby, a seven-pound boy, who had been named Magoma. We asked to see the child. As we took turns holding him, Consolata said she had not written to her husband to announce the birth.

> "I haven't got money for stamps. I haven't got anything, except *chinsaga* [a spinach-like vegetable which the Gusii consider essential to a woman who is immediately postpartum]. No tea or sugar or cocoa. Clemencia [a neighbor who has also just given birth to her fifth child] received all she needed from her husband [a cousin of Nyamwange, also working in Mombasa], but mine doesn't even know his child has been born! Here we have no *obokima,* no bananas. My mother-in-law hasn't any maize left, either. My breast milk isn't coming in the way it should. The baby's hungry all the time. It is terrible when a woman gives birth and has no food!"

I sent Consolata's eldest son, Gichaba, off to the market to buy tea and sugar, without which Gusii women nowadays believe the breast milk cannot begin to flow properly. Consolata thanked me at the time, but never alluded to my contribution again.

Magoma, conceived in the abundance of harvest, had been born at the most difficult time of year, when supplies were exhausted and the new maize was scarcely in the ear. For at least a month after childbirth Consolata literally ate nothing besides boiled vegetables. Any extra weight she had gained during pregnancy melted away. The rains were particularly heavy that year, and the weather was very cold. The children, including the baby, had upper respiratory infections for weeks on end. Kwamboka, who at the best of times suffered chronically from worms, got pneumonia and was incapacitated. Thus Consolata found herself with much more than her usual share of work. Nyamwange, who was ultimately informed of the birth of Magoma, responded with a money order for sixty shillings. It was sitting in the post office in Kisii and to get it Consolata had to borrow bus fare for herself and her brother-in-law Obiri, who would act as her witness, and go to town to stand in line for hours.

"And what good will sixty shillings do me? Other women who have husbands at Mombasa receive 300 shillings at one time. They say I should send that money order back! I shouldn't accept so little! But I'm lucky if I get 300 shillings in a whole year. By the time I've paid what I owe to the school fund so Gichaba and Obamba will be allowed back to class, I'll only have ten shillings left for maize. [The fact that Nyamwange is currently unemployed and must have borrowed even the pittance he has managed to send carries no weight with her.] You see this baby here, how long his hair is? People ask, 'Why don't you cut his hair?' Well, it hasn't been cut since he was born because I haven't got money to buy beer, and you can't cut a baby's hair without offering beer to your mother-in-law and the barber. [Babies' heads are usually shaved within the first month.] I tell you, at the time I married I didn't know life would be like this. I eloped here with Nyamwange, and when my father came to take me back home again, I begged him to let me stay. I told him this was a good place, and he was convinced and let me stay. I was so young, and I knew nothing about men. I'd never played about with boys. I was afraid of them. People told me Nyamwange was a good man, and I believed them, so I came here with him. A child, that's all I was." She laughs. "I remember when I menstruated for the first time. I was in the *shamba* weeding maize, and when I saw the blood I ran to my sister Mokeira and stayed there with her until the bleeding stopped. My son Gichaba is like me. He's afraid of growing up. He hasn't been circumcised yet because he says he fears those spears which men point at boys' heads during the circumcision rite, and he's a big boy, as you can see." As she talks, her brother-in-law Obiri passes by. Later in the day they will meet at the post office in town so that Consolata can get her money order cashed. Consolata watches him disappear from view. *"Omongiti!* He's a miser. He earns a good salary as a teacher, and yet he'll never buy a single bar of soap for my children. He's spending his own money to get to Kisii, but the minute that money order is cashed I'll have to pay him back for his bus fare. My brother-in-law at Mombasa is the only good one. He once sent me a dress. Obiri is a bachelor, but he spends his money on himself and on presents for his girl-friend. You see them walking up and down the road together, but he can't marry her until she's finished secondary school." In-side her house a child starts to cry. "She's hungry, that's why she's making such a noise. But her uncle Obiri doesn't care. He won't even lend me money to buy maize for my children." The child's screams get louder. "Last night I bought two shillings' worth of flour and we had *obokima* for supper, but it's all gone now and the children are hungry again. I'm hungry too, and I don't have enough milk for Magoma." Mary urges Consolata to roast some maize. "If I pick it now then we'll be hungry later," Consolata retorts. She gets up and goes into her house to the screaming child. "Magoma is such a pretty baby," Mary whis-pers to me, "but he won't stay that way, not in a house like this." Consolata comes out again, pulling her weeping daughter by the hand. As she sits wearily beside us, heaving the child onto her lap, she remarks, "I should go to the fields today, but if I did that I wouldn't have strength left for anything else. Who would cook or collect firewood or watch these children if I didn't? The old woman has gone off to Sotik to attend a funeral, so I have to do all the work. She said she meant to get maize from her brother's granary. If she gets it, we'll be able to eat again. Though she is old, my mother-in-law can still take grain from home because her family is well-to-do. I can't do it, though. Since my father died, my mother is a poor woman. My brothers do not care for her as they should. If I asked her, mother would have nothing to give me."

But one afternoon toward the end of July I could see even from a distance that Consolata was euphoric.

"We have food!" she calls. "My mother-in-law brought maize from her brother, and now we have harvested our first *wimbi* [finger millet]. We shall grind it and make *obokima* for supper." Kwamboka, who is sitting under a tree shelling beans, grins from ear to ear. "We shall eat well this evening. We shan't wait for our husbands to taste our first *obokima*. In the old days a man was angry if his wife tasted before him, but our husbands are far away. Of course we cannot wait until they return."

Kwamboka was home again and in charge; the family had plenty to eat, and before my eyes Consolata was gaining weight. These days in the fields, harvesting with her mother-in-law or in the homestead preparing food, Consolata was very quiet. She was replete and cared for. For the moment she had nothing to complain about and thus nothing to say. Kwamboka, meanwhile, filled our sessions with a stream of information and gossip about the progress and misfortunes of relatives and neighbors. Except in the heaviest planting season and at harvest time, she was always visiting relatives. She went for a night or two here, a week there, decked out in a pink and green dress, with a *kitenge* cloth thrown over her shoulder, a gift from one of her sons. Consolata listened to all Kwamboka's stories and smiled when a smile was appropriate but rarely commented. Whole sessions went by in which she barely spoke at all. She was like a girl of eleven or twelve who, having not yet discovered the pleasures of boys, still devoted all her time to the mute and adoring service of her mother.

The reality, however, was that Consolata was a married woman, mother of five children, and her husband showed no sign whatever of coming to greet his new son. Nor did he send any more money. But Ogaro, the brother with whom Nyamwange was living, came on leave from Mombasa. He announced that he intended to marry, and sure enough within a few days he brought home an illiterate girl of eighteen named Josephine. The girl was dull and plain, and her new husband admitted after the first night together that he did not love (i.e., desire) her much, since he found she was blemished (she had a scar on her back). Nevertheless, he stuck by his decision to make her his wife because she fulfilled his other requirements; namely, she was unintelligent and uneducated and thus, he believed, would not give him any trouble when he entertained other women or interfere with his drinking habits or his association with men friends. Because she knew neither Swahili nor English, she would not even be able to understand what people were saying. He wanted to marry in order to provide himself with children and a permanent housekeeper, and Josephine showed immediately that she was competent and conscientious (she even managed to conceive before Ogaro's departure). Thus, after a couple of weeks, having presented Josephine with two new dresses, Ogaro returned to Mombasa well satisfied with his choice. As soon as he had earned enough money, he would send for Josephine to join him.

But while the focus of attention in the homestead was upon the bride in her new dresses, Consolata was languishing without word from

Nyamwange. One day one of Kwamboka's daughters came home for a visit and insisted on discussing at length Nyamwange's irresponsibility toward his infant son.

"I'll tell you why he hasn't come!" Consolata laughs bitterly. "It's because I'm a bush woman. I haven't washed since I gave birth, and so I stink. He has so many clean women in Mombasa to make him happy, women who are brown because they live idle city lives, not black as I am from working in the sun day after day. If ever I hear he is coming home, I'll cover myself in red clay, as widows did in our grandfathers' time. I'll have my revenge. People will laugh at him for neglecting me so long! I have had five of his children, and he lets them grow like weeds. He doesn't care if they're *kebago* [wastrels] when they're big. They're that way already."

The euphoria of harvest time was passing now. The new school term had begun, but Consolata was in arrears with building fees, and her two older boys were not readmitted. We met her coming with her mother-in-law from the fields. As Kwamboka washed herself and got ready to go off to the power mill, Consolata told us in a low voice that she too wanted to go, but she had no money with which to have her maize ground.

"Why won't Kwamboka give you a shilling?" I ask.
"Because my husband has been weaned!" she retorts. [I.e., he is an adult and should be independent.] "Once the *omongina* gave me malaria medicine, but she never gives me money. I have to provide for myself. We have a large piece of land, but we never have any money. We have many mouths to feed, so mostly we plant maize, very little coffee, and pyrethrum. Our cash income is very small. Well," she sighs, as she sits to nurse Magoma, "I think I'll go and weed a few hours for a neighbor, enough to earn money for the power mill." But then, squinting at the sky, she remarks, "Look, it's going to rain. I can't go to my neighbor today. Anyway, there's a little flour left over from yesterday, enough for supper. Maybe I'll go to work tomorrow."

Other women as impoverished as she were constantly running here and there, earning a few shillings from better-off neighbors. Consolata went once and afterward asked us indignantly, "Why should I tire myself weeding another woman's pyrethrum when I have my own to weed?" Never, to my knowledge, did she go again.

> Magoma, who is four months old now and very beautiful, waves his arms to get his mother's attention. Consolata nuzzles him, singing to him briefly. I ask if he is the most beautiful of her babies. "They were all like this. I loved each one in turn when he was small."

But now it seemed she found them nothing but a burden, an irritation. She was always complaining about Gichaba, who, in the absence of any suitable girl child, acted as *omoreri* to his baby brother. "He's useless," Consolata told us whenever we visited. "He puts that baby down and forgets him altogether. He's like his father, irresponsible," she added, glaring at Gichaba, who looked away into the pumpkin patch. Often we came upon Consolata waving a stick. She had either just beaten Gichaba or was on her way to do so. Only our arrival gave him a chance to escape. Consolata was very dependent on Gichaba, her eldest child, and his failure to meet her demands kept her in a constant rage. I had plenty of opportunity to observe Gichaba, both under the surveillance of his mother and, more significantly, when he was taking care of his siblings by himself. Given that he was only nine years old and a boy, required to perform what are generally considered female tasks, I would say Gichaba did rather well. He was an easy target, however, for Consolata's feelings of discontent and deprivation. It was possibly true that, though Kwamboka shared all the food she had with her daughter-in-law, she refused to lend her money. Certainly Consolata complained about the situation. But Kwamboka was too strong a personality, too powerful in terms of what realistically she could give out or withhold, for Consolata to dare to express anger to her directly. With Gichaba, on the other hand, Consolata engaged in something approaching mortal combat. "*Kebago*," she shouted at him, ten times a day. Given the way his mother treated him, it seemed rather likely that he would indeed grow up to be the delinquent Consolata already judged him to be.

On the day Magoma was five months old, Consolata's mother sent word that she was coming at last to greet her new grandson. I gathered she had had to wait until the very end of the old harvest before she was able to afford all the gifts a mother should bring to her daughter after she has given birth. For her part, Consolata contributed three pots of *busaa,* and the celebration lasted twenty-four hours. I myself came only by chance toward the end, when everyone was sprawled about under Kwamboka's shade tree, replete and exhausted from having been up all night. This was the one occasion when I saw Consolata's mother, and my impression of her was worth little, given her fatigue and inebriation. She was quite youthful in appearance, small, slim, and very quiet. She left soon after my arrival. Of the group of more than a dozen women—mostly her sisters-in-law and the cowives of her mother-in-law—Consolata was the only one in a reasonable condition. Even the children, with the exception of Magoma, were all drunk, and they either tottered about or lay on top of one another in the grass. Consolata looked content.

Her task on this occasion, having first received her mother's gifts, had been to cook for all the guests. Everyone agreed that she had cooked well, that every visitor had been well taken care of. It had been her day, and so much attention from so many women, especially from her mother and mother-in-law, had permitted her to be energetic and generous with a good grace.

But a week later, when the excitement had passed, we found her hunched over her cooking fire complaining of malaria. As we took our places beside her, on the tiny hardwood stools that Gusii people have in their houses, Consolata burst out, "My husband is *kebago!*"

It seems she has heard from her brother-in-law Ogaro in Mombasa that Nyamwange has been employed in a permanent job as a watchman with a commercial firm for the past three months. "And yet not a cent has he given to me! He hasn't written to me, he hasn't come to greet his child, and Magoma will soon cut his first teeth. It is very bad indeed if a father does not see his son before the teeth come out. The other children are in rags. If I wash their clothes, they have nothing else to wear while these clothes are drying. I haven't had salt for a week. My flour has run out. My mother-in-law refuses to lend me money for the power mill," and so on. Magoma, who has fever also, is fretting in her arms. "I've never had a man beside my husband, but now I think I shall go to the camp and get myself a construction worker. Dorcas, my mother-in-law's cowife, goes to the camp. She got a head-tie and a dress from one of those men.

I shall do as she did." She whispers, "If my mother-in-law heard
what I'm saying, she'd chase me away from here. But she knows
what kind of man Nyamwange is. She would know that what
I'm telling you is true." Consolata smiles. "I wouldn't go to any
uncircumcised man. I don't like that foreskin." "But do you
know how to behave like an *omotari* [prostitute]?" I tease her.
She says in broken Swahili, "'I am a young girl, I have no
children.' That's what I'd say," she laughs bitterly, "and if my
husband heard, he'd divorce me." "When you first knew him,
what did you think of him?" I ask her. "His friends said he was
a good man, but of course he wasn't. In fact I ran away from
him when I was pregnant with Gichaba [i.e., before the
bridewealth had been paid]. But he came after me and begged
me to go back to him. Even then, at Kericho, when we were
first married he would roam about like a dog. In recent years
when he has come home on leave for a week, he has no interest
in staying here with me. He's always out, with another woman
or in a bar. Last time he was here, I was lucky to conceive
Magoma. He was out each night until the early hours of the
morning with a girl in Geterere, who was his cousin."

But it seems that Consolata, as she sees things, has no choice
but to stay. "My father has been dead eight years, and at home
there is only my younger brother, who wouldn't feed me. He
scarcely feeds our mother properly. My mother couldn't take me
in. She was already past childbearing when my father died, and
she has no *omochinyomba* [leviratic husband]. Then, Nyamwange
has paid for me. He paid eight cows, and my elder brother
would refuse a divorce because then he'd be obliged to pay back
those cattle, which he used long ago to marry himself. So I have
only one choice, to go to Mowlem and earn money from those
men, and that is no choice at all. Thus I must stay here at home
and hope that someday along the road or in the market I may
find another husband. Until the day comes that I elope to the
house of another man, I must remain in this poor place." She
knocks at the kitchen wall with a stick. "This husband I have is
not a real husband. He didn't build this house, and he doesn't
repair it either. He leaves it to his younger brothers to do that.
He doesn't care if the roof leaks! I tell you, the only person I can
rely on is my sister Mokeira. It is to her that I must send
Gichaba to beg money for the power mill. Mokeira gives it to

me when she can, though she knows very well I won't be able to repay her." She jumps up and pushes past us to the door and yells at the children playing outside, "Either go up the hill or down. I can't stand your noise." As she sits down again she says, "They make my head ache. This is a miserable homestead, a wretched place. When my husband comes I'll cover myself in clay and stand before him. But I shan't say a word. I don't want Kwamboka to hear anything. I just want Nyamwange to understand what in truth I am—a widow." Outside in the yard we hear Kwamboka talking to Obamba. "Forget what I told you," Consolata laughs, "I was mistaken; this is the best homestead."

She followed us outside to bid us goodbye, and as we walked away down the hill she shouted one last remark, "Remember I told you all my children are *kebago!*"

But a week later a relative arrived from Mombasa bringing clothes from Nyamwange for his mother, his wife, and all his children. Consolata was exultant in her new red dress. She sashayed about for our inspection. In spite of her delight in her appearance, not once did she express any feelings of gratitude toward her husband or indicate that she understood why he had been so long in sending presents. In fact he had only been employed a short while, and it had taken that long for him to save enough money to outfit his family. The relative who brought the things also brought presents to Josephine from her husband, so clearly Ogaro's intentions toward her were firm. Thus we were entertained by a fashion show as everyone, Kwamboka included, paraded before us.

Two days later when we passed through the homestead, we saw Gichaba sitting dejectedly outside his grandmother's house. His mother's house was locked. "Where is Consolata?" we asked, and Gichaba replied that she had taken Magoma and little Jean and had set out to accompany Josephine to Mombasa. They had taken the night bus to Nairobi on the first part of the long journey. "Yes," Kwamboka agreed when we met her on the road, "they have gone." She glowed with pride. Her sons had behaved correctly; they had sent for their wives. And yet when we had been in the compound two days previously helping to celebrate the arrival of the gifts, Consolata had not spoken of the receipt of money or of any impending journey. Could it be that she was actually ashamed of how much she had maligned her husband, that she could not reveal to us the full extent of his generosity for fear of appearing in our eyes all the more indiscreet and ungrateful?

Possibly, but I think it unlikely that Consolata experienced remorse at her earlier confidences to us about Nyamwange. Rather, she kept quiet about her impending journey. To talk about it ahead of time would have been to boast of her good fortune. She treated me, an outsider, as if I were as untrustworthy as any Gusii neighbor, as if my jealousy would be as easily aroused as theirs. She herself had never been beyond Kericho, let alone to Mombasa. There were women around whose husbands worked there just as hers did, but they had not been summoned to go there as she was being summoned. And so to wear her new clothes was as far as she dared go. She would make her preparations with the barest fuss and climb on the bus when it passed through Morongo after dark. Then in the morning, when she was well on her way, let the neighbors discover she had gone.

III

Five months later Consolata returned, after being summoned by Kwamboka, who complained that Gichaba was giving her too much trouble. In fact, all this time the old lady had been taking care of Consolata's three older children without receiving any communication whatsoever from their mother. When the new planting season came, she felt she had had enough and demanded that her daughter-in-law come home to resume her responsibilities.

On the morning after Consolata's return we found her angry, agitated, and depressed. She gave us scant pause for greetings but poured out her tumultuous feelings about being home again, as if the long hiatus just past were merely an afternoon's interruption. She was wearing two wrappers or lengths of cloth over her dress. One was tied under her armpits, the other draped about her head and shoulders in the manner of coastal women. Her appearance was quite dramatic.

"My husband made me come home. I didn't want to. He bought me a train ticket and forced me to leave." I say I gather she has enjoyed living in Mombasa. "Oh no, it's too hot! You sweat all the time. We had one small room for which we paid fifty shillings in rent, and for that, though we shared a water faucet with other people in the compound, we didn't even have electricity in our room; we had to buy all our food. It was very expensive. Next door lived a prostitute. In fact there were two, one on each side of us. My husband is quite used to them, of course, but I'm not. He runs after them all the time. I want to go back to Mombasa as soon as possible to try to stop that kind of behavior. Anyway I'd rather see what he does with my own eyes than imagine what goes on."

She paced about the yard, tossing her cloth over her head, catching it when it slipped, tossing it again. She moved on from the subject of Nyamwange's taste for prostitutes to something which weighed more heavily on her mind.

"I have to go back there because he didn't give me what I wanted. I came home with one blanket and no clothes for the children, who are so angry that I came empty-handed that they refused to fetch water for me from the river this morning. I had intended to stay there until I had got from him dresses for myself, things for the children, several blankets. Well, he didn't get rid of me that easily. I shall just stay here long enough to finish the weeding. Then I'll go off again to Mombasa. This time I'll take Gichaba as well as the two little ones. If Nyamwange won't let me stay, I'll threaten to leave all the children with him. Then we'll see what he has to say!" She grimaces in disgust. "I'd got used to living in a concrete house with piped water, but now I'm back again in the same old leaky hut. Still, it's nice to be cool. I do dislike the heat and getting malaria so often. I think I'd like to spend half the week here and half at Mombasa, where we used to sleep naked at night, and in the day I wore only a cloth."

A few days later we found Consolata shivering in her fireless kitchen while outside the rain pelted down.

"I hadn't wanted to go to Mombasa in the first place, mind you. It was Nyamwange's business to come here to greet Magoma, not mine to go there. But this relative came with presents for us. You'll remember. And he had been told to give me money to accompany Josephine. [Is it true she hadn't wanted to go? Why had she looked so delighted that day five months ago, when we had seen her in her new red dress from Mombasa?]

I was so angry with my husband. My mother-in-law was on my
side. It was his business to come home. But then some relatives
here persuaded us, saying, 'The child's teeth have come out, let
her go,' so I went. Ogaro was so delighted to see Josephine, and
months later when I left them, he was still happy with her. But
Nyamwange! He wanted me to leave again almost as soon as I
had arrived. He gave me nothing! Just these two cloths, which
cost twenty-five shillings each. They were secondhand. When he
received a letter from his mother complaining of Gichaba, he
bought me a ticket and took all my boxes to the station. I
refused to go with him. For two days I refused. In the end I did
leave, but I took with me everything he had in that room of his,
every cup and plate! But he didn't get rid of me. I'm going back
in a month, with all the children, and we'll stay there until he's
given me what I need. I told him that if he doesn't send me
money for my return journey, I'll go and find a construction
worker. I warned him! Here I am again in the miserable house
with his children, who are like wild beasts. My mother-in-law
could control them. She bit them if they wouldn't behave! But I
can't control them myself."

I told her children usually behaved badly when the mother returned
after being away for some time, but Consolata was unimpressed.

"They're like that; it's their nature, whether I'm here or not."
She turns to yell at Obamba and Gichaba, who are pummeling
one another on the floor. They separate and Consolata gives us
her attention again. "I come back here and find my mother-in-
law hasn't planted any *wimbi,* only maize."
"But it's not too late to plant *wimbi.*"
Consolata looks at me scornfully. "There isn't any space left.
The old woman used up all the land. Of course she did things
the way she wanted," she adds angrily.

Consolata made no mention of the fact that Kwamboka had done all
the digging and planting herself. She had done her daughter-in-law's
share of work as well as her own, to make sure Consolata and her
children would have something to eat. But Consolata could only
complain about what her mother-in-law had not done. She had no
gratitude for what, despite rheumatism and chronic intestinal problems, the old woman had accomplished.

"One thing I can promise you," Consolata bursts out. "I'm not going to have any more children. If it ever pleases Nyamwange to pay a visit to his home, I shan't be here to greet him. I'll go and stay with my mother. Five children are enough for me! If I never saw that man again, I wouldn't mind. I don't miss him." I ask if she missed anyone here at home when she was in Mombasa. "Why should I?" "Not even Kwamboka, who loves you so much?" Consolata shrugs. "No, not even her."

Consolata's depression permeated the homestead. She strode about scowling and silent except for her outbursts against her children, who sat for hours on end like tense little rabbits under the shade tree. When their mother shouted at them, they jumped. As for Consolata, she took to extremes her tendency to dwell upon adversity to the exclusion of good fortune, her own or anyone else's. One morning, for example, we found her frowning into the distance. One of Nyamwange's sisters, a young woman widowed young and previously unable to conceive a child by a succession of leviratic husbands, had finally become pregnant, and we knew her to be at the end of her term. Consolata said gloomily, "Nyaboke fell into the latrine yesterday. They had great difficulty in pulling her out. She suffered very much." Only later did we discover that in fact the fall had precipitated labor and Nyaboke had given birth that night to a son, a most joyous event, since by her original husband she had had two daughters, followed by years of infertility. Kwamboka was delirious with happiness, but Consolata sat in silence, her back to us, her nose in the air. Her sister-in-law's good fortune was more than she could bear. Eventually she turned toward us and announced she was not feeling well. She had cramps in her stomach. When I teased her that she might be pregnant, she denied this and launched into a monologue on the subject of why she so much disliked menstruating. Sitting beside her was Obamba, aged eight. But his mother was oblivious to him. She described her experiences and her objections in detail. Even when her son, before whom, according to Gusii customs of avoidance, she should never mention such things, burst into nervous giggles, she ignored him.

But then, as usual, the true source of her irritation and anger emerged.

"I haven't heard a word from Nyamwange. Yesterday I sent him a letter enclosing a stamped envelope. I told him the boys have no school uniforms. Perhaps he will deign to answer me this time." She is throwing little twigs into the lush grass which grows around her yard. "I can't go to Mombasa now. I have to weed the pyrethrum, but one day I'll take all the children. We'll go to Kisumu by bus and board the train to Mombasa," she says, her voice rising, "and then we'll go to the place where Nyamwange works. I'll line up the boys unwashed in their shirts alone, without shorts, and I'll say, 'Here are the naked sons of that man. He gives me nothing but children.'" She laughs wildly. "It's a good plan, don't you think?" and she repeats it, changing a detail or two, embroidering here and there. "When I was at Mombasa we fought every day about money. He has so many clothes himself! So many pairs of trousers. He even left two pairs here when he last came a year and a half ago. They were extra, he didn't need them. But to me he gives nothing, a single dress and forty shillings [each time Consolata talks about what she did or did not get at Mombasa, the list of items changes and the sum of money is reduced], and expects me to come back here content. Well, I tell you, I left him with plenty of trouble! I took the key to his room with me, as well as all his utensils. Why should I even try to be friends with a man like that? If he comes here, I barely see him. He's off with someone else's wife, giving her soap with which to wash her children. He wouldn't give *me* soap to wash *his* children. I haven't got any soap at all at the moment. It's my mother-in-law who keeps me here, but one day that man will come and he'll find I've run away. Who cares where I'll go! To my home, to Kisii town."

Meanwhile Consolata's third son, Omae, had been trying to snuggle up to her. Several times he tried to put his arms round her, to comfort her and himself too. But she pushed him roughly away, shouting at another son, Obamba, for his failure to fetch firewood from the bottom of the hill. When Magoma awakened from his nap and was brought to her to nurse, she put him to the breast without once looking at him directly. Nothing could distract her from her bitterness.

"I'd like to tie up the penis of Nyamwange! Tie it tight so that it won't work any more. We never get along, even when we're together. When I see him I don't care for him. If I feel anything special for him, it is that I dislike him more than any other man. Other women whose husbands earn what he earns [though she concedes she doesn't know the actual salary; she's never dared ask] are treated a hundred times better than he treats me. Their husbands send money home for them, and they build beautiful houses—and still they go running after other men. But I stay, fool that I am, bearing his children. I wish I had daughters, not these sons who so exactly resemble their father!"

A month after her return from Mombasa, Consolata was as angry as ever. Everyone in the compound, with the sole exception of Kwamboka, seemed afraid of her. One morning we were talking in the yard when Jane, Nyamwange's youngest sister and Consolata's only acknowledged "friend," came out of the house wearing one of Consolata's *kitenge* cloths. Consolata looked at Jane icily, and Jane, her head bowed, untied the cloth and handed it over. With a sweep of her arm Consolata draped it over her head and instantly became a coastal woman, poised, queenly. But then as Jane vanished in shame into the garden, Consolata slid off her pedestal, back into the stream of her familiar complaints. We had been talking about the possibility of going to her home. Consolata had not seen her mother since the occasion many months ago when her mother came to greet Magoma. "But I can't go home now," she insisted. "I need sugar and tea and meat. How can I buy those things? I tell you, I came from Mombasa with nothing!" The *kitenge* cloth slipped from her head and shoulders to the ground, uncovering her dress, the red dress which had been new for the journey to Mombasa. Now it was smeared across the front, the hem was coming down, there were large dark patches at the armpits.

"No, I can't go home now," she repeats, angrily, as if I am the one who is somehow preventing her from making the trip.

Her preoccupation with her marriage or, more properly, with her husband's failure, as she saw it, to fulfill his obligation to her had pervaded and spoiled every aspect of her life. No relationship was untouched by her bitterness. She had even withdrawn from her infant son, a sunny child whom she admitted everyone loved, "including his father." Magoma had got his siblings and cousins closely involved with him, and for a time their attention might help him navigate the space his mother seemed to have vacated.

I wondered what role, if any, Mary and I played in her life. We came repeatedly, irritatingly. She would barely greet us, turning instantly from us the moment we said that we were about to leave. She told us once, in passing, that she shared her feelings about Nyamwange only with her sister-in-law Jane. She did not mention that she also shared those feelings with us. Indeed she treated us time and again to seemingly uncensored diatribes in which she included every imaginable prurient detail of her husband's life. These outpourings were frequently preceded by long silences which made me, for one, very uncomfortable. It was as if we came each time as strangers.

On one occasion, however, I happened to be talking to her without Mary, but with another assistant. We were asking her routine questions about her childhood, how many siblings she had, how well she knew her maternal grandmother, and so forth. As she considered her answer to a particular question, Consolata wandered over behind where I was sitting and suddenly I felt her playing with my hair. She braided it and unbraided it again, fingering it idly. She did not say a word about what she was doing, and yet after such a long period in which she had studiously, determinedly, refused to grant me any meaningful existence, her attentions suffused me with feeling. She was doing to me what she might have done to her own sister or perhaps to her daughter. I imagined her mother used once to do it to her. I never saw Kwamboka caress Consolata's head. It seemed to me that this kind of caress was used only between women who were related by blood. "Doing" another woman's hair, combing and oiling and plaiting it into a hairstyle, was something quite different. Consolata touched my hair not in order to perform a service but for pleasure. We were talking about what her childhood had been like, whom she had slept with, whom she had loved most; and in that context, one which encouraged reverie and regression, this proud but woefully immature woman was able to express her desire to be close to me. It was the only time this or any similar expression occurred.

In the following session she was as cold and angry as ever. The previous night several women who worked in a bar at Morongo had been arrested and taken to jail. Consolata said she wished she could have been among them.

"That way at least I could have got away from my children! Gichaba was told to watch the other children, and he ran off. When I catch him, I'll cut off his foot. That'll stop him from running away again! I tell you children are nothing but trouble. If it weren't for them, I'd have gone off and enjoyed myself at Mowlem." When the conversation turns to a divorced woman whom we know to be pregnant, Consolata remarks, "She gave birth last week. But she kept her legs together during delivery and squashed the child's head with her knees so that it died."

She spoke matter-of-factly, as if it were a chicken which had died. In her current mood she found children, generally so much desired by the Gusii, unutterably burdensome. I reminded her that today Magoma was a year old. She shrugged, "Yes? I had forgotten." Even though Gusii people pay no special attention to birthdays, her lack of any spark of interest was extraordinary.

Up to the time I left the field Consolata's mood did not change. She heard nothing from her husband; her sons remained out of school for lack of fees. Gichaba, aged ten, possessed not a single pair of shorts. His nakedness was a pitiful sight to see. Several incidents, however, brought temporary diversion. The most exciting was the arrest of Consolata and another woman for selling *busaa* without a license. They were subsequently jailed at Keroka for three days. So Consolata got her wish, namely, a holiday away from her older children, but on her release and return home she admitted that the holiday was hardly worth it. There had been no *obokima* in jail, and they had been forced to sleep on the floor without blankets. At least at home she, Jean, and Magoma shared a blanket between the three of them. At the court hearing the judge gave them a fine of 100 shillings each, but when they wept and made a tremendous racket, he released them and sent them home without payment. Thus Consolata, who had viewed herself as a victim in the saga, having sold beer for her mother-in-law's profit, not her own, derived considerable satisfaction from the gullibility of the magistrate. She felt she put one over on him and, for a brief afternoon, was in good spirits.

A second event, which perhaps affected Consolata more deeply, was the psychotic breakdown of her stepbrother-in-law. This young man had been working in Nairobi when he became ill and was escorted back home in order to consult a diviner concerning the cause of his affliction. The *omoragori* told the family that the *ebirecha* (ancestors) first required the sacrifice of a bull before permitting the man's recovery; but Oyugi,

the patriarch, refused either to finance the sacrifice or even to participate in the occasion. Meanwhile his son sat at home, hallucinating in
his mother's compound. The mother, Anna, who was Kwamboka's
senior cowife, managed to borrow money for the bull from her own
brothers. Once the animal had been purchased, she organized her
cowives to put pressure on their husband to play his prescribed role in
the ritual. Thus Kwamboka and Consolata brewed beer for Oyugi in
the hope that, if drunk enough, he would capitulate, which in fact
turned out to be the case. He performed the sacrifice, and his son
speedily recovered and returned to work. However, Consolata, who had
herself put a lot of effort into the persuasion scheme, pleaded illness
and did not attend the ritual occasion, an event of major importance in
the lineage. Perhaps she identified too closely with her piteous, impotent brother-in-law, whose crazy behavior she described to me in
detail. Whatever demons had deranged him might have been familiar
to Consolata as well. Thus, while other family members could risk the
assault on the consciousness which the sight of the psychotic boy and
the slaughter of the bull together entailed, Consolata stayed away.

IV

When finally I told her I would be leaving the
community in a week or two, Consolata made no comment. On the day
I said goodbye, she accepted with a formal smile my gift of a set of
underclothes—garments which I know very well, from her numerous
complaints, she lacked. As she turned away I experienced the absolute-
ness of her failure to connect with me. But in fact she was relating to
me, a stranger, in the same way she related to everyone. If a person had
something she believed should be hers and it was denied to her, she
experienced rage and frustration. During the time I knew her, at any
rate, disappointment invariably elicited from her the same response.
But she was certainly not the only woman in her area to be locked into
an unsatisfactory marriage, and hers was not the worst situation I
encountered, by any means. In fact she had many things going for her:
she was young and strong; she was the only wife and likely to remain
so, for Nyamwange had never shown the slightest inclination to marry
a second wife. Thus her children did not face the prospect of sharing

what little there was with a slew of half-siblings. But most important, she was lucky in that her mother-in-law, though garrulous and intrusive, was a warm and responsible woman. No one in the neighborhood ever hinted that Kwamboka was malicious or dangerous in any way. But unfortunately Consolata seemed unable to derive much comfort from this relationship. I only met her mother once; I never saw the home she grew up in. I suspect, however, that her early experience had given her little to grow on emotionally, that she had emerged so narcissistically self-involved and with such an all-pervasive sense of deprivation that no circumstances in the imaginable future would be likely to change her angry hauteur and spurious pride.

5

Zipporah Bochere

I

I came to know Zipporah Bochere because she was related by marriage to Suzanna Bosibori. Their husbands were second cousins, and Zipporah, who was pregnant at the time, would sometimes visit Suzanna while I was there in the afternoon. She would sit serenely, her hands on her stomach. She had a presence, a certain style, even though her dress was faded and worn. I noticed particularly that she was not shy of asking me what she wanted to know, and her questions were always serious. It was quite rare for Gusii women to ask for information. Usually they showed no overt interest in me or in the customs of my homeland. Sometimes they asked about my children or my father—whether he had many cattle was a common question—but even when they had known me a long while and the time of deference to a stranger was passed, they still did not feel free to question me very much. From the start Zipporah clearly enjoyed our conversations, both having a chance to express herself and listening carefully to what I said in reply. I decided that once she had had her baby I would include her in my clinical study, aware though I was that this might invite complications in my relationship with her cousin Suzanna. They lived about half a mile from one another, however, and it was possible to reach Zipporah's house without passing Suzanna's.

As Zipporah told me the first time I met her, her husband, Makori, was *richara* (a feebleminded person). She said intently, "He is a drunkard and beats me very often, especially when I'm pregnant, as I am now." Suzanna, who was cooking in the corner, burst out laughing, from anxiety as much as mirth. Whereupon Zipporah laughed heartily also. This was always her way: she suffered, but the very fact that her husband was so bizarre and unreliable gave her some power and discretion in the family which other women, with normally functioning husbands, did not have. Zipporah could laugh at Makori's bizarreness because it allowed her a measure of freedom. Whether Makori was actually retarded or emotionally disturbed, whether he suffered from alcoholic deterioration or a combination of such afflictions, was very difficult to tell. His mental condition was further complicated by the fact that he had had two head operations, one of them a month before I met him. He suffered from excruciating headaches—which the operations, of course, had been intended to relieve—and spent most of the day drinking in order to "help his head." He did this even though the *omobari* (head surgeon) had strictly forbidden Makori to drink again until his scars were quite healed. "If you drink, you will kill yourself," he had been told, but a week after his second operation he had resumed his old habits.

During the twelve months and forty sessions in which I met with Zipporah, Makori was present a great part of the time. My efforts to see Zipporah alone were usually futile, since Makori, initially suspicious of me and later, I believe, genuinely fond of me, usually made sure he was present too. He would suddenly appear round the corner of the house, having been last seen at a beer party half a mile away. When a child told him I had come, he would leave the party and run, with his long loping stride, down the narrow, flower-strewn paths to his homestead. There he would greet me with an enormous smile and deposit his lanky body in a chair next to mine. Thus I inadvertently found myself working with both husband and wife. Over the course of the year, I began to realize that this unlikely couple, Zipporah the Seventh Day Adventist and Makori the non-Christian ("Let them bury me as an *omogusii;* no one even tried to convert me"), the compulsive worker and the profligate, provided one another with the kind of companionship that I scarcely ever saw elsewhere between a Gusii husband and wife.

Zipporah's own home was only a mile away on the road to the

Seventh Day Adventist church. Her father had died when she was seven years old, and after that, although her mother took a leviratic husband by whom she had several more children, she was on her own financially. She had to bring up her children as best she could without help from her husband's relatives. Zipporah, the eldest, had a daughter, Tabitha, out of wedlock. At that time illegitimate pregnancies were still a rarity, and a customary marriage for such a girl would be difficult to arrange. Makori presented himself, offering six cows as bridewealth, and Zipporah's mother forced Zipporah to accept Makori, whose reputation as a feebleminded drunkard—already deserted by one wife—was well known. After a period of resistance, Zipporah agreed to go to Makori. For a year after her marriage she refused to speak to her mother. Mother and daughter would see one another in the market several times each week, but they did not greet one another.

Meanwhile, on becoming Makori's wife, Zipporah discovered in short order not only that her husband was usually drunk and frequently violent, not only did he never bathe, but he was essentially impotent. It was for this reason that his first wife, a woman of another tribe, had left him; but she had gone back to her own distant tribal area, and it seems Zipporah was unaware of Makori's condition until after her own marriage had taken place. Her mother refused to agree to a divorce because she had already disposed of Makori's cattle. So Zipporah stayed with Makori. His brothers consulted diviners on his behalf and performed many sacrifices to placate the ancestors who were thus afflicting him, and over ten years Zipporah had produced five children. Rumor had it that none of these children were fathered by Makori. At least two of them, however, had Makori's unusual hair: his hair was softer and more loosely curled than anyone else's in the neighborhood. Zipporah allowed that Makori had benefited somewhat from all the sacrifices performed on his behalf, and even though he was not like other men, occasionally he was capable of having intercourse. According to Gusii custom, if a man is incapable of impregnating his wife, she has the right to find another man by whom to have children, and those children are always regarded as the offspring of her husband. Traditionally, however, the husband would himself select a relative to "service" his wife. His substitute would be of his own choosing. In this instance, I learned, Zipporah had the reputation of going to whomever she pleased, and her alleged promiscuity kept Makori in a constant state of suspicion and anger. Indeed everyone in the neighborhood awaited with interest the birth of the child Zipporah was carrying when I first met her. For months after birth the infant, Omae, did not seem to resemble anyone in particular, not even his mother, but eventually when he was about nine months old some loosely curling hair appeared on his hitherto bald head, and it was agreed he probably was Makori's child.

These days Zipporah's mother, Kemunto, was a pillar of her church, an active member of Dorcas, the Seventh Day Adventist women's group. Her younger children were all going to secondary school on the proceeds of their mother's maize business. But twelve years ago, when Zipporah had given birth to Tabitha out of wedlock, Kemunto had still been a traditional woman who wanted a good husband for her daughter, and she perceived Makori's family as a "good" family. None of them was educated or even baptized, but they had land and they had cattle. More recently this still remained true, for while their neighbors had become Christians, educated their children, and rationalized their farming methods, Makori's family had changed their goals and life-style very little. Of the four brothers, one had become a tractor driver, moved away, and bought land elsewhere; but the others were much as before, their land underexploited, their skinny native cattle producing too little milk to justify their pasturage. The three remaining brothers spent a great deal of time and most of their money drinking beer. However, while the other two behaved with respect even when drunk, Makori, the *omokogoti* (youngest), was generally regarded as a comic figure, someone of an age to be given respect, but undeserving of it.

His mother, Nyaboke, was still alive, aged about eighty. Her husband had been killed in the First World War, and all her children were by a leviratic husband, Obaro, who for most of their life together had had no wife of his own. Eventually Nyaboke had persuaded him to marry "properly," but this was not until Nyaboke was herself well past menopause. Obaro had died fairly recently and was deeply mourned by Nyaboke and her young cowife, Moraa. As Nyaboke told me, "Obaro and I were best friends." Her other great love, the one who remained with her, was Makori, her youngest child. The Gusii believe that women tend to infantilize their lastborn children, to nurse them longer and to indulge them throughout life, and as a result *abakogoti* are often spoiled (*basandikire*). This stereotype certainly fitted Makori. The relationship of mother and son was intense and stormy. Nyaboke was a small, ramrod-straight old lady, with a thousand wrinkles creasing her face. Makori was very tall, extraordinarily thin, and round-shouldered. One would invariably come upon this pair walking swiftly, one pursuing the other, both talking volubly, neither apparently paying attention to what the other was saying. Nyaboke interfered endlessly in the relationship between Makori and Zipporah, sometimes in defense of her daughter-in-law, sometimes in opposition, but her basic stance never altered: her aim was to keep the marriage intact. Her son had to keep a wife in order to have children. If Makori behaved outrageously, Nyaboke made it her business to protect Zipporah. If she perceived Zipporah as the offender, Nyaboke made every effort to bring her into line.

II

The first time I visited Zipporah in her own house I found Nyaboke, arms akimbo, in the middle of the yard. That day she dominated the conversation so completely that Zipporah scarcely had a chance to speak at all. She was about to give birth, but she did not complain of feeling tired. Indeed she looked very well. She roasted maize for me and served it with care. As I was to learn, Zipporah was always a gracious hostess. Although she was very poor and was in a constant state of anxiety about money, never a session passed without her offering refreshment of some kind. As Mary, my assistant, said, "Zipporah really knows how to entertain visitors." Two days after she gave birth, our physician brought with her some American visitors when she came to examine the baby. As the visitors walked up the path, Makori was beating Zipporah in the kitchen. When he heard the strangers' voices, Makori fled through a back window, whereupon Zipporah emerged bruised but smiling to greet her visitors and insist on cooking for them.

On this my first encounter with Nyaboke, I saw Zipporah smile as she listened to what the old woman had to say. Nyaboke was a little drunk, for it was mid-afternoon already, and she gave a histrionic account of her husband's family's migration to the area and of her life with him, accompanied by dramatic gesticulation. Apparently she remembered her husband's age-mate, Mary's father-in-law, with affection, and even though he had died at least forty-five years ago, time was telescoped in her memory so that it seemed to her he had been dead only a short while. She insisted, therefore, that Mary must remember him as well as she did herself, when of course Mary was not married to Nyagama until a few years ago. Zipporah looked at several points as if she were about to guffaw with laughter, but she pressed the back of her hand against her mouth and controlled herself. She always had respect for her mother-in-law, whatever treatment she received. Currently, as Nyaboke disclosed, Zipporah was having to sleep in the old woman's house in order to avoid Makori. He had resumed drinking almost immediately after his head operation, and the effect on his temper had been disastrous, at least for Zipporah. Thus Nyaboke had given her daughter-in-law and most of her grandchildren house room so that when Makori returned drunk after dark, he would find his prey had escaped. He would curse and shout for a while, but then he would fall into bed and sleep.

A couple of weeks later Makori, whom I still had not seen, beat his mother late one afternoon when he returned home drunk. I found Nyaboke hobbling about, frowning in pain. "I went to my eldest son's house and begged to be taken in, but he refused me. He said my place was with Zipporah, my lastborn's wife. But could I go there? Makori would find me and beat me again, so I went to my cowife's house and slept there, with Moraa."

So Makori was on a rampage. Zipporah, who was nursing her new baby, told us Makori was in a vile temper not just because he was drunk. Though he invariably beat his wife, it took more than beer to make him beat his own mother. He wanted to rent out their one small pyrethrum field to raise money for a third head operation, but Nyaboke and Zipporah were doing their best to prevent this. Thus Makori was creating an uproar at home.

> Everyone is out of favor with Makori except Tabitha. "He has never beaten that girl, since the day I brought her here. Perhaps he *should* beat her after all, for she is bound to get into trouble before long. She goes off in the morning in her uniform, but she doesn't go to school. She hides behind the hedge and waits for boys. She's more interested in boys than in learning. I myself beat her but it makes no difference."

Perhaps Zipporah saw her daughter already headed along the same path she herself had taken as a girl, but in this case Tabitha seemed to have her stepfather's tacit encouragement. Neither Zipporah nor Makori had ever spent a day at school themselves, but to Zipporah, some of whose siblings were currently in secondary school, education was of primary importance, for girls as much as for boys. "You can see for yourself," she seemed to be saying to me, "what a place I have married into." She was setting herself apart. She did not say that she herself was superior to her in-laws, only that *they* were inferior, and I was left to draw my own conclusions. She went out of her way to criticize her cousin-in-law, Ongaki, Suzanna's husband. She described how he used to behave when he was employed, how he drank and spent every penny he earned (unlike her own teetotaling, parsimonious family, her mother and her mother's cowives, all of whom scrimped and saved and invested everything in their children's education). Mary heard these stories and said to me later, "Should we believe what Zipporah says about Makori? Gusii people are always telling lies behind one another's backs." As it turned out, Zipporah's stories did seem to be true. Mary had a point, however; Zipporah was too quickly indiscreet about her husband's relatives when we still scarcely knew her.

It was not until the fourth session that I met Makori. As we sat talking under the arbor of passion fruit vines in Zipporah's yard, Makori came up the path, a wide, pleasant, silly grin on his face. The stories I had heard of his bizarreness scarcely prepared me for what I saw: he was wearing ancient green overalls, the legs cut off at the knees. There was a long ragged rent diagonally across one buttock. Over his hair he wore a blue kerchief tied in a knot above his forehead. He extended one huge, bony hand to me in greeting and stood a while, looming over me as he talked in a most friendly—though disjointed—manner about his recent head operation. His legs, as Zipporah had described, were caked with dried mud. ("He does not like to go to the river. I have never known him to wash. He thinks to be clean is something very bad.") His feet were a match for his hands. Had he worn shoes, he would probably have needed a size fifteen. He told me that he needed another operation: "I can't stop drinking, so there is no point in anyone telling me to stop. Even if I get dizzy and fall down, I must drink."

He first had headaches more than twenty years ago, he told me, grinning all the while. Then five years ago he hit his head on the door jamb (a very common cause of skull fractures and chronic headaches in this area), and two years ago he paid 150 shillings for an operation. He told me the name of the surgeon and where he came from, as if he were giving a social history. Zipporah, who was standing beside me, shook her head violently in disagreement at certain points. "You did *not* pay 150 shillings," she said, but Makori did not deign to look at her or speak to her. The children, however, clung to him. They had run to greet him when he first came into the yard, and now he had one hanging from each arm and another holding the cloth of the seat of his boiler suit. The little ones seemed very attached to him and he to them. He swung them round as he talked to me. Zipporah's skin and eyes shone. She looked as if she was about to burst with scorn or laughter, but apart from the one remark she made about the operation fee, she kept silent and soon went into the house to roast some maize for us. When Makori appeared she relinquished center stage to him, but it was at a psychological price she seemed hard put to pay. Other women, warring with their husbands, would fall into a glum dense silence when they reappeared. But Zipporah's silence today and on many other days was so agitated that I had the sense that she was screaming, and her lips were wrapped over one another, squeezed shut to prevent any sound from escaping.

She often behaved in the same way when her mother-in-law was holding forth. When we arrived for the fifth session Nyaboke was drunk again.

"Why is my son sleeping and not drinking beer?" she exclaims. "It is already the ninth hour, and I have been drinking since the fifth, and yet my son has still taken nothing." At which Makori appears in the doorway, dressed in a new pair of shorts and a shirt. He has scarcely greeted us before seizing a length of barbed wire and charging off across the yard after his eight-year-old son, Gichaba. The boy flees from him, squealing with laughter. I am certain that the father is about to lacerate the son for no reason I know of, but then I realize this is just Makori's game. Gichaba is not afraid after all. When Makori lumbers back again, his mother tells him, "Go and drink beer, my son. If you haven't any money, I will give you some. I have drunk so you, too, must go there. I've paid two shillings for you. Go and drink what they have kept for you." Makori grins at me and does as he is bidden. Watching him depart, the old woman remarks with the utmost satisfaction, "Now all three of my sons are drinking." And she turns and goes toward her own house fifty yards away.

Zipporah, who has been observing the scene, shrugs her shoulders.

"He didn't sleep at home last night. He was drunk. He never reached this house. But you saw his new clothes, didn't you? I bought those shorts months ago with money my brother-in-law gave me for Makori. Makori wouldn't wear them until today. Yesterday people laughed at him in his rags at the beer party, and so at last he agreed to take off that thing he was wearing. His shirt I got in payment of a chicken. He has already torn it, as you saw. As for that cloth on his head, he wears that to hide the place where he had his operation. The wound is not yet healed. He talks of having another operation, but even now I cannot manage him. Usually I cannot sleep here because he gets so drunk at night. He drinks heavily to help the pain. What would happen if he had yet another operation?"

Zipporah almost allowed herself to be sorry for Makori. His headaches were truly terrible, she agreed, but still the principal sufferer was herself, who had to live with a madman, one who chased his child with barbed wire. Before our very eyes her mother-in-law had sent her husband out to drink again, to get drunk as he had done the previous night and every other night. She, Zipporah, tried to provide for Makori by getting reasonable clothes for him so he would not be a laughing stock, but he refused for months to wear the clothes she bought for him, and when he did so he tore them so that in a moment he was almost as comical as before.

Makori monopolized the conversation in the sixth session. I found him sitting in front of his house, a child in the crook of each arm. He had never spoken to a white person before, which might explain his lack of inhibition with me. Perhaps he wanted to display himself for my admiration, my amusement. His loquaciousness in itself marked him out as deviant in a culture where men are very circumspect and careful to preserve a dignified image. But Makori told me at great length, and with little elicitation on my part, about his first marriage.

He described how his wife left him because he was drunk all the time, how he kidnapped her child in order to force her back to him, but without success. In the end she left him and the court awarded him back his bridewealth, though he never was able to reclaim all the cattle involved.

In telling his story, he elaborated on his own idiosyncrasies. "I, Makori, do things in such and such a way." It was as if he were doing publicity for himself. He was bombarding me with *his* version of his life, "I am a drunkard"—so that I would not listen to the version he must have known Zipporah was telling me, namely, that he was *ritiba* (impotent). On this occasion he clearly wanted to prevent me from having a single private word with Zipporah, and in fact it was many weeks before he allowed us to be alone again for more than a few minutes. At times I thought that to continue my visits was pointless. I would spend hours watching a clown show in which Makori performed for me, played the buffoon, the *fou-savant,* while Zipporah moved like a shadow behind him, looking always as if she were about to burst into some great outpouring of mockery or angry tears. All she said, however, under her breath, again and again, was, "Lies, he tells only lies." But I continued because I knew no other couple like these two. Makori was the most traditional man in our sample. He had never been employed, nor had he ventured out of the district. He had rarely been to Kisii town and never to the hospital. In recent years he never even went to Morongo market for fear of being stopped by the tribal police and asked for his *kipande,* his card showing if he had paid his hut tax. Of course he had not paid it. He roamed about within an area about half a mile square, and thus he had confined himself for three years past. Mary, who lived a short distance away, had never seen him before she came to work with me.

One day as he sat in front of his house telling me how he had worked so hard on his farm to pay for Zipporah (while she, husking maize at his side, whispered, "Lies, all lies. His brothers paid for me"), a little girl came up the path into the yard. She had come to take a glowing coal from Zipporah's hearth to light her mother's fire.

Makori leaps to his feet and sashays across the compound, imitating the child. "See how she walks, like a woman. This is because she has chiggers. As soon as her mother takes one chigger out, another jumps right into the hole. That woman is a slut. She never sweeps or smears her house. [This from Makori, who has never been known to wash his own feet. But perhaps his soles are so callused no chigger could embed itself there.] Sarah, how can I see my children do not get chiggers?" "Get a job and buy them shoes," I reply, teasing him. "Why should I do that? I do quite well. I work very hard." "Is it you who works, or Zipporah?" I ask him in mock seriousness. "I graze the cow so that"—he points at the infant Omae—"can have milk. Sometimes I pick coffee. Anyway, if I had more energy, I wouldn't go somewhere else to find employment, I'd stay at home and work harder here. I was born to stay here. It is the most beautiful land in the world." "How do you know what the world is like," I ask, "if you've never been to Kipsigis country or even to the land of the Luos?" "At least I know the world is round." "Why do you say that?" I tease him. "Most people say it is flat." "I'll tell you how I know," he says. "Once I went to the river and looked into the water, and from the way it was flowing I knew the world was round. Why should I bother going anywhere else to check when I am already certain? I shall live and die here, at home. But," he adds with pride, "I used to have two bicycles. I chased after my first wife on one when she ran away to a relative at Nyagneba. I rode there to kidnap her child. Oh, yes. I used to travel about in those days, but even then I didn't look to left or right. I saw neither tree nor hill nor flower. I pedaled to where I wanted to go, and then I pedaled home again. But these days," he shook his head regretfully, "I have no bicycles. They fell to pieces." Then he laughs not, I think, because he like me finds himself comical but merely because my attention makes him feel good. He catches my eye, preens himself, and laughs again.

He said his head operation made it impossible for him to work. He had nothing to do but drink, or wait at home until the hour of the day when drinking starts. If he had initially made a point of being at home when I came in order to prevent Zipporah from talking with me, now he found this opportunity to display himself so pleasurable that he certainly was not going to forgo it. He also, evidently, was getting some kind of advantage socially from having me as a visitor. While some of the women tried to conceal their relationship with me from their neighbors, Makori seemed to be flaunting it. Indeed he had been telling people that with his recommendation they could bring their children to our pediatric clinic, even though registration had long since been closed. One afternoon a child came into the yard and, seeing me, ran off instantly. In a little while she returned with her mother, who said Makori had told her to come to speak to me about getting medical care for her children, even though her homestead was outside our area. I had to refuse her while Makori looked on, grinning. If he was humiliated by my refusal to accept this woman, Teresa, after his assurance to her that he would "fix" things for her, he certainly did not show it. Zipporah watched this scene in silence, the usual explosive expression on her face.

But gradually Zipporah did begin to participate in the conversation. Perhaps as Makori, the gatekeeper, got used to me, he could allow his wife more access to me. Instead of Makori's monologue, what now evolved were dual conversations: both Makori and Zipporah talked to Mary and myself, but they did not talk to one another. Each listened to what the other said, then contradicted what had been said, directing his comments to us. We were the wedge between them, the no-man's-land, making verbal rather than physical combat possible. For example, one day we were talking about Makori's nonpayment of the local council hut tax. Makori told me he had been excused because of his head injury. "That's a lie," Zipporah interjected. Makori ignored her. He said he had not paid the tax for four years. "Four years!" Zipporah exclaimed. "In the ten years since I came here he hasn't paid it, Sarah. The police caught him once on the way home from the coffee cooperative, when he had cash on him, so they made him pay. Never since that time. But one day they'll come here and catch him." Makori nodded. "It's true what I tell you. I have been excused."

A little while later Zipporah was talking about her mother's relationship with her cowives. She got on well with one but badly with the other.

> "She told me never to accept a cowife, if I could avoid it. Tabitha's father had another wife, and that is why I refused to marry him, even though he wanted me. Then Makori's *omosigane* [go-between] came and I accepted." As she says this, her face is contorted with feeling. Makori remarks that he is considering getting another wife. "I have two cows. I need three more. Perhaps my first wife will come back to me. She has only two

children, which is good. Zipporah does nothing but produce *chimbaba* [rats]. I want family planning myself."

"That's the first I've ever heard of it," Zipporah exclaims.

"Women are always against it," says Makori. I ask where Zipporah could get birth control pills. "Oh, pills aren't any good," Makori says. "Women suffer with those. They have pains; they vomit. There is nothing for it but for Zipporah to get more rats." I say birth control is his responsibility as well as Zipporah's. Makori laughs, "How can that be? When I'm having sex I am sweaty and tired. I don't think at all of the rats which will come." "What about abstaining from sex?" I tease him. "How can I do that? When the two of us are alone in bed in the dark, and no one is watching us, I have to have sex. And then the rats come."

"If he doesn't want rats, let him sleep alone from this day on," Zipporah says. "He should have stayed with his first wife, the Maragoli woman. She can't have any more children."

Later, as we were leaving, Makori insisted on escorting us. He growled into my ear, "Zipporah is a dog. If I don't have intercourse with her, she'll go running about." He was a centimeter from me, and very agitated. In an effort to distance him a little, I remarked that it was getting late and asked whether he did not intend to drink that day. "Oh, yes, I'm on my way now. I must drink and feel full as if I have eaten *obokima*. Beer is like tea to me. But don't listen to Zipporah. She will only tell you lies." "She says the same about you," I pointed out. Makori snorted and veered off down a little path in the direction of a homestead where a beer party was in progress.

During this session, Zipporah and Makori had seemed equally determined to gain my support. They watched me and my reactions throughout, but they did not look at one another. Once, when Makori went out of the house for a moment, I asked Zipporah, "Which is better, to have a husband who is feebleminded or to share a clever man with another woman?" but I did not get an answer because Makori loomed in the doorway.

Conversations such as this one made me anxious. I was torn between leaving and staying. I felt that I was taking unfair advantage of a man who, because of his emotional condition and his intellectual inadequacy, was unable to censor himself. He talked about things that a

Gusii man should not mention to a stranger, much less to a woman. To save his face, so that he might salvage some self-respect, I should leave. But Makori did not seem at all uncomfortable. On the contrary, he *wanted* me to stay and listen to him so that he could persuade me that he was potent as other men, that the children were all his. I stayed and listened to this message repeated many times, but I found I was compelled to structure things in order to keep a distance between us both physically and socially. I found myself teasing him, setting him up as a buffoon, to Zipporah's delight. A Gusii man with *amasikane,* a self-respecting middle-aged man, would find my behavior intolerable, but Makori encouraged me whenever we met, even in other homesteads where I sometimes found him drinking beer. During the early part of December, when beer was plentiful and the community was preparing for circumcision, I came upon Makori several times a day. I would turn a corner in the *rikori* (cattle path), and there he would be, grinning, lying in wait for me. I found his unpredictable presence disconcerting, almost threatening.

It was not until the eleventh session that I managed to see Zipporah alone. Both husband and mother-in-law had gone to drink, and Zipporah settled down with Mary and me under the arbor. She reported two dreams. In the first, she and Mary were talking together in the yard, and Mary said to her, "Put on your underpants." Then in the dream a neighbor came and Zipporah awoke. She commented that she always slept naked. Makori and the children did too. In her own home it was the same. Most uneducated people slept naked; they covered themselves with blankets, but clothing they found uncomfortable. Since she had not seen Mary for a week, she was surprised to dream about her.

In the second dream a young neighbor of Zipporah's who worked in Mombasa came home on leave. The next morning she saw him on the road, so he had indeed come home, and Zipporah had had no idea he was due for leave. She commented she was happy to see him. She knew then that she had dreamed "right," though generally she was alarmed when what she dreamed came true. She noticed this happened quite frequently, and it worried her. Clairvoyance was not a gift a person could feel happy about. For example, if she dreamed someone died, he invariably did so. She believed there were other people who had this same ability to foretell the future in dreams, but she had not talked with any (not even, apparently, with her friend Suzanna, who was similarly burdened. These women shared their dreams only with their husbands, and now with me.). She told her neighbor she had dreamed of him, but that was because she met him by chance. She would not have gone out of her way to look for him (if she heard he had come home) in order to tell him of her dream.

So Zipporah too believed she was clairvoyant. Moreover, she had dreamed that Mary, a woman of Bogoro like herself, told her to put on her underpants. Mary, we have established, lived near a half sister of Zipporah, a woman who, being a little younger than herself, was educated and had become a nurse. Erena was her name, and she was proud. She had beautiful clothes and a well-to-do husband, and she refused to check Zipporah's children if they were sick, even though she was their aunt. Mary was the same age as Erena. She spoke English and lived an ordered life with her progressive husband. No doubt Mary wore nightdresses and slept in sheets, as Erena did. Perhaps she too would despise Zipporah, as her own sister despised her, for being a bush woman who slept without clothes. In the dream Mary told Zipporah to dress, to hide the most intimate part of herself, i.e., to control herself. Just at that point a neighbor came, breaking into the privacy and overhearing the secrets Zipporah was revealing. Instantly, in order to keep those secrets hidden, Zipporah awakened. And so it seemed that Zipporah was ambivalent about the relationship with us that she had been easing herself into these past four months. Perhaps Makori's chaperonage had been quite welcome to her. It slowed things down. But now there was much beer to be drunk, and Makori's head was better. He was out much more than before, and Zipporah would in the future be finding herself alone with us, with nothing to impede the revelation of secrets. In part she was eager for the revelations, and in part she was afraid. She dreamed about Mary, my interpreter and intercessor. Zipporah, it seemed, needed help in handling her erotic impulses. Perhaps Mary would supply those controls. But what about me? How did she regard me? Could she engage me also to control her impulses?

She said she had never known any Europeans before me. She was not sure what white people were like, but Makori told her white people quarreled and divorced just as Africans did; he said everyone was the same the world over. Makori knew this because in Kisii town Euro-

peans locked their houses. "They are afraid of thieves here," he told her,
"because they have been forewarned by their experiences with thieves in
their own country." He also said Europeans introduced the practice of
divorce. They quarreled with their wives and sent them away, and so
Africans followed their example. "Makori claims to know everything,
even though he's never been anywhere," Zipporah said, belittling him,
but clearly she had paid some attention to her husband's opinions,
despite her skepticism.

If Europeans had thieves, they must have witchcraft too. Zipporah
had seen photographs of crippled white children. Since crippling was
always caused by witchcraft, obviously Europeans, just like the Gusii,
felt jealous of one another and resorted to witchcraft to get even with
their enemies and people who had been successful. "Everyone is jealous
of the success of others," Zipporah said. I pointed out that in America
there were many educated and wealthy people who thrived without
incurring afflictions. But Zipporah had a ready answer. "Even in Kenya
there are many educated and wealthy people, and many thrive. But
that is because not everyone can die. Some survive even witchcraft."

And so it seemed that if Zipporah was leery about trusting Mary, a
Gusii, she was equally reluctant to trust me. Europeans were mortal.
They were like other people, like Africans, like the people of Bogoro
whom Zipporah did not trust. She was the only woman in my study
who did not idealize Europeans; on the contrary, she assumed that
Europeans were like herself, as likely to experience jealousy and *to be
motivated to malevolence by jealousy* as Gusii people were. When later her
relationship with Makori and his family became tortuous and strained,
and Zipporah continued to tell a different story from everyone else in
the community, I would wait, unbelieving, for her to "tell me the
truth," to make a clean breast of it, since after all no one believed her
version. But she always clung to it. Better to stick to her lies regardless
of the evidence piled up against her. Her code appeared to be definite
on this point: never concede guilt, never voluntarily admit your culpability. You cannot trust anyone not to kick you if you are down, even a
foreigner who has no investment in the community and with whom you
have a generally warm relationship. If no one else will save your face for
you, then you must save it yourself, and if you have no other means,
then the most threadbare lies must suffice. You can tell all you know
about someone else, your husband or your son; you can incriminate

them freely. It is expected and ultimately acceptable. But you never incriminate yourself.

One day we passed Makori doing a "contract," i.e., day laboring on the house a relative was building. We were glad to have a chance to see Zipporah alone. She told us Makori had earned fifteen shillings from his relative but had already spent it on beer and his woman friend. She remarked casually that Teresa, the woman who came asking to be registered at our clinic, and Makori had been lovers for the past eighteen months.

> "And she is not the only woman he has. He goes with any-
> one, especially old women others do not want." She lists a few
> women of at least fifty-five years of age whom it is hard to im-
> agine having a sex life any more. "He has so much energy with
> them. They drink and then they go to have sex. But with me he
> only wants sex once a month. I don't like his having other
> women, but what can I do? And anyway, I don't like him to
> have sex with me. He is so dirty, and this way he leaves me
> alone most of the time. Really what I do not like is that any
> money he has he spends on those women, on beer and soap for
> them. But meanwhile I have no soap." She says the older chil-
> dren are well aware of Makori's behavior. "Once Teresa was
> drinking *changaa* here when I was at the market. When I came
> back, Teresa, who was very drunk, said, 'You should cook for
> Makori.' I had no vegetables, so I went to a neighbor to get
> some, and while I was gone a certain old lady, Bosibori, came
> and knocked at the door. It was locked and from within the
> house Teresa called, 'Makori has seduced me.' Bosibori was very
> shocked, and she often reminds me of this incident. When I
> myself returned with my vegetables, I found Teresa sitting in
> the yard, but her skirt was all wet. Women who are drunk when
> they are having sex often urinate because they can't control
> themselves, and this is what Teresa had done. That was two
> years ago, nearly. These days I stay away from Teresa as much as
> I can. [I remember a time Teresa came into the yard and Zip-
> porah had her "bursting" look on her face.] When Omae was
> born, Makori took Teresa ten shillings but gave nothing to me.
> We often quarrel about Teresa, and she is not the only one,
> either. Areba's wife comes here—he has another wife where he
> lives in the settlement scheme—and the mother-in-law of
> Marisera, whom you know. They are both old, but they still

come looking for Makori. I don't know what they are coming for, whether beer or sex. When he was married to the Maragoli woman he was impotent, and her child was by another man. Even now, after all the sacrifices made for him, he can only ejaculate once, and then he waits a week or two before he can have sex again. People say my children are from outside, from other men. Certainly Makori believes this. He is so jealous of me. He follows me wherever I go to see if I am meeting men."

"But you said just now that Makori is very energetic," I say. "How can he be energetic if he scarcely ever can have sex?"

"When I told you he had so much energy, maybe I was hiding the truth and waiting for you to get the real story."

"Well, what do you think Makori is doing with these women?"

"I told you, I don't actually know. But can you keep a secret? My second child, Suzannah, is not his. Not only was Makori impotent with his first wife, but with me too. I couldn't wait. I ran away to another man. While I was gone Makori slaughtered yet more goats, but even though he improved a little, he is not really like a man, even now. I don't like to have sex with Makori. I always fight him. I can't be sure any child of mine is his, though Robina [aged two] looks like him. She has his hair. Makori says Omae must be the son of Obao [a cousin] because once he found Obao drinking beer here. Makori is waiting to see what kind of hair Omae will grow. But he is wrong; Obao and I never had sex together. Obao seduced Makori's niece, Maria, not me, Makori's wife. But of course it is I whom he accuses, not Maria.

"Do you remember that time Makori called the children rats? Well, he came home in a rage that evening because I had said in front of you that he always tells lies. He does not want me to talk to you." Zipporah gets up and looks about her as if she expects Makori to appear at any moment, but he is still to be seen safely on the far side of the valley, at the construction site of his relative's new house.

"Sarah," Zipporah turns to me, "how often do white men want sex?" but she barely listens to my answer. "Makori's much taller than I am," she bursts out, "but he never digs or weeds or helps me in the garden. He is a weakling. Those women only like him because he buys them beer. He is no more good for them than he is for me. My mother, who forced me to come here and to remain here, now tells me I should leave and find another husband. She says that Makori treats me badly in every way. He never gives me anything, and if I buy something like a blanket for the children with money from my chickens, Makori only takes it for himself. But I can't listen to my mother. I have six children, so I must stay here. I do not want to spoil my name."

I had already heard several people say that Makori was impotent and Zipporah's children were fathered by other men, and here Zipporah was confirming the neighborhood gossip. I rarely heard other Gusii women, married and living with their husbands, admit to having extramarital relations. They might fantasize about going with other men, but always they would make quite clear that I should not misunderstand them. Though they often thought of taking lovers—out of revenge, usually, against their neglectful husbands—they never conceded that they had actually done so. The expectation was that a wife should be faithful, regardless of her husband's behavior, and even though the entire community might be aware that a woman was promiscuous, she would protest her fidelity face to face. Later Zipporah would retract this admission of infidelity, but at this point in her battle with Makori it was very important to her to win my support. She was prepared to admit adultery, while making the point that her failings were far less shameful than Makori's. If she sought other men it was for a very good reason, a reason which was acceptable in the culture— namely, her husband was impotent. He was of no use to her. She hated him for this and was willing to have me hear the secrets of their marriage in order to win me over to her side and have *me* scorn Makori's protestations of virility, of his capacity to sire "rats" ad infinitum, just as *she* scorned them.

For most of the month of December, the month of eating and drinking—and consequently of quarreling and fighting—I was in Europe, and when I returned I found that Zipporah had quarreled violently with Makori and gone home. I met her mother-in-law, Nyaboke, at the *okwarokio* (the coming out after circumcision) of two little girls, cousins of Makori. Nyaboke was the *omokorerani*. She was guiding the children through the ritual and was thus much absorbed. But I did get from her that, on discovering that a tin of her *wimbi* (finger millet) had been stolen, she had gone to a diviner. The diviner had told her that the grain was stolen by Zipporah and her friend Marisera, a young English-speaking woman whom I knew quite well and who was married to a second cousin of Makori. Other guests at this party had different suggestions as to who might have stolen the *wimbi*. One said Orindo, a local man who had been in prison many times already for stealing from his neighbors, was probably the thief. Another said, "How could it be Zipporah? No one has ever accused her of stealing before. She is not that kind of person at all." But Nyaboke was adamant. "Zipporah will be back before long," someone remarked. "She has to take care of her *shamba*." And indeed, after a little more than a week she did return. When I visited her she was pleased to see me.

> "I came back because I heard my children were suffering. Makori didn't beat me when I returned, but he hasn't spoken to me, and neither has my mother-in-law. Makori has been sleeping somewhere else at night. He takes his mother's side entirely, of course. But I didn't take that tin. Why should I? I have plenty of *wimbi* of my own. So has Marisera. Marisera's father is bringing the case to the *abaturetti* [ward heads], in order to clear his daughter's name. He doesn't want this slander to continue. I believe my sister-in-law took the *wimbi*."

On the day the case was to be heard, Mary and I had some difficulty in finding any of the principal participants. We had been told the *abaturetti* would assemble in a certain field at a certain time, but the field was deserted. We met Nyaboke, the old lady, but she was thin lipped and silent. She passed us, marching purposefully in the direction of a beer party. Eventually we found Zipporah with a relative. She took us back to her house, whispering that Makori was continually bringing cases to the *abaturetti*. It was his favorite pastime. These cases were always about her talking with strange men. However, this one, since it did not concern his own honor, he had left to Marisera's father to bring. Makori had no interest in clearing Zipporah's name. He was delighted to have her vilified. In fact he had done as much as possible to stop the case from being heard at all, because it suited him very well for people to continue to say bad things about Zipporah.

> "He has been running around today trying to change the minds of the *abaturetti*. Perhaps, if he gives them beer, they will forget to hear the case at all, or so he thinks." She confides that she herself is very afraid of the case and almost wishes Makori

could prevent the hearing. "I am so afraid of standing up in front of all those people. I shall shake with fear. They say that if we are convicted we shan't have to pay a fine. They intend to shame us, that's all, and the shame will prevent us from doing such a thing again."

Though she ceased to protest her innocence, this admission of fear and dread of shame was as close as she ever came to admitting her guilt. Word reached us that the *abaturetti* were assembled at last, not in the field but in someone's house, and Zipporah should go there "so the case may be solved, once and for all." Zipporah nursed Omae, tidied up her living room, and then, reluctantly, she handed the baby to Tabitha. When we came to the house we found the *abaturetti* had been served beer *before* the hearing instead of waiting until afterward, the usual procedure. And it was obvious from the din emanating from within that everyone was already either drunk or well on the way. Marisera and Zipporah hovered behind me, their faces completely impassive. At no point did any one of the elders speak to them. I asked to see one of the *abaturetti,* and he came out in due course to tell me the case had been delayed until the following week. He smiled apologetically and went back to his beer. As we wandered away, we were overtaken by one of Mary's brothers-in-law, an elder of the community, who took it upon himself to explain what had occurred.

"There is no doubt that the two women are guilty. But the case had to be settled in the homestead. It won't be heard next week or ever. Everyone is from the same family. You cannot pursue such a case to the chief or to the police. Even the *abaturetti* should not hear it, for cases such as these tear families apart. The father of Marisera, who is himself an *omoturetti* in another area, knows this well enough. And so he saved everyone's face: he brought the case—to save his own and his daughter's face. Then he bought beer for the *abaturetti* to allow them to agree to let the case go before they had even heard it; thus the women went unindicted. And yet they have been sufficiently frightened that this incident may be a warning to them not to try anything so foolish again." "And their motive, why did they do it?" I ask. "It is because of Makori. He gives her nothing. With Marisera's help Zipporah stole that *wimbi* so she might sell it and buy things she needed for her children."

And so it seemed that everyone, though certain Zipporah stole from her mother-in-law, appreciated her motive, sympathized with her, and thought it right that she be let off with a warning. As for Makori, we met him a little later, jubilant. "Of course they stole it, and everyone knows this to be true. See, they did not even bother to have a case. Those women are thieves."

Four days later we found Zipporah at home alone. She was sitting glumly under the arbor, Omae on her lap. Omae, who was five and a half months old now, was small and scrawny but very alert, as were all Zipporah's children. Though she did not play with them much, when Zipporah talked to them she was almost always gentle, however tired or upset she was. Omae had found a playmate in his sister Robina, who spent a great deal of time coaxing him to laugh and giggle while their mother looked impassively over their heads. Sometimes the children were absorbed in their games for long periods, and Zipporah paid them almost no attention at all. Today she was heedless of their squeals of laughter.

"The *abaturetti* dropped the case, you know," she says in a tight voice. "Makori bribed them with the money he'd earned digging Obeita's latrine. He wanted the case stopped so that everyone would continue to think I was a thief. Yes, he *wants* people to believe I am a bad person. Also he is afraid of Mari-sera's father, Chweya, who is a sorcerer. Makori wanted Chweya to go to his home and never come back. Now, with the case stopped, Chweya has gone home for good, and Makori is happy once more. He has started eating here again. He even talks to me once in a while, though mostly he talks to his mother. He has agreed to plant the old woman's *wimbi* when the planting season comes." (Gusii men very rarely have anything to do with *wimbi,* which is considered women's work.) She takes out her breast to nurse Omae. As she looks down to see if he is sucking properly, she remarks bitterly, "I wish the case had gone to the chief and he'd put Makori in prison for bearing false testimony against me. Makori is always bringing cases against me."

I ask her what he charges her with. She answers indirectly: "If I am late back from the marketplace, he asks what man I have been having sex with. My mother tells me I should pack up and go home, but I am afraid to leave the bigger children here [as she would have to do, since Makori has paid bridewealth for her and therefore has proprietary rights over the children]. Makori can't be trusted to take care of them. Last time I went home he fried fertilized eggs for them. In fact the chicks were about to hatch. He took them from under the hen. He doesn't give me soap. He spends his contract money on bribing the *abaturetti*."

I believe Zipporah did steal the *wimbi,* but she never admitted it to me or probably to anyone else, even though, apart from Makori and his mother, people in the neighborhood were quite sympathetic to her. Everyone knew her children went in rags and Makori drank away any money she earned from the cooperative society. All December he had been drinking, and Zipporah did not have a cent with which to pay building fees when the new school year opened the first week of January. No one had any difficulty in understanding Zipporah's motivation. Marisera was merely an accomplice. She helped Zipporah out of friendship, not for personal gain. The consensus in the neighborhood, however, was that such behavior, though understandable, should be strongly discouraged, and this should be accomplished by shaming the two women. And for her part Zipporah *was* ashamed, and frightened too, but once the case had been dropped and everyone had settled down again, she remained bitter and resentful. She went about her business in angry silence. When her beer was ready and she offered it for sale, I found her customers enjoying themselves, the old woman Nyaboke full of laughter and indiscreet gossip in the midst of them. Zipporah padded about with Omae on her back, attending to everyone's needs, but silent, her eyes downcast, refusing to be touched by the hilarity or to guffaw with the others at Nyaboke's jokes.

One Monday morning after a weekend in which I had not been in the community at all, we met Marisera in the road. She pulled us off to one side and spilled out a startling story. The previous Friday, a drunken Zipporah had been found at dusk by a young relative, Simeon, having intercourse in a thicket beside the road with a neighbor, Jeremiah. Now Jeremiah was not only Makori's second cousin but Zipporah's first cousin, since his mother and Zipporah's father were brother and sister. By having sexual relations they thus committed two sacrileges, the first as "brother" and "sister" and the second as in-laws. And what was more, rumor had it that they had been lovers for years, beginning long ago before Zipporah was married to Makori. Some even said Tabitha was fathered by Jeremiah, although Marisera herself did not believe this, as Tabitha looked like another man altogether. On discovering Zipporah and Jeremiah together, Simeon raised the alarm, and Makori, who was drinking nearby, having first rushed home to collect his spear (*ritimo*), went off in pursuit. He was too late, of course, to catch his wife red-handed, but over the weekend he brought the case to the *abaturetti*. At the hearing Zipporah and Jeremiah were ordered to prepare for the elaborate ritual which Gusii custom requires be performed by those who have committed such a sacrilege. Marisera herself had once seen this ritual performed by two cousins of hers. She had been a child at the time, but she claimed to remember (inaccurately, I discovered; Marisera was very agitated as she described the scene) how each had stood over a trench and had cut his or her genitals so that blood flowed, whereupon each had then been directed to taste the other's blood. And this exchange had been followed by sacrifices. Now, Marisera reported, everyone was waiting to hear the date on which the ritual would be performed for the cleansing of Zipporah and Jeremiah. As she left us she remarked, "People have said Makori is impotent, though this I cannot know. However, I do know Zipporah has gone with many men. In this case, with this man she sinned many times, and the fortieth time she was caught."

Six days previously we had seen Zipporah, depressed and angry, serving her customers at her own beer party. Four days ago she had been found in the act of adultery. At the hearing Jeremiah had testified he was "invited," indeed Zipporah had dragged him into the bush and practically forced him to have intercourse with her. She had been drunk but insistent. Naturally Jeremiah would attempt to whitewash himself, to protest his (relative) innocence. On the other hand, given Zipporah's mood following the aftermath of the *wimbi* incident, her alleged behavior might seem credible, in fact, very deliberate. Since she really had nothing of a "good name" left to lose, perhaps she hoped at least to take short-lived revenge upon her husband. While she might run the risk of being caught in the dusk, her adulterous act, though drawing abuse upon herself, at the same time illuminated Makori's shameful condition of impotency. Though neighbors might say, "Zipporah is a bad woman who cannot control herself," they would also say, "She goes to other men, even her own cousins, because Makori's thing is useless, it cannot stand up." If they enjoyed reviling her, they would scorn Makori with even greater relish.

When we go to the homestead we find both Zipporah and Makori in the yard. "I've heard an amazing story about Jeremiah," I say. "Is it true?" Makori throws back his head and laughs, all his long teeth flashing. "You heard how Simeon caught Zipporah in the *act?* I ran with my spear and when I met her on the path I beat her. Don't you see how her legs have swollen?" Zipporah, hovering in the doorway of the house, says, "I've been ill for a week. It is from digging that my legs are swollen." Makori snorts, "Don't you listen to her. I beat her. We had the case here on Sunday, and fifty people came." He grins gleefully. "Jeremiah tried to deny it, but the *abaturetti* said Simeon was telling the truth, for why should anyone accuse his own aunt unless he were speaking truthfully? The *abaturetti* told them both to prepare for *ogosonsorana* [the reconciliation ritual]. You know this is the second time I have had to bring a case against Jeremiah. Last January I noticed his footprints in the mud, next to Zipporah's. I recognized the pattern of the soles of his shoes. But the *abaturetti* dismissed that case because they said *amabarata* [footprints] were not sufficient evidence. But this time she was caught *in the act.*" "Why did you run to get your spear then," Zipporah cried, "instead of coming to catch me? I'll tell you why. Because you knew Simeon's story was a lie. I was only talking to Jeremiah, and indeed, when Simeon came upon me, I wasn't even with Jeremiah any longer. I was with a *woman.* It was too dark for Simeon to see properly." "Simeon got witnesses from that very beer party you'd been at yourself," Makori replies, grinning. He is enjoying himself thoroughly. They all saw you with Jeremiah." "This is the sixth case you've brought against me," Zipporah says bitterly. "Why did you want your wife to be branded a thief and an adulteress?"

Makori ignores the first epithet. Of the second he says, "I have to protect myself from *amasangia.* If I were ill, Jeremiah, being my cousin as well as yours, is likely to come visit me, and then I would die. Is it not true that our neighbor Machoma chased his wife away this month after their baby died? That child died because her mother was an adulteress. It is better that you stand accused before the elders than that I or one of our children die for your sins." He gets up abruptly and lopes off to his mother's house to light his cigarette at her cooking fire. While he is gone I ask Zipporah if she has *rirongo*, protective medicine against *amasangia*. *Rirongo* is the magical potion which Gusii buy and use to protect themselves and their families from the consequences of their adulteries. Zipporah shakes her head. "No, I have none." She seems very close to tears as Makori returns.

"Are these children mine?" Makori asks rhetorically. "No, they come from the world," he says, kicking the mangy cat in the rear. Omae, who has been laid to sleep on a cloth on the ground, starts to cry. Zipporah at this point is inside the house. "Won't you pick him up?" I ask Makori. "How can I do that? If wild animals were to attack us now, how could I protect us with that child in my arms? I have to have my hands free to hold my *panga*," he laughs, mirthlessly. "The child is tired," he yells at Zipporah. "I won't look after these rats. One isn't mine anyway. You brought her here with you, though the rest are mine." "If they are yours, why are you so afraid of *amasangia?*" Zipporah mocks him. "When I give birth, do I give birth in secret in the *shamba* for fear my lover will step over my birth blood and I will die? No, I give birth in the house [i.e., like a faithful wife]. If I were an adulteress I would have died of *amasangia* by now."

The two of them glare at one another. I say quietly to Makori, "What will become of Jeremiah now?"

"I'm going to bewitch him," Makori guffaws. "We'll slaughter a goat and call him to eat, but I'll put *emete* [a certain medicine] in his portion and he will die." He laughs and runs inside to fetch the spear with which he armed himself against Jeremiah. In fact it is not a spear, only a long piece of piping. He shows it to me with pride. "I beat her knees with this," he says.

"Everything he tells you is a lie," Zipporah says harshly. "He and I should hold the *omotembe* tree to see who lies and who speaks the truth." (Traditionally in the native court when two parties gave conflicting evidence, both would be required to take hold of the trunk of this particular tree, one of which was planted outside every courthouse or, before colonial times, in every clearing where cases were adjudicated. Each party would take an oath that he had spoken the truth, and it was believed that he who had lied would be struck dead. Thus, from fear of being put to such a test, anyone who had given false evidence usually retracted his testimony.)

"What is the *omotembe* tree?" Makori mocks. "I have never heard of such a thing."

If Zipporah committed adultery in order to take revenge upon Makori for his public accusation that she had stolen his mother's *wimbi* (part of which, as the wife of the old lady's youngest son, she might expect to be given as a gift, were her relationship with her mother-in-law somewhat different and better), her triumph had been short-lived indeed. In the nineteenth session we found her alone, for Makori had gone off with a *risaga* (community work group). He would never contribute his labor to his family's economy, only to his mother's and on occasion to a neighbor's, provided there was free beer at the end of the day.

> Zipporah pours out her thoughts. Recently we have been her only visitors, the only people who have dared to come to her house, for Makori has prohibited visitors. "The case will go to the chief next week," she tells us. "I want to do this, to clear my name. Makori was telling lies the other day when he said the *abaturetti* believed Simeon's story at the hearing. In fact they told Makori not to pursue the case without sufficient evidence, for after all, Makori has never himself seen me with another man. He claims that footprints or places in the *shamba* where the grass has been flattened are sufficient evidence that I have lain with a man, but the *abaturetti* say no, Makori must catch me himself. I wish I could kill him," she says wildly.
>
> "Kill whom?" I ask.
>
> "That uncircumcised boy, Simeon."

Simeon was in fact a married man with two children, but "uncircumcised boy (or girl)" is the most deprecating name one Gusii adult can call another. I was prepared to believe Zipporah's report of the *abaturetti*'s reaction, for having attended hearings myself I was well aware that their aim was conciliation, not the apportionment of blame. Later, when I spoke to one of the elders about this case, he conceded that Zipporah was a woman of questionable sexual reputation, but since she and Makori were continuing to live together they must be admonished to settle their differences, or at least gloss over them, rather than exacerbating them further. Zipporah also denied that the *abaturetti* had directed her and Jeremiah to perform the reconciliation sacrifice, and in this too she was probably correct, since it is the role of the diviner, the agent of the supernatural, the mouthpiece of the ancestor spirits, to prescribe the ritual. The *abaturetti* are merely laymen who might indeed suggest that the parties in the case consult a diviner, but they are not in a position themselves to order the performance of sacrifices.

> "I have heard of such rituals but have never seen them performed. I only know of *rirongo*. When I ran away from Makori after I had been here a year and returned to give birth to Suzannah, I bought *rirongo* from Nyambusi [the local purveyor of such potions] and sprinkled it on Makori's vegetables, to prevent *amasangia*. I told Makori this is what I had done, and he was happy to eat the food. But for him that was not precaution enough, for I discovered he himself had gone secretly to Nyambusi. She made little cuts on his back and into them she rubbed her medicine. When women commit adultery they always get *rirongo*, or if they don't they invite trouble. Men who have lovers do not get *rirongo* themselves. They expect their lovers to attend to that. I myself only got *rirongo* that once eight years ago. You get it only once, and it should protect you and your family thereafter. But Makori does not trust the power of it. He thinks it has worn off."

Today Zipporah would admit to only the one adulterous relationship, after which Suzannah was born. However clever Mary and I were in our questions, we were never, either that day or at any other time, able to get her to admit more recent adulteries, even those she herself had hinted at in the past. She had once told us she did not know whether any of her children were fathered by Makori, but now she insisted, just as Makori had insisted in the previous session, "All my children are his, except Suzannah."

> "I am so upset, I wish I could die," she tells us, perched on the edge of a chair, her eyes ranging over the yard. "If my home were farther away I would go there, but it is so close. Makori would force me to come back here. I don't know why he wants me. All he does is abuse me. I think in the past three years, he has got crazier than before. Perhaps it is the head operations. We live together thus, with nothing but abuse. The other day

when he came with his spear, hoping to catch me with
Jeremiah, I really fought him. I tore his shirt and I would have
torn his shorts, too, but he was armed and all I had was my bare
hands, so he beat me. I wish I could have torn off his penis and
thrown it into the bush. I ran away across the fields to my
brother-in-law's, and I slept there. Makori searched for me, and
when he couldn't find me he went home and seized the two
youngest children, Omae and Robina. He carried them to the
cooking fire, shouting, 'I am going to burn her rats,' but his
mother pulled them away from him and carried them off to her
own house for the night. I wish I could die. I would be much
better dead.

"Makori tells only lies about me. Jeremiah has always been
my cousin and my friend but never my lover. When we were
children we liked each other very much. But these days, though
we can see each other's homesteads, we meet rarely. When I
married here I was not especially glad that I would be living
near him." She becomes even more agitated. "I've never had sex
in the bush, in an open place, where someone could catch me."
The words are tumbling over one another. "The Gusii believe if
a man is impotent a woman has a right to go 'outside.' Everyone
believes Makori *is* impotent. It is true that since the sacrifices he
can make his thing stand up occasionally, but no one really
knows or believes this. People expect me to find other men.
They don't blame me, whatever I do, as long as I do it in secret.
But Makori is a madman. He wants children, and yet he does
not. He calls them rats. After the third child was born he said
that must be the last. 'No more rats.' He stole my underclothes
and took them to an *omorogi*, to have her bewitch me, to prevent
me from having more children."

"Who was the *omorogi?*" I ask, "She can't have been very powerful for you have had three more children."

"I don't know who she was."

It seemed, then, that the issue between Makori and Zipporah was
not simply Zipporah's persistence in seeking extramarital relationships
to provide her with the children she believed to be her right. Her
behavior, as long as it was discreet, was sanctioned by the culture. It
was expectable and acceptable. It was Makori's reaction to her behavior
which was deviant. Were he a man of respect he would try to make the
best of his affliction with good grace. He would allow his wife to

provide him with the children—in particular the sons—every Gusii man desires. Meanwhile, with dignity, he would fulfill the role of the sociological if not the biological father. But Makori had no dignity, no good grace. Zipporah's sexual activities continued, after ten years, to rankle and periodically to enrage him. For her part it seemed that she was not as discreet as she should be. She was very resistant to Makori in the first place, for reasons which are not hard to understand, and no doubt her resentment had sometimes motivated her to be less than discreet in her liaisons. The flagrancy of her behavior may in fact have been beyond her conscious control, given the force of her resentment against Makori.

But any attempts Zipporah might make to be discreet were further undermined by alcohol. She came from a family which, in her girlhood, had not yet become Seventh Day Adventist. "We went to the Sabbath, but my mother had not been baptized when I married because she was still making beer to support her children." Only after Zipporah left home did Kemunto become a maize trader; then she could afford to give up brewing beer and become a full member of the church. Zipporah herself, even though she had no doubt adopted many Adventist domestic habits and ideals, nevertheless had never been baptized. She had continued to drink even though in her own family, all three cowives of her father with their children had become Christians, i.e., had given up brewing, selling, and drinking beer. Thus, if Makori had a drunkard's habits and reputation, Zipporah was no saint either. Occasionally, if I met her late in the day, I realized she had been drinking, but whereas many women become talkative and disorganized when they are drunk, Zipporah's style was different. She was quiet and unobtrusive. Thus I was never very aware of her drinking or of the adverse effect alcohol had upon her.

In the twentieth session she announced that the previous Saturday she had attended the Sabbath and now she had given up drinking.

> "It is beer which has got me into trouble. If I stay at home and don't go along the paths or to other homesteads, I shall be all right. On Saturday I went with a friend to church. I like to hear the word of God. People may abuse you at home, but if you go to church you can feel well in your heart again."

Makori, it seemed, had not changed *his* habits. Even now he was sleeping off the aftereffects of *changaa*. As Zipporah added, however,

"We are doing better together this week. We've agreed to drop the case concerning Jeremiah and myself. For my part, by staying at home I shall keep out of any more trouble."

For the rest of my time in the field, Zipporah did indeed go to Sabbath from time to time. Occasionally she would brew beer at home to sell and would herself drink a fair amount on the side. She would stay away from the Sabbath for a week or two, until her discomfort had worn off. Then she would go to church again. I once came upon the whole family, the youngest children included, drunk at noon. As usual Zipporah was silent. She smiled as she went back and forth from the house to the arbor where her customers sat. They were being entertained by the *omobari* (head surgeon) who had performed Makori's head operations. (The second operation had evidently been successful, for Makori no longer complained about headaches.) He was playing a horn to which he sang and danced. Makori introduced him to me with pride and bade me sit too and watch the entertainment.

At the time during which relations bewteen Makori and Zipporah had been at their very worst, and Makori had ranged through the neighborhood giving out bulletins on the latest developments in Zipporah's "cases," I had come to know Kemunto, Zipporah's mother, who sat each day in the Morongo market behind her little piles of maize. We had commiserated together over Zipporah's suffering, and Kemunto had invited me to visit her in the near future. So one day when, as Zipporah reported, she and Makori "were doing better" and Zipporah could "afford" to spend a session in this way, after weeks of flooding me with her anxieties, we set off for her home. Kemunto had told us she would take off half a day from her business, but we scarcely saw her at all, since she was busy cooking for us and would not allow us into the kitchen to keep her company while she prepared the food.

What struck me most forcibly about the homestead was its blandness. A mile away Zipporah and Makori lived in a lush, half-tamed place, but Kemunto's acreage was meticulously laid out, every foot used rationally. The house was iron roofed and spotless. Kemunto's youngest child was about ten, and no doubt the absence of young children accounted in part for the orderly atmosphere. Zipporah herself was tense throughout the visit. She seemed like a stranger to whom her mother's ways were foreign. She showed us around the property and introduced us to her mother's cowives, both of whom, turbaned and dressed in their best, were about to go off to a church meeting. The three women had obviously prospered since their husband died. In their new independence they had become Christians and radically altered their life-style, but there was something sterile about this homestead which had been without an *omonyeny'e'nyomba* for such a long time. We ate the meal when it was ready and then drove Kemunto back to Morongo to her appointed position in the market. After twenty years of widowhood, Kemunto's primary role was that of trader, not housewife or mother. She did little digging these days; she hired laborers to do it for her. Her children did most of the housework. Indeed Kemunto herself was scarcely at home in the daytime anymore except after services on the Sabbath, when her church compelled her to rest.

III

With the advent of the rains and the planting season, the atmosphere in Makori's homestead was quieter. Again we found Nyaboke drinking porridge in Zipporah's house. The old lady's visitors sat under Zipporah's arbor, not in her own yard. Makori even dug Zipporah's fallow land, in preparation for planting. "He did it badly," Zipporah commented. "He just turned the sod over without breaking it up. I'll have to dig the whole field again myself." But though she mocked his efforts, she was pleased.

One day she reports a dream about her mother's sister. "In my dream my aunt died. She doesn't have a husband, so my uncles came and took all her possessions back home, and her only child, a daughter, they did not find. The girl was away at boarding school. She had not even been told her mother had died. When I awoke I was very sad."

She commented that this sister of her mother, Mongina, was married once and then divorced because she never was able to bear another child after the one daughter. So she become *omotari* (a prostitute), and she traveled about. She was once married to a man of another tribe in a town in the Rift Valley, but she came back to Kisii town, where she started a shop. The shop had done quite well. Once, when Zipporah was pregnant with Omae, Makori beat her severely in the face. She had to go to hospital for stitches, so she stayed the night with Mongina and saw her aunt's beautiful clothes and her furniture and the way she lived. She was middle-aged, but no one would guess it. She was still pretty, and she had many lovers, especially young men, some of whom she spoiled so they never wanted to marry after they had known her. She had just the one child, a girl whom she loved and provided with everything one could imagine, but she had no son. Kemunto had told her often, "You should buy some land and find a woman to marry and have children for you," but Mongina kept silent. (The Gusii have "woman marriage," still quite common today, by which a senior woman who has borne only daughters, or has been entirely barren herself, will marry a young girl with bridewealth and set her up with land and a house and then arrange for the girl to be impregnated by a particular man, usually a relative of the woman's own husband. The children of this union are considered her children and will inherit her husband's property.) Thus in the dream the woman's brothers inherited her property, since she had no son of her own, and her daughter, still a child and not even present when her mother died, was in no position to defend her rights to her mother's possessions.

Mongina served as Zipporah's role model for a divorced woman. In many ways she was to be envied. She was well-to-do. She had many lovers; she lived in town and led an interesting life. "If I were like my aunt [i.e., a good businesswoman, able to support herself], I would take all my children and live as she does, without a husband." But, though her aunt was completely free to do as she pleased, without a man to constrain her, she was sterile, she had no son. In the dream Zipporah was very sad for her.

She went on to talk about her brother, Nyariki, who was having difficulties with his wife. She was stubborn and lazy and had brought two illegitimate children to the marriage. But Nyariki was rather stupid, and it had been difficult for him to find a wife. He had had to pay eight cows, and even then he did not get a young girl, but only one with two children.

> "That woman is not happy with my brother, even though she has all she needs. We don't understand her. My brother treats her very well; he is very eager for sex, he is very energetic, and still she is not happy."

"What makes you happy?" I ask Zipporah.

"Only children. If you have children you are thankful and you

stay regardless of how your husband treats you. Sometimes I am
bitter that I have Makori as my husband, but really I am pleased
enough. I have six children, and two of them are sons."

So children made life tolerable, but only just.

"I wanted to give up beer, but when I come from the fields I
need *busaa*. I am so tired and lonely. You know that Makori
won't let me have visitors apart from you and my mother and
brothers. And he has forbidden me to go to other homesteads
where people are drinking. He wants me to see no one. He's
afraid I will find a lover or else that I will go somewhere to get
emesira, some medicine to use against him. Makori doesn't want
me to see women any more than men, even though I can't have
sex with them. Of course he's happy if his own friend, Teresa,
comes here. They visit one another very often these days. But I
have to stay here at home. I can run to Morongo and back, that's
all he'll allow. During the daytime Makori and I *are* getting
along better together than during the time of the *chikina,* the
cases against me. But that's because he is sober and I keep very
quiet. But at night he comes home drunk, and he stands in the
doorway and yells, 'I've forgotten nothing. I know what kind of
woman you are—a woman who loves many men,' and then he
comes to beat me and I run to Moraa, my mother-in-law's cowife, and sleep there. There's nothing I can do to make Makori
change his thoughts about me. One day, of his own accord, he
may decide to let me have visitors again, but I can't be sure.
Meanwhile I'll just stay here at home, and if he kills me one
night, let him bury me. Then he'll really have trouble. He could
kill the wife he hates, but that won't be the end of it [i.e.,
because it is a great sacrilege which will bring down upon him
the anger of the ancestors]. I myself don't think of killing him,
but if someone else did so, or if he got very sick and died, I'd be
glad. I would just stay here alone with my children. I wouldn't
want *omochinyomba* [a leviratic husband]. But Makori is a madman. He thinks all the time about men with whom he imagines
I am having sex. Even when he comes home completely drunk,
he'll check the door and the windows to see that they are locked
against my lovers. Once he found a window unlocked in the
morning, and he said, 'There was a man in here last night, but I
was sleeping too soundly to hear him.' If you come, Sarah, in
ten years' time, you'll find us just the same. We'll never change.

This is because we never discuss things. We never solve our problems. Makori's like a hyena [i.e., he's an unsocialized out-cast, always on the move, always snarling and snapping]. Since we were married he has never been to my home. This is because we've never been friends long enough to arrange an occasion. If he sees my mother on the road, he shouts abuse at her from behind the hedge or else he hides himself completely. My sisters' husbands are all friends with my mother. She entertains them. They feel comfortable in my home. But as for me, my husband is a wild dog against whom my brothers and sisters-in-law must protect me."

Even though, when drunk, Makori was as irascible as ever, never-theless it seemed as if the two of them had arrived at a somewhat viable status quo as long as Zipporah appeared to be abiding by his rules. (In fact her two best women friends visited her briefly, having first made sure Makori was out.) Makori was treating her better. He worked on her land, whereas formerly he had helped only his mother, never his wife. He left us to have conversations without interruption, no doubt confident that now that I had been forcibly confronted with the truth about Zipporah's behavior, he no longer had to spend time convincing me himself. On afternoons when Makori was off drinking and Zipporah had returned from the fields, we had time for long, unchaperoned conversations. Zipporah had questions about everything, about how people lived in other parts of Kenya or in Europe or America. One day I brought her a book of photographs of Kenya pastoralists, and she was at once horrified and intrigued by their nakedness. She confessed she had always believed the lowland Gusii were savages, ornamented but otherwise naked, until I told her dif-ferently. She shyly admitted she also believed Europeans only washed with oil until she saw me wash my hands with water before eating in her house.

One afternoon Zipporah laughed out loud as she saw us coming up the path. She started to tell us that Makori had just been released after spending a night in the Keroka jail. On Saturday he had begun cutting the hedge of a very old but influential relative, when the old man tried to stop him. Makori had yelled, "You're so ancient! All your age-mates have died. You haven't got a penis any more," whereupon the old man's son fetched the police and had Makori arrested. Later the old man went to the jail and asked the police to "have mercy" on Makori, and the police, who had seen Makori's matted hair and dirty clothes, thought he was a madman and not responsible for himself, so they released him.

"As for me, I wish they'd kept him there for two years," Zipporah remarks. "But he's home again, though I'm happy to say he was badly frightened by what happened." At this point Makori walks into the yard. When I say I've heard he's just come from prison he denies it vehemently.

"He can't change," Zipporah throws up her hands. "He's always the same."

But the next day Makori talked to me about his experience in jail, in which he found himself, he said, just because he was doing what his eldest brother had told him to do, namely, cut the hedge.

"What's bad about cutting a hedge?" he asks, but he uses the word *okorabiakura,* which is a slang word for the seduction of women. "I'm going to do it again this afternoon." "Then," says Zipporah, her eyes almost popping out of her head in her effort to contain her laughter, "you should sharpen your *panga.*" Makori appears to ignore her remark, and yet he has heard and he has been nettled, for he starts boasting about how he would never do the work of women. Even if he were all alone and needed water to cook with he would never deign to carry water from the river. A woman or a child must fetch water, never a man.

A week later, however, Zipporah told us Makori, despite his bravado, had been chastened by the jail incident: "He isn't fighting me. He is very quiet. Provided I don't dawdle on the road but come straight home from the power mill, he does not bother to find fault with me. Of course this can't last. Makori is a bad dog and always will be."

But for the moment Makori relaxed his vigilance; he was less intrusive into Zipporah's life as he recovered psychologically from his prison experience. In this period of relative ease, Zipporah reported a dream in which she found herself having sexual relations with a man named Magoma. But before her eyes Magoma turned into Makori. She looked up and saw my car parked at the edge of her land, and she wanted to get into it and drive away. When she awoke she was upset that she had wanted to have sex with Magoma. To make herself feel better she thought of telling the madman (Makori), but because she knew he would only abuse her, she did not. In her associations to this dream she said Magoma was a great seducer of women. He had made overtures to her on a number of occasions. Last year he came to her house and said, "Makori tells me you are having sex with six other men, yet you've never let me have a chance. Let me buy beer for you now." She sent him away.

Zipporah remarks that Magoma has grown children, and once he was a teacher, but he was fired. Recently, however, the authorities have rehired him because he is very good at teaching children how to sing. I ask her whether she enjoyed dreaming the dream. "Yes, I did," she says, "until I awoke," and she smiles. "I saw Magoma last week when Makori was in jail. I met him on the road on the Sabbath when Makori had just been arrested. Magoma knew this, for he had seen Makori in the custody of the police. He asked me if he could buy me beer, but I refused, saying I no longer drank beer. Though I didn't tell Magoma this, the fact is I've had to give up beer because I have a madman for a husband who accuses me of committing adultery if I drink."

Zipporah longed to escape either into adultery or through her relationship with me, someone who brought her the information she thirsted for about a wider world. But Makori was the constraining reality of her life. Children were essential to her well-being, to her sense of purpose and self-worth. Her children were Makori's. He had paid for her and therefore for them. She had no viable alternative to staying with them and for them. Adultery offered momentary excitement and pleasure but no solution. If she needed a man to father her child, the community could turn a blind eye, but if she engaged in an adulterous relationship long before the infant Omae was ready to be weaned, and thus long before she might legitimately desire to conceive again, then she was inviting trouble. But even though she was consciously aware of the strict parameters of her life, in her dreams she constantly explored her ambivalence about her lot. This could never be resolved. It rose and fell and was more or less difficult to bear. A couple

of weeks later she reported another dream, in which Makori beat her
with his spear. She nudged him awake and told him what she had
dreamed, but he refused to comment and turned back to sleep again.
She too fell asleep once more and dreamed that her youngest brother,
who had been an infant in her charge just before she married Makori,
had died.

"I loved that boy. He's thirteen now, and I see him rarely. He
hasn't come here since December. I know in fact that everyone is
well at home, but of course I always have to dream of misfortune. I never dream of anything good." Her thoughts are clearly
on her girlhood, before her life was irrevocably blighted. Then
she talks of Tabitha's father, who "is still running about after
women. Perhaps Tabitha will be like him. She hasn't
menstruated, but she looks as if she is ready to elope at any
moment. She loves dancing to the radio if she gets a chance, and
when she sees boys she starts to laugh. She's always liked boys,
even before circumcision."

So Tabitha, like her father, was a highly sexual creature, but the
implication was that she was like her mother too, or like her mother
long ago when she was nursemaid to her little brother and fantasized
about having a man and a little son of her own. What she got, however, was an illegitimate girl child by a womanizer; and after that her
fate, as un unmarried mother, was to become the wife of the maniac
Makori. A few days later Zipporah reported a fourth dream, in which
Makori died from drinking too much bitter beer:

"He died in a grass hut which I did not know. He did not die
at home. I saw a great crowd around the house and heard my
mother crying. 'Although he was *richara,* a feebleminded childish person, in his own homestead he was a man, the head of his
household. Who will watch over his children now?' And as I
watched some men digging the grave, I myself cried. 'It is true
he was *richara,* but now that he is dead I shall suffer. Men will
come to my house and beat me and abuse me and force me to do
what they want.'"

Thus it would seem that this bizarre marriage, though endlessly
fractious, was in a way a haven for Zipporah. She needed Makori with
his paranoia, his accusations and suspicions, to restrict her and protect

her from herself. In her dream she was afraid that once she were a widow, "men" would force her to do what they wanted. But what they wanted must in fact be what she also wanted, despite herself, and if she were to go that way there would be no end for her but self-destruction. Better then not to think too much about that prospect but to say, as Makori said when she recounted her dream to him, "It is nothing at all, just a dream. Perhaps we shall hear today or tomorrow that someone else has died." And so she embarked upon a lengthy account of her financial worries and her failure to extract anything out of Makori for the children's school uniforms. He had been paid nearly 300 shillings by the cooperative society a week previously but had steadfastly refused to part with a single cent.

"It is hidden in the ceiling, at least that sum which he has not yet spent on beer and soap for his friend Teresa."

"Why don't you take some of it if you know where it is?" I ask.

"I'm not feeling well. I have a bad cough," she replies, and adds, "besides, I am afraid of him." And in response to my probing she details how she is managing somehow to provide for her family by her own efforts.

In the midst of this Makori appeared, rather drunk. He yelled at the children and glared at us. His shirt and shorts were in rags. Zipporah whispered to me that he had come from his beer party to find out what we were saying about him. Without greeting us he passed us angrily to weed a line of gum saplings. A few moments later thunder rolled, and rain lashed across the yard. We ran into the kitchen to the cooking fire, but Makori was too drunk or too angry to follow. Soaked to the skin, he stayed outside, viciously weeding the little gum trees.

Shortly thereafter, perhaps as a result of this drenching, Makori caught pneumonia. He refused to go to the Kisii hospital. "I've never been there; why should I go now?" But he was in great pain. Presumably he was reluctant to go to the hospital because, as usual, he was afraid of being caught by the police for nonpayment of the local council tax. He wanted me to bring him medicine, and I did so, but he did not finish the course of medication. As soon as he started to feel better, he stopped taking his pills, and he had a relapse. Meanwhile Zipporah had severe bronchitis. She was thankful when I offered to take her to the hospital, but since she had to continue to do all the housework as well as some farm work, her recovery was slow. Eventually Makori agreed to go to Kisii to get shots—for in his case injections were the only method of ensuring that he took his medication, and after a month of languishing under the eaves he recovered also. Meanwhile, since he was housebound, my sessions with Zipporah necessarily included Makori. Whether because of his poor health or the shock which the jail incident had given him, or because since the Jeremiah case he had experienced an increment in his hold over Zipporah, these days Makori seemed less combative and more able to tolerate a three-way conversation. In the past Zipporah would hover in the doorway whispering, "Lies, all he tells are lies," but now she sat near him, her hands folded in her lap, and the two of them talked not only to me but to one another.

Admittedly most of the conversational topics were introduced by Makori. He was interested in agricultural methods used in America and in how the various food crops were processed. Zipporah wanted to know about house construction, birth control methods, family organization, who lived with whom, who received gifts from whom. But what interested Makori most of all was interracial marriage. "White people never marry Africans," he claimed. When I told him there were several mixed couples here in Kisii District, both African men with white wives and vice versa, he declared that these Europeans had to be a new kind. "The old ones left after Mau Mau," he said (and for the most part he was right; interracial marriage used to be very rare indeed in colonial times, and whites who are involved in them in the contemporary period are mostly newcomers). I evidently was one of the new breed, who related to Africans as equals.

> "Sarah, you must give me a picture of yourself. I'll nail it up in the house, and when Omae is a big boy I will tell him, 'That European used to come and watch you.' By then you will be long gone to your own place, leaving us here in Kisii, the best place in the world, where maize, *wimbi,* and bananas can all grow at once in the same field."

During the last month of my stay both Zipporah and Makori were quite recovered from their illnesses, and Makori resumed his habit of spending the afternoon drinking beer, so I saw little of him. Zipporah was brisk and energetic once more. This year, she said, people were not going hungry as they had the previous year. There were plenty of beans and she had a little maize left, so even though Makori took all but a few shillings of their coffee cooperative money for his own purposes, at least the children had enough to eat. One day on the road she told me her friend Bosibori, who was barren, was being driven away by her husband because he had found another woman to marry, and this new love had an illegitimate child, so the man knew already she was not barren. Zipporah added that the man's mother was fully in favor of her son's divorce and remarriage even though formerly she and the daughter-in-law had always been on excellent terms. "But Bosibori is *ritiba,* so she must go and leave her house to another woman." That was the fate of barren women. They were driven out into the world. But a woman like herself had a function and a role. She then told me a dream in which a neighbor named Mkwa, who in fact had died recently, came toward her, carrying a big stick. He threatened her and she was terrified to see him thus, risen from the dead. In her associations she said,

> "Mkwa was a liar, he lied about me. When Simeon testified at the hearing that I had committed adultery with Jeremiah, Mkwa supported Simeon. He was the one who said I was guilty and thus I should bring a goat to perform the *ogosonsorana* ritual. I was not sorry," she whispers, "to hear he had died. And I was very happy indeed when Simeon was convicted and sentenced to a year in prison for cutting his cousin's maize. I wish that boy had been sentenced to five years. He deserves it. He is such a liar and a trouble maker." Her eyes are shining as she delivers this utterance, which constitutes a most unusual admission for a Gusii. Such an admission must indicate hatred in the heart and consequently malevolence, the desire to destroy one's enemy. But I am an outsider who can tolerate her intimate thoughts, however destructive. "I'm not surprised you're happy," I say. "Simeon is *omochege* [a fighter and a wild man]." I leave her standing on the road. "Do you have to go? Can't you walk with me longer?" she begs. "When you go back to your home, people will suffer," she says sadly, and adjusting the bag of maize kernels on her head, she turns away up the hill toward the market.

When I entered the compound for the last session, Zipporah, to whom I had sent word of the hour I would come, took one look at me as

I came across the yard, holding gifts for her and her children in my arms, and rushed around the corner of the house into her maize. Neither Makori, who had a child on each knee, nor her bigger children admitted to having any idea where she had gone. I waited half an hour and then I had to go, as I had other homesteads to visit. I intended to return the following day, but two hours later, when I was about to leave the community, I saw Zipporah running up the road toward me. "I've cooked; everything is ready. You must come and eat my food."

As we reached her house I gave her the gifts I had brought, for fear that she might disappear again before I had had a chance to present them. She took one wondering look at the underclothes I had given her, thanked me, and ran off to her kitchen. She called over her shoulder that the first time we had come, she remembered she had needed a bottle opener, and she had run off to borrow one from a neighbor. Makori appeared shiningly clean from head to toe and wearing a jacket of Madras cotton, purchased from the trader in American used clothing who offered his wares twice weekly in Morongo market. Omae, who had just learned to walk, was resplendent in a new shirt. We sat in the *eero* waiting for Zipporah to bring out a feast of chicken, *obokima,* and sodas, and when we had finished, Zipporah and Makori presented me with their gifts. From Zipporah I received a chicken and from Makori a package, weighing about a pound, of prime Kisii marijuana wrapped in banana leaves. When Zipporah had swept the room, she sat down with us and we talked peacefully though regretfully of my imminent departure.

And so at the end, as I watched and listened to Zipporah and Makori, surrounded by their children, I had a sense that these two were able, at least at intervals, to provide one another with a kind of mutual tolerance and companionship which was rather rare in this Gusii community. Of the seven women in my study, Zipporah was the only one whose husband intruded forcefully into my relationship with her. And when the time came for me to go, only Zipporah and Makori organized the measured, almost ritualized, leave taking which enabled us to bring our relationship to an appropriate conclusion. As for Zipporah herself, she was engaged up to the last moment with me. The real parting from me took place not bit by bit over many weeks, but only when, having escorted me to the road for the last time, she turned back again down the path to her house.

IV

I found this family more difficult to get used to than any other. The reason for this was that for many months either the old lady Nyaboke or Makori dominated the scene whenever I visited. They assaulted me verbally. I had no time to get my bearings. Neither of them seemed to have the slightest regard, even initially, for the fact that I was a stranger. At least it did not appear so to me. It was only very much later that I came to understand that I had been mistaken. They had indeed reacted to me as a stranger, but in a way which, since I did not expect it, I could neither detect nor interpret. I had expected some initial reserve on their parts. When this seemed to be absent, I ascribed their loquacity in part to alcohol, in part to a form of social deviance which prevented them from approximating the cultural norms of reserve and discretion in the presence of a stranger. I was distracted by their alcoholic state and what I perceived as their socially inappropriate behavior, and then again, I spent considerable time trying to determine truth from falsehood. In this way I paid insufficient attention to the actual content of their monologues and to the real messages which they were so garrulously trying to transmit to me, an outsider who was painfully slow in understanding.

In her long dissertations on the migration of her husband's family to this area, on his virtues and her happiness with him and the fates of his children and grandchildren, I believe Nyaboke was telling me that her primary task, now that she was old, was to ensure the continuation of the lineage. All her sons must have sons to follow them. Her role, then, was to support and protect her daughters-in-law, especially Zipporah, and to discipline them when they needed disciplining. The families of her three older sons needed minimal surveillance on her part, but Makori's wife and children demanded much more of her attention.

The reason for this was what Makori spent so much effort trying to conceal, not just from myself but from everyone in the community (all of whom were of course well aware of it), namely, that his potency was severely impaired and evidently always had been. In consultations with diviners he had been told it was the ancestor spirits (*ebirecha*) who were afflicting him, through no fault of his own. But multiple sacrifices had done little to appease them, and his problem endured with only marginal improvement. Thus my early sessions with both Makori and Zipporah together had been taken up with Makori's accounts of how he strong-armed and bullied his first wife, and with his complaints (and scarcely concealed braggadocio) about the "rats" which Zipporah continually produced. Her rats, after all, were evidence of his potency. No Gusii man with respect (*bw'amasikane*) would brag in this way to a strange woman. But Makori was not *bw'amasikane*.

It is difficult in any society for a man who is impotent to retain his self-respect. Perhaps those who manage to do so are rare. But Gusii culture certainly provided avenues for a man who had impotency problems. In the first place, he could select a substitute for himself, from among his own kin, who would periodically impregnate his wife on his behalf. The resulting children would be universally regarded as his own. But this solution required a solid sense of self-worth, which Makori evidently lacked. A second solution, one of which we knew several instances, was to seek to destroy through sorcery those whom a man believed to have bewitched him. This solution, in theory, was open to Makori. It is true that the diviners had told him his affliction was due not to witchcraft but to the wrath of the ancestors, who, at some point in the distant past, had been dissatisfied. Nevertheless, when he found his condition unalleviated after the performance of sacrifices to the ancestral spirit, he might still have decided that witchcraft was after all the cause of his affliction. Then he could have taken instruction as *omonyanasira,* and his supernatural powers would have made him much feared by his neighbors, with a consequent increment in his self-esteem. Third, he might have become insane. There were several psychotics in the area of whom it was said their madness had been brought on by the *ebirecha;* these men, like Makori, were thought to have been impotent prior to the onset of schizophrenia. But although his level of dysfunctioning varied over time, so that there were periods when he was not merely comical but obviously bizarre, and although his eccentricity was recognized by his neighbors, Makori was not considered a madman. He was tolerated in a community where admittedly the threshold of tolerance was very high. As long as he was not violent away from home and people were not physically threatened by him, they would not reject him. Thus the only solution left to him was to drown his insecurities in alcohol and to give vent at home to his irascible temper and paranoia.

By her albeit reluctant assent to the marriage, Zipporah had committed herself to an almost unworkable situation: Makori wanted a wife in order to have children; Zipporah wanted a husband in order to have children also. For her, as for all traditional Gusii women, bearing and raising children constituted her central and fundamental goal and achievement. However, although Makori's impotency need not necessarily have brought with it great turmoil, in this case it did, for Makori was incapable of a mature adjustment to his condition. Not only did he refuse to legitimize Zipporah's right of access to any other single man, but he spent a large part of the family's monetary resources on the entertainment of other women. Though he probably failed to have any real sexual relationship with them, he expended a great deal of energy and money, for a man in his financial situation, on trying to convince people—himself included—that he in fact did enjoy sexual relationships with them. Meanwhile he was continually suspicious of the sexual activities of his wife. The very factor which had induced him to marry her in the first place, namely, her proven ability to bear children, aroused in him a torrent of jealousy. He hated and valued her at the same time. His violent temper seemed to be seasonal, however. One might guess that he was at his most aggressive when he was most debilitated by his head injury or, again, at those times when he suspected Zipporah of being eager to get pregnant again.

I did not know them long enough to understand the pattern. I do know, however, from the accounts of others and from my own observations, that a period of turmoil and hostility between them would be followed by one of relative calm, in which each seemed quite content with his or her side of the bargain. At such times Zipporah could expect some companionship and help with her farm work, while Makori, in an expansive mood, enjoyed the affection of his children and the meticulous housekeeping of his wife. Meanwhile neighbors, who had watched this repetitive pattern of turmoil and calm over ten years, told me, "They are alike, those two. Makori has no respect when he drinks and he drinks too much. At times he treats Zipporah very badly; he beats her and accuses her of many things. Her situation is unfortunate indeed. But sometimes she drinks too, and then she behaves as she does. Since she has chosen to stay with him, she should do so like a big person. She could behave better than she does for, as it is, she and Makori are too much alike. They are both children."

It would seem, therefore, that her neighbors believed Zipporah did at one time have an option. She could have left Makori years ago, when she understood what the situation with him was. But she stayed to have a son, whether by Makori or another man I do not know, and after that, as the mother of a male child, she was bonded to the lineage of Obaro forever. Why did she stay to have a son? One informant told me that some years before we came to the field Zipporah had, for a brief period, been insane. The *omoragori* said that she had been afflicted by the spirits of the ancestors of Obaro, and after the necessary sacrifices had been performed she regained her sanity. She never spoke of this incident to me, but I am inclined to trust my informant's account. Perhaps Zipporah stayed because, as people said, she and Makori were so much alike. Once married to him she was herself subject to his ancestor spirits, from which there could be no escape.

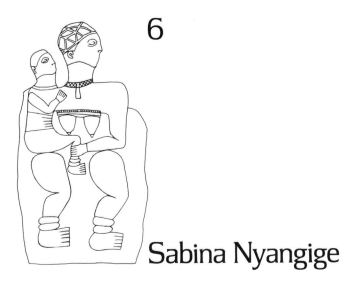

6

Sabina Nyangige

I

From the time that we first came to the field I had been struck by the manner in which women of different ages initially responded to me. While young women were polite and generally reserved, I was often astonished by the brash outspokenness of women in their late thirties or early forties. At first meeting they often seemed to presume a familiarity which did not exist. The fact that my husband had worked with his first wife in the area many years ago when these women were young brides presumably encouraged their frankness, but apart from being a white woman I did not much resemble my predecessor, who had been small with short curly hair, while I was tall with long straight hair. I felt that whatever associations I had for them, those did not explain the liberties some women took with me. For example, seeing me on the road for the first time, one older woman examined my scalp and remarked, "You *are* going gray, aren't you!" Another, on an occasion when I was visiting her compound with others in our research team, called out to me, "What do you think you are doing there, lolling in the sunshine?" When I asked our Gusii assistants for an explanation, I was told, "That is what happens with age. If you had known that woman when she was young, you would have

found her *omokiriru* [silent]; now she has become *omokwani* [talkative]."
I decided, therefore, to seek out one of these talkative ladies, as I was
curious to discover something about the process by which *abasubati
bw'amasikane* (respectful women) might in a few years be so markedly
changed, at least in their social behavior.

After some months I came to know Sabina Nyangige, a woman of
about forty, who was pregnant at the time with her ninth child. She
had been a bride twenty years before when my husband had been
working there, and I had read about her in the field notes of Sara
Nerlove, who had worked in the area in the mid-1960s, but I did not
meet her myself until she came to the clinic our physician ran for
pregnant women. She was a very thin black woman of indeterminate
age. She looked sixty when her face was in repose. Her eyes were
unusually small, and they darted about, the only movement in an
otherwise unexpressive face. But once she began to talk, she was full of
affect. Her eyes and teeth flashed, and suddenly her pregnant abdomen
seemed believable. While I was taking a social history, she suddenly
launched into a remarkable tale of family intrigue and sorcery which
she just as suddenly terminated. She jumped up, explaining as she ran
out the door that she had business to do and could not give me any
more of her time.

A short while later I saw her with a friend at a funeral. They stared at
me for a moment, and then in an intense whisper the friend demanded
to know whether I intended to study them and their families in return
for food and clothing for their children. "You might even employ our
daughters, as you have employed that young woman," she added,
nodding at Mary. Sabina smiled but said nothing. Since the coffin was
about to be brought out for burial past where we all stood with bowed
heads, conversation was no longer possible. In the course of my work I
soon began visiting Sabina, whose child, when it was born, might be
included in our longitudinal sample. But at first I was reluctant to
include Sabina in my clinical study as well. The little incident which
had occurred at the funeral enhanced my fears that to embark upon a
special relationship with Sabina might invite complications, the nature
of which I shall explain.

Both my husband and Sara Nerlove had confined their research to
people from two clans, the Abaseko and the Abasoga, who lived in an
area which was called in publications thereafter Nyansongo. In our

current study, however, we had increased the area fivefold to include people from two other clans, Abagoro and Abatamba. Some older members of these later clans remembered my husband, Getuka, as they called him, but none had really known him, and none of the families in those clan areas had had any immediate experience with researchers. On the other hand, the Abaseko and Abasoga had had intermittent but intensive contact with both Getuka and Sara Nerlove, and on this field trip we quickly discovered a marked difference in their expectations of us from those of the Abagoro or Abatamba.

Even men who had been children in the 1950s or 1960s and women who had not married into those clans until very recently soon adopted the expectations of these older residents of the original research area, who had learned long ago how to exact a quid pro quo from American anthropologists. Their demands, which verged in some instances on rapaciousness, outdid from the beginning to the end of our fieldwork anything which we had to deal with in the other clan areas under investigation. The people of Nyansongo were more uniformly poor than their neighbors (although there were plenty of poor people in the area as a whole). With one or two remarkable exceptions, few Abaseko or Abasoga had managed to establish themselves outside the district. The population density was greatest in their area; alcoholic consumption was very high; people were less progressive, in the sense that more men were living at home, dependent to a greater degree on traditional sources of income.

Sabina, who was married to a man from Boseko (i.e., the clan area of Abaseko), had not yet given birth for the first time when my husband had left the field nearly twenty years before. Indeed he had a photograph of her attending a circumcision ceremony. In the midst of the excitement her face was modest and reserved. Ten years later Sara Nerlove had found Sabina with five children, and from her field notes I gathered Sara had had extensive contact with her. I anticipated, therefore, that my attempts to develop a relationship with Sabina would be complicated by whatever had occurred between her and the Sara of ten years ago. Nevertheless, there were reasons for persistence. In the first place, we had information on Sabina and people in her husband's kin group over a period of two decades. In the second place, she seemed to represent exactly what I had been looking for: she was *omokungu enyabure* (a woman with many children) who was now eligible, having approximated the Gusii ideal, to relax a little and enjoy being cared for after all the years of taking care of others. Thus I put aside my reservations and embarked upon a relationship with Sabina.

During the seven months in which I visited her, I came to understand something of what it was like to be a traditional woman in her middle years, at a point when by rights she should be looking forward to the support and protection of her grown sons; but who found that, on the contrary, middle age offered none of the solace and ease she had been hoping for, but only increasing hardship. While her situation must be very common in Gusiiland at this time, Sabina's response to it seemed peculiarly maladaptive. Her behavior puzzled me throughout our association, and she seemed to mystify everyone else as well, those who were friendly to her as much as those who were not. In the end when she had gone away, her closest friend remarked to me, "Just remember one thing about her. She'll never tell you the truth. Probably she doesn't know what the truth is." It was with relief I heard this. I had struggled to make sense of the stream of consciousness Sabina had poured out to me week after week, asking myself, "Can I believe this? Is this literally true, or is it only her psychic reality?" I was rarely able to tell. But apparently her friends could not tell much better than I.

In all I saw her for twenty-one sessions over a period of seven months. Sabina was the senior wife of Obamba, who for many years had worked for a European-owned timber company in the forests of a neighboring district. For short periods Sabina would visit him at his place of work, but usually, once she had accomplished her purpose—which was to get pregnant—she would return to her husband's home. There she had sole responsibility not only for cultivation but for protection of the property, which had been the source of extensive feuding and litigation between Obamba and his half brother for at least a decade. Her husband came home once a year at Christmas time for a few days. The last time he had come, Sabina told me, he had brought with him the wife of another man, whom this woman had left without repayment by her parents of her bridewealth. By her husband this woman had had four sons, who might possibly compete with Sabina's own six for Obamba's two acres.

Obamba himself had been the eldest of three sons, but one of these had gone off to live in Tanzania, while the other had taken their mother to Uganda. Neither had ever returned. Thus Sabina lived alone on her husband's patrimony in a deteriorated hut. The roof leaked and the walls crumbled. I never saw any evidence of attempts at repair. A short way away was the *esaiga*, the hut which had been built for her circumcised sons. Three of the older boys, however, were living with their father at Kericho and going to school there. Sabina had with her her two daughters, Kwamboka, aged about seventeen, and Josephine, aged four, and three sons, Gekonde, Momanyi, and Musa, aged twelve, six, and two, respectively. She had coffee and pyrethrum, and an extensive stand of banana trees as well as sugarcane, all of which generated a little income. In addition, for domestic consumption, she grew maize and vegetables, and she had some pasture by the river on which she grazed a couple of sheep. She had recently rented out about half an acre of land for the princely sum of 100 shillings (twelve dollars) in order to pay the school building fees and buy uniforms for Kwamboka and Gekonde, who were the only two children attending school. The woman who leased the land had planted pyrethrum and was already harvesting the flowers at biweekly intervals. Thus Sabina would sit and watch a stranger use profitably the land over which she herself had lost all control. For her, as for almost all parents in the area, school attendance was important and sacrifices had to be made, although it was never clear whether in her case such a major step as the renting of her land had really been essential. After all, she too could have planted pyrethrum and earned money with which to pay the building fees. Sabina herself had never been to school and was illiterate. For the past eight years, however, she had been a member of the Lutheran church, a denomination which was only sparsely represented in the area. Her father, a polygamist, had refused to allow any of his daughters to go to school. Although her mother had become a Catholic late in life, when Sabina was a child both parents had been non-Christian. Her marriage to Obamba had been arranged, and for many months after the cattle had been paid, Sabina had refused to go to her husband's house. In the end, Obamba and his friends had come before dawn and forced her to go with them, and since then, as she said, she had experienced little but trouble.

II

When I first began to visit Sabina regularly, I felt she was the most exotic woman I had attempted to work with up to that point. By exotic I meant most obviously different from myself. Unlike the other, mostly younger women, Sabina was quite garrulous by nature, and thus encouraging her to talk was not a problem. I already perceived her as being a somewhat eccentric person, a "character." If I was curious to discover the nature of her preoccupations, her pattern of associations, how she perceived the world around her, I had only to sit and listen to her. And if the stream of information, conjecture, observation, and sheer gossip which poured forth did not reflect perfectly her intrapsychic life, then I trusted I would discover clues by which to illuminate whatever remained obscure.

I visited Sabina for the first time one hot morning. She was sitting in the shade of a large drying mat, propped up against a ramshackle draining rack. Her three young children were all sitting on her lap. Musa and Josephine, the younger two, had beautiful faces, though both were very skinny. Momanyi did not resemble his siblings in looks, nor perhaps in disposition either, for while they were alert and smiling, he scowled blackly and looked away from me. Sabina did not rise to greet us. She was in the eighth month of pregnancy.

> "We have no food now," she remarks, "unless we get money from somewhere and go to buy maize. We're living on bananas. [This is the leanest period, shortly before the harvest.] My husband hasn't shown his face here for six months. He told me to join him in Kericho, but why should I go there to give birth and have my cowife kill me? So I refused. If that woman wants me dead, let her come here and make the *amasangia* here in this house. Let her step over the blood in my house so that I die in my own bed. You see, my cowife loves men. She isn't faithful to our husband. So if she were with me when I give birth, her bad ways would kill me, wouldn't they?" She finishes with relish, removing a pair of scissors from the two-year-old Musa's hand. "You're a good boy, Musa," she says to sooth his disappointment at losing his plaything. She lays his head against her breast and holds him close.

When Sabina spoke of *amasangia*, she referred to a Gusii belief that adulterers can cause the death of those whom they have betrayed. The standard example informants gave is that in which a wife whose husband has been adulterous might be visited during childbirth by her husband's lover. If that woman steps over the birth blood which has spilled upon the floor, the wife will bleed to death. Sabina went on, her eyes gleaming in her black face. (However hot it was or however much she might be sweating, her skin always seemed to have a matte finish.)

"When I reached Kericho last September, to seek this child you see here," she indicates her stomach, "I found my husband with this woman. I had not known of her existence until then. I walked in, and they walked out together, saying they were going to a club to drink. When they came back, they said, 'Have you cooked for us?' After that I stayed for two months, doing all the work, the cooking and shopping and washing. Obamba and that woman have so many clothes, and, as you see, I have nothing." She is wearing a cloth tied under her armpits over her torn cotton slip. "He sends me nothing. Even the school fees for Kwamboka and Gekonde I must pay myself. He thinks it is enough that he educates the three other boys in Kericho. He doesn't provide them with clothes, though. They go about in rags."

Musa interrupted her. He was hungry. Sabina told Momanyi to make a fire so she could boil bananas quickly. Her voice was sharp, and Momanyi refused. She dragged herself to her feet and went with the two smallest children into the house to fetch a raw banana for Musa, but even as he ate it, Musa wept.

"He only wants *obokima,* real food," Sabina remarks, "and where can I get any?" She takes him on her lap again and tries to soothe him as she thinks aloud, "I'll send Gekonde to the market with a few sticks of sugarcane. If he can get a shilling, I'll be able to buy a shilling's worth of maize meal and that could keep you from crying for a day." Then her voice rises again, harshly. "Obamba didn't buy clothes for this young one when he was born, and he won't buy clothes for his follower, either. Why do I continue to have children? Because I dislike menstruating! Who can claim to like that mess each month? People say I am Obamba's wife, but really, I am no one's wife. I have only God to depend on." She is momentarily still, a trifle melodramatically, I think. Then she stretches and smiles to her audience and describes a daydream: "Obamba has two acres of land at Kericho which I planted myself two months ago. When this new child is a little over a month old, I will go to harvest what I planted. I will greet my husband {i.e., she will sleep with him}, and I will conceive. I am very fertile. I have no difficulty conceiving," she adds, smiling and preening. When she smiles her eyes narrow so much that they almost disappear into her head.

In this the first, unstructured conversation I had with her, Sabina paid little attention to formalities. She saw that I was seated, albeit in the direct sun, and then she launched into a recitation of her misfortunes, scarcely looking at me meanwhile. Was she merely picking up where she left off with Sara Nerlove ten years ago? Did she relate to all outsiders in this manner, with only the slightest regard for who they were, other than that presumably they were in some way powerful and might possibly help her with her troubles (and troubles she clearly had)? She listed hunger, poverty, her sudden and recent discovery that her husband had taken another wife whose sons might claim a share of her husband's meager parcel of land. Further, she cited her husband's rejection of her: "He goes to bars with that woman of his, and I am left to do the cooking." Her little boy Musa wept from hunger, and Sabina talked of peddling sugarcane (snack food) in order to earn a shilling's worth of flour to satisfy the child, "if only for a day. Then he will cry again." Without shame she displayed her pitiable condition. From time to time she glanced at my face to make sure that I was listening to what she had to tell me. But then, just as I was wondering how she could survive her hardships, she said, "Soon I will sleep with my husband and conceive again. I am very fertile, I always conceive immediately." She was to be pitied, but she should also be admired and envied. She had given birth to eight children, and none of them had died. She was pregnant with her ninth. She expected to have more still. She had a single great competence! She was continually fertile.

Thus she boasted to me, but given what I already knew of Gusii women, the fact that she felt unconstrained before me, even though I was an outsider, marked her as a deviant. At that point I had no way of guessing the degree of her eccentricity, but, it should be said, during my entire stay she was the only woman who admitted any pride in her powers of procreation. As for these children whom she had produced with such ease and regularity, from what I could observe during the session, she treated the younger two rather like puppies. They cuddled against her and looked out at me with interest. Sabina talked about them but rarely to them. When she wanted to stand up, she shrugged them off her lap. They rolled over, picked themselves up, and trotted after her. With Momanyi, aged six, her relationship was different, clearly a source of tension. He shrank against his mother in a way which she found irksome. When she told him to build a fire, he refused, in part, I think, because this would have meant getting up and going into the kitchen alone without her, and he wanted desperately to be right beside her where, unfortunately for him, she resented and rejected him. Momanyi was like a changeling beside the other two. Did his scowls and whining indicate his anger at being ejected from his mother's favor once he had grown too big to be a mere extension of herself? Or had he never been included in that symbiotic warmth in the first place?

In the next session Sabina again assaulted us with a recitation of her difficulties.

> "Gekonde and Kwamboka have malaria. Kwamboka is very weak. I ran to a neighbor to borrow money for the bus fare to take her to the hospital, but on the way I fell down, and now I am suffering pains in my back, and of course Kwamboka didn't get to the hospital. Obamba never sends me money now. It all goes for that woman, taking her to bars. I used to brew and sell beer, but now I am so heavy [with child], I haven't the strength. I did not replant my pyrethrum as I should have done last year. At that time I was getting pregnant at Kericho." The two youngest children come zooming in from the fields where they have been playing "cars." They greet me and flop down upon their mother. I remark that they, at least, seem well, to which Sabina replies that her mother came the day before with a basket of beans. Once they had eaten, the children were full of energy again.
>
> [If I hadn't mentioned that they seemed lively that day, I am sure Sabina would never have told me about the present her mother had brought. I was learning slowly that misfortune is more readily a topic of conversation than good luck.]
>
> Sabina shifts the children and rearranges herself to relieve her aching back. "You two," she says, meaning Mary and myself, "are good. You don't mind how dirty people are; you still come to visit them."

Sabina's back hurt so much now that she could not walk the steep path down to the river, and since the two bigger children were sick and she had no one to fetch water, she had not bathed in some time. But if she was ashamed of her unwashed condition, why did she talk about it? On the other hand, perhaps she was not ashamed. She wanted me to accept her for what she was, take note of her slovenliness, and admire her despite it. In fact there seemed to be many subjects which, though generally considered shameful, Sabina felt perfectly free to talk about.

> "When I am in childbirth, I like to have many women with me. I like to have them all around me, pulling and pushing. They come from everywhere about here. It is the noise which draws them. They ululate and dance, they come to see how well I have been circumcised, whether my house [i.e., vaginal opening] is big or small." At this Musa and Josephine burst out laughing and roll off their mother's lap. "At circumcision if a girl shows she is afraid the *omosari* [circumciser] only cuts off a little. But if the girl is strong, the circumciser will cut all. So my neighbors lie me on the ground and spread my legs and see that I was strong, I have nothing now. I had a good circumcision, even though it hurt me very much for two months afterward and I cried in my mother's house, where no one could see or hear me. Kwamboka," Sabina adds proudly, "was circumcised well also, and she did not even cry afterward."

What are the most important sources of a Gusii's woman's self-esteem? Her capacity to bear and raise children and even before that, her courage at circumcision. These are attributes admired and envied by others, and in the excitement of childbirth a woman has the opportunity to display both. Sabina told us that "many women" came to be with her: "Even Ester comes from Bogoro." (Ester is a well-to-do woman from the neighboring clan. Normally Ester would never seek Sabina out but, we are told, she too is drawn by the excitement, the celebration of Sabina's womanhood.) With all the other women, she crowded in to see Sabina's house, her store and treasure trove. I, on the other hand, did not have to wait until the day of delivery to become acquainted with the details of her genitalia. She described their proportions with delight. Her pride and excitement in display were extraordinary. I felt literally assaulted by her. Then suddenly she recounted two dreams.

> "In the first, Getuka takes me to the hospital because I am in labor. At the hospital they ask me, 'Who can sign for you?' and I say, 'Getuka can sign,' and thus he does so. I am put in the

ward, but under the blankets I have no clothes, I am naked. When Kwamboka comes to see me, I tell her to go home and bring some clothes for me to wear."

In the second dream, a woman whom she knows only slightly died. Sabina awoke weeping and told her daughter, who said, "Of course it cannot happen."

Sabina said she did not understand why she should cry about that woman's death, since she was not a friend; they happened to live in the same area, that was all. Perhaps she would tell the woman what she dreamed if she should see her, but this was unlikely, as they did not live very close. She added that the day after she had had this dream, Kwamboka had fainted. But Sabina had not been really frightened because she had been reassured by her dream of the previous night: if a person dreams someone has died, then the opposite must be true, so Gusii people say. Thus, when she saw Kwamboka had fainted, *nakuete,* which also means "she died" in Ekegusii, Sabina knew that in a moment or two the girl would be all right again.

Although she had quite lengthy associations to her second dream, Sabina had none about the first, which she had remembered so suddenly in the midst of describing the scene of her imminent delivery. She could talk about the death of a woman whom she occasionally saw "walking all by herself" on the road to the market. Perhaps she identified with that woman, who for so many years had been living among this clan but still appeared to be lonely. Sabina longed to be the center of attention, and she anticipated with joy and great excitement the moment when she would give birth. But what if the women of her husband's clan abandoned her to give birth alone? Then she would have the investigator take care of her. This first dream might seem to a Westerner to be primarily erotic in content and quality. From an excited description of her own genitalia Sabina suddenly remembered a dream in which my husband, whom, in fact, she knew slightly, took her to the hospital. In the absence of her own husband, had she taken mine? She was surprised but not ashamed. It would appear, however, from her later associations, that in Sabina's fantasy my husband, I, and even Mary were really one and the same—a longed-for, admiring, mirroring person. Thus her high pleasure in describing the childbirth scene was not necessarily erotic. Rather, it indicated a wave of exhibitionistic excitement: these strangers were going to investigate her,

her most intimate corners, and they would appreciate and validate her worth.

As we prepare to leave on this occasion, Mary suggested that Sabina roast some of the new maize which was ready. Sabina protested, "There is none yet," so Mary showed her several ears which were ripe. "And there are many more. Your children need not eat bananas alone," she said. But Sabina did not move from her place in the shade of the *richambe* (threshing mat). "She does not want to help herself," Mary remarked when we were out of earshot. She wanted to present herself to us as one who suffered, and we should not spoil that picture by giving her a few simple ideas about how to alleviate her suffering. "I don't understand her," said Mary, shaking her head in disbelief.

A few days later we found Sabina in considerable pain and fright. She had fallen, and the baby in her womb had stopped moving. Our doctor instructed Mary and me to massage Sabina's back until she felt life, so we stayed with her in her bedroom, taking turns massaging her. After twenty minutes she announced, "The baby has sat up," and swinging her legs off the side of her bed, she led us quickly out into the sunshine.

> "Why don't those women who run in the night [i.e., witches] ever fall down when they are with child? They never do. Only good people like myself suffer that misfortune. Twice I have fallen in a week!"
>
> Then she talks about Sara Nerlove. "She was so good to people. She gave them sodas and everything they wanted. She took me to the hospital when I gave birth to my son Samuel."

At the time she reported the dream in which Getuka took her to the hospital to give birth, she had had no associations to it. We knew Sara Nerlove had taken people to the hospital on occasion, although there was no mention in her field notes of her having done so for Sabina. (Later Sara Nerlove wrote denying that she had ever taken Sabina to the hospital.) But the facts were not so important. Of more importance was that Sabina wanted us to know that she, as a good person, not a witch, had been recognized in the past for her virtues. The other investigator had been her friend and had taken care of her as I too had begun to take care of her. Had I not entered her bedroom and without hesitation touched her body repeatedly? I had not been disgusted by the poverty of her room or by her unwashed skin.

She lay down in the shade, and her children cuddled up against her.

"You heard that last night Nyaboke's baby died," she remarks, relieved of her pain and ready now to gossip. "That woman! She was pregnant by a Mowlem [construction company] worker. So many women from Bogoro [women of the clan across the river] go to drink at the club, and when they are drunk, they conceive." Sabina doubles up with laughter, knocking her children off her lap in her merriment. She stands them up again and sends them to sleep in the shade round the side of the house. "Those women are terrible. They will do whatever men want in return for presents of clothes and shoes. They may often consent just for beer alone. They drink, then they go with men and lie down in the bush." She is suddenly solemn. "They enjoy themselves, they have no worries. But I, I have so many worries. You ask me if I dream at night. How can I dream when I cannot even sleep because my head aches with worry? What will I give the children to eat when I give birth? Will my husband send money for sugar then? No, he won't send a cent. He knows that when I am pregnant I need to drink tea, and for tea I need sugar. But he has provided me with neither, so can I expect him to give me these things when I have delivered? I tell you, were it not for this pregnancy, I too would go to find myself a friend at Mowlem. So many women do it!"

And she gave us a list of neighbors who had "got things" from Mowlem workers in return for sex. A number, she said, like the woman whose baby had died that morning, got children along with the presents. Some of those women were not even poor. Their husbands provided very well for them, and yet still they sought men. The implication seemed to be that these well-off women were much worse morally. They did not even have poverty as an excuse for their behavior. They were "hot" for men because their husbands were away from home, but did that excuse them?

"Now that I am a Christian I do not drink beer. But a year ago I used to brew it for the club and even to sell it in my own house. I have lived with beer and I am used to being with men who drink; but let me tell you, if you don't want them to bother you, they won't. A woman living alone will always be bothered by men, but she can stop them. She can keep a *panga* in her house to chase those who come to her door or who try to linger after all the beer is finished. When I used to sell beer here at home, I sold it from midday until five o'clock, and then I told them to go away, I was closing; they should come back again tomorrow. You wouldn't find a man here still at six o'clock. As a woman alone you have to make yourself plain or you'll have even young boys after you. But I do make myself plain. If Kwamboka has a boyfriend, she'd better not play about with him near my house!"

Suddenly Gekonde appeared from school for his lunch break. His mother sent him off to ask a laborer on the road nearby to lend her two shillings for meat. "I long for meat now," she explained, "and that man is my brother. Perhaps he will lend me the money." Later Mary remarked, "Was that man really her brother? How can he be! He is a Mowlem worker. Do those people come from these parts? No, they are strangers, mostly they are not even Gusii. Perhaps that man is the father of the child she is carrying. She tells us so many stories of the women in this neighborhood who make 'beer friends' at the club. Wasn't she talking of herself?"

Possibly at one level she *was* talking of herself, but she was also trying very hard to differentiate herself from her neighbors. She admitted that she used to brew beer, for how else could a woman whose husband did not support her make money to pay school fees and clothe her children? The club had a legal license, and a woman could get a contract from the proprietor to brew so much beer each week for sale on his premises. But he would charge her a large share of her earnings for the privilege of selling her beer in his club. On the other hand, if she were to brew and sell beer illegally in her own home, she could pocket the entire profits. Many "good" women risked arrest to do so. Sabina had been one of them.

So the picture which Sabina wanted us to have of her was now emerging: she was a Christian, a good woman, surrounded by the temptations of alcohol, tobacco, and men, all of which she resisted. An abjectly poor person, a sufferer, she was worthy of our pity, our help, and also our interest and admiration. For her part, she had begun to idealize the entire project, our African assistants as well as the white researchers. During this time she was mostly housebound by the inertia of later pregnancy and then by the need to be with her infant in the weeks immediately following childbirth. She had plenty of time for me and for the project.

For whatever reasons, whether boredom or longing for attention,

Sabina responded to us as if she had literally been waiting for us to walk into her compound and provide her with a focus for her life. She did not seem to differentiate very clearly among the various workers on the project. Since I visited her more often than anyone else, however, I was barraged more frequently and at greater length by what seemed at first like helter-skelter associations, a stream of consciousness. Mary would ask, "When Sabina hops, can you guess where she will hop to?" and I had to admit my confusion at the apparently random nature of her monologues. It was only after a long time that I recognized how focused these apparently scattered thoughts really were: she was continually searching for an increment in self-esteem. She would depict herself as a pure woman, a good Christian, the kind of person whom, she believed, we would want her to be. Meanwhile, by her salacious and incessant gossip she sought to depict others as being worse than she was herself, despite her failings which, however hard she tried to conceal them, invariably emerged in time. She suffered. She was abused by the world and her family, by her husband in particular; misfortunes rained upon her, but they were not of her own making. On one level, therefore, she sought to convince herself, and me in particular, of her worth in comparison with the sinners who were her neighbors. At another, deeper level, I believe she sought from me an intense interest in her body, in her most intimate parts, an interest which, if it could be successfully aroused in me, promised her a sense of completeness and self-worth.

It was rather rare that I saw her with other adults, and on the few occasions when I did, she struck me as being ill at ease. At first I thought this due to the difficulty she might experience in maintaining, for my benefit, what she perceived as an ideal self, in front of someone who was much more familiar with the ordinary, everyday Sabina. Once, as we were coming up to her house, we saw her standing smoking a pipe together with another woman. The instant she heard us, Sabina knocked the tobacco out of her pipe and hid it in her dress. She looked sheepish as we emerged from the path into her yard. Though she did not mention her smoking (which is strictly forbidden by her church) and neither did we, and perhaps she believed she had concealed her pipe in time, she seemed distinctly uncomfortable with us during that session and relieved when we rose to go. There was another reason, however, for her uneasiness at having to deal with us in front of her friends from the neighborhood. This became obvious one morning when we found her sitting with a woman who, it emerged, was divorced, had an illegitimate child, and was suffering from some vague physical complaint. She was short-tempered and scowled continually, but she truly had plenty to complain about, perhaps more than Sabina. Sabina then began what I realized was an effort to convince all of us that on the contrary Sabina, of the two of them, was worse off.

> "Did you have breakfast [i.e., tea] this morning?" Sabina asks the other woman, and when she nods yes, she did have breakfast, Sabina says, "Well, I didn't. There must be sugar in your father's house if you drank tea [for the Gusii never drink tea without sugar], so please bring me half a cup of sugar so that I too may have some breakfast." A little later we hear Sabina complaining that she has no blankets. Since Mary and I have been into her bedroom and have seen blankets there, this is patently untrue. She even boasted to us once that a woman in her church gave her two blankets, out of "respect"; so in this little speech Sabina is telling her unfortunate, afflicted neighbor, "Don't you go envying me because these strangers come to visit me. They come empty-handed. If you think they give me sugar or blankets to cover myself with, you are wrong. I am worse off than you, who at least have a father to care for you, whereas I only have a husband who gives me nothing."

Of all the women with whom I worked closely, Sabina was the most aloof when I met her in public. Her eyes would dart at me and then she would look away. It was almost impossible for her to acknowledge that she knew me. Indeed I often saw her scuttling away as fast as she could go. No doubt this was because she was at that moment engaged in doing something which she believed I would not approve of, but she also was apparently terrified of the jealousy of her neighbors, many of whom had also known Getuka years ago, as well as Sara Nerlove, and yet had not had the good fortune to have been picked out by Getuka's wife for her special attention. The other women I worked with also expressed their fear of inviting the malevolence of their neighbors by virtue of their association with me, but without exception they were eager to greet and talk to me when we met by chance on the road. They would even call out to me if they thought I had not seen them, disregarding the attention they were attracting from passersby.

In the fifth session I found Sabina pacing about her yard. She said she was waiting for her older children, whom she had sent off to look for firewood. She remarked casually that she and her family were unable to collect wood close to home because they were afraid of her husband's half brother, Marco, who would beat them if he caught them there. Just as casually, she added that he almost succeeded in having her killed last year. He was the real tyrant of her life, not her husband, who merely neglected her. Her brother-in-law, on the other hand, had terrorized her for years.

From Sabina herself on our first meeting, and also from other people in the community, I had learned something about the land dispute between Obamba and Marco. After years of intrigue which from time to time flared into violence, the case had reached the district court, and Obamba had been judged to be the true heir. Despite the court order, however, the same pattern of intrigue and intermittent hostility had continued, and since Obamba was away from home, Sabina had had to bear the brunt of Marco's hostility. In the course of this decade-long dispute, Marco had been initiated as *omonyamasera* (a sorcerer), ostensibly to protect himself from the witchcraft he believed Obamba and Sabina must be perpetrating upon him (for he had become impotent, and one of his wives had run away in disgust). Thus, as Sabina had recounted to me the first time we met, she lived in terror of Marco's *emesira* (sorcery), and hence her intense, if inconsistent, association with the Lutheran church—her own attempt to secure divine protection against her brother-in-law's supernatural powers. Marco and his sons would also periodically take physical action against her. For example, they might burn her boundary fence or cut down her maize at night, and her children's safety was always at risk.

In this session, however, Sabina nonchalantly revealed that in the previous year she had undergone a head operation following a beating Utuori, Marco's son, had given her, in which he had fractured her skull. This startling fact emerged because she complained of having a headache. She put her hands to her forehead, remarking that she had to lie down, there was something beating in there.

> "The *omobari* [head surgeon] did not finish his work. When I
> have had my child, I will go back to him again and have another
> operation. The *omobari* is a relative of mine, and thus he only
> charged me 150 shillings, a special price. But that was too much

for work done badly. Next time I shall pay him only fifty
shillings, and he had better do a good job!"

The Gusii have long been famous for the performance of head operations, and the number of people who have undergone this procudure
seems to be very large. Although I never witnessed the operation
myself, I met many people of all ages who had undergone one and
sometimes many such operations. The scars of the women were usually
concealed by their head cloths or by their hair, but in any marketplace
one could see men whose scalps and foreheads bore the dramatic scars of
okobara. The principle involved in this surgery is simple: when someone has migraines or dizziness as a result of a beating or head injury,
the Gusii believe that by cutting the sufferer's scalp and removing some
of his blood, bone, and "surplus" matter, the pain will be alleviated.
Unfortunately surgeons vary considerably in skill. They are supposed to
undergo a long period of apprenticeship, but it is not always the case
that they do so. My husband later interviewed Sabina's surgeon, who
volunteered that he had had a truncated apprenticeship. Sabina's experience with him had not been very satisfactory. Perhaps in Gusiiland,
as elsewhere, if you go to a cut-rate surgeon, regardless of whether or
not he is a relative, you can expect a second-rate operation.

Sabina described her experience thus:

"It was late in the afternoon, just before my children came
home from school. I was looking at my maize. It was the
seventh month then, as now, and we were roasting maize. Then
suddenly Utuori started to shout abuse at me; he jumped
through the fence and came after me with a hoe. He shouted
that I was *richara* [a retarded person], and I was not fit to have
won the court case. Then he brought that hoe down upon me.
He would have killed me, but Gekonde arrived that minute
from school and threw stones at Utuori, so that he ran away.
Next day my family took me to the district hospital, but they
could do nothing for me there, so my brothers arranged with
Motanya the *omobari,* and three days later he operated on me. In
those days Obamba hadn't got himself a second wife yet, so he
stayed here with the children, and I was taken to my home.
Musa was at the breast still, so I took him with me. The operation took place in my mother's house. I was very afraid of what
would happen to me. I had never seen such a thing being done.
There were ten people to help Motanya. When he cut my scalp,

they brought forked sticks and held back the flaps of skin for
him so he could work inside my head. He scraped out blood and
gristle and filled up several little cooking pots with it. Then
when he had finished he used different kinds of leaves to stop the
bleeding. The operation took an hour, they told me, but as for
me, I fainted after a little while, so I cannot remember a great
deal. My head was very swollen from the beating and I could feel
nothing there. I was numb. But at the edges I felt the knife and
from pain and terror I fainted. Afterward I stayed in my
mother's house for a month. She brought Musa to me where I
lay, and I nursed him like that. I urinated into a tin. I never
went outside at all. But when the bandages were taken off and
the cuts had healed and I went home again, I knew I was not
altogether well. When I work hard in the *shamba* my head hurts
me. I think this is because Motanya cut me twice above my left
temple but only once above my right. He must operate again on
the right side, and if the scars are equal on both sides I think I
shall be well again. As soon as I am strong enough after my
child is born, I want Motanya to come here to my house and
perform the operation. Obamba will not consent to leave his
woman now, so Kwamboka will take care of the children in his
stead. Mind you, my brothers will have to pay Motanya. I
haven't any money, so if I am to have this operation again, it
will be my brothers who will pay."

I was appalled by Sabina's revelation. When I had first interviewed
her in our pregnancy clinic, she had given me a dramatic account of the
dispute between her husband and Marco, swelling at length on her fear
of Marco's powers as *omonyamasira,* but it was not until the fifth session
that she mentioned the head operation, the result of the beating she
had received from Marco's son. Perhaps she had not alluded to the
beating or the subsequent operation because until recently the migraine
headaches had not been bothering her. Or possibly she assumed I
would notice the scars just below her hairline and would guess what she
had been through. But given the fact that she consistently presented
herself as a sufferer, someone who was abused and betrayed, it was
strange that until now she had neglected to use this piece of evidence to
emphasize her pitiful condition. At any rate her disclosure was such a
surprise to us that Mary said to me afterward she suspected Sabina of
having concocted the story in order to gain our sympathy. "Those scars
she has are small. They could be from something else." Some discreet

questioning in the neighborhood, however, confirmed Sabina's account, and I was all the more impressed by the extraordinarily precarious nature of the physical and emotional conditions under which she lived. A year ago, almost to the day, she had narrowly escaped being murdered, and following that she had had a head operation, which regardless of its frequency in Gusiiland was nevertheless traumatic. Then a month later she had gone to visit her husband, with whom, she had assumed, she had a stable and supportive relationship—seeing that he had come home to take care of their children during her convalescence—only to find that he had entered an apparently permanent relationship with another woman, the mother of four sons. On becoming pregnant, she had then returned to Morongo, where she had been living within a stone's throw of a man who had tried to kill her. Since she was constantly in fear for her life, it was hardly surprising she often appeared so disorganized.

Now, having described this experience of a year ago, she seemed suddenly to put it out of her mind, along with the headache she had been complaining about.

> She jumped up and paced the yard again, then in and out of her house, obsessing about her cowife. "Obamba had another wife once. When he married me she was with him, but she ran away with a Kipsigis years ago, taking her daughter with her. So I was the only one until now. Suddenly I have a cowife again, but no husband. I have written three letters to him and received no answer. What will become of me when my child is born?" She jiggles up and down, prompting Mary to exclaim, "The child is being born now, by the look of you." Sabina grins, "You think I am in labor because you see me walking like this. I got some snuff from a neighbor this morning. Often women sniff it when they feel the pains, and I think perhaps I'll take some. It is too soon, though. It is three more weeks until my time." "You may have counted wrong; perhaps you made a mistake," I offer. She glances at me disdainfully as she passes. "Would I be mistaken? Do you imagine me to be an old-fashioned woman who dates her menstrual period by whether the moon is full or new, whether the night is dark or light? No, I count by the days of the month so I don't make mistakes. This child is due in the fourth week of July. These pains are nothing. I usually begin to feel them in the seventh month, and none of

my children came too soon; they were all nine-month babies. This one will be too, you'll see."

Sabina's claim to be in labor for two or three months was not unusual among Gusii women. I myself knew one woman who had contractions for an extended period every day for six weeks. Eventually she gave birth to a normal, full-term child.

I was due to go on vacation just at the time Sabina would give birth. She knew this and scolded me as the time drew nearer.

> "How can you go away and leave me? I am afraid without you." "You managed very well eight other times. You are an expert! And anyway, our doctor will be here if you need her. She knows a hundred times more about childbirth than I do." "But I am not used to her as I am used to you, Sarah. [In fact she has known both of us for an equal length of time.] I am used to you as I was used to the other Sarah. Did you tell me she married? Has she got children?" Sabina is wandering about her yard. She has heard about Sara Nerlove's marriage and the birth of her son several times already. She muses, "If this baby of mine is a girl, I shall call her Sarah, and if it is a boy, I'll call him Robert." She goes on dreamily, "Kwamboka started life as Barbara. That was Getuka's first wife. She was a good woman, so I named my firstborn after her." Kwamboka is sitting quietly in the yard. She is a stolid young lady who appears to be the sensible caretaker not only of her younger siblings but of her mother also. When I have a chance to speak with her alone, she seems intelligent and sensitive. Currently she is very religious and spends her weekends at meetings of the Church of God, a Protestant sect fairly active in the area. She left the Lutheran church, into which she was baptized as a child, and is now undergoing instruction prior to admission into this fundamentalist church. (Her mother's only comment to us about her daughter's independent religious venture is, "Maybe I should follow her example. Those Lutherans were disappointed by me. I should start with Kwamboka's new friends. They'd take a while to find out about me"; i.e., she would enjoy a period of illusory virtue and acceptance before the ministers of the Church of God caught up with her and she fell from grace.)

I doubted that Sabina had really called her first child after my husband's first wife, and when I asked Kwamboka she shrugged, "I

don't remember." I sometimes saw Kwamboka smiling wryly at her
mother's remarks, but despite the abuse which Sabina heaped upon
her—accusations of stupidity and laziness— Kwamboka rarely appeared hurt or annoyed. In fact she seemed to be very attached to her
mother, while for her part Sabina sometimes admitted that she valued
Kwamboka. "I have six sons and only two daughters," she would say.
"Would that it was the other way around!" She often recounted conversations she had had with Kwamboka, indicating that the girl was a
source of comfort to her. Indeed in the last month of her pregnancy, as
Sabina became progressively disorganized, most of the burdens of running the household fell upon Kwamboka. Sabina had so many physical
complaints: she had stomach cramps most days; she had scabies on her
buttocks; she usually had a headache. In minute detail she described
her discomforts.

She seemed more intent than ever on representing herself as a
virtuous sufferer, i.e., in the image desirable to the Lutheran missionaries, who were the only white people other than anthropologists
whom she had ever known. She maintained repeatedly that she no
longer drank beer, and yet one day Josephine, her four-year-old, asked
her mother for beer while we were there. Sabina whispered to her to be
quiet, but since the child was demanding beer, one can only assume it
was something she was getting used to. Another time we met
Momanyi with tobacco in his hand. He said his mother had sent him to
buy it, and yet Sabina volunteered on more than one occasion that she
did not smoke. She also declared she never had been to a diviner in her
life, despite all her troubles with Marco. "If I am sick, either God will
see fit to cure me or else I shall die," she said. She knew that Getuka
attended sacrifices and divinations, and yet she seemed convinced that
I, like the missionaries, would disapprove of her having to do with
anything of that sort. Indeed, before I had even asked her if she went to
diviners, she took pains to dissociate herself from them.

> "*Abaragori* lie," she declares. "There is a woman here who
> could not bear children and, oh, she slaughtered so many goats
> in vain. Those diviners, they tell you one thing and another, and
> always that you must buy goats to slaughter for the ancestors.
> But this woman, she began to think perhaps it was her hus-
> band's fault, that he was *omoreba* [sterile]. Now she goes with
> other men to see if she can get a child that way. She has not

conceived so far, but who knows, perhaps she will. At any rate those goats did nothing for her but waste her money."

I knew that her own family had consulted diviners about a sister, Maria, who was barren and seemed also to be retarded, but I never had any evidence that Sabina herself had used divination for help with her own problems. It may be that in this respect at any rate she did conform to her church's views and prohibitions. While she claimed that diviners were frauds, however, she certainly believed in the powers of witchcraft and sorcery. By her own admission, it had been in order to secure protection against Marco's malevolence that she had been baptized in the first place, though in the ten years since her baptism, I gathered that her involvement with the church had waxed and waned. When I knew her, Sabina often gave her health as an excuse for infrequent church attendance—the Lutheran church was several miles away—but not so long ago her attendance had been regular, and her attempts to live a Christian life had been rewarded by the friendship of other church members, especially that of a widowed stepsister-in-law, Evalyn, who had been baptized on the same day as Sabina and had remained a passionate and devoted believer. This woman came from another tribe and despite many years in Gusiiland always experienced herself as an endangered alien. During the period in which I worked with Sabina, she scarcely went to church at all. Nevertheless, even though Evalyn lectured Sabina about her return to sinful ways, she continued to help her when and as she could, particularly by providing milk for the younger children.

Sabina herself evidently viewed her current behavior as a "return to sinful ways." She sometimes said with a cackle of laughter that she was *omosatani* (a follower of Satan). She would look at me boldly, and yet with the question in her eyes: Would I reject her, or could I continue to be her friend and to visit her, given how "dirty" she was? For months she tried very hard to maintain the fiction that she was the puritan her church demanded she should be, the puritan she assumed I and all white people insisted she be if she hoped to keep our *amasikane* (respect). This need of hers to present a virtuous image gave rise to increasing tension between us. Mary and I continually found clues indicating that she was not conducting her life in quite the way she maintained that she was. Children had to be hushed up, objects had to be hidden, she even hid herself. In fact, in the week before I went away on vacation, I never found her at home. She had said repeatedly that she wanted me to be present at the birth, but on the three or four occasions during that week that I went to her house, she was never there. Once I caught a fleeting glimpse of her across the river. I called to her, but she turned away and disappeared into the house of a woman who I knew held beer parties twice a week. It seemed that in the last dog days before her child was born Sabina was out drinking from morning until dark, but she was not prepared to admit it to me. Other women whose lives were as disorganized as hers showed little if any shame about themselves. Sometimes one might apologize mildly for herself: "I drink and I wish I didn't, because I get into trouble when I'm drunk"; but another would be completely straightforward: "I drink and I like it. Beer is good." Only Sabina took pains to conceal her habits from me.

It was true that her efforts to convince me of her virtue were sometimes sabotaged by her children's tactlessness, but when I did find her home, she would spend an enormous amount of time pointing out the shortcomings of her neighbors—in comparison, presumably, with herself. She might be found wanting in many ways, but other people whom we all knew were equally wayward. Her flow of gossip was sometimes overwhelming. I would come out of her compound gasping for clean air, my head reeling with images of violence and greed, lust and malevolence. Though Sabina might begin by praising someone, her story would invariably twist about so that in the end that person had to be seen in a shameful light. One day, for example, she told how much she admired one of the project assistants, a local woman, who had been kind to her. She asked about the woman's husband, her children, her in-laws. Surely she must be one of the best, the most generous people from these parts. But then Sabina confided in us that this woman's father had stolen a large sum of money from the coffee cooperative to which she herself belonged. "What am I to do? I shall need my share in order to buy tea and sugar when I give birth. Now Obongo, that thief, has taken everything from me and so many other poor people as well!" The "theft," only the merest rumor, was disproved a day or two later. Nothing had been stolen. Sabina got her money, but this incident illustrated something very typical of her behavior with me. She would talk warmly about someone she imagined I was close to. Then suddenly she would produce some unflattering information about that person or a relative of his, in effect eradicating the earlier pleasant impression she had given of him. Her underlying message was clear: "I may be devious and underhand, but everyone is at least as devious and underhand as I."

Sabina gave birth to a daughter the night after I left on vacation. She was attended not by a crowd of neighborhood women, as she had fantasized, but by two female relatives. When our physician went to examine the baby, who, though full term, was small for gestational age, Sabina announced she was angry that Sarah had abandoned her, and thus, she said, she had named her child Suzannah after the doctor.

I went to see her immediately on my return two weeks later. My contacts with Sabina had been particularly intense. In the last weeks of her pregnancy, I had watched and listened to her in the hot sun, fascinated by her reveries and her exhibitionism. I had been profoundly impressed by her emotional and physical ordeals of the past year. I had wanted to be with her for her delivery and had been disappointed that this had not been possible.

"The baby's name is Suzannah," she says as I walk into the yard, for first she must snub me. I apologize for not being there for the birth. She grins, "Anyway, it's good you're back again," and it is clear that she is glad. She rattles on. "I have had so many visitors, and they all brought food." In other words, she did quite well without me. However, Obamba doesn't know that the baby has been born. "Why should I spend money on a stamp when I need that money to buy soap for my child? When I was pregnant, didn't I write him three letters, and he never replied? So why should I expect anything from him now? How can I get family planning? I'll never go to where he is at Kericho again, but he'll come here eventually." A neighbor sitting with her remarks scornfully, "Can we believe her? Of course not! When that child is the size Musa is now, Sabina will take herself off to Kericho to get another. She won't wait for Obamba to come home." Sabina's eyes gleam. She barks out her laughter. "I tell you, I don't want any more children," but she is excited by the attention she is attracting to her remarkable facility for conception. "Was childbirth so bad this time?" I tease her. "Didn't you and your friends enjoy yourself?" "Friends? There were only two of them. Why should I want a lot of women here while I'm giving birth? You have to be careful, you know. One of them might scrape up some of my blood and take it off to use against me. I don't care about *abaragori* [diviners], but I do fear witchcraft, though I trust God will protect me from those who use it against me. Those diviners! They cause nothing but trouble and expense. You go to them because you are sick and they say, 'It is the ancestors. They need a sacrifice. You must spend fifty shillings on a goat'; or else they say, 'Your sister-in-law is bewitching you,' when you are ill from natural causes. So then you start to hate your sister-in-law for nothing. I have nothing to do with either kind, diviners or witches."

Why did she give birth so privately? When she had Musa, a throng of women had encouraged her and urged her on. Perhaps this time the lateness of the hour had accounted for the lack of supporters. She had been attended by Evalyn, whose strong religious faith gave her courage to brave the darkness, and Kerubo, the midwife and a herbalist, who walked without fear at night. The fact that Sabina had delivered at three o'clock in the morning, however, need not have been a deterrent to her friends. They would have come had they been summoned. But Sabina had chosen not to call them. Presumably she had been feeling less secure this time than two years ago when Musa had been born, and thus she had not been willing to expose herself unnecessarily. So Suzannah had arrived almost in secret, and it had not been until the following morning, when the placenta was safely in the latrine and Evalyn had swept and cleaned the house, that the news of the birth had been carried across the river to Bogoro and women had come to greet the baby and her mother.

Two weeks after childbirth, Sabina was still tired. Most other Gusii women would have been harvesting their fields again. Sabina's finger millet had been flattened by the wind and rain, and if it were not picked soon, it would spoil. Kwamboka, on vacation from school, had the main burden of providing for the household. She offered to roast maize for us, and while we were waiting her mother complained, "That girl is so slow. She doesn't know how to do anything, even though she has been taught." She called into the kitchen, "You'd better marry a rich man who'll provide you with a cook. But of course he'll divorce you. How could you stay married when you're so slow?" Sabina's initial excitement at seeing me and describing the events of the past weeks had evaporated. She was irritable. "This mess I have," she continued, forgetting Kwamboka, "this blood. How tired I am of it! It goes on for such a long time!" In the past she had used leaves of a particular bush to catch the flow of the afterbirth. The leaves were soft and absorbent and still widely used in Gusiiland, but this time she had an old dress which she tore into rags.

When Kwamboka brought us the roasted maize, her mother exclaimed, "It is raw, just as I said it would be." Kwamboka impassively offered us *obokima* instead, and Sabina wolfed it down. Though a month ago, at the end of her pregnancy, Sabina had gone hungry, now in the middle of August there was plenty of food. Musa and Josephine were already fatter and content. "They are happy to have the new baby, and they are eating well. Why shouldn't they be content?" Sabina shrugged, launching into a stream of personal complaints. Before she had given birth she had had plenty of complaints too, but at the same time she had generated a tremendous liveliness, despite her physical condition. She relished our attention and rewarded us for it. She had amused herself and us as well. But now I sensed her depression. Although in the past she had talked a great deal about her husband's rejection, perhaps the child moving in her womb had warded off the full impact of the blow. Now the child was separate from her and lay under the dish drainer in the shade, where Sabina paid her little attention. In passing she remarked, "She's very small, isn't she? That's why I suffered so. The baby never grew big enough for my stomach. She knocked about inside me, instead of filling the space and lying still." She had given birth to a runt.

A week later she reported she had enough energy at last to do a little farm work. There was finger millet and pyrethrum lying out to dry in the yard. Still Obamba knew nothing. She had not written to him, but he had not inquired about her, either, and he must have known very well she was due in July. Their oldest son had come home for a visit in May and had seen how big his mother was, and he must have told his father. These days she was washing the children's clothes without soap, she said, and though she had *obokima*, she had no vegetables or beans to eat with it. She stood, hands on hips, a distracted expression on her face. She did not look at me. She might have been talking to herself. She wore no head cloth, and it seemed as if her clothes were disintegrating before my eyes. Or perhaps it was that she was disintegrating. Suddenly from above us we heard the loud explosion of a car's exhaust. Sabina jumped in terror.

"That frightened me! Three years ago there was an accident up on the road. The driver was killed, and the woman beside him was badly injured. People ran and stole everything from the car as she lay there. They took blankets, *wimbi,* beans, and all their money. The woman just watched them do it. I was very shocked, and so were many others. But we knew we could not stop the thieves. We didn't try."

First Sabina had said she needed beans and money, and then she had gone on to describe an episode in which people plundered a wrecked car and stole those very things. They did it even though they were being watched by their neighbors: they did it blatantly. They took whatever they wanted. I had also witnessed similar incidents, in which a house or a vehicle had been stripped by people who, seeing property unprotected, had not hesitated to seize whatever they could lay their hands on and make off with it. At such times people are propelled by greed, and by rage if anyone should try to thwart them. It is the Hobbesian apocalypse of each against all. Sabina had been an onlooker, but her impulse to run and join those violators, her neighbors, people like herself, had been so strong at the time that even in recollecting the incident she was extremely agitated. She needed things which should have been hers by right. She had a right to expect her share of her husband's resources, but she was being thwarted by that interloper, her cowife. As she, like the woman in the car wreck, lay debilitated (by childbirth), her husband's new woman was grabbing the money which Obamba should have been sending to his legitimate wife, the mother of his nine children.

She wandered about the yard, jumping from one subject to another. The two youngest children started to squabble, and Sabina took a stick to hit Josephine. But the little girl retreated, so Sabina threw the stick away, remarking, "She's going to leave me anyway [i.e., to marry into another clan], and it is Musa who will bury me." (In a patrilocal society a son will always have the right to live at home with his mother.) She settled herself down under the eaves to talk about a neighbor who had had a difficult labor during the past week and had been taken to Kisii hospital by my husband.

"That woman Theresa once had a breach birth, and ever since she insists on giving birth outside her house. The *abaragori* told her to do all kinds of things, and after that the child came out feet first. She had to sacrifice and brew beer for her husband's relatives. All this to make the ancestors happy. Those *abaragori!* The things they tell you!"

When Sabina gave birth, Getuka had been far away at Mombasa. Theresa, on the other hand, was taken by Getuka to the hospital in just the way that, in her dream, Sabina had been taken to the hospital. But in the same breath Sabina said, essentially, that Theresa was a pagan bushwoman who blindly did what the diviners told her to do. She wasn't worthy of our friendship or respect or even of our help.

To cheer Sabina up a little, I told her that she was looking slim now, like a young girl. Huh! She wouldn't be here if she were a girl. She'd be at home drinking tea in the mornings with her mother (i.e., she would be unmarried).

"As it is, I haven't been home for a year. I had *chinsoni* [shame] for my father because I was pregnant. [Younger Gusii women claim not to experience shame in appearing pregnant in front of their fathers, but Sabina is of a generation which, with very few exceptions, still observes all the rules of avoidance with the parental generation and probably also experiences the discomfort and sexual tension these rules are designed to handle.] My mother hasn't come to see me since I gave birth because she hasn't money to buy sugar and meat, flour and vegetables which she must bring when first she comes to greet my child. Last week Suzannah was sick, so I sent Kwamboka to my mother for *eriogo ri'emete* [herbal medicine] but she came back empty-handed."

Sabina had been disappointed by her husband, Getuka, me, and even her own mother. The world was a hostile place. Even the nurse at our clinic had treated her badly when she had taken the children there.

"I know that woman Priska from years ago. I met her in the hospital. She abused everyone, she and another one called Joyce. They were cruel to all the women. As for Priska, she has grown so fat. I don't like fat people at all. [Didn't I just admire Sabina for how slim she had become?] Thin people never smell, even in their vaginas, but fat people, when they don't wash, they stink.

When fat people walk they make a strange noise. It is their thighs slapping together. Sometimes they are incontinent like my huge neighbor Evalyn. She even urinates in church; she can't control herself. My brother's wife is very fat also. She has to give birth in the hospital, and there she uses special powder and sweet-smelling soap so that she won't drive everyone away with her stink. I am thankful I don't have to have my children in the hospital, as she does. I would rather die than be abused by those nurses."

A month or two previously Sabina had longed to deliver her child in the hospital. She had dreamed about it and talked about it often. But she had given birth at home, without any celebration or excitement, and she had to handle her disappointment in the best way she knew: by making a virtue out of necessity. How fortunate she was that her good health and strength guaranteed she would not be thrown at the mercy of those arrogant women who called themselves nurses. People who, like her obese sister-in-law, had to have their children in the hospital were to be pitied. Her "huge neighbor Evalyn" was none other than the Evalyn who helped deliver Suzannah, and Sabina was very dependent on her for material and emotional support. Then why did Sabina mock her gratuitously? She rambled on, stopped, stared across the valley, began to talk again. We seemed to be eavesdropping on her interior monologue. And yet she wanted a response. She wanted us to be shocked by the tales she told of other people. She wanted us to think less of them, even though we might think no more favorably of her.

A few days later we found her sitting in her yard with another woman, Moraa, who, it emerged, had rented most of the rest of Sabina's land. Indeed Moraa had already begun to plough her rented plot, without even waiting for Sabina to harvest the maize which stood on it. The maize stalks were lying in the field, but so far Sabina had not harvested the cobs. Sabina said she decided to rent out the land because Kwamboka and Gekonde had been sent away from school for lack of building fees. (She did so without consulting Obamba: "It's his own fault. He hasn't sent me money.") In addition, Gekonde had got into a fight a couple of days before in which he was badly beaten, and Sabina had had to raise some cash in order to take him to the hospital. Therefore she agreed to rent her land to Moraa for two years for 100 shillings. Moraa corrected her: 280 shillings for three years were the terms. Once Moraa had dug the land, she intended to plant pyrethrum there. Sabina shrugged. She would not argue with Moraa's figure. She was lying wrapped in a blanket, full of lassitude.

The reasons she gave for parting with her land seemed odd to us. There was no doubt that Sabina was chronically in need of cash, especially in recent months if, as she claimed, her husband had sent her little or no money. However, 280 shillings was not a reasonable compensation for the use of her land for one year, let alone three. According to Sabina, before he had taken another wife Obamba used to send money for school fees, and only in the past year had he stopped doing so. Perhaps her impulsive decision to rent this land, which for so many years she had defended against Marco, was really an act of vengeance against her husband. Of course Sabina lived there, but it was to Obamba that the court had awarded the land title, not to his wife. Perhaps she hoped to wound him and to force him to reassume his responsibilities to his family.

When Moraa asked for soap and water to wash with before going home for lunch, Sabina laughed, "There's water, but no soap. How can a woman who has no husband buy soap?" Moraa rebuked her, "You have a husband just as I have a husband; otherwise where would you have got all those children?" Then, as she splashed water over her feet to wash the heavy soil away, she remarked, "You planted maize, but you never weeded it, did you?" In other words, Sabina did not know how to help herself. Her maize grew sparsely because it was choked with weeds. Sabina grimaced, "It's true, I never weeded," and she offered Moraa a rather puny ear of boiled maize. She did not seem offended by Moraa's straight talking. "Sit and eat anyway," she urged, and, forgetting her children crying for her at home, Moraa accepted. The two women seemed like old friends already, and yet as I understood it, they scarcely knew one another. It was apparently possible for a Gusii woman to speak her mind to a stranger and be direct in a way she would never dare to be, for instance, to her sister-in-law. Moraa could tell Sabina she exaggerated her troubles. She could accuse her of being lazy and profligate, and yet a moment later the two were gossiping happily together about someone else's troubles. In exchange for her land Sabina got company as well as cash.

Meanwhile, an elderly woman had been sitting in silence on the far side of the house. Eventually she came a little closer and was introduced to me as Sabina's mother, Clemencia, who, on hearing of the beating Gekonde had received, had come to see her grandson. I gathered that the emergency had made it possible for her to come to her daughter's home even though she had not brought any of the gifts that a mother was required to give to her daughter after childbirth. She sat around the corner of the house because, as a traditional Gusii woman, she was constrained from entering or even approaching the *egesaku* (main door) of her son-in-law's house. She was about sixty years old and very thin but vigorous. She was black like Sabina, and round her neck she wore an immense crucifix. Neither at this time nor on subsequent occasions did she speak to me, despite my attempts to engage her in conversation. Unlike her daughter, she was quiet. Long ago she had been rejected by her husband, and though she still lived in his homestead, they had had nothing to do with one another for years, and she had the shyness of someone who did not count for much. Occasionally she interjected a remark into the discussion, but the younger women seemed to ignore her. They had returned to the issue of how Sabina used her land.

"Why don't you plant beans?" Moraa asked her, "Then you won't need to buy them; you'll have your own." Sabina is silent. Throwing her corn cob into a bush, Moraa gets to her feet. "Well, when you didn't plant beans you were making a big mistake," she pronounces as she takes her leave. Sabina stares at the bare earth of her yard for a moment, then she giggles to herself, "I'll go to Kericho, that's what I'll do. Not this New Year, but the next is when I'll go. When I've been to the *omobari* [head surgeon]. I must go soon. I have such pains in my head. It shouldn't cost more than sixty shillings," she adds, for her mother's benefit. Clemencia must relay to her sons at home that Sabina needs their help in paying for this second operation. Suddenly Moraa reappears from the banana trees. She's come back to ask for a drink of water. "You should take that baby of yours to Kericho," she teases, "so your husband can greet her" (i.e., so that Sabina and Obamba can sleep together again). The two women cackle with laughter, while Clemencia remains modestly quiet. "Do you think he's missing me?" Sabina cries. "I tell you, he is, but I'm not missing him!" She is still giggling and muttering to herself under her breath when Moraa, having quenched her thirst, leaves again, this time for good. But

Sabina's attention is taken by Momanyi, who is hanging about near her, looking angry. "You stink!" she exclaims, and he hits her hard on the back and runs off into the garden. "Why didn't you leave him with his father?" Clemencia asks from seventy feet away. Sabina rubs the place where Momanyi hit her. "That child is something very bad." Clemencia nods in agreement. "He's so ugly. When you were a child, you weren't ugly as he is." "I couldn't leave him at Kericho. His father wouldn't keep him. He was always running away into the forest with Kipsigis boys. Then Obamba would search for him for two days at a time. Gekonde is very bad too. I don't know what to do with my children. Now I've rented most of the land here, I should send my remaining sons to their father and stay here at home with my daughters. There'll be enough to eat for just the four of us." "Why ever did you rent your land for 100 shillings?" Clemencia asks. "Your brother got 200 shillings for a much smaller plot." Sabina says she wants to get ready to go out for the afternoon, and so her mother, giving up on the rental issue, goes back to Momanyi. "That child is a Kipsigis because his father was a Kipsigis [i.e., he has been going so long among an alien people that he is no longer a Gusii]. Nobody likes him." Momanyi scowls under the eaves. But today Sabina can't be seduced even by such a favorite topic as Momanyi's bad character. She wants us all, including her mother, to leave so that she can be on her way "to a fund raising in Getutu," as she claims outrageously. But we know perfectly well that nobody goes to a fund raising on a weekday in a place far away from her home. Of course Sabina is going to drink beer.

It seemed that Sabina's latest folly was at least as puzzling to her mother and her tenant as it was to us. A woman who no longer receives any support from her husband has no option but to cultivate her garden, to maximize its productivity. To rent it out at a pittance (the exact sum always remained a mystery) everyone agreed was madness. "I'll go to Kericho," she said, laughing, "after I've had my operation," while Moraa told her, "Take the child there so her father may greet her," but they were surely joking. Obamba had not even bothered to find out if the child had been born. Meanwhile his wife had not the self-discipline, the foresight, or the energy to collect the maize that was lying on the ground, where it would be rotted by the afternoon rain.

Instead she put her old dress over her torn slip, tied her infant on her back, and went off across the river to look for beer, so that at least for the remainder of the day she would not have to think very clearly about her situation.

But next morning she was faced with it again. Five weeks after Suzannah's birth she observed,

> "My husband doesn't like me anymore. But that isn't so im-
> portant. The children are well, they have enough to eat, and I
> have a new baby. I have no need at present to go to Kericho to
> look for another child. My three big boys there are weaned.
> They can take care of themselves. If one should die, then he will
> come home again as a corpse. Otherwise none will come. My
> eldest son David is fifteen. He knew I was pregnant, but he has
> not come to see me, even though the schools are closed and he
> would have the chance to come if he had the interest. He's a
> man now. Why should he come? I don't miss my husband. Even
> if the baby finished three years without ever seeing her father it
> wouldn't matter. She doesn't have to see him. If I had the
> money for my bus fare, I would go to Kericho to harvest the
> maize I planted in April, but I haven't any money, so my cowife
> will harvest it for me. Let me stay here at home without a hus-
> band. Why should I go to Kericho? The road is so dangerous I
> might get into an accident. I am old now. If I went there, what
> would I go for? For meat, for sugar, for sex? Do I need that?
> My family would laugh at me." She has no need of Obamba, nor
> does he have any need of her, or he would have brought the baby
> clothes a woman has a right to expect from her husband. "Now-
> adays he only comes once a year. In the past when I refused to
> join him at Kericho he went to harlots, but he never took
> another wife. You must expect a man to use prostitutes. He
> cannot go for a year without sex. But now he has taken a wife
> whose sons are all big [i.e., circumcised], so they sleep in an-
> other house. Obamba and their mother are free to be like unmar-
> ried people. They can enjoy themselves [i.e., they have no need
> to be surreptitious when they have sex]. They have sex every
> night. They eat well and drink beer together. My cowife is old,
> as old as Rosa [a neighbor], and fat, and she can no longer
> conceive and bear children. But even old women can elope with
> other people's husbands." Suzannah wakes crying, and Sabina
> puts her to the breast. "This child is so small. I have pains in

my breasts. My milk is not good. I can't spend any money on
the bus fare to Kericho, for I must buy food and milk for my
children." Musa, who has been with her all this time, starts
peering under his mother's skirt. She pushes him off as if he
were a fly, but he keeps returning. Finally she explodes, "Leave
me! Can't you see I'm nursing the baby!" She explains to me,
"He does that because he wants me to get up and go to the
kitchen to cook *obokima* for him. He will annoy me until I do as
he wishes."

She turned her back on us and on the rest of her children and bent
over the baby. She was tired. At mid-morning her shoulders sagged.
She had nothing more to say to us.

Almost a month went by before Sabina harvested her maize, and by
that time most of it was rotten. One day we found her in the *shamba*
planting pyrethrum on Moraa's rented plot. "Moraa is pregnant, don't
you see. She isn't strong, so I'm helping her."

She laughed and joked with Moraa, who sat watching her landlady
do her work for her. Meanwhile Sabina's own maize and pyrethrum
were rank with weeds. A little while ago, in our hearing, Moraa had
told Sabina that she should be weeding her garden, but her words went
unheeded. So now she was delighted to accept Sabina's help. It seemed
Sabina needed the emotional support of the other woman, and even
though she was too depressed to help herself, she had energy enough to
secure Moraa's friendship by doing her planting for her.

Today Sabina's dress was very short indeed. Hitching her skirt even
higher, she sashayed away from us across the *shamba,* swinging her hips
and singing a circumcision song. She didn't want to talk to us!
Couldn't we see she was working? Her children watched her in silence.
The older boy Gekonde, who, his mother so often complained, was a
rogue (*ekebago*), obediently held the baby. When the child cried, he
hushed her, "Mokeira, Mokeira, kira." "So her name isn't Suzannah,
after all," I said. "It is Mokeira. She has been Mokeira from when she
was born," Gekonde answered, smiling. "Suzannah" was just the name
Sabina called her child in front of us, to please us. "Suzannah is the
kind of name you give to a bus, not a baby," said Kwamboka. All
Kenyan buses had names, and a local bus, which passed through
Morongo many times a day, had "Suzannah" written along the side of
it in large uneven blue letters. Sabina's children were lined up like a

chorus, watching their mother. "You can see for yourself how she is," the older ones seemed to be saying to us. "Would she tell you the truth?"

Hours later Sabina was still in the fields. But this time when the baby cried, she came into the yard to nurse her. It was for the baby, not for us, that she left the *shamba*. "She has no respect for us now," Mary remarked, and indeed when some women who had been working nearby came to ask for drinking water and Sabina told them to fetch their own from the river, they said the same thing: Sabina had no respect; she was not behaving these days as she should. She was as garrulous as ever, but her disconnected flow of words seemed designed to drive us away, rather than to engage us. "She wants to go to drink beer," Mary whispered, "She doesn't want to sit here with us."

Sabina thrust the baby into Josephine's arms and went down on her knees beside a mat where her maize, most of which was already spoiled, was drying. She picked out the rotten kernels with jerky movements. "If there's any that is good, I'll take it to my pastor." She laughed harshly. It was wise to placate the elders of the church when one had fallen into evil ways. She jumped up and ran to wash herself after her hours of digging. She wanted to dress and go out looking for beer, but the Europeans had come and they were preventing her from doing as she wished.

> "I live too near the road," she says. "I wish I had a fence so that people would not see me and I would not see them either." As she scrubs her legs she criticizes her children. "You, Kwamboka, you wouldn't help anyone, even if they were about to die. You wouldn't know what to do for them, would you? You and Gekonde have wasted the day in idleness. If I'd known you were going to be let out of school so early, I'd have seen to it that you went to weed our maize."

Momanyi came back from a neighbor's with an armful of borrowed clothes for his mother to wear. It was fairly common for women to lend one another their better clothes for special occasions. Women were afraid to refuse if they were asked, because a refusal would indicate a pride in their possessions and a desire to conserve them which might provoke the malevolence of others. And thus, though those who were better off complained bitterly in private about being forced to lend their possessions, they did so nevertheless. "I have a cough," Sabina remarked, defensively; "I don't want to go anywhere." With a frown she inspected the clothes Momanyi had brought. "They aren't even clean," she complained, but she carried them into the house just the same. Later, when she had got rid of us, she would go to her beer party.

How long would she maintain the fiction that she was a good church member, one who had forsworn beer and who took the little maize she had harvested to her pastor? Had we not seen her disappearing into a house where a beer party had been in progress months ago, even before the birth of Suzannah Mokeira? Did she believe that we had not heard her children's remarks? Why did she lie so blatantly, saying that she wanted to go to a fund raising when everyone knew that she, who was so poor, would never go to a fund raising in her own community, let alone in another location? Why did she say she had a cough when we had been with her for an hour and never once heard it? We rarely found her at home, and when we did she always tried to get rid of us, so she could be on her way to drink. And yet long after a point at which, if she reflected at all, she would have known we knew the truth about her habits, she fiercely pretended that she did not drink. She conceded that she used to, before she was "saved," but that had been long ago. Why was our "good" opinion of her of such importance that she had to hide from us or drive us away in order to conserve it? As the weeks drew on without word from Obamba, she spent longer stretches of each day drinking. And as she became more disorganized and more neglectful of her tasks at home, her need to have and keep the European's approval was more intense than ever. But apparently she believed that the only way she could do this was by avoiding us almost entirely.

I continued, however, to visit her, even though more often than not I found a turned back or a deserted compound. I waited to see how this deadlock would be resolved. It was not my place to confront her deliberately. I was not her therapist. My task was to observe how she handled the pressures of her life, not to help her handle them more effectively, unless she chose to use me in that way.

In the end the confrontation took place by chance. I went to see the mother of a child whom we were considering including in our longitudinal sample. This woman, whose name was Maria, was a well-known brewer of beer. She lived across the river from Sabina, and it was into her house that I had seen Sabina disappear when I had been looking for her one afternoon several months ago. As Mary and I came into the yard, we saw little Musa staggering about with a mug in his hand and the mushy residue of beer all over his face. In the house Sabina sat nursing her baby, Josephine and Momanyi beside her. When she saw me, she signaled Musa to hide his mug, but her friend and hostess laughed, "Why hide it? Why pretend you do not drink beer? Why try to conceal that your children drink also?" Maria was drunk herself.

Sabina was also drunk, but not drunk enough to be free from shame. She pushed Josephine and Momanyi toward the door, whispering to them to go home and take Musa with them. She must have assumed that though we would be shocked to see her in this condition, we would be even more horrified at seeing her children drunk, for most Gusii people deplore beer drinking by young children, although it is a fast-spreading phenomenon. "Don't you know," Maria cried, "Sabina always tells lies? She does not know how to tell the truth!" As she spoke a great clap of thunder shook the house, and rain crashed against the iron sheets of the roof. There was no chance that anyone could escape until the storm passed, and so we sat together for forty minutes. Conversation was impossible because of the noise of the rain on the roof. Although Maria and another woman continued to drink, Sabina took nothing more. She sat red eyed, giggling to herself from time to time. She would steal glances at us, but she did not speak to us. But when the weather cleared and we got up to go, she cheerfully agreed to be at home the following afternoon. I emerged into the cool evening believing that an important milestone in our relationship had been reached.

As we went up the steep path to Morongo, we met a man slipping and sliding in haste on his way down from the market. He called to us as he passed that a woman had been killed by lightning just twenty minutes ago. While we had been sheltered from the storm in Maria's house, a lightning bolt had struck her Seventh Day Adventist neighbor. At her conversion this woman, like Sabina, had forsworn alcohol, but unlike Sabina she had maintained her abstinence ever since. Her burial provoked an enormous amount of controversy, absorbing the interests and energies of the community for several days. It emerged that on two previous occasions the same homestead had been struck by lightning. Once a tree had been killed, and once a child had been struck, although he subsequently recovered. In neither case did the family consult a diviner or perform the sacrifices Gusii custom prescribed. Therefore people viewed this latest tragedy as the inevitable consequence of the family's refusal to placate the ancestors on the two earlier occasions. In cases of death by lightning, Gusii custom demanded the completion of a complicated series of rituals and sacrifices before the corpse could be removed for burial. Immediately following the death of this woman, members of her husband's lineage set about finding the right *omokorerani* to oversee the performance of these rituals, and they began to collect money to pay for the sacrificial goats. The following day, however, when neighbors and relatives gathered at her house to mourn the dead woman, who still lay where she had fallen at her front door, I witnessed a confrontation between those who wanted to follow Gusii custom, with all the expense and delay involved, and the elders of the Seventh Day Adventist church, who demanded she be buried as a Christian, i.e., immediately, and without "pagan" ritual of any sort. The elders successfully persuaded the widower, a man known to be feebleminded, to follow their dictates. As I watched, almost every one of the mourners rose in fear and disgust and went away, saying to one another that by prohibiting the placation of the ancestors the elders had condemned the family to yet further tragedy.

Later that day I went to see Sabina. I found her running up the road near her house, waving her fists and yelling at her son, Gekonde. She accused him of having stolen and sold her pyrethrum. The boy raced past us as his mother faltered and angrily gave up the chase. Apparently, while she had been drinking with Maria the previous afternoon, Gekonde had taken down the sack of flowers from the storage area in the ceiling of his mother's house and sold it at Morongo.

> As he retreats up the hill the boy shouts, "You went off to drink. You weren't at home. How do you know it was I who was the thief?" "Unless you bring me that money you shan't set foot in my homestead again," Sabina yells back. "If he doesn't do as you tell him, what will you do about it?" Mary asks her. Sabina doesn't reply. She seems close to tears as she leads us angrily and at great speed to her house. "That boy thinks I am *richara,* so feebleminded that I won't notice that he has stolen my pyrethrum! He should be at Kericho with his father. He's always lived here because he was attending school here, but I doubt he even goes to school these days, though I pay for him to

go. It seems he has forgotten what he learned at school and has
become a thief. He stays away from home for weeks at a time.
He claims he's washing glasses in a bar at Morongo because he is
fed better there than at home. It is true we never see meat in my
house. He only came home to steal my pyrethrum."

Back in her own yard she flopped down, reaching into the neck of
her dress for her breast. By nursing the child perhaps she would calm
herself. Her words tumbled upon one another. Even Mary found it
virtually impossible to understand what she said. She did not mention
our meeting the day before. Gekonde had shouted, "Yesterday you
were gone drinking beer," but Sabina herself said nothing about it. She
did, however, talk about the funeral, and in the light of the opinions
she had so often expressed about sacrifices, what she said was interesting. She was very shocked by her neighbor's death. Indeed this act of
God, or of the ancestors, as the Gusii believe, provoked a good deal of
soul-searching in the community. How many people suddenly remembered sacrileges for which they had never made retribution?

"Even though those people are Christians, they should have
sacrificed," Sabina says. "What difference does Christianity
make? When the catechist was so ill he slaughtered goats, and
he is a man of God."

In the abstract, divination and ritual sacrifice could be scorned, but
when the threat of destruction was so close Sabina unambivalently
endorsed traditional practice. Yesterday I had come upon her and her
children drinking only minutes before the storm broke. She had tried
to push her children out into the yard, out of my sight. Meanwhile, at
that exact moment a few hundred yards away, her neighbor had been
struck by lightning as she ran out to secure her cow before the storm.

After our meeting at Maria's, Sabina's attitude toward us changed.
This was not to say that she stayed at home in order to see us, for in fact
she was out drinking more than ever. But when we did find her she was
relaxed, hospitable, and happy to amuse us with her tales. Alcohol
carried her through the day and night, so that she scarcely had a sober
moment in twenty-four hours. Her problems receded. They were not so
noxious now that she was drunk so much of the time.

"I have heard no word from Kericho since Mokeira was born.
[She has forgotten now that the baby should be Suzannah in
front of us.] I don't miss him. I am old now. He will come

eventually, though I may have to wait ten years to see his face," she says evenly, without bitterness. "He wasn't here when Musa was born, either. I am used to living alone. I have food enough. You ask me if I dream. Well, I don't dream nowadays. When I was pregnant I was always dreaming of the hospital, fearing that I might die there, but even then I never dreamed of my husband. Never in my life have I dreamed of him."

She talked about her life plan. In the future she would live as if she had no husband. She would have to rely on her friends and her children, though how could anyone know if her children would be reliable? Her eldest boy, David, would soon be out in the world, but who knew if he would choose to help his mother? There was a woman nearby whose son was employed in Nairobi, and yet she went about in rags. The boy gave his mother nothing. As for Gekonde, Sabina had sent him once to Morongo for meat.

"You, Sarah, were here. You saw him go. Well, he never came back for a month! He stayed in a bar at Morongo for a whole month! And now I'm waiting for Kwamboka to come back from school to take my coffee beans to the cooperative. But Kwamboka must be dawdling on the road. Time is passing. The office will be shut for the day. Marco's son cracked my head open, but it wasn't because I was a witch. I'm a good person. Yet even so I have no child to help me."

When Kwamboka appeared in the yard, Sabina was angry with her, but only for a moment. Her complaints were numerous, as usual, but she enumerated them without venom. Perhaps her pain was easing at last. Obamba had rejected her after she had borne nine of his children and had had her skull cracked in defense of his property, but, as she said, she had food enough. She was unusually loving to the younger children. She played with the baby, bouncing her and singing to her. She cuddled Musa. She even joked with Momanyi, the Kipsigis, the child whom she could not abide. Then Suzannah Mokeira, who had diarrhea, soiled his shorts so badly that he had to change into a pair of very ragged pants, by which he was deeply humiliated. But Sabina said gently, "Momanyi, pretend they are bell-bottoms [*chibelli*]. They'll be fine until we've washed your shorts." The bushes around the yard were spread with drying clothes which she had washed earlier at the river. A little timidly, she showed me her new dress.

"Women who have husbands will get maxi-skirts for Christmas. As for me, I have this." She spreads out an American cowgirl's dress of red and green cotton. "Out of my pyrethrum money I paid twenty shillings for it in the market from the man who sells secondhand clothes. It is an old person's dress. I borrowed the money from Thomas, Maria's husband. I can depend on him for everything, for paraffin, aspirin, soap. He knows my troubles, and he always helps me."

Who was this Thomas, who evidently paid so many of Sabina's expenses? He was a shopkeeper, whose wife was the woman in whose house we found Sabina drinking beer. Apart from the drinking relationship between the two women, I was curious as to why Thomas, a man of the Abagoro clan, should be obligated toward Sabina, whose husband was Omoseko, that is, a man from a different clan. I had heard many stories from Sabina about the adulterous behavior of the Abagoro women, and I wondered whether in fact the truth was closer to home. Sabina, after all, had lived apart from Obamba for most of her married life. Her claims that she did not drink were patently untrue, so perhaps her protestations of sexual virtue, equally strident, were also untrue. We learned, however, that if Sabina had been unfaithful, it had not been with Thomas. It emerged that shortly after Sabina married Obamba she was *omosigane* (the go-between) in the marriage of her half sister to Thomas, who at that time already had a wife whom he had married in the Catholic church. This woman warned him that if he took another wife, she would kill her, and when he ignored her threats and went ahead with the marriage, she killed her new cowife with an axe when they were harvesting finger millet. The murderess ran away to her home and never returned. She was tried for her crime and set free after a priest testified that the Church did not countenance polygamy, and thus the accused's murderous rage was in part justified. Thomas married Maria, his third wife, shortly thereafter, and she brought up the children whom the murderess had left behind.

But the children of the first marriage were not the only residue. After the second wife was killed, her father, who was also of course Sabina's father, came with his sons and destroyed Thomas's homestead. They demanded the performance of certain sacrifices which are dictated by Gusii custom in cases of the murder of one cowife by another, considered among the Gusii to be one of the greatest sacrileges of all.

But Thomas refused to follow the custom on the grounds that he was a Christian, though a polygamist, and believed that once the criminal had been tried for the crime, that was the end of it. However, he found himself responsible for Sabina, his dead wife's sister, and accordingly over the years had often helped her financially. His third marriage had been extremely stormy, and no doubt Thomas's refusal to perform the necessary sacrifices was one major source of conflict, for one of Maria's own children had had meningitis as an infant and as a result was severely retarded. There was little question that Maria's tolerance and indulgence of Sabina was motivated by the fear that the ancestors might exact yet further retribution upon her husband through their children. If she took care of Sabina, as a substitute for her murdered sister, Maria's other children might be spared. Thus, apart from being at liberty to send Momanyi across the river to "borrow" flour, matches, and every other household necessity, Sabina could drink beer for nothing in Maria's house several afternoons a week, at a time when in Gusiiland beer was no longer being offered gratis except on ritual occasions. Perhaps the truth was that in her home Sabina was marginally better off with the help given her by Thomas and Maria than she would have been in Kericho with her husband.

In the weeks before the new harvest, Sabina's tranquil mood continued. She told me one day,

> "From the time when I was very young, my mother always had cowives, and though she quarreled with my father, she got on well with her cowives. I too expected that when I married, I would have a cowife, and we would sit together and chatter. Indeed, when I first was married against my will to Obamba, whom I thought old and black and ugly, he had already another wife. We lived together happily at Kericho, but after a year she ran away. I knew she was *omotari* [a prostitute], as I'd seen her talking to men at the river, but I liked her anyway. She didn't do *me* any harm. If a man is clever and has money for bridewealth, then he should marry a second wife if he chooses. Of course this woman Obamba has now was married to her husband with twelve cows, and Obamba cannot possibly repay him. But even so, if she were to come here with her four sons somehow we would have to share this little piece of land between us." She laughs shortly, "But she won't come! She likes *kimbo* [oil] with her vegetables, and we have to boil ours. There's no *kimbo*

here. Divorced women like to eat and be fat. They don't care for
the lean life, which is what we have here." She is used to the
reality of having a cowife, and the reality is tolerable, provided
the two women don't have to live together. Suddenly she jumps
up. "The bedclothes are wet. I forgot to put them out to dry.
All the children urinate at night. Momanyi even wets the bed in
the daytime if he happens to be sleeping there. One day I'll take
a thread and tie up his penis. How it will swell!" She laughs
gleefully. "No, I can't do that. The child would die. I used to
beat him but it was useless." (Bedwetting is said to be a common occurrence among Gusii children and even adults. Once a
child ceases to sleep in the same bed as his parents or perhaps his
grandmother, who might have strenuously objected, he is generally left to outgrow the habit. His siblings are usually more tol-
erant than adults.) "He's just following the example of Gekonde.
Gekonde still does it. Even Obamba does it when he's drunk. I
told him once, and he said he hadn't realized what he'd done.
After that I just put the blankets out to dry, along with the
children's."

Who would want a husband who in middle age still wets his bed?
Certainly she did not! And yet why should she tell me this shameful
thing about Obamba? She said she was glad to live alone. She had food.
But the wound must still smart. Obamba was a drunk, who wet his
bed like a child: she had never wanted to marry him in the first place.
She was forced to go to him. And yet, despite all her protestations to
the contrary, she was bound to him still.

III

Gusii children are circumcised in the first or
second week of December, as soon as the schools are closed for the long
Christmas vacation. The circumcision ceremonies take place on the four
or five days following the last day of term. The children then go into
seclusion, the healing period, for up to four weeks. In some cases they
emerge from the seclusion in time for Christmas, in others not until the
New Year. At their coming out (*ekiarokio*), they are greeted with
almost as much excitement as that which surrounded them at the
circumcision ceremony itself. They are then ready for the next school

year when it begins in the first week of January. December is therefore a time of great rejoicing. The harvest is beginning, and much beer is drunk in the course of celebrating the traditional and the Christian festivals which fall during the month. In our research community alone that year, more than sixty boys and girls were circumcised. In some instances, the parents had known long in advance that their children were to be initiated. In others the children themselves suddenly insisted that they too wanted to be circumcised, perhaps together with a slightly older cousin whose initiation had long been anticipated. If parents aquiesced to such demands, they would have to make all the preparations for the ceremonies in short order.

In the last week of November, Sabina received a letter from David saying that Jomo, aged about ten, who had been living at Kericho with their father, wanted to come home to be circumcised. He asked Sabina to make haste and prepare the circumcision beer and arrange for the *omosari* (circumciser), for they would be home in a week's time. Sabina eagerly showed us the *chinkara* she had made which would be the base of the *amarua* (beer). However, a week later, when all the other children of the area had already gone into seclusion, Jomo had still not come home. Presumably Obamba had vetoed the boy's circumcision, on the grounds that he was too young still.

At eleven one morning Sabina was already rather drunk. She had been drinking beer at the circumcision ceremonies of her neighbors' children, but the *chinkara* she had prepared for her own son's beer she had put away in the rafters. "Never mind, it will be of use to me later. I'll make beer for myself and my friends," she said, but her nonchalance did not hide her disappointment. I had brought my camera to take pictures of her with all her children, assuming the ones from Kericho would have arrived by now. Sabina shrugged, "We might as well have our pictures anyway. We'll forget Gekonde. I haven't seen him since he stole my pyrethrum." She collected an assortment of "Sunday" clothes and tried them on the little children. Finally they were all more or less ready for the camera. Of herself she said, "I am all right for a picture. I have my new dress." But the dress was already split down one side. Musa's shoes were much too small, and he cried as his mother forced his feet into them. Then he smiled joyously, admiring his feet, and later, after the photographic session, he refused to take the shoes off again. In the middle of the proceedings Momanyi, hurt because I had called him *ekebure,* meaning one who has lost his two front teeth, ran off into the banana trees, crying inconsolably. It was a long time before he could be brought back. Kwamboka insisted on having her picture taken alone "for her boyfriend-to-be." Perhaps she had it in mind to elope with some young man who could offer her a happier life.

Afterwards Sabina wandered about in her torn dress, and again we seemed to be eavesdropping on an interior monologue.

"When Sarah first came I was a Christian. I didn't drink. Then I started to drink a little. Then more, and now I am drinking very much. I am *omosatani* [a sinner]. Now that it is the time of circumcision, I drink even *changaa.* In the past I didn't drink it. Next I shall go to Mowlem and find myself a man at the construction company. In fact, the baby is the child of a Mowlem worker. Her shirt is a present from my 'husband' there. Obamba has gone to Tanzania [i.e., people who go to Tanzania, like one of her husband's brothers, never come back again]. These days I drink in the club, and formerly I would only pass through there to greet people. Now I stop and drink with my friends." She squats under the eaves, her hand on her forehead. "My head hurts. I want another operation. I should have had one. I was planning to have one, but my brothers had no money to pay the *omobari.* My sister fell out of a tree when she was picking guavas, and so they spent their money on taking her to the hospital." She cradles her head with both hands. "I feel dizzy and have headaches all the time. I am missing my children at Kericho. I want to see them again. I have no strength to weed or to dig. What will become of these children of mine? I am neglecting them; I am *ekebago* [a bad person]."

I saw Sabina for the last time, the twenty-first session, at the end of December. While I had been gone in Europe, our assistants told me they never found Sabina at home. Today, at nine o'clock in the morning, Sabina had to be summoned from Maria's house. While I waited for her, I talked to her three sons who had all come from Kericho for Christmas. They were polite boys, reasonably dressed, and they looked well fed and cared for. They said their father had changed his mind at the last moment about the circumcision. This year they had come home without him almost a month ago, and they expected to go back to Kericho in a day or two, in time for the opening of school. When at last their mother came stumbling up the hill from the river, she was quite drunk. "Thomas sent for me early in the morning," she protested. "I didn't go to drink of my own accord." She thanked me profusely for the small presents I had had delivered to her before Christmas, and she swept me into her house to give me tea. "Obamba said I had to visit him," she giggled. "He's not going to come here to me. He wants to greet the baby before she has teeth." "If you go," I said, "be careful, or you'll get pregnant again." "Why should I go?" she laughed.

But four days later the house was locked and she had gone. Her friend Maria told us,

"Sabina came here carrying a pot of beer mixed with *changaa*, as a going-away present. She said she had hired laborers for her *shamba* here and she was going to Kericho to weed. She took all her children with her except Kwamboka and Gekonde. She said Obamba had bought two acres of land and she was going there to prepare the ground. She would be back in March. Yesterday when I saw some women weeding her *shamba*, I imagined they were the laborers she had hired to take care of her garden while she was gone, but those women told me they weren't laborers at all. They had rented the land for two years. And it is true, Sabina has rented out all her land, every yard of it up to the eaves of her house, so now she has nothing left to cultivate herself. Everything she had in her house except the beds she took to Evalyn for safekeeping. I tell you, she has gone, and she told no one what she was doing. I don't believe Obamba even knew that she had rented her land to Moraa three months ago, let alone that she has made this latest arrangement. He certainly did not tell her to come to him at Kericho permanently. For a visit, yes, but not for good. Sarah, as I have told you before, Sabina tells so many lies. When I was married here I found Sabina already in the habit of coming over to my house. This was because her sister was once married to Thomas. She would ask us to lend her money and then go and spend it not on maize and paraffin, necessities, but on big things like clothes which a person need not have. She would pay us back when she could, though often she could not. She always complained that Obamba didn't send her money. But that was a lie. Oh, the lies! Even the *ritinge* she says Obamba has taken as his wife is not his wife. She is the wife of a Kipsigis man who owns the bar where Obamba goes to drink. Sabina calls her *ritinge* because she is the wife of another man, but she does not live with Obamba as his wife.

Sabina has no cowife. She tells these tales, but her big children say they are not true. I have continued to be friends with her, despite the lies, because she is a good woman. She will always do an errand for you, and unlike most Gusii, she is not jealous. She will lend you whatever she has. But she is drunk so much of the time that you rarely find her sensible. She said she wanted to say goodbye to you, Sarah, but she never did because she was ashamed."

Maria's sister-in-law, who had been listening, remarked, "She was ashamed because as a woman with so many children [*omokungu enyabure*], she should not have been pursuing her husband. She should have stayed on her own land and planted pyrethrum. She has many troubles, so she ought to go slowly with her left hand, not unthinkingly with her right. She even put all seven children in one vehicle to go to Kericho, instead of dividing them up, half in one bus, half in the other in case one crashed. And then she leaves Kwamboka here. A big girl like that needs to be watched by her mother, or she will get into trouble."

So it seemed that Sabina's behavior made no sense to her friends. As for Kwamboka, who was now living with her maternal grandmother and walking the long distance to the Morongo school each day, when we met her on the road she burst into tears.

"My father sent word for my mother to come for a visit, but she went off for good. I don't know where she is living, for my father has no house of his own and no land. I miss her very much. I don't like living with my grandmother at all."

One day Kwamboka went to visit her mother and returned with scraps of news and greetings for me. But the roof of Sabina's house sagged unattended after the heavy rains of April and May, and her tenants' maize grew ten feet tall across her yard and right up to her padlocked door. She never came again before we left the field.

When Sabina was still at Morongo, my assistant was frequently indignant about her lack of regard for the truth. "She's not even clever in her lies! Can we believe anything at all she says? Is it that she *cannot* tell the truth?" It was not that Mary expected to be told the truth; rather, she was angered at being told such obvious lies. That Sabina could not be bothered to be more skillful Mary took as a mark of disrespect. But I was interested in how Sabina functioned in the particular circumstances of her life. If it turned out that she lied to me, that was as important diagnostically as if she told the "truth." I knew her for only seven months, which was a shorter period than for any of the other women in the study. She left before I had begun to make efforts to know her relatives, nor had I, at that point, questioned people in the neighborhood about her. My attention was still focused on what she chose to reveal to me intentionally or unintentionally. But after she left, and I waited incredulously for her to return, I tried to learn more about her and how she was regarded by her relatives and friends. It seemed that, uniformly, those who knew her liked her. She was regarded as a *good* person. She had no enemies apart from Marco, her brother-in-law, and his family, and even their hostility was not really personal: she was a stand-in for Obamba. No one intimated that she was malevolent in any way, despite her darting eyes and habit of talking to herself, both witchlike behaviors. People were not afraid of her, and therefore they had no reason to attribute supernatural powers to her. In this she was quite an exception in her neighborhood, where witches and sorcerers abounded. If people agreed that Sabina's behavior was puzzling, they had a simple explanation: she drank too much. She did not know what she was doing. She could not behave "sensibly."

As for myself, as I had got to know her better I had become certain that Sabina was not just eccentric: she was in a state of emotional collapse. Possibly because I was an outsider and therefore not "jealous," and because she had had a special relationship, or at least imagined having had one, with Sara Nerlove in the past, she revealed herself more readily to me than to other people. I saw her at home, and thus in a more disorganized condition than she allowed most others to see her. When I met her away from home she was less talkative. She did not ramble on as she did in her own house. She was invariably neatly if shabbily dressed. "She tells you stories, and she leaves her maize unweeded because she drinks so much," her friends and neighbors told me. Once a person starts to drink heavily it is very difficult, Gusii people say, to tell if he or she is *omotindu* (a drunkard) or *eberimo* (a crazy person), since the two often behave much the same. Madmen drink and drunks appear frequently to be mad. By her own account Sabina had gone through bouts of heavy drinking, interspersed with periods of devoted church attendance. Gossips said—and since in Gusiiland almost nothing can be truly kept a secret, I must at least entertain the notion that they spoke the truth—she had carried on a lengthy adulterous relationship some years ago with "a beer friend" in Bogoro. Again, it was hinted that Momanyi was the son not of Obamba but of a neighbor. When Sabina had suspected she was pregnant, she had gone pell-mell to Kericho to cover her tracks in her husband's bed. Certainly Momanyi did not look much like any of his siblings, and Sabina clearly disliked him. She abused him constantly, and he seemed an exceptionally unhappy—and for a Gusii—overtly angry little boy.

There are indications, then, of irregular behavior on Sabina's part in the past, between stretches of devoted churchgoing. But as far as I could tell, she had never been so neglectful of her farming work before, nor had she done anything so dramatically self-destructive as to rent her land and take herself and her children off to the life of the landless peasant in the lumber camps of the Mau Forest. For it turned out that Obamba had not bought land there after all, and the parcel he had previously been lent had been taken by the Kipsigis owner for his own use. I last heard of Sabina was that she was living apart from Obamba and working as a laborer for an African tea planter, while sharing a tiny cabin with two other women and their children. The day after her mother left Morongo, Kwamboka told us that her father had no land of his own. If Kwamboka knew this, then surely Sabina must have known the truth also, before she set off. And yet she told everyone Obamba had bought two acres and she had been summoned by him to prepare it for planting. It was in this way that she had justified her abrupt departure. She had been in Kericho many times before, though briefly, and she knew very well what kind of life awaited her. And yet she was determined to go there. She preferred to suffer all kinds of indignities in Kericho rather than stay at home, even though at home, with the help of Thomas, Maria, and Evalyn, she was sure of something quite a bit better.

I hoped that her relatives would provide me with some insights into her behavior. I had known Pacifica, Sabina's younger sister, for some time and came to know her much better after Sabina left. Both women claimed to be good friends as adults, even though as children they had fought like cats and dogs. Certainly Pacifica had come within two weeks of Suzannah's birth, with gifts of food and a little money for Sabina. She kept in touch with her sister and would often give me news of her at times when I myself had been unable to find her at home. Pacifica, who was about five years younger than Sabina, looked quite like her. She too was very black and very skinny. But in personality they were utterly different. Neither woman had spent a day at school ("Our father didn't think girls should waste time there"), but Pacifica, whose husband was a progressive farmer and a tailor, was enormously energetic. She had an ulcer, but this did not seem to hold her back. She worked constantly. She was an exceptionately warm and lively person, loving, if exacting, with her children. Pacifica was a highly competent woman, but her sister seemed to crumble before one's eyes. In Sabina one saw something of Pacifica's style but little of her substance. Sabina might be blown away by the wind. Or she might get on a bus one day with seven of her children and vanish. Of her departure Pacifica said, "She has taken the child to greet its father." That was a reasonable enough thing to do, but her sudden decision to rent all her land, thereby making her return impossible, was much harder for Pacifica to explain. She shrugged her shoulders. "I don't know why she did it," she said, but she did not seem particularly surprised, nor was she indignant for the children's sake. "Do you think Sabina hoped to drive away her cowife if she too insisted on living at Kericho?" I asked her, but Pacifica shrugged again. She was even uncertain that Sabina had a cowife. She herself had never met the woman. "Who knows why Sabina did what she did," Pacifica seemed to be saying, "but you can be sure she had her reasons, even though you and I don't know them; she was justified."

One day she took me to her and Sabina's childhood home. We met their father digging at the top of his land with his third wife, the only one he had anything to do with anymore. Pacifica greeted him and talked to him briefly. As we walked on she said, "You see how I didn't shake hands with him? That is because he is a traditional man, and he cannot shake hands with his children, as many Gusii do nowadays. He feels *chinsoni.*" In the past, customs of avoidance prohibited physical contact between generations, but those who observe the old rules now are relatively rare, at least in this part of Gusiiland, which has the reputation of being a progressive area. "As I told you, our father has never allowed any of his daughters, even the youngest ones, to go to school," Pacifica added, by way of explanation. Although he had originally inherited twenty acres, the old man had three wives and at least a dozen sons, and his plot had been divided and subdivided, so that every few feet one crossed property boundaries, and everywhere the ground was planted with two, three, even four different crops.

We came finally to Clemencia's house, and there we found Kwamboka waiting for us. During the afternoon I met three of Sabina's brothers, and they were all much like Pacifica, active in their church and cooperative societies. From time to time they had all been employed "outside." Even Sabina's retarded sister was sociable and open. I felt that I knew where I was with all Sabina's siblings. They entertained me, and they made efforts to understand me when I spoke—something Sabina had rarely bothered about. She would turn to Mary for translation rather than ask me to repeat what I had said. Later they gave me a tour of their property, listing what crops they grew, showing me their stretch of river bank and the stand of trees they had planted there. But their mother, Clemencia, scarcely appeared at all, and when she did she was too shy to speak to me. She scurried back into her kitchen. Her house, though kept in reasonable repair by her sons, was disordered inside. This might in part be explained by the fact that several young grandchildren lived with her, but it must also have reflected her own personality, self-effacing, low in self-esteem. Pacifica told me, "The brother who follows me was lucky to be born. Even then my parents were quarreling, and my father hardly ever came to my mother's house. After James was born, my father never came again."

So by the time Sabina was about seven, her mother was already a rejected wife, entrenched upon her little bit of land, waiting for her sons to grow up and take over their father's role as protector and provider. This was the same role which, toward the end of her time at Morongo, Sabina had convinced me she had accepted for herself. But then she had picked herself up and gone off. Of her departure her brothers had little to say. She had married long ago, and her eldest brother had married his wife with Obamba's cattle. She had continued to visit fairly frequently, depending on whether or not she was pregnant. She came to drink beer with her mother, and yes, she had had her head operation in their mother's house eighteen months ago. They had no idea what she was doing at Kericho or when she might return. She had not written to them, and they did not expect to hear from her unless Kwamboka went to see her mother during the Easter holidays.

My visit to Sabina's home was short, but I found it helpful. Sabina did not seem to resemble any of her relatives except possibly her mother. Her siblings appeared self-assured and certain of their place in life. Even her retarded sister was a sturdy individual. My impressions, of course, were most superficial, but if I made nothing else of the visit, at the very least I had to be struck by how unlike Sabina her brothers and sisters all were. Then again I was impressed by how unconcerned they were about Sabina. Like Pacifica, they seemed to find her behavior unremarkable. They agreed that Sabina drank a lot of beer and had had a head operation following a beating. Otherwise they were very vague, for example, about whether Obamba had land or whether he had another wife. Of course he was only their brother-in-law, whom they probably had not seen for years, so their vagueness was hardly surprising.

But others who knew Sabina better were just as vague about the facts of her life. Maria told us Obamba had bought land, but Kwamboka denied this. Maria scoffed at the idea of Obamba's taking a second wife. She said he had a girlfriend who still lived with her husband. Then Kwamboka came back from her Easter visit to tell us that her father's new woman, far from being anyone's wife, was just a prostitute who came and went from one tea estate or lumber camp to another. "She never stays long," Kwamboka said. Then what had caused Sabina's "breakdown," for thus I had come to view her depression?

During our time in Gusiiland, we slowly learned that the most important factor in any given situation is often the one most carefully obscured. Sometimes no one mentions it at all. Neighbors and relatives may know what is going on, what the score is, but outsiders like ourselves remain confused and mystified. In Sabina's case I understood that her usual social psychological adjustment had been marginal. At her best she fortified herself with the teachings of the Lutheran church, and with the support of other church members, she attempted to live what she understood to be a Christian life, in the hope that God's power would prove greater than that of her enemies. At her worst, she drank a great deal and was negligent in caring for her family and farm. Neither her personal deterioration, however, nor her abrupt departure and plans for a long-term absence from Morongo were adequately explained by Sabina or anyone else. Throughout much of the time in which I was visiting her, she was obsessed about the way in which her husband had rejected her. If I was not completely deceived by her theme, at least I was distracted. It might well be that Sabina did suffer a great deal on account of this, but that suffering flowed and ebbed. As she said, she had been brought up expecting a cowife; indeed she had had one once, and when I last saw her she was rather calm about her polygamous situation. Why then did she not settle down at home like a "big woman"? Instead, rejecting all "good" sense, she rented her land and went to join her husband and, presumably, the other woman, whoever she was, wife or girlfriend, permanent or temporary. She never explained her decision to me, and no one offered a credible explanation on her behalf. I assume, however, that her motive was obvious to everyone except myself: she rented her land, thus making it impossible for Obamba to send her home again, at least for the two years of the rental agreement, because she had no intention of returning.

The most important factor in her life was not Obamba's treatment of her but her terror of Marco. Months ago, at our very first meeting when I was taking notes for a social history in the pregnancy clinic, Sabina had told me her brother-in-law wanted to kill her, he was *omonyamasira* (a sorcerer). She never herself mentioned this again, but when I was collecting material on land disputes in our area, Sabina's account was corroborated by several sources—that he was a sorcerer was widely known in the community. Two months later she mentioned (so casually that for a moment I thought I must have already been told and had forgotten) that she had been beaten almost to death by Marco's son. She talked of the operation which followed and of her aching head, but never again of the beating. Nor did anyone else mention it to me. I believe that whatever kind of sexual relationship she had discovered Obamba was involved in when she had gone to Kericho to get pregnant with Suzannah, Sabina had already been anxious, and anxiety had increased when the time came for her to return to Morongo to await the birth of her child. Marco and his son had not killed her yet, but surely they would try again. Moreover, Marco's *emesira* might drive her mad.

I had been afraid that her earlier relationships with other researchers would encourage Sabina to be extremely demanding of my time and resources. I was mistaken, however. Although she sometimes importuned others in our project, she scarcely ever asked me for anything. If initially she fused me with Sara Nerlove, this soon passed. In fact, her relationship with my husband twenty years ago had been quite superficial, and apparently Sara Nerlove had known Sabina only a little better.

In my own case, having welcomed me to begin with, she later made persistent attempts to avoid me, for she wanted to maintain an ideal image in my eyes. I had chosen to work with her because I had hoped to understand how, over twenty years, a reserved young girl becomes a talkative, opinionated woman ready to speak her mind at every opportunity.

From having known Sabina, however, I cannot say I was a great deal wiser. For one thing, she was scarcely typical of her age cohort. In fact she was not nearly as loquacious as I had imagined. She could be very talkative, but she was moody and selective about when she chose to talk. In public places she was reserved. Of course, there were times at home when she poured forth a seemingly unedited stream of primary process material. A "big" woman, though talkative, would have been careful about what she said, unless she were drunk. But Sabina's un-inhibited manner at home was not due to advancing age and senior status so much as to anxiety. Her goal was not just to titillate her listeners but, rather, to maintain her balance by sharing a fraction of the dissociated ideas which teemed through her mind. Was she psychotic? When she was drunk, she would flash from one forbidden topic to another—forbidden, that is, by Gusii conventions. For example, why should she talk, in a high gleeful voice, about her husband's habit of wetting his bed and of a neighbor's urinating in church? Was it merely to shock me or to excite me as she herself seemed to be excited? I think not. Rather, she was talking about her own fears that she was losing control of her mind as well as her body. She was drinking many hours a day to drown her terrors, but her terrors remained with her. I would find her wandering about, one breast hanging out of her dress, talking to herself, the conventional Western idea of a madwoman. And yet she was not quite mad. True, she was disorganized, but her children were fed, and by no means was Kwamboka wholly responsible for the house-keeping. Sabina harvested her maize and finger millet herself, eventually, before it was all rotten. We knew of women, bewitched by their enemies, as the local people believed, who let their crops rot completely while they wandered bare breasted not in their own yards but on the public highway. Her neighbors and relatives said Sabina was a drunkard, not a madwoman. Gusii society could still tolerate marginal people who, in our own society, would have been labeled mentally incompetent and summarily removed from their families.

Sabina had standards for social behavior even if she did not meet them. She wanted to be a good person, *omokungu bu'amasikane* (a respectable woman). For months she tried desperately to convince me—and herself—that she was respectable, but in the end she confessed that she was *omosatani, ekebago* (a sinner, a wastrel). However, there were limits as to how far she could bear to let herself go. When she reached those limits she still had energy enough, both physical and emotional, to organize her own departure and to escape the hell in which, as a brutalized victim as well as a sinner, she had been living.

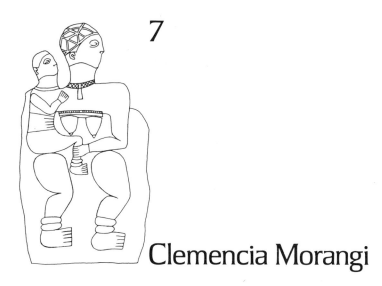

7

Clemencia Morangi

I

Clemencia Morangi's tenth child, a son named Pious, was the last infant to be included in our longitudinal sample. In this way I came to know Clemencia fairly late in our field study. In all I knew her for a little over a year. At the time when Sabina Nyangige vanished so precipitously, I had already spent a good deal of time with Clemencia while observing her child. I decided to begin visiting Clemencia as a replacement for Sabina in my case studies, since she was of similar age and experience in mothering. I thus worked closely with her for only twenty sessions over six months.

Like Sabina, Clemencia had been a bride when my husband had lived at Morongo twenty years before. Even though he had known of Clemencia, however, he had no clear memory of her, since she had been living with her husband James Nyagari outside the district, and the two of them had come home on leave only rarely. But in those days, as in this more recent period of fieldwork, my husband had had intensive relationships with other members of James's family. This experience, together with Sara Nerlove's material, gave us a good deal of information about the family. Indeed, given the amount of contact my husband and I had had with her father-in-law, the senior Nyagari, and his wives and progeny, it was surprising that I had not met Clemencia sooner. But she kept herself to herself in her homestead by the river—whereas the rest of the family lived on higher ground near the top of the ridge—and my first contact with her was when she came, in her seventh month, to the pregnancy clinic.

Although Clemencia was as shabbily dressed as any woman in the community, she had unusual poise. At forty years old, she was still rather pretty, with a small, attractive brown face. She had told me that her husband had worked for many years in the Kenya police force and that during that time she had lived with him in various places all over Kenya. At this point he was employed by the *Daily Nation* in Nairobi, but Clemencia remained at home on the land with their children, since life in the city was very expensive for such a large family. She said she already had too many children, but her husband, who had only one full brother, had insisted on having ten children.

"I am tired and now that he is realizing his ambition, perhaps he will let me rest," she added, laughing. Despite her mild complaint, however, Clemencia was clearly very satisfied with her achievement: nine living children and a tenth about to be born. As for her own ambitions for them, she said she hoped to see them all educated to as high a level as their abilities would take them, an unusual admission for a Gusii mother, who almost invariably conceals her hopes for fear of inviting accusations of arrogance and pride. She herself, she said, had gone to school for only four years because her mother had died when she was very young, and her mother's cowife had not wanted to see her well educated. She later conceded that she had never in fact been to school at all, but at our first meeting she wanted to give me a good impression of herself—she wanted me to see her as a somewhat "better" type of person than was generally found in the community.

Certainly her years in Nairobi and Mombasa as the wife of an up-and-coming police officer, a man who was the friend of Europeans, had had a profound effect on Clemencia. She too had had an opportunity to observe white people at close quarters, even though I doubt she had had immediate social contact with them. From the first she knew how to talk to me, slowly, in such a way that I could understand, and she would listen closely to what I had to say in reply. She wanted to communicate with me directly, not through an interpreter, and even though she attempted, at times successfully, to make use of our relationship to various ends, her warmth toward me and her pleasure in our sessions was undoubtedly genuine. She lived a rather isolated life. Her nearest neighbor was a sister-in-law much younger than herself, a flagrantly volatile and immature woman, with whom Clemencia had an obvious personality clash. For companionship and support she relied mainly on her eldest daughter, Agnes, aged eighteen, an intelligent and sensitive girl who spoke good English, but there was certainly space in her life for me. As for myself, I had quickly come to value her sweetness and warmth. I was attracted by the unusual reciprocal nature of the relationships she had with some, if not all, of her children. She seemed to seek out and be capable of sustaining the kind of intimacy with which I was familiar. Thus, even when she persistently presented herself as a sufferer, escalating her demands on me for money (demands which, incidentally, she alone of the women in my clinical sample presumed to make), I nevertheless continued to be charmed by her. My assistant found Clemencia's begging shameful and in private was critical about her. I was aware, therefore, of how Clemencia's behavior toward me would be viewed within her own culture, but even so, I looked forward to our time together.

Clemencia's parents were both long dead. She had one older sister, married into the same clan, though living at a distance, and the sisters scarcely ever met. Clemencia sometimes saw one of her father's brothers who had a half share in a power mill at Morongo, but apart from him she had almost no contact with her family of origin. Her life centered upon her children, her farm work, and the church. She had been brought up a Seventh Day Adventist but had converted to the Catholic church at marriage (a common occurrence in Gusiiland, despite the wide theological differences between the churches. Girls are told to follow where their husbands lead them, and in most cases they do so). There was no resident priest at Morongo, which was served each week by a European from a distant mission, there being a very serious shortage of priests in this primarily Catholic district. However, Clemencia was strongly attached to the Gusii catechist, a man who, though he and his family had suffered and continued to suffer many afflictions, nevertheless rejected the use of sorcery in his own defense. Clemencia identified closely with him and his struggle against the forces of evil which surrounded him.

James, her husband, had been one of the first boys in the area to receive an education. He had attended Catholic schools and followed his father into the police force. His career, however, had been terminated for reasons which were not entirely clear to us, and when we first came to the field he had been unemployed and at home and had begged my husband to hire him. Later a relative had got him a job in Nairobi at the *Daily Nation* as a file clerk or office boy. Though in a menial position, he earned a regular salary, enough to pay his children's school fees, if insufficient to have his family live with him near his place of work. The main thing from Clemencia's point of view was that he was employed. He had one foot in the door. Who knew what prospects the future might hold? In the last month of her pregnancy Clemencia could say, rather grandly, that she expected to deliver her baby in a Nairobi hospital. Her husband would come any day now to fetch her, for he did not like to have any of his children born at home. James, however, did not appear to take her to Nairobi, so when her time came Pious was born in her kitchen at home.

The Nyagari family into which Clemencia had married was in a peculiar social situation. Jacob, Clemencia's father-in-law, had been one of the first men from the area to go into government service years previously. His position as a corporal in the Kenya police had given him prestige and, by local standards, wealth. The little amount of money he actually earned, however, he spent in the traditional manner: he had had four wives and in addition was the *omochinyomba* (leviratic husband) of a fifth. Since his retirement he had lived on a small pension, which was woefully insufficient for the education of his younger children. Thus their expectations of privilege, as the offspring of one of the first men to be employed "outside," were brutally confounded. James, as the eldest son of Jacob's first wife, had fared much better than the half siblings who followed him over a period of more than forty years. But his career, which had begun with such promise, had come to nothing, and when we left them James was once again unemployed, and the prospects of his ten children were problematic, to say the least, even though they were almost unique in the community in having not only an educated father but a literate grandfather as well.

For all his early advantages and innate abilities, James Nyagari was a wastrel. Clemencia had known this for a long time, though she did her best to conceal it from other people and even from herself. During the period in which I knew her, I watched her attempts to deal with this reality: her initial confidence, even complacency, that everything seemed to be going well; her suspicion and dread that she was being deceived; her very short period of psychosomatic breakdown; and then, once the truth was irrefutable, her personal reintegration and determination to cope alone, as for all purposes it seemed she would have to do.

II

James and Clemencia's house was in need of repair, but it was nevertheless superior to the houses in neighboring compounds. James had built it as a dwelling suitable for a man of high status. It had three large rooms, louvered windows, and strong doors and contained a fair amount of furniture, including some chairs lacking a leg or an arm or perhaps a cane seat. Outside there was a separate building which housed a kitchen and a bedroom for the bigger boys; and in the large and attractive shrubbery, containing a pretty arbor and many flowering trees and bushes such as one saw in European settler gardens, were no less than three latrines, one for the children, one for James and Clemencia, and one for visitors. A path through the shrubbery sloped down sharply to the river, and to one side was a lofty tree, the favorite resting place of a flock of tiny chattering birds. The homestead was entirely surrounded by thick foliage which allowed for almost total privacy. It was indeed the home of an *omosongo* (white man).

The first time I went specifically to talk to Clemencia rather than to observe Pious, now a beautiful six-month-old, I found her sitting under the eaves in the late afternoon surrounded by her younger children. When I asked after her health, she frowned and said she thought she had worms.

"Yesterday I was quite well, but today, suddenly there is this pain."

"Clemencia," I tease her, "it isn't worms. Do worms come so suddenly? It's *oborogi* [witchcraft]."

"How did you know?" she exclaims. "Last night, before it was quite dark, we were having supper when a man's face appeared at the window. When Bernard [her eldest son] opened the door, he saw a black man running naked in the dusk."

"Who was it? Joshua?" (Joshua is the incorrigible rapist of

Morongo, a man who has been incarcerated many times for his crimes but who currently is at liberty. He always rapes light-skinned women, and Clemencia is very light skinned.)

"No, Joshua is brown. This was another. We went to bed as usual, but in the middle of the night I became violently ill with diarrhea, and I knew I had been bewitched." She sits clutching her stomach, in her old maternity dress, used these days for farm work.

"May you recover [*ochie obwene*]."

Her eight-year-old daughter Serafina was taking care of Pious. Before Christmas Clemencia had expected the girl would be circumcised, but she had not been. "James forbade it. He says he doesn't want any more of his daughters to be circumcised."

This was the first instance I had heard of in Gusiiland of a parent's refusal to allow his child to undergo the central and most important ritual in the culture, without which no Gusii can become a self-respecting adult. While in Kikuyuland female circumcision was being given up in some areas, the Gusii were still far from following suit. "Serafina agreed with her father. She did not want to be circumcised either." Then Clemencia mentioned two very prominent men from Nyagari's clan. "None of their daughters are circumcised either, though of course they live in Nairobi," i.e., among uncircumcised Kikuyu, Kamba, and European girls and far from their tribal area, where to remain *chisagane* (little girls) would necessarily invite dreadful humiliation. So James wanted to follow the example set by his kinsmen who, unlike himself, could afford to insulate their daughters from the social consequences of their progressive beliefs. Serafina, on the other hand, had to go to school with circumcised girls at Morongo.

"She may yet be circumcised," her mother adds. "She is very young. There's time." From this I gather that she is ambivalent about the matter. But she does not clarify her own position; perhaps she thinks that to express her disagreement with her husband would make me view her as old-fashioned, and she wants to impress me with just how sophisticated she is.

I take Pious from Serafina, remarking on his beauty and weight.

"All my children were like that as infants," Clemencia says. "When Agnes was a baby, we lived in Nanyuki, and there we met an American, a black man called Charles, who used Agnes in a film about babies. That was 1958, and he paid us 175 shillings. He was a very kind man, Charles. When he went back to America, we wrote to him and he to us. He would tell us what it was like to be black in your country. It was not good."

As she talked she became increasingly animated, and her stomach pains seemed forgotten. She talked at length about life in Nanyuki, at the foot of Mount Kenya. She asked many questions about conditions on the upper slopes, at which she used to gaze from the police camp. She had seen snow but never touched it. She herself would be afraid to climb so high. Then she questioned me about the circumstances of my mother's death, and when I asked her about how her own mother had died, she assumed a mournful expression, in abrupt and rather melodramatic contrast with that which preceded it.

"My father had a leviratic wife by whom he had two children, but his brothers urged him to marry a wife of his own, so he married my mother. When I was less than a year old, my mother was bewitched and killed by her cowife, who later killed my father as well. Then that woman and her son took all my father's land. But that boy was not my father's actual son. He had land from his real father. My father's land should have been inherited by my uncles' sons. But my stepmother was a witch, and she made my father love her too much, and then she killed him. She and her son still live on his land." "And who took care of you?" I ask. "My father did, until he died." "Even as an infant, a child as young as Pious?" "Yes, my father took care of me," she insists. "You have suffered much from witchcraft, even from infancy," I say. She sighs, "It is true."

She went on to talk about her sister-in-law, Margaret, who these days loudly proclaimed her fear of witches. She had very recently moved into her new hut by the river and was now living only a couple of hundred yards from Clemencia.

Clemencia was of two minds about this development. Though no one could suspect Margaret herself of witchcraft, she was a hysterical, dependent young woman who knew no better then to seek the companionship of certain older women whom Clemencia believed to be witches. Clemencia protected herself from the powers of evil by keeping very much to herself, but Margaret, whose third child everyone knew had been killed by witchcraft, continued to keep the company of evil women.

> "Then she complains about them. What can you say to her? Now Margaret says she has worms, though she hasn't actually seen one in the latrine. But she insists there are worms, and they are the result of witchcraft. She goes everywhere begging for medicine, your medicine too. But there's nothing wrong with her," Clemencia says scornfully, by way of contrasting the behavior of her silly sister-in-law with her own.

Margaret was actually a bright, rather appealing girl. Her marital and financial situation was very poor indeed, and from the time we first came to the field she had done her best to extort from the project milk, medicines, clothes, money, and transportation. Her unflagging and often annoying attempts to involve us all inextricably in her life had been quite successful. She was an operator, but an operator of more than average charm. Clemencia was obviously well aware of my involvement with her sister-in-law and was eager to illustrate for me Margaret's foolishness and manipulative tendencies. But of course her own situation was only slightly better than Margaret's, and she herself was quite as needy. Looking at me out of the corner of her eye, Clemencia proceeded to describe her own current difficulties in getting medical treatment for her children. Whatever Margaret needed from us Clemencia needed just as direly, but she would try to be more subtle in her approach.

Because we were already at ease with one another when I began to work with her intensively, Clemencia touched on sensitive subjects more quickly than did most of the other women. On one hand she demonstrated her experience of the world gained through the fortuitous circumstance of being married to an educated man, but on the other she hinted at the price she had to pay for these advantages. She was surrounded by her husband's relatives, all of whom (except Margaret's husband John, James's younger brother) were peasant farmers, bitterly jealous of James's successes. Why should he be so blessed and not they? Unfortunately for her, his success was only relative. He had not been successful enough to be able to settle his wife and children permanently outside the district. He had forbidden Serafina's circumcision, but he lacked the social or financial position to be able to protect her from the resulting ridicule and shame. Thus Clemencia believed that the next year or the year after he would capitulate, and before she was over age the child would be circumcised. If, on seeing her house, her yard, and her many thriving children, I should conclude she were fortunate, she quickly corrected me. She had lived in continual fear of the malevolence of others. Jealousy had deprived her of her mother. "My father brought me up," Clemencia explained, but he also deserted her. He too was powerless in the face of the same greed and jealousy which had killed his only "real" wife. So from girlhood on Clemencia had been an orphan, forced precociously to depend upon her own resources and yet forever in need, forever longing to be given to as a little child should be given to, unambivalently, as a matter of course, by virtue of being a child.

Ten days later Clemencia reported that the witch was continuing to come each night. She jumped up to show me what he did.

"He knocks on the roof with a stick, and he rattles the door handle. Sometimes he throws stones on the roof, too. Only once, the time I told you of, has he looked through the window at us." She lowers her voice: "He's been coming for more than a year, almost nightly."

"Do you know who he is?"

Clemencia ignores me. "John and James told both Margaret and myself not to join *egesangio* [a work group] for digging. All our neighbors are witches. Our husbands said we should dig together, but Margaret paid no attention. She joined the *egesangio* of Nyamaito, the wife of our uncle Mogere, leaving me to dig alone. Nyamaito and Mogere are famous witches [I had heard this from several sources], and yet Margaret loves them. As for me, I am so afraid. I would take my ten children and go to James in town, but I cannot. Life is too costly. So I must stay here. The catechist tells me I should pray when I hear these noises at night, for if I do so the power of the *eriogo* [spell] which perhaps the witch is putting in my walls will turn back upon himself. Now prayer is my only weapon, for I am here alone. But once when my son Bernard was sick, James happened to be at home. He went to where his relatives were drinking and told them, 'If you bewitch my son, I will kill you,' and immediately Bernard recovered. If you face them, you can sometimes frighten them so much they will leave you alone for a time. But we are surrounded by them. Once we had a cow which one of them bewitched out of jealousy. It became very vicious and kicked us all, so we had to sell it.

You can find husbands as well as wives in *egesangio* together, as in the case of Mogere and Nyamaito, though not always so. For example, my father-in-law is not a witch, though his wife Bosibori, who killed Margaret's child, is one. My father-in-law has told her he will kill her if he discovers her again bewitching anyone within his homestead, so she waits until he has gone to visit one of his other wives who lives beyond Morongo, and then she goes about her evil business." She puts her head close to mine. "We know who comes here at night. When my son Clovis was in seclusion at the top of the hill after circumcision in December a year ago, he peeped through a hole in the wall and saw the youngest son of old Elizabeth coming home in the middle of the night. That young man is very black, like the man who looked through my window. What could he have been doing then at midnight, except witchcraft? He is the one who comes here even now."

But this young man was only a distant relative, which diminished his power to harm her and her children. (Were he an uncle or a mother-in-law, Clemencia's anxiety would have been greater.) The power of prayer might indeed be enough to keep her and her family safe from the malevolence of a mere boy who probably ran in the night more for the thrill of scaring women living alone than anything else. A cousin of hers who lived downstream, Faustina, had had much more serious trouble than Clemencia. For Faustina's cowife was in league with their mother-in-law against Faustina and their husband Musima. Faustina and Musima had at last driven the junior wife away, but for a long time they had lived in terror of their lives. Clemencia should be thankful she did not have a cowife. Once, for a period of time, James did have a second wife at his place of work. She was a barren woman of another tribe who ran away as soon as James lost his job with the police force. But she and Clemencia never had to live together here at home. *Engareka* (jealousy between cowives) could lead to terrible things.

The rains were beginning now, and Clemencia looked forward to planting not only her own land but also two garden plots she had rented the previous year. James was employed; the older children were in school; and if she had been badly scared by the witch, she recovered her spirits once her attack of diarrhea passed. She enjoyed her conversations with me, for she could talk freely of times gone by when she lived in a European style. If she were to reminisce about those times with her neighbors she would invite trouble, but she knew I would not be jealous when I heard the details of her bathroom in Nairobi and saw the photographs of her children in their school uniforms, photographs she kept hidden in a box at the back of her closet.

"We lived in a wonderful house in Nairobi. The other houses in other towns were good, but the Nairobi house was best of all. It had three bedrooms, a gas cooking stove, electricity, and a flush toilet. Anyone seeing me now in rags as I am wouldn't believe I'd ever lived in such a house. Once some neighbors from home came to spend the night on their way to Mombasa. They ate very well, very much *obokima*, and they each stayed very long in the toilet, but they didn't know how to flush it or, indeed, that it should be flushed, and the shit piled up so. After they left it was days before that toilet was properly clean again and the stink had gone. But really the best thing about that house was that the walls of each room went up to the ceiling, and you couldn't hear the noise of other people." (In her own house there is a gap of several feet between the top of the mud room partitions and the iron roof.)

"But even in such a house as that one in Nairobi, Gusii people must observe the same rules as they do in the reserve. [Clemencia, who lived outside Gusiiland in colonial times, always uses the colonial expression "the reserve" when referring to Kisii District, an area which the British administration reserved for Africans and in which Europeans were not permitted to own farms.] If James and I were living in such a house nowadays, with its private rooms, even so our sons Bernard and Clovis could not stay with us. They would eat with us, but they would be obliged to sleep elsewhere. You see we feel *chinsoni* [shame] with our circumcised sons, even in Nairobi."

At this time a young cousin of mine, an anthropology student, was living and working with us, and Clemencia had seen him on the road. She was curious to know where Eddie slept and was relieved to hear he usually slept next door, not in the same house as my husband and myself. I explained that we do not experience the shame which Gusii people feel in relation to our children and to relatives of our children's generation, and Clemencia replied that though she knew our customs were different, she could not imagine herself ever losing *chinsoni*.

"Europeans are so different from us, and yet in ways they are much the same. Once I went to a nightclub in Mombasa with James. I was young and pretty then. I only had one child. A white sailor asked me to dance and I accepted, and afterward he asked me three times in English to visit him at the harbor to drink sodas and talk. The fourth time he spoke in Swahili and I understood, so I told him I was married and pointed out my husband, who was frowning at us in the corner. I was afraid he'd jump up and beat the sailor, but I excused myself and went to sit down with James. Until then I hadn't known that white and black people had sex together. I'd thought white men wouldn't want us Africans. I was very ignorant. A little while after that, at Nanyuki I heard a story about something which happened during the emergency [the period of the Mau Mau rebellion]. I heard that two British soldiers on a lorry on the Nyeri road stopped an old Kikuyu woman and had her put her load down." Clemencia demonstrates how Kikuyus carry their loads on their backs, unlike the Gusii, who carry theirs on their heads. "They gave her a soda to drink, and then they seized her and carried her across the *omotara* [drainage ditch] and into the bush, where they raped her. Then they jumped into their vehicle and drove away. But a man on a bicycle heard the old woman wailing, and he took her to the police station in Nanyuki, where a doctor examined her and removed the sperm from her vagina. The police telephoned to Nairobi to stop all army lorries coming from Nyeri, and the whole convoy was sent back to Nanyuki. They lined up all the soldiers and brought out the old woman, who recognized the men who'd raped her. The judge sentenced those men to two years in prison, and afterward they were sent back home. These days no one does anything to stop army boys from rape, but the British were better. When they were here they tried."

In the course of our work, we got the impression that most older women and almost all people of both sexes under the age of thirty had only the vaguest notion of the nature of British rule. Because Gusiiland was a reserve with virtually no permanent British residents, many people knew nothing of Kenya beyond Gusiiland, much less of the colonial status of the country. Only when politicians started coming to the marketplaces to shout through bull horns about *uhuru* (freedom) did the people realize that they were being ruled by Europeans. Their contact with authority had always been through the African chiefs who administered the district at the local level. British officials were rarely seen in the bush, and thus there were very many people at the time of independence who had literally never laid eyes on a white man. Some Gusii men had worked outside the district, where they had contact, sometimes even intimate contact, with Europeans, but they were a very small minority. Since this was a country whose indigenous population had been subject for sixty years to a colonial government operating primarily for the benefit of the settler community, I had expected to encounter some residual bitterness toward British rule. But in Gusiiland this was not so. The large majority of the adult population had been ignorant of the existence of British control—and therefore oblivious to its evils or benefits—at the time, while those who had been exposed to it directly remembered it with a mixture of amusement, slight scorn, and a good deal of admiration. This was not Central Province, the heartland of Kikuyu country, where every family had been touched by the Mau Mau rebellion. The Gusii had been remote from the harshness and humiliations of colonialism.

As for Clemencia, who had spent the early years of her marriage as the wife of a British government employee, she remembered those times with nostalgia. The British were efficient; they did things properly. In the twilight of their rule James Nyagari's hopes had been high. Twelve years after Independence James's fortunes were distinctly diminished in luster, but Clemencia still clung to the aura of earlier times. As I left her that afternoon, she remarked that I would not find her after the end of the month, since she expected to be going to Nairobi with the seven younger children. They would spend April with James and then return in time for the opening of school in early May. It would be good for the children to see Nairobi, which even these days relatively few people in the community had seen. Clemencia seemed to imply that Nairobi, after all, was where they should be living. That they were not was merely a trick of fate. But then, as she escorted me to the gate of her homestead, she whispered,

"James sent 100 shillings to me, but I used it all to pay school building fees. I know I will receive more from him within a few days, but I have prepared the ground for planting, the rains have come, and I have nothing with which to buy seed maize. I'm afraid I shall be late if I wait longer. I expected James to come last weekend—he usually comes on the first Saturday in the month with his salary and returns to Nairobi on the Sunday, which is why you haven't had a chance to meet him. You rarely come to Morongo at the weekend, do you? But he didn't come as I'd expected. I know he'll come at the end of this week, and then he'll bring his salary, as usual. But, Sarah, could you lend me money for seed? If I could plant this week, I should be very happy. By next week the rains may be so strong they'll wash out the seeds. I'll repay you as soon as James comes."

I tell her I will ask my husband, but I warn her that we have a policy not to lend money to people in the community. "I understand," she says, "but you'll ask Getuka anyway, won't you? For Clemencia."

For the first eighteen months in the field, we did not lend anyone money. Though the sums requested of us were small, from the first we had stuck to the principle that our quid pro quo should be one equally available to every family in the community, and thus the pediatric clinic which cared for all children under the age of six was the single continuous service we offered. We were afraid, of course, that a practice of payment for interviews, loans, or gifts of money to individuals would invite trouble. As we neared the end of our work, however, we became a little laxer and occasionally made exceptions to our original policy. The Nyagari family benefited more from our revised practice than any other family. Other would-be beneficiaries were quite persistent but less so than the Nyagaris, which indicated certain characteristics about them as well as about us and our receptivity. Their maneuvers were familiar to us, and though we recognized them for what they were and warned one another, we allowed ourselves to be seduced nonetheless. The Nyagaris' previous contact with Europeans set them apart from most others in the community, and I think we were homesick for the familiar and so we rather often acceded to their requests.

Thus Clemencia got the twenty-seven shillings she requested and immediately bought and planted her seed corn. She was immensely grateful. But though James came home at the weekend as expected, he left her with nothing when he returned to Nairobi.

> "He says two weeks ago he sent 100 shillings to me by way of a friend of his, but the money certainly never reached me, and if his friend pocketed that money himself, James has no more to give me. I'll have to wait until the beginning of next month to repay you." Clemencia seems distracted and upset today. She tells me a dream in which her brother-in-law John, Margaret's husband, died. "I couldn't tell him what I'd dreamed because he wasn't here. He was in Nairobi."

John was a poor husband to Margaret. He gave her nothing at all financially, as he had another wife with four children in Nairobi. It was Margaret's father who supported her. Her father told her that with three sons she could not leave John, so she should cultivate her husband's land and raise her children as best she could while he himself provided her with money for the barest essentials. But Margaret was not resigned to her lot. She shared her anger, indignation, and depression with anyone who came her way, ourselves and of course Clemencia, who lived next door, in particular. And Clemencia found Margaret's explosive behavior disturbing. She maintained that Margaret brought these troubles upon herself. She agreed that John was irresponsible but maintained that nevertheless Margaret could have handled her difficulties better than she did. She should have drunk less, talked less and to fewer people, worked harder, and taken better care of her children. But no doubt Clemencia's criticisms were partly powered by envy, for while Margaret had a father ("a good man who, though a Catholic, not a Seventh Day Adventist, never drinks beer"), Clemencia was an orphan with no one to protect her from the vicissitudes of her husband's favor or fortunes.

Clemencia suddenly shifted to her own situation. Her marriage to the senior of the two Nyagari brothers had been far from smooth. She started to tell me how James happened to lose his job with the police. I had heard from several sources that he was retired on a small pension long before he was due for retirement because he was a chronic drunkard. Clemencia's version, however, was rather different:

> "James was a grade-one inspector in Kisumu, where he was the only Kisii man amongst many Luos [the neighboring tribe].

The Luos were always jealous of him; they wanted his job for one of their own. Then one day a certain man came to Kisumu from Uganda. He got in a fight when drunk, and he was put in jail. But this man's brother was a policeman, who begged James to let him go, which James did. This man, after he returned to Uganda, wrote a letter to Queen Elizabeth telling her what had happened, that he had been released without trial. The Queen forwarded that letter to President Kenyatta, and James was soon charged with misconduct. He admitted his mistake and resigned. They begged him to reconsider his resignation, but he refused, and so he came home with a monthly pension of 100 shillings, and he was here at home, unemployed, for five years before a relative found him a job with the *Daily Nation*. That was a year ago."

Did Clemencia want me to believe that James ruined his career through altruism? Was she trying to convince herself that her husband was a man of principle, a man she could respect? She dreamed that John, James's grandiose and erratic younger brother, was dead. If James shared some similar personality characteristics, perhaps this dream represented her wish that the "bad" James should vanish, leaving only the "good" James, who placed pity for his friends above loyalty to an impersonal bureaucracy and when caught refused clemency, taking his punishment like a man. Clemencia was much more anxious on this occasion than I had previously seen her. She reassured me that James's failure to bring money with him when he came at the weekend could easily be explained: he was gullible; he had trusted someone who was untrustworthy. She did her best not to blame him or to let me blame him. "Wait, you will get your money," she told me, and with a sinking heart she tried to convince herself it would be so.

But four days later Mary saw Clemencia in the beer club at midmorning. She was drinking and said irritably she was on her way home to help another woman weed her fields. Three days after that we found her at home drunk in the afternoon. She immediately told us she had been working in her *shamba* since early morning.

"Really, Clemencia?" I say, and she slides out of her first story and into her second, namely, that James has come home on leave, and so they bought beer to celebrate his arrival. "But as for myself I only tasted, and when I was in the club I was only tasting. How could I work in the fields if I had drunk deeply, and as you see I have certainly been digging," she begs, seeing my skepticism. We argue about the difference between drinking and tasting, and eventually she concedes they are the same. She looks very ashamed of herself, and as she turns away I tell her I drink too, after work on days when my husband is at home. She nods as she puts her hoe under the eaves. While washing the mud off her hands and feet, she tells me, "James hasn't been paid yet. It isn't the end of the month. He came on leave before receiving his salary. I can't repay you yet. I am so sorry." She takes Pious from Serafina to nurse him, and once he is settled she asks, "Could you take me to my original home near Keroka one day? I would like you to see my home." I agree that soon we shall go, when arrangements can be made.

"You see, my father had two farms. One here at Morongo and one at Keroka. We used to travel back and forth between the two. The farm here belongs now to Morema, the son of my father's leviratic wife by her real husband. The other farm, the one at Keroka, was taken by another of her sons. But I think of that land as 'ours' though I have no share in it. I would like to see it. I have not seen it in a long while." Her eyes are blood-shot, and she speaks very fast, on and on about what became of certain European farms after the settlers left, how various power-ful Gusii men bought them, how profitable they are, or so she's heard. She talks with awe of James's "patron," who owns such a property these days; she rushes on with tales about that man's marriage, his divorce, the chaos in his family life. Then abruptly she asks me, "Could you employ my daughter Agnes for the month of April, the school holidays? She will do any-thing you ask of her. When you come home at night, everything will be so tidy." I refuse her as gently as I can, saying I have help enough at home. "If you can't give her work, can you have pity on her and help her with clothes or shoes? The child has nothing. Her uniform is torn, and she has but a single dress to wear for every occasion."

When it was time for me to leave, Clemencia thrust Pious into his sister's arms and pursued me down the path to the river, begging me for help, laughing hysterically, clutching at the branches of bushes to prevent herself from falling on the slippery hill side. As I climbed up the far bank, she was still calling to me, proclaiming her anxiety to anyone who happened to be within earshot, just like her sister-in-law, the despised and volatile Margaret who could not keep her troubles to herself but shouted them across the river when she was drunk, and even sometimes when she was sober.

A few days later, I met James for the first time on the path. He looked glum and avoided eye contact. He spoke only Ekegusii, though he was fluent in English. I gathered that he was on his way to Nairobi, though he expected to return the following Saturday.

When Mary and I went to see Clemencia for our seventh session, we found her digging in the fields. She immediately told us about her dream of the night before:

> "I was walking along with many people, all of us employees
> of an industrial company. We were going to enter the factory,
> but a policeman stopped us, and we ran away. We never got
> inside the fence of the factory compound." She comments that
> when James was fired from the police, she dreamed about it
> beforehand, but in this case her dream is *only* a dream. "Some-
> times you dream the truth, sometimes just the opposite of the
> truth."

> I ask her what James told her when he was last at home.
> "Nothing. He hardly spoke to me. He was out with his friends
> most of the time."

> "I wonder why he keeps going back and forth to Nairobi.
> Three times he has come this month. Does he usually come so
> often?" I ask. "Could it be that he has no work to keep him in
> Nairobi now?"

> Clemencia's face is flushed. "That's exactly what I said to my
> daughter last night. 'What if it's true, and he's been fired?' I
> said to her. 'How shall we ever manage?' James came last time
> without *anything.* Not even a loaf of bread, let alone clothes for
> the children. He had money for his bus fare back to Nairobi,
> that's all. If he's been fired, how will he ever get another job?
> He hasn't got a sponsor. The man who helped him get the
> *Nation* job wouldn't help him again. I know. He can't work
> again for the government. Once you've resigned from the civil
> service, you can't ever be hired again. [She says resigned but she
> means fired.] This means he must find work in a private busi-
> ness, but no one would take him. He is getting too old [he is
> about forty], and there are many younger men with relatives to
> help them. James has no one." As she talks, she stands beside

me in the midst of her pyrethrum, picking at the earth under her fingernails, but then she seizes her hoe and frantically starts to dig again. "We paid 500 shillings over the past six years to rent this piece of land. Now I'm pulling up the pyrethrum because it's time to replant. These flowers, they only yield for two years; then you must let the land rest and replace the plants. But how will we be able to go on paying our rent if James is unemployed?"

Gradually, as she talks, she grows calmer.

"You know, Sarah, two neighbors asked me why you come to see me so often, and what I talk about with you. And so I told them, 'I tell Sarah things I would only tell to someone I liked very much.' Don't leave me now. Sit in the *shamba* and talk to me while I dig. I haven't time to go home right now, but we could still talk, couldn't we, where we are?"

And so we sit with her, and she tells us all about a talk just given by an American woman to the women in her church.

"It was about how we could improve our lives. She told us each child must sleep separately, and if we haven't blankets enough, then we should cut up those we do have so that every child has his own piece. What do you think of such advice?" And after a moment Clemencia is laughing and giggling as she swings her hoe in the morning sun. "I like to see you two," she says. "You ease the heart."

At the eighth session, which again took place in the fields where Clemencia was weeding her *wimbi,* we heard that James had not returned from Nairobi.

"I've received nothing from him, not one word. I am so worried. Last night I dreamed some men came in the night with *pangas* to kill me and the children. I shouted to my daughter to pick up a rake to defend us, and then I awoke. I was terribly afraid and upset. I tell you, nights are frightening for a woman living alone without her husband. Some do very well, but I am not so brave."

She told a long story about a Gusii woman living on her farm in the settlement scheme who cut off the head of a thief whom she discovered in the barn trying to steal her cattle. "But I couldn't do such a thing. I couldn't use a knife as she did." This woman, about whom Clemencia dreamed, was well known for her energy and wealth. She farmed her own land. Her money was hers to use as she wished. Though she once had had a husband, she had nothing to do with him now. She was successful and independent. But Clemencia was less tough. She was fearful alone at night, surrounded as she was by malevolent people. Perhaps she was saying that for all his faults, she would welcome James's return, his enforced idleness, if indeed he had been fired. But if in fact Clemencia knew the truth, so far she had not told us. It was probably that James had been evasive with her, as with everyone else. Gusii people do not state the obvious, especially if it is shameful. They leave even their closest kin to gather clues and draw their conclusions. And even though their families are very quick to detect indications of misfortune, they are slow to admit that these signs add up to anything.

Clemencia talked at length about life as it was lived on the large farms of the settlement scheme, to which many of the progressive people of the district had moved in the 1960s as soon as land became available to Africans after the departure of the British. One of her relatives lived there with his fifth and youngest wife. He left the four older wives here near Morongo.

> "He is a big man, a proud man," she remarks. "He has five wives and so many children. Sarah, what do you think of polygamy? I have heard you do not have it in America, but here people say a man with only one wife must sit near the door at a beer party, for if word is brought that his wife is in trouble, he must run home as fast as he can to save her, his only help-mate. If he's sitting far from the door, he might break his neigh-bor's beer pot in his haste. You see, people laugh at a man with only one wife. They pity him; they despise him."

Perhaps Clemencia was afraid that, with nothing to do all day, James would be subject to pressure. His cronies would mock him for having only Clemencia, an old woman now, worn by childbearing. The acquisition of a younger woman would lighten his spirits and make him feel like a man again: she rested on the handle of her hoe for a moment. "You're lucky in America. These Gusii men who want to marry wives, they bring only hardship to their families."

Six days later I found Clemencia sitting huddled in a blanket in her yard. She looked wretched. She had malaria, and her mouth inside and out was covered with sores. She said she had been unable to work in the fields since John came from Nairobi the previous weekend. He told her that six weeks ago James had been "stopped from work," and since that time James had been living with a relative and traveling back and forth to Morongo, not daring to tell his family he had lost his job.

"Whenever James came here, I would ask him how things were at work, and he always answered, 'Fine.'" Clemencia cradles her forehead in the palms of her hands. "He was afraid of the thoughts I'd have if he told me the truth. I remember when he was unemployed the last time. For four years he did nothing from morning to night. He just sat. He didn't help me in the garden. He refused to dig. He didn't visit other villages in Boseko." "And did he drink?" I ask. She shrugs, "James doesn't like *busaa* [native beer]. Only Tusker, European beer." (Even in the midst of this latest disaster Clemencia must still claim to me that her husband is too sophisticated to drink what everyone else drinks, especially unemployed men who cannot afford anything better. She has evidently decided to forget that Getuka drank *busaa* with James in this very yard only last month.) "How will he ever educate these children now?" she moans. "Perhaps James's pension is enough for soap and paraffin, but nothing else. At this very moment I haven't even money for soap, let alone for tea and sugar, which I need in order to get well again. The sores in my throat are so painful. I can't swallow porridge." As she speaks, her face changes color rapidly. She flushes, goes pale, then flushes again.

"I dreamed last night that James brought home many secondhand things—mattresses and clothing and other things tied up in boxes. Secondhand! He won't be bringing home anything at all in the future, not even secondhand nor even fifth-hand! I heard this news from John, you know, not from James. He is afraid to tell me. He hasn't even come home for three weeks. John was afraid too. He only told me because I forced him to. When he came here on Friday, I asked him straight. So he had to answer. Then of course Margaret ran about telling the rest of the family. My father-in-law came to say he was sorry. He says it must be that *ebirecha* [the ancestor spirits] are angry; otherwise, why should his sons suffer so much misfortune, and some of his daughters also? His brother Mogere came as well to say *pole sana* [sorry]. Perhaps Mogere wasn't really sorry perhaps he and his wife [both of them are witches] were really glad. We have rented their land for years, and now we cannot afford to continue. We are brought low as they are. But who knows, perhaps Mogere *is* sorry. He and many others used to be glad James was employed, because when he came home on leave from Nairobi he would always buy beer as a way of greeting his relatives and neighbors. He can no longer greet them now. My cousin Faustina also came to say sorry, but so far she and Mogere and Nyagari are the only ones to have done so. Once James himself comes, and he must surely come soon, then everyone will hear of it. Then we shall find out if people are sorry or secretly glad."

For the past year or so Clemencia had been living in fear of Mogere and his wife Nyamoita, both *abarogi abanene* (big witches). But now those two had no more cause to envy James or, by association, his wife Clemencia. In Gusiiland each small advantage lays one open to the malevolence of others. Thus to lose one's advantages had its compensations. In the future Clemencia might live in dread of hunger but with much less fear of witchcraft.

Two days later Clemencia's sores were still painful, but her fever had gone. In part her recovery was due to the chloroquin I had given her; in part, no doubt, to the profound relief she undoubtedly experienced in knowing at last where she stood. For a week after John confirmed her fears, she sat shivering under the eaves, unable to weed or to pick her pyrethrum. Agnes cooked and went to the river and the power mill while her mother suffered. But now Clemencia was pulling herself together. "I can swallow again," she said. "I ate *obokima* last night. Even without tea I am recovering," she laughed. "My daughter told me it was worry which made me sick, but what use is there in sitting still? When my husband comes home, he will find me strong."

For the moment, however, she could sit a little longer with us in the house and wait for the afternoon rain to pass. Then she would go to weed.

"Sarah, you shall see us suffering. Last time James was out of work he used that little pension of his on the daughter of Nchogu, the man from Bogoro across the river. Nchogu is *omonyamasira,* he has money. Every day James would go there to drink *busaa* and *changaa*. Sometimes he drank until late, and so he would sleep there and come home in the morning. [This is the first time Clemencia has volunteered that James not only drinks *busaa* but a great deal of it.] Nchogu had liked James in

the days when he was a police inspector because James used to
give his friends beer when he came home on leave and had
money. When James no longer had money to spend on his
friends, Nchogu still liked him. Nchogu had a daughter, and he
wanted James to marry that girl. She and James were friends.
He would stay with her in the bush until dawn. The girl got a
daughter with James. The child is four years old now. But
Nyagari forbade James to marry Nchogu's daughter. He said if
the girl came to live with James on our side of the river, he
would kill her with his own hands. When my father-in-law said
this, and he said it many times, James wouldn't answer him.
Once Nyagari hid in the reeds by the river and sprang out upon
James as he came from sleeping with the girl before the sun rose.
Still James refused to speak to his father about what he was
doing. 'How can you, a man without employment, take a second
wife?' Nyagari would shout. Of course Nyagari has had many
wives himself, but he married them when he was in the police
force. James would look at the ground and be silent. I didn't ask
James about his plans. I didn't quarrel with him. There was no
point in fighting him.
  "Then one day he went off to Kisumu with the girl and
remained there for two weeks. While he was gone Nchogu came
and seized two sheep which belonged to me. These were presents
to me from a cousin of mine, but Nchogu didn't care. He took
them in payment for his daughter. I never got those sheep back,
even though James returned Nchogu's daughter. Eventually she
gave birth. James went to Kisii and spent his pension on soap
and talcum powder for the baby. The children saw the taxi stop
on the road and James get out of it. He was carrying a box,
which he hid in the bushes. Then he came home and was so
friendly to me. 'Clemencia,' he said, 'you're cold.' And he sent a
child to get milk for tea. 'You need tea to warm you,' he said.
While I was in the kitchen boiling water for that tea, James sent
one of my children to get the box from its hiding place and carry
it to Nchogu. 'Never tell your mother,' he told Clementina, but
though Clementina fetched the box, she didn't take it to
Nchogu. She hid it again and told me, and later we used
the soap here at home. James never said a word about that box.
Nor do I know if he went to see his girlfriend again. When
James's child was three months old, the girl eloped, and she's
been with her husband these past four years.

"Since that time James has not wanted to marry another wife, but he has never stopped pursuing women. Years ago when we were first married, he was all right, but once we went to live in Nairobi he changed. He started to spend money on bar girls. He even had European women at different times. Once there was a teacher. Another time he had a girl whose father was an English army officer. There's a photograph of her in our book. I showed it to you once. [On that occasion Clemencia said the blonde girl in the picture was a "friend of the family."] James never brought these women home with him, but I heard about them from others. As far as I know, only once did James live with a woman as his wife. That was the Maragoli woman. Since she ran away I have been the only wife, but who can say if I shall remain so? Other men sometimes urge James to marry. My sister-in-law Margaret would be delighted if she heard I had a cowife. Then I would suffer as much as she, for whatever difficulties I have already would be doubled if I had a cowife."

Last time James had been fired, Clemencia had seven children. Now she had ten. She had paid tuition for the older ones up until the end of the school year, but in December her daughter Agnes would finish elementary school, and now James was unemployed. Even if Agnes passed her examinations, who would pay her tuition? A year behind her came Bernard, and after him eight more siblings. And yet from previous experience Clemencia knew that poverty, rather than being a deterrent, acted as a spur to James's need to flaunt his manhood. Ten hungry mouths, ten children in need of an education would not stop him from seeking out a young girl to bear him yet more children. His father had protected Clemencia's interests so far, but Nyagari was growing old, and James was about to start a period of idleness in which, being too proud to work with his hands on his land, he would boost his spirits with drink and womanizing.

When James finally came back for good, he slipped off the bus and down the hill into his homestead. It was some days before he showed himself on the road or Clemencia would admit that yes, he was home. One day my assistant saw a pair of long trousers drying on the clothes line, but when she asked if James had come from Nairobi, Clemencia denied it. "Those belong to Bernard," she said. That same day when I myself went to visit her, Clemencia denied to me also that she had seen James.

"But a cousin, who came from Nairobi, told me James is being sent on leave for a while as a punishment because he left some company money in a cupboard at work and went away in the evening without remembering to transfer that money to a safe. Of course in the morning he found the cupboard had been broken into and the money stolen. Perhaps he is only temporarily without work. They will take him back again when he has learned not to do such a thing again."

When at last Mary met James in the market, he told her he had been back at Morongo for several days. Why then did Clemencia so strenuously deny his return? All the neighbors and relatives would certainly have heard of James's arrival the moment he got off the Nairobi bus. But perhaps Clemencia felt that as long as his presence could be concealed from Mary and me, who though outsiders had nevertheless become important in her life, she too could deny the reality of her situation for a few more days.

When eventually we found both of them together in the compound, Clemencia's manner was immediately different from that to which we had been accustomed. Her voice was higher, she smiled more, she fluttered about, encouraging James to talk to us. He, meanwhile, sat dressed in his best clothes on the sturdiest of their chairs. He looked as if he were about to go off to an office to perform the duties of a government official. He remained, however, elbows on the arms of the chair, legs crossed, listening to this women's conversation but rarely participating himself. Clemencia anxiously scampered around us. "We are suffering, Sarah. James needs to go just once more to Nairobi to settle his business there once and for all. And yet he has no money for transport. Could you or Getuka help us?" She wrung her hands, her face flushed. Meanwhile, James stared at the ground. I replied that when next one of us went to Nairobi he was welcome to go with us. I would let him know when we had plans to go. Clemencia chattered her thanks, and James was silent.

The first few weeks after his return we often found James silent in his yard. When he did speak he never used English. His presence prevented us from having anything but the most superficial conversation with Clemencia, who clearly experienced great strain at having to interact with all of us at the same time. She had been critical of her husband when he was still far away in Nairobi, but now that he was home she seemed to have great difficulty in treating him with wifely subservience, especially in front of us, to whom she had given so complete an account of his shortcomings. She persistently asked our help for James. He frowned, tapped his foot, nodded his head to indicate his support for her requests, but never spoke on his own behalf. Clemencia blushed continually, and after a few painful encounters we took to greeting the two of them and going quickly on our way.

When eventually we found Clemencia alone, though less anxious than she had been lately in the company of her husband, she was still guarded. James had gone to Kisii the day before and had not yet returned, but he was expected momentarily, she said. I recognized the same propriety in Clemencia when talking about her husband now as I had noticed in other women whose husbands were living at home. As long as their men were in Mombasa or Nairobi, women were free to be as disloyal as they pleased, but the closer husbands were to home, the more constrained were their wives. I knew one woman whose husband regularly slept in Kisii town during the week because he owned and operated a bar there. If I talked with this woman on a Monday, she would reveal all kinds of intimate information about her husband, but by Thursday she was more discreet, and by Friday morning, when she expected him home at any moment, she would be unwilling to talk about him at all.

Thus, though Clemencia had a great need to talk at this time, she could not bring herself to raise the marital problems that so concerned her, because she expected James's return shortly. So instead she told me a long story about a neighboring family in which the senior wife, Teresa, had murdered her cowife. She concluded by saying of herself, "I am so different from Teresa. Whenever James was about to take a second wife, I kept quiet. I made no threats." So far, of course, her compliant approach had paid off; even if her husband were a wastrel, at least she had him to herself. She told me with pride that she had never thwarted James's intentions, but I knew her compliance to be quite the exception in Gusiiland, where a woman commonly would put up tremendous resistance to her husband's attempts to marry another wife.

Clemencia's passive position might be explained in part by her early history. As an orphan she had had no protector. When she grew up her father's family, whom she scarcely knew since she had been raised by her maternal grandmother, were interested in her solely for her bridewealth. Once she was married and her father was dead, they were no longer concerned with her. They were certainly not going to bother defending her rights against any other wife her husband might choose to acquire. Margaret's father remained intimately involved with his daughter in her struggles with John, and when Margaret ultimately drove her cowife away her father was her staunch ally. But Clemencia had nobody to protect her interests. If Nyagari thought fit to intrude upon James's affairs and Clemencia benefited from her father-in-law's involvement, that was sheer luck. As an orphan Clemencia had no outside support in hard times. She literally had no home to return to. Her only ally was her husband. Her interests, therefore, lay in placating and promoting him. As the aging mother of five sons, she had no other option.

As long as we were in the field James was profoundly depressed and consistently failed to comply with her efforts to promote his interests, but that did not stop Clemencia from making plans on his behalf. She swamped me with entreaties for work, any kind of work for even the shortest period. At least four times she arranged for James to travel to Nairobi with someone on the project so that he could look for a job, but every time James failed to show up at the appointed time and place. After each snafu Clemencia would shrug her shoulders and come up with some new scheme, though in none of them did James himself show any interest. In fact, after a few weeks of sitting despondently at home, he began slipping into his old pattern of drinking in the homesteads of Bogoro. We saw him much less. It was easy now to find Clemencia alone, and when we talked she spoke not just of employment possibilities for James but of her own plans to start a maize-trading business with capital borrowed from myself. "Sarah, it would take only 100 shillings." I was sorely tempted to "lend" her the money but did not do so.

One day, however, I took Clemencia and James, in their best, to visit Clemencia's relatives. Although Clemencia had told me she would send word of our coming, as it turned out she had not done so, she explained, because she had not had enough money for bus fare for one of her children. As we drove along, Clemencia revealed that she had not been to her home for fifteen years. Her response to my inquiry as to why she had stayed away so long was garbled. She did say, however, that since her maternal grandmother, not her father, had taken care of her after her mother died, she had visited her father's family only infrequently. Most of the time she had lived at her mother's home. Her father died shortly after her marriage, and although Clemencia did herself go once to his home after his death, James had not come with her on that occasion. To this day he had never visited those paternal relatives. I gathered the marriage negotiations had been with the members of the family who had settled at Morongo, not with those whom we were about to see who lived at Keroka. Thus, nineteen years after marriage, James was going to his wife's home as a "bridegroom."

Indeed it had been so many years since Clemencia was there that she did not recognize the turnoff, and we had to stop and take in a local man who guided us to the place. As we walked up the hill Clemencia laughed and cried all at once.

> "When I was here last there was no pyrethrum, there were no passion fruit vines. People in the Nyaribari location had never seen such things. These fences are new. The land was all open when I young. There were no European cattle, only African cattle then." She pauses a moment, her eyes very bright as she looks at a house standing at a distance from the path. "*This* was my father's land. That woman, my stepmother, took it when he died. That house must be her son's house."

Then she led the way to the gate of a second house. We clustered about her, looking over her shoulder into an immaculate compound. In the countryside around Morongo I had never seen such a homestead, with its chicken coops and flower garden, its bath house and cattle barn. In our research area only Clemencia and James's house approached its charm. In front of the main house a woman stared at us incredulously. Then Clemencia greeted her and the woman, almost overcome with amazement, ran up to us to draw us into her house.

There then followed an afternoon of excitement, joy, and confusion as we went from one house to another on the hill side. Every homestead of this Seventh Day Adventist family was as pristine and ordered as the first we had entered. The men were mostly Clemencia's first cousins, all but one of her uncles having died. They seemed decidedly prosperous. In one house we found an aunt by marriage, an *omoragori*, in whose living room the accouterments of divination were displayed. The old lady was drinking beer with some other elderly people, and once Clemencia and James had settled down to drink it was extremely difficult to get them to leave. The *omoragori* told me she had given up divination—and beer—at baptism, but shortly thereafter she had fallen ill, and the ancestor spirits told her this was because she had foresaken them. Thus, for her health, she had reverted to her career as a diviner and left the church. "Beer is good for me," she laughed. "You too should drink with us now that our daughter has come home."

But Mary and I asked if we might be shown round the lineage land, as we were eager to see what crops were being planted in this area, which was a few hundred feet higher than Morongo. So Percepta, the first woman we had met on our arrival, offered to take us on a tour. Thus we had a chance to ask her why Clemencia had not come home in fifteen years and why James had never come at all before today.

> "Clemencia was never paid for. Can a woman continue visiting her home if her bridewealth is not paid?"

> "But Clemencia told me James paid six cows long ago, before she ever went to Nyagari's place as a bride." (Indeed Sara Nerlove, who made a study of bridewealth in the area, had listed this payment as having been made for Clemencia.)

> Percepta shrugged and turned away. "There we have planted more tea, but we are not yet picking it. We shall wait until the ninth month, and then we shall start."

When we got back to the house of the *omoragori,* we found everyone rather drunk. James smiled silently into his mug of *busaa* while Clemencia wept into hers. The *omoragori* led us into another room to talk and explained that though James had indeed paid in full for Clemencia, instead of bringing those cows home to his brothers as he should have done, Clemencia's father had given them all to his leviratic wife.

> "Here we got nothing, not even a hen. For a time my brothers-in-law wanted to bring a case against Clemencia's father, who had used their cattle heedlessly, but he died and then they could do nothing, so they were defeated. One of the sons of that woman married with Clemencia's cattle. You passed his house as you were coming here. He is a big trader now; he's done very well for himself. He does not greet us, nor do we greet him."

It seemed from the gracious way in which her relatives welcomed Clemencia that they felt no bitterness against her personally or against

James. I noticed that they were extremely delicate in the way they handled the fact that James had never before visited them. They were being tactful for their own sake as much as his. They said, "Of course you haven't had a chance to come here before because for so many years you were working out of the district. Now that you are on leave you at last found an opportunity to come to greet us." No mention was made of the fact that for four years (1970–74) James had been unemployed at home. I am certain, moreover, that Clemencia's relatives were aware of James's employment history, for even though there had been no direct contact between them and the adult Nyagaris, Clementina, James and Clemencia's second daughter, had once been sent as *omoreri* to look after the children of Clemencia's cousin who was working at the time in Mombasa. Had James still been in the police force at that time, Clementina would have been living with him in comfortable circumstances. She would not have needed to look for work as an *omoreri*, presumably in return for school fees, for her own parents would have provided school fees. Only families who have fallen upon hard times send their daughters out to work for relatives.

Until today, however, for fifteen years Clemencia had not herself set foot in the place she considered her home. Possibly her anxiety about James's loss of work was so great that she was finally prepared, with the excuse of "showing the white stranger her home," to seize the bull by the horns and take the first step in her plans to involve her prosperous relatives in her welfare and that of her family. She hoped that after such a long time their anger against her father and, by association, against herself and James had diminished. But meanwhile, until she was convinced that she was truly welcome in her own home, Clemencia felt compelled to say repeatedly during the course of the afternoon that we had come for *my* sake and that I, not she, had initiated the visit.

In the session immediately following our trip to her home, Clemencia was euphoric. She thanked me profusely for having made the visit possible. Then she gave me her own account of how her bridewealth cattle had been "lost" to her father's family. She explained that because, before marriage, she had been living with her maternal grandmother, James had brought the cattle to the old lady, and her father had collected them from there. Her father had inherited his leviratic wife from a cousin when he was a young man and looked upon that woman as his wife, treating her children, who had been very young when he first moved in with their mother, as his own. He had married Clemencia's mother only in response to pressure from his brothers, not because he was dissatisfied with the arrangement he had with the wife he had inherited. His union with Clemencia's mother was brief, and until the day he died he always behaved as if his leviratic wife were his "real" wife, even though according to Gusii custom she was not. He therefore gave her Clemencia's cattle and steadfastly withstood all his brothers' efforts to get him to transfer the animals to them for their use.

> "Those cows brought *me* nothing but trouble. All these years my uncles have ignored me because *they* didn't get the cattle, while my stepbrother, who did get them and used them to marry his first wife, also ignores me when I meet him occasionally in the market."

But today, in the aftermath of a visit which could be the beginning of a fresh start in her relationship with her father's family, Clemencia was in high spirits. In great good humor she described the furor which had been going on next door these past few days between Margaret and her cowife, whom John had been foolish enough to bring home when he came on leave from Nairobi. Then later, as we left, Clemencia ran after us to ask in a whisper whether James had yet come to see Getuka about a job. I told her no, he had not come.

> "In two weeks I must pay building fees at school," she cries, "and with what am I supposed to pay? Every day James says he is going to see Getuka, but he does not go. I tell him, 'Move yourself, wash, get dressed, go,' but he hides behind a bush beside the road." Clemencia jumps off the path and demonstrates the cowardice of her husband. Then she jumps back, laughing. "I tell you, his head is full of nothing but wool. He has the thought but no strength to do anything about it. Maybe the *omogaka* Nyagari is right when he says James has been taken by *ebirecha*. And John also. Those two brothers: one is as foolish as the other." Suddenly we are caught in a shower of rain, but Clemencia keeps following us up toward the road, talking and laughing about her troubles in such a way that one can scarcely believe she suffers. "Come soon to see your Clemencia," she calls after us.

There was an unreal quality about Clemencia at this time. She was too gay, too quick to be intimate with Mary and myself, and for a woman with ten children, too readily indiscreet about her husband. One morning we found her singing in the fields. The sun was shining, and the hills were fresh after the night's rain. When she saw us Clemencia threw down her hoe and brought us into her yard. I remarked upon the new fence between the shrubbery and the open space surrounding the kitchen. "Oh, that. James built it. That's the only work he's consented to do." James was standing in the doorway listening, his face expressionless. Clemencia led us past him, insisting that we sit under the arbor. "This is the place for conversation," she said gaily. Today Clemencia wanted to entertain us in proper fashion; she and her husband and their guests should enjoy the fresh morning air under the passion fruit vines, even though she had no refreshment to offer us.

For a time James sat with us as Clemencia told us of the latest developments in the saga next door between John's two wives. Then James went into the house, and without lowering her voice, Clemencia remarked, "He does nothing to help himself. It's all up to me." James reemerged carrying a pile of photographs he had taken in the past of the children and Clemencia and the different houses they had lived in when he was in the police. At some point in his youth he had learned photography, with the thought that he would one day set himself up in the business, but he had never had the capital to realize his dream. Now he did not even have a camera anymore, only a pile of photographs to show what once he could do. He handed the pictures to me one by one, answering my questions patiently. When he had shown them all, he brought out another pile of pictures, these commercially produced. They were all colored photographs of bare-breasted Masai and Samburu women. It was as if he were saying, "See, I am like a European. I also find women's breasts exciting," unlike most African men who find the buttocks, for example, far more erotic. Meanwhile Clemencia was sitting next to me, her face burning, overcome with shame.

When James had lovingly examined the last picture, Clemencia said loudly,

"Sarah is going to Nairobi next week. She'll take you there for nothing and bring you home again. Will you go with her?" But James will not meet her eyes, or mine either. Wordlessly, he carries his picture postcards back into the house. "Last year,"

Clemencia says bitterly, "we had enough to eat. But this year we will go hungry. Last year I rented land in Nyoosia on which I planted maize. This year I could not pay the rent for that land. All we shall harvest is the little field here at home for which you gave me seed money. Sarah, in America women don't have as many children as I, do they? No, of course not. They could not be so foolish."

I set off for Nairobi as planned, but James was not waiting on the road for his ride. He appeared in our clinic an hour after I had passed by. In a state of great agitation he told my husband that he had narrowly missed me. "I saw the car go by above me as I was climbing the hill." And there he stood, abjectly miserable, until my husband "lent" him 100 shillings with which to make his own way to Nairobi, so that he could make the rounds of those people, friends in better times, who just might help him find some kind of work.

On my return to Morongo, I found Clemencia ill with pneumonia. She lay under an ornamental tree in the shrubbery. Three of her children had severe upper respiratory infections also, and they had all been sick for several days, without medicine of any sort. James was still in Nairobi.

"My father-in-law is certain James's troubles are due to *ebirecha*. Indeed he believes the suffering and disappointment of all his children, his sons and his daughters, are due to the anger of his ancestors. Last week while you were gone Nyagari sacrificed a goat and a bull, because the *abaragori* told him he should do so. 'Your children misbehave as they do because of *chimoma* [sacrileges],' the *abaragori* said, 'and so you must make retribution.' I myself did not attend the sacrifice, nor did I accept any of the sacrificial meat. I wouldn't allow any of my children to go either, but James was forced to attend by his father, even though he says he doesn't believe in *ebirecha*. Then he ran off to Nairobi. As for John, he refused to attend. He went to Nairobi before Nyagari could stop him. Only Margaret ate the meat from that homestead and James from this one. Such sacrifices do not change a person's character. If they are the kind who misbehave, they will continue so."

"What do you mean?" I ask. "In what way did James misbehave?" Clemencia blushes. "He didn't misbehave. He made mistakes. He did favors for people, then this last time at the newspaper he was forgetful. He forgot to lock up that money."

But I insist, "You said he misbehaved. I have heard this too."

Clemencia watches my face intently. "What did you hear? That he drank ten bottles of beer at once? It is true. He won't get rehired at the newspaper. He wasn't sent home on leave. He was fired once and for all. He won't find another job, either. He hasn't the courage to go to important people to ask them to sponsor him. He is ashamed. You know yourself that he talks of asking Getuka to help him find a job, but he has never gone to ask Getuka. James cannot help himself. He is ruined. And I, I am *omoiserwa*, I am so poor. How will I educate my children?"

She is seized by a fit of coughing. She moans and covers her face with her hands. Her little son Clifford, aged about three, strokes her shoulder, pleading with her to look at him. This child loves his mother overtly in a way familiar to a Westerner but rare among the Gusii. Distracted by the demands of nine of her children, Clemencia often seems to ignore his chatter and periodic attempts to hug her, but the fact that he devotedly persists must indicate that from time to time Clemencia does respond. "Mama, mama," he croons softly, peering round her shoulder. I expect to see tears escaping from her fingers, but all of a sudden she jumps up, laughing. She hitches up her rags. "I feel better now. A little while ago I was at death's door, but you always make me feel better."

She begins to talk now about a nephew of Nyagari's after whom the baby Pious was named. During his life time this man was very good to Clemencia, out of gratitude because he had been orphaned as a young child and James's mother had taken him into her house and brought him up.

"He never forgot what James's mother did for him, and he tried to repay her after her death by caring for her children and her grandchildren. He died a little while before you came here, Sarah. He was a tall man, very fat. He died in the hospital after an operation." She stops and looks at me. "You're very quiet. You're thinking of your mother, aren't you? [This is true, I am thinking of her.] Don't be sad. Don't think of her now. When I was a child if someone said something cruel I used to become quiet like that in the middle of a conversation. No one could have guessed, though, that I was hurt," and she shows how she would withdraw and hang her head. "People thought I was tired suddenly. They couldn't tell I was suffering." For a moment she is silent, looking away toward the river. When she turns back to me, she is suddenly animated. "Sarah, I am so poor. If you helped me no one would know it but we three, you and me and Mary. You could do it secretly. If I had 100 shillings I could start to trade in maize. Couldn't you help me?"

"You know my husband gave your husband 100 shillings last week."

"I didn't know that. James told me Getuka gave him transport money. He did not name the amount," she insists. It is perfectly possible that James did not tell her how much money my husband gave him, and even if he did tell Clemencia the specific amount, Clemencia knows she does not stand a chance of getting her hands on any of it. Any "loans" James might cajole from my husband he will use for his own purposes.

"Please, Sarah, if you cannot lend me money, at least let me and my children have medicine. You'll send some down to us, won't you?" As I get up to leave she pleads, "When you go to America, you won't forget me, will you?"

III

In the two weeks before I left the field, Clemencia bombarded me with requests. I felt, as we drove away that last day, that I had barely escaped, that if I turned round and looked back down the road I would see Clemencia running after me, her hands outstretched, begging and beseeching, "I am so poor, I have nothing."

I have always found leave takings in Africa stressful; but on this occasion, after a long period of fieldwork in which I had experienced more intense relationships than on previous occasions, the process of termination was especially painful. Insofar as these feelings focused on Clemencia, I felt that she had rewarded me both as a research subject, who had provided me with rich material, and as a friend. For if, as she said, "talking to you eases my mind," this experience was mutual. Though she was several years my senior and her children covered a much greater age range than did mine, nevertheless, because of her unusual capacity or perhaps courage in empathizing and identifying with other people, our relationship was closer to that of equals than was the case with any of my other subjects. I knew very well the realities of her life, including the personalities of her husband and his relatives. As was true of everyone in the community with whom I had become familiar, I was apprehensive about her future economic circumstances. Conditions were hard, and they were likely to grow progressively worse in the face of world inflation, increasing land shortages, and soil exhaustion.

In short, I left Clemencia with a heavy heart, knowing I would miss her and worry about her. From her point of view, I had been rather like the goose that laid the golden egg (though in fact I had given her little money, a few clothes for her younger children, and, at the end, a dress for herself). As long as I was still with her, she could hope that I would pay the school fees of her daughter Agnes, a fine young woman who surely deserved a sponsor as much as anyone, and that I would give Clemencia herself the wherewithal to become financially independent of her husband, whose earning days were probably now at an end. Other women in the community demanded these guarantees from me, and I was forced to refuse them gently at first, less gently as they persisted. But Clemencia was more difficult than most to refuse because, as she danced before me those last weeks, as she smiled and sang and did her best to seduce me with indiscretions about her husband and his family, I felt that her wiles arose not just from a frantic need for goods or money but also from her fear of the loss of our relationship.

When I first got to know her, I had found in her a certain quality which resonated with something in myself. I think it is most easily described as a sense of "after the fall," that alert preoccupation with loss. Superficially Clemencia was concerned with her exclusion from the world of detribalized, urbanized Kenya, but at a deeper level with her childhood deprivation of a regular family. She had had a grandmother whose importance she minimized. "She was good," Clemencia would say, "but she is dead now." However good she might have been, her grandmother could not make up to Clemencia for the loss of her parents, her mother through death, her father through lack of interest. Clemencia had learned to manage quite well without a mother or a father. "I would be quiet, and no one would ever know that I was hurt." She had come out of her childhood with a fair degree of self-esteem, a reflective intelligence, and a depressive personality which permitted her to function well provided she had the rather minimal support which was all an emotionally impoverished childhood had conditioned her to expect. When I came to know her, she relied on her church and the catechist, two female cousins who had married a little way down the river, the intermittent interest of her father-in-law and an uncle, the companionship of her eldest daughter, and the all-pervasive structure which providing for a large family imposed upon her time. But I believe her contacts with me stirred up deeper needs.

I knew her at a time when her world was collapsing, her hopes for her children's future and thus for her own (since Gusii women can only expect security once their children are grown up and can take care of them) were turning to ashes. I had come out of nowhere with an overriding interest not in her husband or her children but in herself. I had begun by spending long hours observing her youngest child; but then when Pious was six months old, the age she had been when her own mother died, I stopped listening to Clemencia with only half an ear and started to give her my exclusive attention. And Clemencia loved it. She would talk with care so that I might understand her and my assistant-interpreter could be dispensed with. She was hungry to see me and for me to see her. She wanted to be admired not for her appearance—she wore rags and frequently referred to this fact—but for her expressiveness. Just as she would play with Pious, smiling and nuzzling him, watching his delight, listening to his laughter, in that same way she demanded that I notice her responsiveness to my attention and that I in turn reflect back to her what I had seen.

As the time approached for me to leave, she repeated incessantly, "I am so poor." Though the harvest had begun, she offered me nothing to eat. Within the context of our relationship, I alone had the power of generation. If I gave her something, then she could blossom. She could take my medicine, get well almost instantly, and go to work in the fields. She could put on a dress I had given her and dance. But the cycle had to be initiated by me. If I gave, she responded with joy and she reciprocated. That time in which I could give to her, however, was strictly limited, and the threat of an ending to it panicked her. What she wanted was a continuation of this mirroring process, and no amount of used children's clothes or seed money would suffice. She came looking for me in the market and, when she could not find me, said to my assistant, "Tell Sarah I have not eaten for two days. Tell her she must help me." My assistant reminded Clemencia of the appropriate decorum for a woman of her age. "Enough is enough. You must stop asking now, Clemencia." And Clemencia, shocked and angry, turned away in disbelief. But while Clemencia pursued me, James just as surely avoided my husband and myself. We never saw him at all in the last month of our stay. Instead of being full of bravado, the most common social defense of someone in his culture who had undergone an abrupt loss of status and respect, in our presence James suffered from crippling shame. In contrast, Clemencia, whose need to be given to, enormously intensified by James's loss of a job and the regression which her relationship with me invited, did not experience shame. Or if she did, her need to extract from me attention of all sorts was so great that it overrode any inhibiting sense of shame completely. In the end, in the consternation and pressure of our departure, it was I who hid from her.

8

Psychological Functioning in Social and Cultural Contexts

In the foregoing chapters we have seen how each of seven Gusii women of one rural place in southwestern Kenya—not necessarily typical of their people but representing a broad range of variation among contemporary married women—reacted over an extended period of time to a foreign investigator of her own sex and to a significant issue or incident in her life as wife and mother. By visiting *their* mothers I was able to form an impression, however blurred, of the earliest relationship in their lives. By meeting with these seven women regularly over periods ranging from six to seventeen months and letting them talk to me as they would, I was able to gain a more distinct and detailed view of their current relationships and their handling of both routine events and crises during the time I was living there. In this slow and laborious way it was possible to discover how they drew on Gusii traditional culture in their struggle for survival and psychological well-being.

some characteristics of the case material

The relationship between the investigator and each subject may be seen as an arena in which the subject was permitted to reveal herself. While each of the seven women had her own idiosyncratic mode of self-expression, there were nevertheless some features characteristic of all of them.

Their habitual mode of expression was to describe actions and events rather than thoughts and feelings. They would generally give accounts of what had been going on in their lives since the last interview, leaving out their personal reactions, opinions, and judgments concerning these events and actions, even when they obviously had strong feelings about them. They seemed to assume that the behavioral description conveyed an implication of what they thought and felt about what was described, without their having to explicate these matters or refer to them directly. This practice is characteristic of Gusii disclosures in general: my participation in many social situations with Gusii women leads me to believe that this is the way they talk among themselves. At one level it is a social convention, but individuals can and do use it for private purposes. It is particularly convenient for someone attempting to disavow potentially unacceptable intentions. Most of the women I studied seemed regularly to be taking advantage of the convention: they portrayed themselves as passive participants in events and avoided assertions of personal responsibility for what was happening, reflecting their assumption that taking responsibility for actions is dangerous and should be avoided in discourse; they evidently felt safer deleting their own intentions and volition from their self-disclosures. This must be seen, particularly in a relationship of increasing intimacy, as representing their defenses against anxiety as well as their conformity to a conventional mode of discourse.

Trufena, for example, could describe in detail the hostile behavior of her female in-laws, while deleting almost entirely her own contribution to the breakdown in her relationship with them. The only aspect of her behavior which she admitted might have helped bring about the impasse was her refusal to allow Cecilia to sleep in her house. She had a perfectly legitimate reason, however, which anyone in her right mind would sympathize with, namely that Cecilia, like a puppy, was not housebroken. Despite, or possibly because of, the fact that Mary, her aunt, was always with me, Trufena apparently felt compelled over time to reveal less and less of her obstructionist behavior and the feelings which motivated it, even though she must have known very well that Mary was a witness to all she did. Whatever the objective truth of her situation, it was essential for Trufena to present herself as one who had been wronged. Thus her public strategy, and—as far as I could tell— her private stance also was to focus on the mote in the eye of her persecutor while discounting entirely the beam in her own.

A second striking example of massive denial, under pressure, of any personal culpability was the incident in which Zipporah was accused by Makori of having committed adultery with her cousin Jeremiah. Previously, Zipporah had indicated to me that she had sought out other men to father the children she so urgently desired but whom Makori could not be relied upon to provide. But the instant that she was publicly charged with adultery, she claimed not only before the *abatureti* but even to me, whose sympathy she might have known she had won and on whose support she could rely, that she was a virtuous woman. Suddenly Zipporah was asserting that this current adversary situation had been brought about entirely by Makori. She had become his victim, as a result of his suspicions, just as Trufena had become the victim of her female in-laws, whose jealousy over her superior education and family background was driving them to get rid of her.

In both cases I believed that I had developed a relationship of trust with these women, since they had previously shared with me confidential information. But while my role as an outsider had allowed them to confide in me on less pressured occasions, in time of crisis my marginality was not enough to render me harmless. Their need to exclude me was unyielding, and from a privileged position I was relegated precipitously to that of a distrusted neighbor. Though it is ambiguous whether the women actually believed their own stories, it seems clear that their assertions of innocence were automatic. As an outsider I was puzzled and even hurt by my sudden exclusion from trust, but Mary understood perfectly: a Gusii could scarcely be expected to accept responsibility for an immoral act, regardless of the evidence and regardless of his awareness that neither his friends nor his enemies gave credence to his denial.

The affects these women expressed overtly in my presence were generally limited in range, and although this changed in some cases as I came to know them better, their social behavior was often difficult to fathom, owing to the maintenance of a very strict control over both facial and emotional expression. For example, despite the sorrows and anxieties all of them bore, I saw only two of them weep, Suzanna and Trufena, while Trufena, a maverick and an intransigent misfit, was the only woman I heard readily verbalize hatred. At the same time they rarely expressed delight or even emphatic satisfaction, except on the receipt of something of value from someone of particular social significance. Consolata was thrilled by the new red dress which her brother-in-law had brought from Nyamwange in Mombasa. She valued it not merely for its newness, its style, and its color but for what it represented: an expensive contribution from a long-neglectful husband and an indication that he was fulfilling, at least in part, his marital obligations. But when I gave her a present, while my gift no doubt elicited many feelings, delight was not one of them. I did not belong to that category of significant people by whose attentions she measured her self-worth. In the same way Trufena was euphoric after receiving money for milk from her husband's uncle Nyagama. The money indicated that Nyagama was taking responsibility for her and that her position in the family was therefore permanent; but when her son Geoffrey was sick and our medicines made him well again, though relieved at his return to health, Trufena appeared to be not especially grateful and certainly not euphoric. Despite Trufena's constant contact with people on the project, particularly at times when she was otherwise beleaguered and isolated, none of us achieved such importance that we could elicit a significant expression of pleasure from her. Thus, given the norm, Clemencia's behavior was particularly striking, for having allowed herself to become more closely attached to me than did any of the other women, she not only expressed her gratitude for the medication that the project had given her when she had pneumonia but made it clear that her delight at having recovered so quickly was intrinsically involved in the pleasure she derived from her relationship with me.

While I saw all seven women either at the birth of a child or shortly thereafter, only Suzanna and Phoebe displayed unambivalent delight in their new offspring. Suzanna had given birth to a son after three daughters, Phoebe to a daughter after two sons, and thus each acknowledged to me that she had achieved her heart's desire. While at least in my presence Clemencia showed no special pleasure in Pious, this might have been due to his being her tenth baby, born at a point where she confessed to being both tired of childbearing and chronically anxious about how to support her large family. This is not to say that with some of her older children she had not been every bit as joyful as were Suzanna or Phoebe, for Clemencia's contemporary relationships with Clovis and Agnes at least seemed to indicate an enduring delight. But the other four women appeared to take their newborn children as a matter of course, one more rung up the ladder to successful mother-hood. While to bear children bountifully and without undue interval was their common goal, the new infant did not seem automatically to constitute a source of joy just for himself alone and his own unique characteristics. In these cases an instantaneous pleasure in the special significance of this particular child to this particular mother seemed, at least at an overt level, to be absent.

I have already alluded to the tendency of these women to see them-selves as innocent victims: their in-laws or neighbors were to blame for their misfortunes, or their brothers or fathers had compelled them to remain in a miserable marriage by refusing to return the bridewealth. This helpless attitude, while indicating the importance of projection and evasion in their defensive system, also tells us a great deal about their preconceptions concerning their place in society. After a child-hood readying herself to leave her father's homestead, at marriage a woman exchanged one marginal position for another; she became the most junior member of her husband's lineage and was obliged to spend a lifetime working her way up through the female hierarchy until eventually, as the mother of adult sons, she achieved a position of permanent authority. Until that point she was beholden at every turn to the judgment and authority of her seniors. Although in fact she took the major share of responsibility for the day-to-day maintenance of her family, socially she was a dependent. While within this sample we seemed to have polar opposites in Phoebe and Consolata, as far as their levels of maturity and performance are concerned, nevertheless, on closer examination, their attitude toward men and toward their hus-bands especially, as the primary authority figures in their lives, were not so very different. Phoebe, for all her competence, did not question Kepha's right to have her do his bidding. If he decided to send her to

Morongo, where she was a stranger, and to have her shoulder all the burdens of his farm, she had to comply. In the same way Consolata also, resistent though she was, boarded the train at Mombasa and came home because Nyamwange told her to. Ultimately a woman must obey her husband's commands since she is powerless to resist, just as in girlhood she was powerless to resist those of her father.

In no relationship does a woman perceive herself as more victimized than in a sexual one. This is especially true of a girl before marriage. While Phoebe conceded that if approached by a boy, a girl had the option to submit or to run away, she was the exception. The others seemed to see themselves either as having been seized by passion (and therefore deprived of will) or deceived and violated, like Consolata by Nyanwange, who, with his friends, tricked a guileless fourteen-year-old into an elopement. This was Suzanna's story also regarding her first marriage and again, some years later, her abduction to Kericho by a wealthy businessman. With Ogaro at last she had exercised some volition—"her blood had warmed to his"—only to discover later that he had used a love potion to force her into staying with him. As for Sabina, Zipporah, and Clemencia, their marriages had been arranged and they had had no choice, regardless of their personal feelings, but to cooperate. Whatever the exact circumstances, each woman with the possible exception of Phoebe could subsequently claim that the decision to marry had not been entirely hers—under pressure she had capitulated, usually, as it turned out, against her own best interests.

The fantasy life of these women, insofar as they revealed it to me, seemed restricted. They all knew I was interested in dreams, for example, but while all of them reported at least one dream each, only three offered their dreams with any consistency. These three, Zipporah, Clemencia, and Suzanna, were the women for whom I assumed the most positive emotional significance and who seemed to want to please me most. To the extent that the seven women shared their daydreams with me, and again some did so much more freely than others, they tended to use me as a sounding board for their fears rather than their hopes or aspirations. Suzanna could tell me about how, as a young girl, she had wanted to be the only wife of an educated man. Now that she had achieved that desire, she spoke of the disappointments and hardships of her current situation, not of escapist fantasies for the future. She knew what life was like with Ogaro and that it was unlikely to change for the better. In the same way Consolata railed against Nyamwange, but while at times she fantasized about becoming a bar girl and luring men to her bed in broken Swahili, for the most part she obsessed about the trials of her daily life. Only Zipporah, convalescing after an attack of bronchitis, liked to question me about the great world and laugh about her own erroneous preconceptions. The rest were concerned with daily living, with how to plant and harvest, how to feed and educate their children, and how to handle those most crucial relationships of all—with their husbands and their mothers-in-law. For the most part these relationships were never stable or secure: rather, pressure was constantly to be resisted; rights were to be established and invoked. One could never really trust a husband; even Phoebe said matter-of-factly that some secrets should not be shared, for who could know her betrayer was not at hand?

Within the constraints of enduring ambivalence, there was not a great deal of latitude for sexual fantasy. Traditions of puritanism and inhibition prevented these Gusii women from sharing their thoughts about such things. At first Trufena, the exception to so many rules, flaunted her sexuality before me and her mortified aunt, but this seemed to be the residue of courtship which, when relations with Ombui deteriorated, vanished precipitously and never reemerged, at least in my time. While Phoebe could say that in her girlhood she had craved sex, her current interest seemed substantially reduced. Four celibate months were no burden to her now. Sexual pleasure belonged, for a woman, to a short period of irresponsibility. At marriage a woman reordered her priorities. Sex became a serious business, the only means to the most important end of all. If at the same time as conceiving and bearing children a woman could prevent her husband from squandering on other women those economic resources which should be reserved for his family, she counted herself lucky. A wife had no real expectation of securing her husband's sexual fidelity as well as his financial support. Thus sex was a commodity in return for which a man could be urged to fulfill obligations of various sorts. The women worried about their side of the bargain and were concerned as to whether the benefits accruing to them would be in proportion to their own contribution. But if they fantasized about the pleasurable aspects of their commitment, they were for the most part extremely reticent in sharing their fantasies with me and, I believe, with other Gusii women as well. In certain circumstances they could joke about sex in an impersonal, conventional manner, but rarely did they choose to speak about their own sexual experiences. There was a hysterical element about their attitude, as if they were disavowing any voluntary participation. As I came to know them better, the inhibitions they had about speaking of sexual matters in some cases relaxed a little, but for the most part they found it easier to talk about the social consequences of sex than the act itself.

If our sessions were a stage on which these women might reveal themselves as they wished, the role which they chose most frequently was that of the sufferer: "Ninchindagete" ("I am suffering"). Having complained at length, however, they very rarely asked me for advice. Perhaps in part this was because I was so far removed from their world that, while they imagined they could teach me about it, I could never learn enough to become an expert. In addition, I had no place in the familial hierarchy. A Gusii woman expected to go to certain people for advice and judgment but not to others. She consulted her in-laws or, in some instances, her parents, but not a European woman who, however much she knew about one, had no place in the lineage or in the authority structure.

Thus I was a mirror and a sounding board but never an oracle. I was someone to whom they were at liberty to complain, and that in and of itself was gratifying. They drew me close, while at the same time limiting my involvement: they shared their disappointments, but it was rare indeed when they spontaneously offered me good news. I had to pick up the clues and ferret out their secrets. That they so carefully guarded news of any good fortune must have reflected the cultural belief that if a neighbor detects that a person has some advantage, his jealousy might motivate him to bewitch the person. This belief is so powerful and pervasive that it restrains a Gusii man or woman at both a conscious and an unconscious level. Thus, since those who know one best are those whom one most fears, as my relationships with these women grew closer, their tendency to complain to me, and of course to Mary, their neighbor, a Gusii like themselves, became if anything more pronounced. If I discovered something favorable had come their way, it was probably because I had learned to detect and interpret the clues rather than that the women divulged to me the good news themselves. For example, when Ogaro at last got a job, Suzanna could not tell me this. Rather, I noted a sudden reduction in her fear of her mother-in-law and realized this could most probably be explained by Ogaro's finding employment.

THE INDIVIDUAL IN HER SOCIAL SETTING

1. *The Stage of Life.* While each of these women as I observed her was the product of both her individual life history and her current situation, in at least one important respect all were similar: they were all of childbearing age, struggling to handle their multiple roles of mother, wife, and cultivator. Moreover, while required to shoulder the burdensome responsibilities of these roles, they were still apprentices in their husbands' lineages: authority was due a person in accordance with her age, not with the extent of her responsibilities. Thus all of them, including Clemencia, whose mother-in-law had died long ago and who herself was the mother of ten children, of whom five were sons, occupied subordinate positions in their husbands' families. Only when her eldest son, Bernard, married and had children of his own would Clemencia, for example, graduate from being *omosubaati* (a wife), to being *omongina* (a female elder), a fully constituted authority figure in the lineage.

Even though the seven women were all dependents in many respects, however, they varied in age and in the legitimacy of their marriages, falling into three classes: brides whose bridewealth was not yet paid, young wives who had been paid for, and older wives whose children were approaching maturity. A sense of permanence and belonging, or lack of it, affected both the way they thought about themselves and their behavior. Suzanna and Trufena, both mothers of sons, had not yet been paid for, and this, it emerged, was the main focus of their thoughts and fantasies. The enduring illegitimacy of their positions confronted them at every turn. Like most of their contemporaries, they had eloped with men of their own choosing with the expectation that in due course their husbands would produce the bridewealth required to ratify their marriages. Both these young women were preoccupied with the anomaly that, having provided their husbands with sons, their bridewealth was still not forthcoming. Thus their status was not only subordinate and dependent but marginal as well. While each could assert defiantly that nothing bound her to "this poor place" and that she was free to go if and when she chose, nevertheless both knew very well that that option was not really theirs, for they had been compromised by their male offspring. Those sons whom they had so desired had in fact compounded their marginality. They were no longer at liberty to find themselves other husbands, for no man in his right mind would take another man's son (*ekerentane*, a "brought" child); they had to stay where they were, tolerating as best they could an insecurity of tenure which might continue indefinitely, depending on their husbands' ability or willingness to pay.

Though there was no significant difference in their ages, Phoebe, Consolata, and Zipporah had already achieved that legitimacy which Suzanna and Trufena sought. For a number of reasons, the husbands of these three had been able to pay bridewealth, either at the time of marriage or shortly afterward, in Consolata's case at the birth of her first child, who was a son. In this way they were properly married women and for better or worse felt compelled to remain in their married homes. As it happened, each considered her husband's homestead inferior to the place in which she had grown up—with reason, as I saw for myself—while to varying degrees each was ambivalent about the in-laws among whom she was obliged to establish a permanent niche. Even Phoebe regretted her isolation from her parents and siblings. Tactful and outwardly conciliatory as she was, she still found the conduct of relations with her sisters-in-law burdensome. One had to take great care, to make every effort to be conciliatory, but even so one invariably antagonized. Hence the rift with Dorothy, who over many months watched Phoebe smearing her house but never offered to assist her.

Legitimacy, then, entailed its own problems, which Suzanna, entangled as she was in an irregular union with a landless drunkard and feeling that no one's lot in life could be worse than her own, was not in a position to appreciate. Though she might envy the correct marital status of her cousin Zipporah, if not the marriage itself, in fact Zipporah's discontent almost equaled her own. Suzanna could still fantasize fleeing home to her parents, but Zipporah knew that that route was closed to her and had to find her escape in dreams of adultery or periodic sexual escapades after beer parties. Meanwhile, though she did not seem to regard her mother-in-law, Nyaboke, as malevolent, nevertheless Zipporah's relationship with the old lady was quite as ambivalent on a day-to-day basis as was Suzanna's with Kwaboka. The difference was only that Zipporah knew full well that she was committed to her erratic husband, to her senile mother-in-law, and to poverty and hardship. Thus she had to make the marriage work, while Suzanna could still toy with the fantasy that she had some latitude, some alternative base.

Consolata, Zipporah, and Phoebe, then, were in the "settling down" period of life, when, while a woman might regret certain aspects of her fate, nevertheless, she sees she has no alternative other than to make the best of her situation. This Phoebe optimistically set out to do. Zipporah was far more ambivalent about her commitment, but she conceded that at times she and Makori "agreed." Indeed I had a chance to observe the companionship which they periodically offered one another. Only Consolata, mother of five, seemed to find her situation intolerable. Ten years after her marriage she was irresolute and resentful. She still railed against her husband, seemingly unable to come to terms with the nature of the man; meanwhile she remained incapable of finding satisfaction in either her children or her work.

By the time I knew them, Clemencia and Sabina had both been married almost twenty years. I had to delve for accounts of their marriage ceremonies, since the details seemed to have slipped their minds. The issue of commitment had been resolved for each of them long ago. Sabina's parents-in-law had been dead for years, while Clemencia had never known her mother-in-law. Both of them had many sons, and yet neither had yet achieved much consequence in her husband's family. I knew them during difficult times when, though they were no longer receiving financial support from their husbands, their eldest sons were still schoolboys, several years short of being wage earners, capable of helping their mothers. A generation ago when land had been more plentiful and economic pressures less compelling, Sabina and Clemencia might already have been enjoying relatively comfortable lives: they would have had adequate land and many children to help them work it. But today, apart from whatever else was burdensome, economic stringencies made their circumstances very difficult indeed. So instead of having leisure to spend with supportive kin, they handled their anxieties for the most part alone, behind the thick hedges they had grown to exclude their enemies, who happened also to be their husbands' closest relatives.

2. *Current Relationships.* It sometimes seemed that many of these women survived almost on a starvation diet, insofar as relationships of trust were concerned. With the exception of Phoebe, none of them had established a marital relationship that was with any consistency supportive. During the entire time I knew her, Sabina had no contact whatsoever with Obamba, while Consolata's visit to Nyamwange at Mombasa was fraught with conflict and mutual recriminations. If in the past Clemencia and James seemed to have derived a good deal of gratification from their marriage, currently the relationship was severely strained, while the relations between Suzanna, Zipporah, and Trufena and their respective husbands pursued a dramatically uneven course. Of the seven only Zipporah's husband lived at home permanently; the other couples had to deal with the complications of migrancy. That the men were absent for long stretches further compounded the difficulties of marital relationships, which at the best of times would have been ambivalent given the nature of marriage in that culture, i.e., it is a contract: a man provides his wife with children and with land on which to support them.

Moreover, in a society in which males are valued so much more highly than females, girls almost inevitably emerge into womanhood believing themselves inferior to all men who have authority over them, that is to say, the adult males in both their families of origin and their married homes. While they may presume to measure themselves against other women, they can scarcely compare themselves with men, whom at the deepest level they perceive as being more powerful than they are. The least competent man has an edge over the most competent woman, simply by virtue of his sex. Thus, however else they thought of their husbands, these women perceived them as enormously powerful; and that power could as easily be used for their destruction as their benefit. Their husbands were tyrants whose favor might be wooed, but whose wishes could scarcely be thwarted. It was hardly surprising that companionship and emotional reciprocity, as we know them in our own society, were neither expected nor sought.

Who, then, could provide a married woman with emotional support? If she were fortunate, she might find in her mother-in-law an ally and a friend. The Gusii have many tales and proverbs, however, demonstrating the antipathy likely to exist between mother-in-law and daughter-in-law. In this sample only Consolata and Phoebe enjoyed relationships with their mothers-in-law in which ambivalences were kept within bounds. This seemed possible in Consolata's case because she was so dependent and immature that she had never attempted to assert herself, while in Phoebe's case the roles had been reversed, and of the two the younger woman had become the nurturer. As for those other three whose mothers-in-law were still alive, Zipporah and Suzanna were both at odds with their husbands' mothers for extended periods during the time I knew them, while Trufena had scarcely anything at all to do with her mother-in-law.

In most cases, on the other hand, sisters-in-law provided some companionship, though even these relationships had to be carefully monitored. Since too much contact seemed inevitably to lead to mutual suspicion and jealousy, one remained if possible at a judicious distance. Suzanna, the most gregarious and open of the seven, appeared to be closest to her sisters-in-law: she could even be friendly to Drucilla of the evil eyes. At the other extreme, Trufena had managed to alienate totally both her husband's young sisters as well as her brother-in-law's wife, Sabera. The others, meanwhile, out of emotional and practical necessity, were in fairly continuous contact with their sisters-in-law, but even so they easily expressed to me their ambivalence about these women with whom, only days ago, they might have been "best friends." Indeed it seemed that the childbirth experience of Trufena highlighted the ambivalent nature of a young woman's relationships with her in-laws. Her sister-in-law Sabera pleaded incompetence, while her husband's aunts and mother were dilatory in their attentions to begin with and brusque and intrusive later. While Trufena's position vis-à-vis her in-laws might have been especially equivocal, nevertheless the behavior of these older women during her labor and afterward is fairly typical of what might occur when a young Gusii woman gives birth. Far from being supportive and nurturant, their culture permits the female in-laws full expression for their hostile feelings. They may freely taunt, abuse, and even slap the younger woman.

Thus it would appear that these women, like most others of their age group in Gusii society, are bound to live psychologically and physically isolated lives—alone, for the most part, with their children. Tradition-ally a married woman always lived separately, in her own *enyomba* (house); however, in the past *amasaga* and *ebisangio* (neighborhood work groups of various types) ensured women social contact of a mutually supportive sort. Since for numerous reasons these work groups have largely been abandoned, women seemed to be condemned to rather solitary lives in which they pursued their daily activities alone for the most part, with little opportunity to meet with others in neutral circumstances. If a lack of trust was always a feature of Gusii culture, the contemporary social and economic situation has further emphasized this characteristic.

As the current relationships of these women with other adults ap-peared to be suspicion-laden and ungratifying, what then might have been the nature of their earlier experiences, particularly their relation-ships with their mothers? While the personality is necessarily the product of multiple factors and influences, nevertheless an examination of the mother-daughter relationship might throw some light on the issue. I met the mothers of six of the seven women in the study toward the end of my work, and I already had some idea of what they might be like, based on what the daughters had told me—or had omitted telling me. Suzanna clearly idealized Moraa, who had taken care of her and suffered for her; indeed Suzanna spoke about her rather as a ten-year-old might speak of her mother, but at the same time I sensed some hesita-tion, as if she knew that Moraa's maternal concern was not uncondi-tional but had to be earned.

Sabina and Zipporah told me little about their mothers, and when they did I sensed their disappointment and even anger, provoked, I imagined, by the fact that parental pressure had forced both women into marriages not to their liking. Consolata and Phoebe spoke least of all about their mothers. Consolata told me once that her mother was poor—and therefore of little use to her, since she could not feed or house her daughter; while Phoebe once reported a dream in which she took maize from her mother's granary and then, in recounting her dream, disparaged her own dependency wishes.

While my contacts with the older generation were superficial and impressionistic, they nevertheless seemed to bear out many of my preconceptions. Suzanna, the most trusting of the seven, loved and was beloved by her mother, whose warmth and openness were evidently reflected in her daughter. In personality style Suzanna so closely resembled her mother, in fact, that one might presume that in infancy at least she had both gratified and been much gratified herself. At the opposite end of the spectrum, Consolata, who appeared chronically chilly and self-absorbed, rarely spoke of her mother to me and refused to take me to her home, and when I did have a chance to meet her mother she neglected to introduce me. The older woman did not speak at all in my presence and struck me as being at least as emotionally depleted as her daughter. I met her when she came to greet her new grandson, i.e., on a joyful occasion, but while the other people present, including Consolata herself, were replete and content, the mother was silent.

In contrast, Phoebe's competence and levelheadedness, as well as her tenderness, were instantly detectable in her mother. Mother and daughter loved and respected one another, but their slight reserve with one another seemed appropriate for two people, both adults, who valued each other's autonomy. The mothers of Trufena and Zipporah were also obviously competent women, able to handle their affairs efficiently, and their daughters had identified with that aspect of their mothers' personalities. In both instances, however, the warmth and gentleness which one immediately detected in the mothers of Suzanna and Phoebe were absent. While Trufena's mother seemed powerful and discerning, she inspired awe rather than desire to reach out and confide. Perhaps without making enough of a preliminary investment before the next baby came along, she had expected too much too soon of Trufena, her eldest child. At any rate, I wondered if the toddler Trufena had been pushed aside: though her mother's directive may have been that she become independent, and she had gone off into life with considerable resources to meet that expectation, at the same time, she behaved as if she had been shortchanged. Thus, at least when I knew her, she seemed to be taking out on her in-laws a debt which properly belonged to her own family.

It always rather surprised me that Sabina's mother was still alive, since Sabina herself appeared so worn and old. In addition to the marked physical resemblance, the two women were alike in other respects as well. One sensed in the older of the two something of the same depression and lack of self-esteem which Sabina only partially concealed with her manic behavior. Perhaps one might conclude that

Sabina had not been fueled sufficiently in the first place. It should be borne in mind, however, that I knew her during a time of great psychological stress; at other points in her life, Sabina might have more closely resembled her sister Pacifica than her mother. Her neighbor Clemencia, meanwhile, was the only orphan in the sample, and yet she was the one who both demanded intimacy with me and tolerated it best. While the loss of her mother in infancy had marked her for life, nevertheless she had a discriminating warmth and emotional energy lacking in the others, so one might presume that her grandmother had not been such an insignificant figure after all.

A demonstrable capacity to bear and raise many children, especially sons, is the primary criterion by which a Gusii woman defines herself. Since none of the women under consideration had encountered a problem of infertility, or failed to produce at least one son, regardless of the other restrictions and disappointments in their lives, with all of them this main source of self-esteem was intact. But if their own formative experiences had left them by and large with a pervasive sense of distrust in other people, how then did they relate to their children? Once again these women varied both in their expectations of reciprocity and in the degree to which they found their children gratifying in this respect. Sabina and Clemencia depended on their eldest children, both daughters, for a great deal of emotional and practical support. Gusii mothers expect to be close to their eldest daughters, although this special relationship tends to become important only after circumcision, when girls have reached a responsible age. Zipporah was disappointed that at ten years old Tabitha was turning out to be *ekebago* (a bad girl) rather than a companion to her mother, while Suzanna's eldest daughter, Flora, was still *egesagane* (uncircumcised), and Suzanna had not quite made up her mind if she liked her or not. One wondered whether Flora, who like Tabitha was the child of an earlier sexual relationship, might not also become a scapegoat as she grew older, rather than a companion and sharer of burdens. Meanwhile Consolata complained incessantly about having to employ a son rather than a daughter as her *omoreri* (child nurse), but if Gichaba was a disappointment to her, she found her other children no more gratifying. A child herself, she wanted to be mothered rather than to have to do the mothering. But among the seven she was an exception in this respect, for the others, even Sabina in her disorganized condition, identified positively with their mothering role; that is, for the most part they enjoyed taking care of little children. Of course they complained about sleepless nights and having to contend with bouts of diarrhea, but at the same time they took obvious relish in the daily routine of mothering. However, they did not seek from their young children the sort of emotional reciprocity and interdependence with which we are familiar in our own society. Their own mothers had not expected it of them either. Rather, they saw their preschool children as extensions of themselves: they cared for them physically as best they could, but only when the children became *abangaine* (they had sense) did these mothers expect emotional support. A mother went through a long investment period before she reaped the rewards of reciprocity.

CULTURAL INFLUENCE AND PERSONAL EXPERIENCE

What can we learn from the case studies about the influence of Gusii culture on the personal experience and psychological functioning of these women? They had all grown up in Gusiiland, isolated from other cultural influences until adulthood, but their explicit knowledge of traditional lore was limited or at least inaccessible to direct ethnographic inquiry; hardly any of them would have made a good anthropological informant. At times I wondered, particularly of the younger women, if they were not members of a deculturated generation that had left much of Gusii culture behind without putting anything else in its place. Yet their personal beliefs and attitudes, as revealed in words and actions over the entire period of observation, bore the unmistakable stamp of Gusii medical and religious beliefs and Gusii morality and social conventions.

The women believed, for example, that the malevolent jealousy of one person could kill another magically and that some of their neighbors were witches (*abarogi*) or possessors of the evil eye (*ebibiriria*) against whom magical or spiritual protection was needed. They believed that love potions (*amaebi*) could cause one person to wed another and that marital infidelity could cause the death of a spouse under the conditions of illness or childbirth specified in the Gusii conception of *amasangia*. Their personal inhibitions, strongly motivated by shame and fear, were experienced in terms of norms of kin avoidance (*chinsoni*) and self-presentation which form the collective context of interpersonal encounters for all Gusii. The fact that a majority had been raised as Protestant Christians, some in strict Seventh Day Adventist homes, makes the indigenous quality of their individual experience all the more striking.

This is not to say that they accepted everything in Gusii tradition. Some openly rejected divination and mocked the advice given by diviners. Most understood that conception does not occur during menstruation, as stated in traditional belief. They generally practiced a more relaxed form of kin avoidance than had been required when their parents were young adults. Some resorted to new "medicines" designed to prevent *amasangia*, the magical punishment for adultery, from working. A few flaunted Gusii social conventions (up to a point) and suffered social stigma (to some extent). For the most part, however, they saw the world in indigenous terms and constructed solutions to their personal problems with ideas and concepts received from previous generations.

One way these women used Gusii cultural belief in the service of intrapsychic defense can be illustrated from the case of Suzanna Bosibori. A critical episode in this case concerns Suzanna's growing fear that her mother-in-law was killing her through witchcraft. The proof offered of the older woman's being a witch was a small pot (*egetono*) discovered in a field by Suzanna a year earlier; her mother-in-law acknowledged having lost it and was happy to recover it. In her state of anxiety, Suzanna represented this kind of pot as a receptacle for witchcraft potions, but it later emerged that diviners also used such pots (for benign purposes) and that the mother-in-law as a former diviner would naturally own one without bringing legitimate suspicions of witchcraft down upon her. Suzanna knew her mother-in-law had been a diviner and, as the granddaughter of a senior diviner herself, was well aware of the apparatus used in divination. What is the meaning of this misrepresentation of *egetono* as an attribute distinctive to witches when it was an attribute shared by witches and diviners? The following cultural analysis, based on the ethnographic study conducted in the same area during 1955–57 provides some context.

The parallel between the female diviners meeting together, training and inducting novices, and the female witches who also meet, recruit and train, is a striking one. The diviner group seems to be a socially acceptable version of the witch group or, conversely stated, the conspiratorial witch group may represent a deviant, dangerous and perhaps fantastic version of the actually functioning group of diviners. [Robert A. LeVine, "Witchcraft and Sorcery in a Gusii Community," in *Witchcraft and Sorcery in East Africa,* ed. J. Middleton and E. Winter (London: Routledge and Kegan Paul, 1963), pp. 232–33]

In other words, the shared beliefs of the Gusii represent diviners and witches as similar in many respects: female, generally older, organized in a local group, possessing secret powers, meeting secretly, inducting and training secretly, with the older women dominating. Although the earlier study concluded that "[no] diviner in Nyansongo was accused of witchcraft and no alleged witch became a diviner" (ibid., p. 233), this was not borne out twenty years later; some diviners of the earlier period were said to have become witches after they had ceased practicing divination.

Suzanna was not alone in suspecting a former diviner to be a witch. In the cultural environment that constitutes the context of her personal beliefs, such suspicions are highly plausible, particularly on the part of a daughter-in-law, who is in a position to observe her husband's mother close at hand. Under stress, Suzanna had recourse to a culturally constituted ambiguity concerning the attributes of beneficent diviners and malevolent witches. She must have known the little pot to be part of her mother-in-law's divination equipment, but interpreting it as proof of witchcraft enabled her to locate her acute distress concerning an irreversible marital transition in an external figure for which there is a clear cultural prototype and a clear customary remedy—antiwitchcraft measures. This interpretation served not only to organize Suzanna's fear and anger in a socially acceptable manner but to restore her sense of control over her life at a moment when she must have been experiencing it as lost. Thus she exploited the interpretive possibility provided by Gusii culture to defend herself against the shattering perception of being responsible for the failure to attain her cherished goals. In retrospect this defensive fantasy was used to manage a personal crisis and was set aside when the crisis was experienced as being over.

Suzanna's defensive belief that her mother-in-law was bewitching her was particularly striking because we all considered her more open and trusting and less suspicious and defensive than most women in the community. She was not a "paranoid" personality, yet her response to stress induced by personal crisis was to imagine a family conspiracy causing her illness, suffering, and eventually death. Perhaps Gusii culture provides such elaboration in the projective beliefs for organizing affects induced by stress, and so few alternative beliefs that even someone like Suzanna had no other coherent cognitive response available to her. Insofar as this was true, her reaction reflected her enculturation rather than the most salient, enduring, or repetitive dispositions of her individual personality.

On the other hand, perhaps the cultural beliefs she employed had some deeper resonance with her personality. It may be that she had an unconscious distrust of older women, a distrust from which not even diviners were exempt when she was under stress. According to this line of analysis, reversibility in the images of witch and diviner reflects an ambivalence toward maternal figures which, though perhaps universal in early childhood, has not yet been resolved in those adults for whom "the good mother" is transformed so easily into "the bad mother." If Suzanna, whose relationships with her mother and other older women in her own family seemed unusually positive and strong, showed this ambivalence on occasion, it must be widespread among those whose ambivalence is more visible and should constitute an influence favoring the propagation of the belief system in which diviners and witches are mirror images.

This is speculation; in the realm of a community's ethos, culture and personality join, reinforce each other, and are not easily disentangled. The Gusii ethos includes the premise that no one with power can be trusted to use it benevolently. This is as true of sorcerers and other medical practitioners as of diviners; they are suspected of using magical means of doing away with their enemies. The case of diviners is particularly significant, for they are the indispensable mediums between the living and their ancestral elders, communicating the most authoritative messages from the world of the lineage founders. That the legitimate role of these publicly respected women makes them subject to suspicions of witchcraft shows how pervasive is the concept that persons with extraordinary power are potentially dangerous to those around them. This premise may be attributed to the culture of the Gusii or to their personalities, but it is not farfetched to claim it as an assumption shared by the Gusii which would not be propagated unless it met their needs as individuals. In Suzanna's case we have seen how it met the needs of one individual under stress.

In a somewhat different vein, the use of cultural belief in intrapsychic defense can also be seen in the way these women concealed information about their advantages and portrayed themselves as afflicted sufferers and pitiable victims.

In behaving this way with me, they were conforming to a Gusii convention regarding routine encounters: it is socially acceptable, particularly for women, to complain but not to boast. The cultural rationale for this convention is more pragmatic than moral: boasting arouses envy in others and is therefore dangerous; complaining displays oneself as unworthy of envy and is therefore safer. It would be a mistake, however, to see the conventional behavior of the women as superficial conformity to a code of etiquette; their rigid adherence to the rules, exceeding the formal requirements of etiquette, suggests that this code represents emotional needs deeper than the wish to conform. Their disinclination to admit being pregnant illustrates this point. Suzanna Bosibori was the only woman who volunteered the fact of her pregnancy before it was clearly visible. We discovered that Gusii women generally do not disclose this information, even to those in their own homestead who might be expected to share their joy.

What is the meaning of this concealment? Our first hypothesis was that it represented sexual modesty in accordance with the norms of kin avoidance. Pregnancy is interpreted as sexual in certain social contexts, and several of the women with whom I worked refrained from visiting their natal homes while pregnant because of the shame they anticipated feeling if their own fathers should see them in that state. But this reticence did not apply to those with whom they lived, who interacted freely with them during pregnancy. Our second attempt to explain the concealment was based on the cultural rationale, taken at face value: if you tell people you are pregnant, you arouse jealousy in those less fortunate who have few children or who have reproductive difficulties, and they may bewitch you. This belief certainly played a part in Trufena Moraa's concealment of her pregnancy from me and my assistant Mary, of whose reproductive problems Trufena was aware. Although Trufena made many personal disclosures that were shameless by Gusii standards, she stopped short of telling us she was pregnant for fear that Mary, her husband's kinswoman, would envy and perhaps bewitch her. But ethnographic interviews showed that this reticence was not limited to situations defined by reproductive inequality. Informants agreed that they would not mention being pregnant even to a woman with many children and grandchildren, even in private where no one else could overhear. Thus it was not simply a matter of withholding the information from those who might reasonably be supposed to react to it with jealousy.

It eventually became clear that Gusii women did not in fact regard silence about one's own pregnancy to constitute a withholding of information. On the contrary, they assumed that those around a woman would be able to tell, without being told, that she was pregnant. They would hear her vomit in the morning or see her refuse morning tea because of nausea. In any event, "they will soon see, so why tell them?" This struck us as the reverse of our attitude, which might be represented as "they will soon see, so why *not* tell them?" The concern of the Gusii woman was that she did not *volunteer* the information; she must avoid the appearance of "boasting" at all costs. Her fear was not that others would discover she was pregnant but that they would see her announcing good news about herself. The very idea of such self-aggrandizement or self-assertion is terrifying to many Gusii women, arousing the fear that personal disaster or destruction will inevitably follow. Thus the fear of self-assertion lies behind what we took to be the concealment of being pregnant.

The declaration "I am expecting a baby," made to one's intimates, seems from a Western perspective to involve a minimal degree of self-assertion. In the Gusii context, however, it has the connotation of boasting, flaunting, gloating, as if to display good fortune at the expense of someone else, including the hearer. This is true of any visible attempt, especially by a woman, to show pride in oneself or to seek admiration, congratulations, intense pleasure, or power of any kind: it is presumed to be gained at the expense of others, on whom the display of pride or self-aggrandizing intent will have a highly destructive impact. The exhibition of a woman's desire for personal satisfaction or distinction, however minimal or transient, is interpreted as an indication of her wish to abandon or destroy her intimates and betray her relationships and obligations as wife and mother. In the concept of *amasangia,* for example, a wife's adultery is believed to result in her husband's death if she approaches him when he is ill; a man who suspects his wife of infidelity confronts her by saying, "Why are you trying to kill me?" When a wife uses *amaebi* (a love potion) to obtain her husband's favor, this assertive act is regarded not only as hostile to her cowives and their children but also to the husband himself, who will inevitably suffer from having a wife exerting power over him. The witch is portrayed in Gusii belief as an exceptionally assertive woman who seeks power at the expense of her own family, intrudes after dark into other people's houses, graves, and ultimately their bodies, and acts willfully to satisfy her own cannibalistic greed and hostile wishes. The diviner, in contrast, is portrayed as being forced by affliction into her role as spirit medium, sacrificing goats rather than people to qualify, and using her power to help anyone who hires her. She is as free of the taint of self-assertion as anyone with supernatural power can be.

Given this cultural context, Gusii women fear their own self-assertive impulses, imagining themselves stripped of protective relationships and exposed to a hostile environment should they give the slightest hint of actively seeking positive attention from others. Most of them crave the safety that comes from an appearance of passivity in interpersonal relations. This "low-profile" strategy involves minimizing social visibility, avoidance of taking initiative if there is any risk that it could be interpreted as self-aggrandizing, and limiting personal responsibility to those tasks imposed by authority. Complaining of personal difficulties is consistent with this strategy, not simply as an exemption from enviability but because it portrays the self as more acted upon than acting. Thus women complained to me of being abducted and raped by men, but these disclosures were more comfortable for them than admitting they had ever taken the initiative in sexual relations.

Departures from the low-profile strategy in the case material are either instances of passive resistance through the traditional mode of "privileged obstruction" or situations in which a woman has dared to act boldly on her own behalf because those who are formally responsible for her have defaulted on their obligations. Trufena Moraa, in failing to fulfill Gusii norms of hospitality toward her husband's family, seemed to be acting not only boldly but self-destructively. In retrospect, however, she was actually putting pressure on them to legitimize her marriage through the payment of bridewealth. She was saying in effect,

"If you won't pay the bridewealth even though I have given you sons, I won't fulfill the basic social requirement of a bride toward her husband's kin," and she was doing so with the security of customary prescription behind her. In this sense her behavior was a form of privileged obstruction as described by Philip Mayer ("Privileged Obstruction of Marriage Rites among the Gusii," *Africa* 20 [1950]: 113–25) for traditional Gusii wedding ceremonies, which can be held up by an essential participant who extorts gifts from the other parties in return for permitting the ceremony to continue; this is a practice paralleled in many situations of Gusii social life.

The other type of departure from the low-profile posture is exemplified by Zipporah Bochere, whose extramarital sexual liaisons and theft of grain, while apparently brazen acts of self-assertive deviance, occurred in contexts publicly considered to support their justifiability: in the first case, the wife's right to be impregnated when her husband is sexually incompetent; in the second, the mother's right to feed her children from the homestead food supply when her mother-in-law and husband have failed to make it available. Finally, the apparent self-destructiveness of Sabina Nyangige in renting out all her husband's land for a pittance, while neglecting her own food crops, can be understood as reciprocating, and calling attention to, her husband's neglect—a kind of retaliation which is justifiable, if unwise. Thus when these women appeared to be asserting themselves in a self-centered way heedless of social sanction, their obstructiveness, retaliatory neglect, and other misbehaviors were usually designed to invoke Gusii norms of kinship on their behalf. Laying responsibility for their own acts on the failures of their husbands to fulfill basic material obligations, they intended their indiscretions to dramatize these failures, heaping disgrace on their husbands in order to force their compliance with the norms.

This style of maneuvering, in which a woman misbehaves in order to dramatize her plight as a neglected or abused wife, carries with it the implication that only the husband is a person of sufficient public importance to have something to lose by her disgraceful or destructive conduct. In this drama, she is nothing more than his appendage, and her only power lies in her ability to thwart, hurt, or disgrace him. If she dresses in rags, lives in a crumbling house with a leaky roof, has malnourished, ill-dressed, and disorderly children—it is *his* reputation that should suffer. Her misconduct is simply a more intense attempt to advertise his neglect. Consolata Nyaboke fantasizes prostituting herself to get the money her husband does not send. She goes on, "When my husband comes I'll cover myself in clay [a funeral symbol] and stand before him. . . . I just want Nyamwange to understand what in truth I am—a widow." Like many other Gusii women, she imagines that dramatic hyperbole of this kind will shock her husband out of his indifference to his family responsibilities. If not, she feels she has nothing to lose by behaving badly herself.

The preference of these women for the appearance of passivity in routine interaction and domestic relationships was based in part on their recognition of the status of women in Gusii society, i.e., as satellites of their husbands and sons without the right to define their own interests separately or pursue them autonomously. Barred from the assumption of formal responsibility, they had learned they could be safer avoiding it. The emotional basis for this inhibited posture as an aspect of individual defense is fear, an affect which is heavily elaborated in Gusii culture. The Gusii belief system provides highly developed metaphors to organize the individual's experience of fear and other negative emotions like hostility and shame, without corresponding cognitive organizers for positive emotions. Gusii witch beliefs, for example, give a name, a face, a vocabulary, and a conceptual structure to the individual's deepest fears, and the kin-avoidance ideals provide a powerful metaphor for the organization of shame. There are no equiv-alent cultural fantasies or elaborated metaphorical structures for love or personal enjoyment. To describe the intense passion of her early marital relationship, Trufena Moraa repeats, "We were like crazy people" but adds little else. It is as if that degree of positive emotional intensity must be classified as mental disorganization in the Gusii context.

In the case studies of this book, as in other Gusii materials, pleasure-seeking activities most often appear with negative value at-tached to them or in a surreptitious social context. The beliefs associ-ated with them are not symbolically elaborated. On the other hand, Gusii medicine, for example, has a large and refined set of associated beliefs, organized largely around the affect of fear. In her study of rituals of kinship among the Nyakyusa, an East African people similar in many ways to the Gusii, Monica Wilson made a related finding.

> The preceding chapters are full of the pagan fear of death, menstruation, childbirth, and shedding blood. The rituals ex-press the fear and teach men what they must do to be saved. . . .

[That] the nature of man's fears is culturally determined is clear
from the Nyakyusa evidence, for Christians and pagans alike are
agreed that "the Christians fear much less" than do pagans, and
the Christians do in fact ignore taboos which the pagans feel to
be binding. But the rituals do not create fear out of nothing. All
the situations in which they are performed—birth and death,
marriage, and misfortune—are situations of emotional tension in
all societies. The rituals heighten the emotions and canalize
them. They both teach men to feel, and teach them what it is
proper to feel. [*Good Company,* p. 232]

For the Gusii there is evidence that the teaching of culturally
appropriate fear begins in early childhood. Here are relevant ethnographic statements from the study conducted in 1955–57, when most of
the women in this book were themselves small children.

A common way of quieting older infants is to frighten them.
When a one-year-old on a nurse's back begins whimpering, she
will say, "Aso, aso, esese," which is a way of calling a dog.
There may or may not really be a dog nearby, but the calling of
it . . . is intended to make the child think that the animal will
come and harm him if he does not stop crying. This often works
to silence him. The infant is prepared to respond in this way by
his mother, grandmother, and other caretakers, who often point
out animals of any kind—cows, chickens, dogs, insects—and
label them all *ekuku,* who "will bite you," a name . . . which is
supposed to inspire terror in the child. The mother and grandmother believe that this fear is good because it will safeguard the
child from actual harm incurred by animals, and also explicitly
because it can be used by a parent to control the child's behavior, particularly excessive crying. . . . Such fear training begins before the child can actually speak and is one of the first
verbal cues learned by the infant. [LeVine and LeVine, *Nyansongo,* pp. 124–25]

The general picture of the Nyansongo child as he emerges
from infancy is that of a dependent, fearful individual, capable
of making demands on his mother and other caretakers for
food and protection, but unaggressive, quiet and timid in
his approach to the physical environment and to strange
things. [Ibid., p. 129]

This early and apparently effective fear training was continued after
infancy, with a shift to unseen dangers:

[Mothers] give instruction in the dangers of the night to instill what they consider a healthy fear of the dark. Half the mothers interviewed said they mentioned hyenas, although there are none in Nyansongo, in their warnings. One said, "I used to frighten Okemwa by saying, 'If you go out, a hyena will take you. I saw a hyena waiting for you by the fence.' I did that so he wouldn't go out at night." Another reported, concerning her daughter, "I'd warn her, 'Don't you go out at night; you'll be taken by hyenas.' I know hyenas don't take children but I said it to frighten her from going out at night." Most of the mothers who did not report warning of hyenas mentioned witches, "wild things," "something which will eat you up," "men and animals who will take you away," or unspecified dangers. Although they do not themselves believe most of the specific warnings, Nyansongo women are genuinely afraid of the dark and convinced that witches who might kill children are outside at night. [Ibid., p. 146]

Finally, there was the absence of an equivalent degree of arousal or concerted effort at training on the side of positive emotion:

Even an indulgent mother, by Nyansongo standards, does not initiate nurturant interaction with her child. . . . [She] does not ordinarily proffer goods or emotional comfort unless she has been asked to do so. Praise is extremely rare, as mothers believe it can make even a good child "rude and disobedient." . . . Only two out of 24 mothers said they praised their children for good behavior. [Ibid., p. 147]

Gusii mothers of the generation under consideration in these quotations believed that the development of fear in a young child would assure his or her physical safety as a toddler and obedience as an older child, while praise and excessive attention would subvert the tractability necessary for participation in the domestic labor force. Parents tended to be stern taskmasters, frequently ordering their children about and giving them the impression that playing was disapproved and must be pursued out of the sight of adults. In the early experience of Gusii raised during or before the 1950s, then, fear was deliberately socialized by parents, who attempted a symbolic elaboration of that affect as the keystone of later development, while the positive affects were driven underground, as it were, outside parental training and organization. For persons who grew up this way, fear—organized in normative conceptions of respect for authority, intergenerational modesty, and the terror of witches—is an accepted part of the social self, a resource available for social adaptation and intrapsychic defense. The pleasure-seeking impulses of greed, lust, and narcissism, however, tend to be publicly disavowed, unaccepted by the self, and relatively unelaborated in cultural symbols. Their rigid censorship in conventional social interaction leaves these impulses less socialized and less integrated with valued parts of the self than fear and shame.

This view of affective development among the Gusii at the time the seven subjects of the present study were children helps to clarify both the inhibitions and excesses observed in them as adults. The fear of self-assertion I found in these women, for example, seems to have its roots in the pattern of early experience described above. If a girl is taught to fear the unknown from infancy, required to be an obedient worker in the family labor force from early childhood, given no praise for conformity or accomplishment, provided no parental approval for play or noninstrumental activities, and punished for deviation from parental command, she will become wary of calling attention to herself. Having learned that displaying good behavior does not result in positive attention, whereas misdemeanors—particularly seeking fun with friends instead of performing chores—inevitably result in punishment if discovered, she will adaptively develop the "low-profile strategy" of social interaction as a means of staying out of trouble. The timidity acquired in her earliest years provides no basis for risking parental disapproval later on. Having received no encouragement for seeking admiration or any other kind of special attention from her parents, she will consider this a gratuitous form of risk taking, more likely to result in negative than positive consequences. Pride will seem a vice rather than a virtue, certainly an attribute that goeth before a fall, as in our tradition. Furthermore, she will come to associate her own personal enjoyment with parental disapproval, something to be denied rather than admitted, hidden rather than shared, and felt to be justified only when someone else initiates it or even forces her into it. The passive position seems the only safe one; to initiate self-seeking action is fraught with real and imagined dangers, and any woman who would do so is to be feared herself.

From this perspective it is possible to understand how the women I worked with had come to see even the announcement of being pregnant as a dangerous boast. Having a child is something each woman wants intensely and selfishly—for her own benefit. She is therefore convinced that taking public pleasure in it could bring her nothing but massive disapproval, not at the news itself but at her excessive pride in flaunting it. She will wait until others notice her condition, and then grudgingly, with eyes averted and voice lowered, concede that she is expecting a baby.

Other selfish desires and pleasurable activities are experienced as equally problematic, not easily integrated into the life of a respectable married woman. Sexuality, for example, was expressed in the censoriousness of Phoebe Bonareri, who believed that a wife who would engage in daytime coitus with her husband would come to a bad end; the obscene ramblings of Sabina Nyangige; the prostitution fantasies of Consolata Nyaboke; Suzanna Bosibori's complaints of being abused; and Zipporah Bochere's extramarital encounters. Perhaps only Phoebe displayed an acceptance of her own desires, of the Gusii moral restraints on their expression, and of her sexual relationship with her husband. For the others, sexuality was often an element of disorder or suffering: a symbol of wantonness or exploitation. The place of drinking in the life of these women was similar. Their behavior ranged from abstention to indulgence, but on the whole drinking appeared more often as a sign of personal disorganization than as part of an organized life. The struggle for impulse control seemed to swing like a pendulum, rarely coming to rest in the center. The more intense forms of pleasure, tempting but dangerous, were neither accepted nor relinquished by the majority of these women.

The early experience of Gusii children in the 1950s, with its deliberate fear training and exclusion of praise, did not foster self-confidence in the face of difficulties and challenges. Both boys and girls felt vulnerable and looked to their older siblings and peers for support and encouragement. For boys this was a continuous process, reaching into adulthood, and when combined with awareness of their higher social and economic position, bolstered their self-esteem and sense of personal efficacy. But girls had to give up their social supports at marriage, just when their emotional need for them was greatest, at the time when they were obliged to move to their husbands' homes. In that strange and sometimes hostile situation, their sense of vulnerability was heightened, and their low level of self-confidence seemed inadequate to protect them from panic. In adapting to this situation, they fell back on the inhibitions developed in childhood—the low-profile posture—

and adopted as their primary defense the belief that others were responsible for their lives, their welfare, their conduct, and—under stress—their health. In time, their success as mothers and their establishment in a support group at their husbands' homes bolstered their self-esteem and enabled them to take a more active posture toward life. But it was a long and by no means certain process, as the cases of Sabina and Clemencia illustrate.

The lack of trust that some of these young women displayed toward the older women in their lives can also be illuminated by reference to their early experience. I have pointed out above that, though most were attached to and admiring of their own mothers, they were often suspicious of women in their husbands' homes and found it plausible that diviners might actually be witches; this seemed to represent an unresolved ambivalence toward maternal figures. If we assume that their mothers behaved toward them as described in the earlier study of "Nyansongo," it is possible to conceptualize the process by which this occurred.

It would appear that their mothers initiated and manipulated their fear of dangerous creatures, including witches. They imposed obedience and discipline on them in early childhood, but at the same time they volunteered no support and withheld praise. If there is any truth at all in the notion that individuals learn the basic trust they carry into all their relationships within the context of the mother-child situation, there is at least the suggestion here that the acquisition of basic trust was incomplete for these women and others of their cohort. Perhaps they could never be sure as small children that they had the unqualified support of their mothers. Perhaps this uncertainty remains with them as adults, preventing them from extending toward new maternal figures the unqualified trust that might be expected. This would explain the suspicion that tends to pervade relationships between brides and their mothers-in-law and the accusations of witchcraft that sometimes emerge.

CONCLUSION

To some, the women in these case studies may appear to be immature or psychologically unstable. The reader might therefore assume either that they have been misrepresented or else that the investigator must have attracted a sample of marginal people, scarcely representative of their culture or society as a whole. While it is no doubt true that my relationships with the women grew out of a mutual interest—mine to discover and understand and theirs to engage my attention and possibly my help—and while it is also often true that the outsider tends to draw to him those who are in a state of need, nevertheless I was in the community long enough to know many other women almost as well as these seven. I could use my knowledge of the larger group to reevaluate the personality characteristics of the women in my sample as I perceived them, and I concluded that as a whole they *were* representative of contemporary Gusii women of their particular age and stage in life. The two who might be exceptions to this were those whose turbulence had perhaps appealed to me most directly to begin with, namely, Trufena and Sabina. I certainly responded to their eagerness to engage me, but with them as with the others, while their evident desire to befriend me gave me an opening, thereafter my relationships with them depended upon their capacity to tolerate an increasing intimacy. In both cases I lost them, for their turbulence, while drawing me to them at the outset, ultimately turned me away. If she had to forgo her mother-in-law's support, Consolata also might have appeared in her own way as deviant as either Trufena or Sabina, but her social situation permitted her a good deal of dependency, and thus, while I might speculate about the nature and degree of the turbulence within, she appeared narcissistic and constricted rather than manifestly disturbed.

Despite their heavy responsibilities, these women were still, at forty years of age as at twenty-one, in an apprenticeship stage in their husbands' lineages and therefore people of little social consequence. Their society expected them to be mothers, cultivators, and wives, in that order, but if they fulfilled these roles less than perfectly, indeed even if they failed grossly to approximate the ideal, their neighbors shrugged: they were without *amasikane* (respect). The community did not condemn Sabina, for instance, for neglecting her children or her farm, while Nyagama reminded the angry women in his homestead that Trufena was still very young. This tolerance was a reflection not merely of the anarchic conditions that prevail when a society disintegrates but also of the way in which the Gusii have traditionally regarded women in their childbearing years: they must serve a long novitiate before being held truly responsible for their behavior. In the same way, only after menopause would they be expected to be experts either in the culture of their husbands' homes in particular or in Gusii culture as a whole. Only then would they be in a position to become *abakorerani*, that is, directors of rituals of various sorts. But the women in my study were not fully accountable, and thus, if to the reader they might appear somewhat insubstantial, this is partly because, according to the lights of their society, they *were* as yet insubstantial. In the same way, if they might seem as a whole unreflective, this was in part because the capacity for reflection and self-examination was not yet much developed, which is not to say that, if I were to seek out Suzanna in thirty years' time, I would not find it in her, just as we found it in her grandmother the diviner.

Bibliography

Bohannan, Laura, and Bohannan, Paul. *The Tiv of Central Nigeria.* 2d ed. London: International African Institute, 1969.

Colson, Elizabeth. *Marriage and the Family among the Plateau Tonga of Northern Rhodesia.* Manchester: Manchester University Press, 1958.

Dieterlen, Germaine. "Parenté et mariage chez les Dogon." *Africa* 26 (1956): 107–48.

Douglas, Mary T. *The Lele of the Kasai.* London: Oxford University Press, 1963.

Earthy, E. Dora. *Valenge Women: The Social and Economic Life of the Valenge Women of Portuguese East Africa.* London: Humphrey Milford, 1933.

Field, Marjorie J. *Social Organization of the Gá People.* London: Crown Agents, 1940.

Goody, Esther N. "Conjugal Separation and Divorce among the Gonja in Northern Ghana." In *Marriage in Tribal Societies,* ed. M. Fortes. Cambridge: Cambridge University Press, 1962.

———. *Contexts of Kinship: An Essay in the Family Sociology of the Gonja of Northern Ghana.* Cambridge: Cambridge University Press, 1973.

Harris, Grace. "Possession 'Hysteria' in a Kenya Tribe." *American Anthropologist* 59 (1957): 1046–65.

———. "Taita Bridewealth and Affinal Relationships." In *Marriage in Tribal Societies,* ed. M. Fortes. Cambridge: Cambridge University Press, 1962.

Kaberry, Phyllis. *Women of the Grassfields: A Study of the Economic Position of Women in Bamenda, British Cameroons*. London: His Majesty's Stationery Office, 1952.

Krige, Eileen J. *The Social System of the Zulus*. London: Longmans Green, 1936.

Krige, Eileen J., and Krige, J. D. *The Realm of a Rain-Queen: A Study of the Pattern of Lovedu Society*. London: Oxford University Press, 1943.

Kuper, Hilda. *The Swazi*. London: International African Institute, 1952.

La Fontaine, Jean. *The Gisu of Uganda*. London: International African Institute, 1959.

————. "Ritualization of Women's Life Crises in Bugisu'." In *The Interpretation of Ritual*. London: Tavistock Publications, 1972.

Leis, Nancy B. "West African Women and the Colonial Experience." *Western Canadian Journal of Anthropology* 6 (1976): 123–32.

————. Women in Groups: Ijaw Women's Associations. In *Women, Culture, and Society*, ed. M. Rosaldo and L. Lamphere. Stanford, Calif.: Stanford University Press, 1974.

Leith-Ross, Sylvia. *African Women: A Study of the Ibo of Nigeria*. London: Faber & Faber, 1938.

Mair, Lucy P. *An African People in the Twentieth Century*. New York: Russell & Russell, 1934.

————. *Native Marriage in Buganda*. International African Institute Memorandum no. 19. London: Oxford University Press, 1940.

Mayer, Iona. *The Nature of Kinship Relations: The Significance of the Use of Kinship Terms among the Gusii*. Rhodes-Livingstone Papers, no. 37. Manchester: Manchester University Press, 1965.

Oppong, Christine. *Marriage among the Matrilineal Elite: A Family Study of Ghanian Civil Servants*. London: Cambridge University Press, 1974.

Ottenberg, Phoebe. "The Changing Economic Position of Women among the Afikpo Ibo." In *Continuity and Change in African Cultures*, ed. W. Bascom and M. Herskovits. Chicago: University of Chicago Press, 1959.

Paulme, Denise. "The Social Condition of Women in Two West African Societies." *Man* 48 (1948): 44.

————, ed. *Women of Tropical Africa*. London: Oxford University Press, 1960.

Powdermaker, Hortense. *Coppertown: Changing Africa—the Human Situation on the Rhodesian Copperbelt.* New York: Harper & Row, 1962.

Reining, Priscilla. *Village Women: Their Changing Lives and Fertility—Studies in Kenya, Mexico, and the Philippines.* Washington, D.C.: AAAS Publication no. 77–6, 1978.

Richards, Audrey I. *Bemba Marriage and Present Economic Conditions.* Livingstone: Rhodes-Livingstone Institute, 1940.

———. *Chisungu: A Girl's Initiation Ceremony among the Bemba of Northern Rhodesia.* London: Faber & Faber, 1956.

———. *Land, Labour, and Diet in Northern Rhodesia.* London: Oxford University Press, 1937.

Shostak, Marjorie. "A !Kung Woman's Memories of Childhood." In *Kalahari Hunter-Gatherers,* ed. R. Lee and I. DeVore. Cambridge, Mass.: Harvard University Press, 1976.

Smedley, Audrey. "Women of Udu: Survival in a Harsh Land." In *Many Sisters: Women in Cross-cultural Perspective,* ed. C. Matthaisson. New York: Free Press, 1974.

Smith, Mary. *Baba of Karo: A Woman of the Muslim Hausa.* London: Faber & Faber, 1954.

Sudarkasa, Niara. *Where Women Work: A Study of Yoruba Women in the Marketplace and in the Home.* Anthropological Papers, no. 53. Ann Arbor: University of Michigan Museum of Anthropology, 1973.

Wilson, Monica H. *Good Company: A Study of the Nyakyusa Age-Villages.* London: Oxford University Press, 1952.

———. *Reaction to Conquest.* London: Oxford University Press, 1936.

DATE DUE			
DEC 1 9 1990			